SO-BRP-177

THE
RESPONSIBLE
REPORTER
2nd Edition

For Roberta, Steve, and Katie

THE
RESPONSIBLE
REPORTER

2nd Edition

Bruce J. Evensen, Editor

VISION Ⅴ PRESS

ABOUT THE EDITOR

Dr. Bruce J. Evensen was a reporter, assignment editor, news director, and bureau chief during thirteen years as a journalist. He worked as a national news editor, based in Washington, D.C., and as Middle East Section Chief, operating out of Jerusalem. He has written three books and numerous articles on newswriting and journalism history. He is Associate Professor in the Department of Communication at DePaul University in Chicago.

Copyright © 1997, by Vision Press.
   All rights reserved. No part of this book may be reproduced in any form without the prior written permission of the publisher.

Vision Press
P.O. Box 1106
3230 Mystic Lake Way
Northport, Alabama 35476

Printed in the United States of America

THE

RESPONSIBLE

REPORTER

2nd Edition

CONTENTS

EXPANDED CONTENTS

FOREWORD
TO SECOND EDITION

When readers in the 21st Century attempt to understand what it was like to live late in the 20th Century they might miss the significance that can be attached to the strange story of Richard Jewell. Historians might also be forgiven if they fail to move the plight of the 34-year-old security guard up from the footnote. But what happened to the man often named and never charged in the bombing of Atlanta's Centennial Park during the 1996 Olympic Games is a clinic on what has gone wrong in competitive journalism and the price the profession pays for its misconduct through the loss of public confidence in its media institutions.

The experience left Jewell "numb, in shock," and with an overwhelming sense of "helplessness." For three months following the July 27th blast that killed one and injured 111 others he had been afraid to leave his mother's apartment. He had not been charged in the bombing and no physical evidence connected him to the crime, but that didn't stop the press from renting an apartment opposite his and spying on his every move, while digging up any dirt that could be found or imagined in the man's unspectacular past. Sources who had never met him were cited as expert evidence that Jewell was a frustrated police wanna-be who created the Centennial Park drama to soak up the media spotlight. Bulletins interrupted normal programming to erroneously report swat teams were breaking into Jewell's apartment, while other watchers were let in on the media-know. "The security guard who seemed so brave," the bad writing went, "now seems like something else."

i

No physical evidence ever connected Jewell to the crime scene and despite the F.B.I's public assertions Jewell had not been charged and wouldn't be anytime soon, the press continued its stakeout. When police entered Jewell's apartment, the press claimed it proved Jewell's arrest was imminent. Only later did it concede police took the step fearing souvenir hunters in the media horde had taken some of Jewell's personal possessions. Jewell's neighbors, pestered by the press for daily quotes, and greatly annoyed at their own loss of privacy, finally did the right thing and obtained a court order to kick the press out. The press might have charged the neighbors were in on the conspiracy but spared themselves any further humiliation.

The cost of botching coverage of the Richard Jewell case was high. Four-fifths of early respondents didn't think the media frenzy had served any good purpose. Their verdict coincided with a study done by the *Los Angeles Times/Mirror* Center for the People and the Press. That probe listed six major criticisms the public has about press performance. They include lack of objectivity; emphasis on bad news; sensationalism; invasion of privacy; over coverage; and inaccuracies. Each of these problems is on lurid display in the story of how the press aimed to get Richard Jewell and how it exposed its own unprofessional conduct instead.

Any police reporter will tell you that in every criminal investigation authorities are developing suspects. Several may be "targets" of official probes, meaning a case is being built with that suspect in mind. The overwhelming majority of these suspects are never charged. That is why some newspapers and a few broadcast news operations have a rule that no suspects should be publicly named by the media until they're formerly charged. In balancing the legal rights of those under investigation with the public's right to know, they reason that no greater good will be served in raiding high school yearbooks for every criminal case that comes up and then publishing those pictures, with viewers and readers asked to cast their votes on who looks the most guilty. The press is not the prosecutor. The public is not a jury. Had that simple logic been shown in the Richard Jewell case it would have saved NBC half a million dollars and the rest of the press the unhappy obligation to justify their rush to judgment.

Some have argued that the Olympic bombing, coming as 14,000 credentialed reporters gathered in Atlanta, is an unusual case reflecting competitive press passions. But it's that very visibility that serves as such a sobering lesson for tomorrow's responsible reporter. The story began badly when the *Atlanta Journal-Constitution* came out with an extra edition on July 30, 1996, in which un-

ii

named sources cited Jewell as a suspect in the bombing. CNN rushed the report on the air, with an anchor reading the newspaper's story verbatim. A feeding frenzy followed with cameras and microphones closing in on Jewell and his elderly mother. Exclusives were hard to find, but that didn't stop some. Former law enforcement agents and psychiatrists not connected with the case were quoted when they agreed Jewell fit the profile of a mad bomber. The fact they had never met Jewell, nor interviewed anyone who had, hardly stopped these sources from saying something and only encouraged reporters to report their experts "seemed certain" Jewell was their man. Suddenly, Jewell was "bathed in a spotlight of suspicion" and his decision to be "less talkative" to bothersome reporters proved his guilt beyond a reasonable doubt. When NBC's Tom Brokaw mistakenly reported "the FBI is close to making the case" and that "they probably have enough to arrest him right now" his eruption became the coda of a mass mediated cacophony that had many readers and watchers tuning out.

At a press conference on October 28, Jewell, now publicly cleared by the FBI as a target of the probe, struck back at the media monster. He hadn't called himself a hero in finding the Centennial Park bomb. They had. He had never studied how to make a bomb, although they said he had. He had passed a polygraph test, but few had bothered to report that. His voice had not matched the voice of the man who phoned in the bomb threat and neither his finger prints nor hair were found on the phone, but still there were those in the press who didn't let that get in the way of a good story. Jewell had felt "like a hunted animal" who now sought to retrieve his reputation.

The media's second mistake in the Richard Jewell case was its failure to admit it made a mistake. NBC issued a statement on December 9 saying it had agreed to a cash settlement after negotiations with Jewell's attorneys, but only to protect the confidentiality of its sources. The network offered no apology or retraction. Editors at the *Atlanta Journal-Constitution* stood by their story and blamed the FBI. Their allies in the press charged the whole affair wouldn't have happened had the FBI "kept its mouth shut," even though the agency never admitted leaking Jewell's name and publicly claimed the opposite. Blaming someone else obscures the central issue in the Richard Jewell case, and that is, what is the responsibility of the reporter in a high profile case, when competition encourages putting out rumor and allegation in the absence of any formal charge. In the aftermath of the Richard Jewell story, the editor of a big city daily told this author that once a rival names names, his paper is obligated to do the same to save

iii

face with its readers. The readers of this book are asked, whose reputation is saved or tarnished in the long run when we run with information that is incomplete, half-baked, and untrue, all in the interests of making a buck?

The contributors to this second edition of *The Responsible Reporter* have had to ask themselves this very question during distinguished careers in journalism and in teaching journalism. What they write in these pages is guided by our collective belief that journalists who begin their careers at the close of the 20th Century and the beginning of the 21st Century will need to reinvent the profession if we are to reclaim anything approximating the confidence we once enjoyed from the American public. Your relationship to your public is like that of a partner in a marriage. When trust is gone the marriage is gone. And the poll data we now see on public attitudes toward journalism should make us all pause. Either we restore the profession to its sense of public responsibility or reap the consequences of a public increasingly alienated from the public life of the nation. Those are the stakes. And it is with that messianic zeal that the authors of *The Responsible Reporter* have undertaken their mission.

Bruce J. Evensen
Chicago
April 1997

iv

WHAT THE POLLS SHOW

The primary problem for today's journalist is winning and maintaining public trust. Barely three Americans in 100 rate journalistic honesty and ethics as "very high," and fewer than one in four rate it "high" or "very high."

In the first edition of *The Responsible Reporter*, we observed that "poll data demonstrate that the field of journalism is experiencing a crisis in public confidence. Whether we measure public confidence in the reporting process, or in the ethical standards of journalists, or bias in the news media, or public trust in the fruits of interpretative journalism, the findings are consistent. The public is not satisfied with its newsgatherers, and that dissatisfaction is growing." Unfortunately, there is little in poll data developed in the last two years to comfort those alarmed by the growing breach between journalists and their audience.

Only three respondents in 100 rated journalistic honesty and ethical standards as "very high," ranking journalists with car salesmen and labor union leaders in terms of public confidence. Twice as many surveyed thought funeral directors had "very high" ethical standards compared to journalists. These findings emerge from two polls regularly taken by the Gallup Organization. Since the mid-1970's we've measured public confidence in basic American institutions and in a second poll we've analyzed the public's perception of the honesty and ethical standards of individuals who work in different professions. In the first survey, respondents are read a list of institutions in American society and are asked to rate how much confidence they have in each one—a great deal, quite a lot, some, or very little. In the second poll, respondents are asked to rate honesty and ethical standards as being very high, high, average, low, or very low. Survey results are not encouraging for journalists or those planning to make a career in journalism.

Only 17 percent of respondents gave a high or very high rating when asked how they viewed the honesty and ethics of newspaper reporters. That ties a fifteen year low. In the late Seventies more than half of all respondents had a great deal or quite a lot of confidence in newspapers. Today that number is less than one third. One in eight surveyed said they had a great deal of confidence in television news. Only one in nine said they had similar confidence in newspapers. In fifteen years, newspaper reporters have seen the number of people who thought the press had high or very high ethical standards nearly halved. Only one in 50 Americans believe newspaper reporters have "high" or "very high" ethical standards.

Nearly one in four Americans say they have very little or no confidence in newspapers or television news. Put another way, twice as many respondents said they had a great deal or quite a lot of confidence in the much maligned American military and the nation's police force than have confidence in its print and broadcast journalists. Television news and newspapers rank with organized labor and big business in terms of public confidence and just ahead of Congress and the criminal justice system. Newspaper reporters are now in a statistical dead heat with lawyers and business executives in terms of their perceived honesty and ethical standards. They rate slightly ahead of labor union leaders, real estate agents, and Congressmen, but lag behind local officeholders and far behind public opinion pollsters.

It is fair to say there is a great of latent distrust Americans have for many institutions in the country, but it is also true to say print and broadcast journalists and commentators have suffered a greater erosion of public confidence than have many other professions. What may be particularly disturbing for those planning careers in journalism is that public distrust of their profession has consistently fallen since Watergate with little statistical evidence that journalism is making a rebound. In fact, from their lofty heights in the middle-Seventies, journalists can hardly fall much farther. Twenty years ago four times as many Americans trusted journalists compared to car salesmen. Today that number is two to one. The gap between journalists and insurance salesmen and advertising practitioners has narrowed by a similar percentage. It is not that respondents suddenly have more confidence in Congressmen, salesmen, and admen, it's that they have

vi

less confidence in journalists.

The collapse in the public's confidence in its print and broadcast journalists is not strongly related to the respondents' gender, race, or political orientation. Each group seems increasingly dubious about press performance. Younger people do have more confidence than older people in newspapers. That's good news if younger readers remain impressed by what they're reading and bad news if growing disenchantment is associated with the more one reads. Two years ago we observed an increasing trend toward tabloid journalism and a growing sense that news organizations were not independent, but were controlled by powerful people or organizations, might be connected to journalism's fall from grace. On the heels of press coverage of the O.J. Simpson case and the rush to judgment in the Richard Jewell case, the skepticism of the American public may well have deepened. Now would seem a perfect time for those entering the journalism profession to consider how they can restore it to its previous place in public confidence.

RICK GARLICK, Research Director for the Gallup Organization, specializing in media research, and **BRUCE J. EVENSEN**

1

REPORTING
AND RESPONSIBILITY

The public's growing discontent with the performance of reporters places a special responsibility on journalism students planning to enter the profession. The public's distrust of the news media stems, in part, from the failure of the press and of broadcast journalists to take their social responsibilities seriously. This chapter focuses on the reporter's responsibility to readers and listeners and identifies several values that beginning reporters should consider in giving their public the news they need to know. Reporting the world today requires journalists who know what they are doing, who know how to interview, how to contextualize material, how to write effectively, and how to arrest the attention of news consumers not through tricks but with the kind of information that audiences know they need to know.

The news media come in for loads of criticism because they are so critical to American society. For generations, the public has looked to reporters to provide them something they can't get for themselves—a picture of the world upon which to act. That requires students entering the profession of journalism to consider what is required of them. To get ready for a career of public service, you must be well-educated, be connected to the world around

BY BRUCE J. EVENSEN

you, and know what it takes to find news and to write it fast and well, always keeping in mind what you owe your reader or listener.

The Responsible Reporter has been designed to help you do this. Each chapter is written by someone who started where you are now and became, through years of professional journalism experience and teaching careers, masters of their craft. To their words we've added perspectives from nationally prominent men and women inside and outside journalism. These chapters and essays will teach you how to become a journalist and how to fulfill your obligations to your audience.

The eve of the 21st Century is an extraordinary time to consider a career in the news media. As Rick Garlick points out in our preface, never in recent memory have readers and viewers believed journalists less. As Alf Pratte notes in this book's concluding chapter, rarely has it been more difficult for graduates to get a start in the news business. In between these words of warning, contributors to *The Responsible Reporter* offer a variety of perspectives on the problems and opportunities beginning reporters face in gathering the news. A serious reader will finish this text knowing what ails the profession of journalism, what it offers, and how you can prepare yourself to contribute to its future.

What unites the authors of *The Responsible Reporter* is our abiding respect for the work of the journalist and our hope the next generation of journalists will restore the profession to its previous position of service. The business of news gathering and dissemination is constitutionally protected because this nation's founders understood the importance of a fully informed electorate to make the decisions that make democracy possible. That is why journalistic responsibility and ethics play such a large part in so many of these chapters. And that is why the goal of our authors is not only to help you gather, write, and edit the news, but to help prepare each of you to play your part in contributing to the creation of a civil society.

Although some students go into journalism for the money, when they see how little there is to be made in it, and the hours they must keep, and the sacrifice to family and personal life that journalism often requires, beginners often go on to something else. Those who remain generally do so because they cannot imagine anything else quite so satisfying. For when it comes to feeding your intellectual curiosity, or giving you a chance to write a lot and well, few things can beat a career in journalism. Nor will you quite get over the good feeling of doing something that demonstrably benefits others. Beneath a certain skepticism, many journalists will tell you the big payoff comes in doing stories that permit people to exercise authority over their own lives and to make decisions that intimately affect those lives.

Not that job satisfaction among journalists tops the charts. Far from it. The eager idealism of many a beginner is shattered by the crass commercialism that has infected much of the profession. In an era of the disappearing daily, the competition between broadcast and cable, and the promise and uncertainties of the "Net," it is not surprising that all too many search for the least common denominator to increase market share. Economic scarcity in the 1990s rewards news operations that can do more with less. This development has threatened the quality and standards demanded by increasingly sophisticated news consumers. They are retaliating by putting down their dailies and turning off their televisions. When they overwhelmingly tell pollsters they do not think journalists have high ethical standards, they are telling beginning journalists to do a better job of regaining that trust.

The consequences of ineffectual journalism are incalculable. Without a picture of the world that allows us to act sensibly, how can we act? If readers and viewers and listeners cannot turn to journalists to provide them with information they need, where can they get that information? The future will allow news consumers to call up selections from a menu of choices in their homes or workplaces by computer. But the information "super highway" that the pop magazines keep buzzing about will still require journalists who know what they are doing, who know how to interview, how to contextualize material, how to write effectively, and how to arrest the attention of news consumers not through tricks but with the kind of information that audiences know they need to know.

British journalist Malcolm Muggeridge has observed that there has never been a time in human history when technology permitted us to go so many places and yet we have so little of substance to say. Anyone who has endured the inordinate, blanket coverage of the O. J. Simpson murder case, the Menendez brothers' murder trial, the strange celebrity of the Bobbitts or Madonna, the Michael Jackson sexual molestation charges, the excruciating details on Jeffrey Dahmer, or the rush to judgment of Olympics bombing suspect Richard Jewell may have wondered where this noisy bustle of celebrity and crime reporting is taking us. It is perhaps for this reason that recent poll numbers placed journalists next to funeral directors in terms of public confidence, a profession journalists all too often resemble. The effect that heavy trafficking in fantasy reporting has on journalism's relationship to its audience has been devastating. Americans are saying in unprecedented numbers that a news media that exploits the sensational, while marginalizing the meaningful, is a news media that isn't fit for a democracy.

As beginning journalists, you need to know that public skepticism is what you're up against. You are up against readers and viewers who don't take you fully seriously. That is why every page of this book was written—and should be read—with the journalist's reader and viewer in mind. That means, if beginning journalists are to be taken seriously by those inside the profession and those outside it, they must earn that respect by proper preparation. As this book takes you through the stages of how a reporter goes about his or her business, open your mind to the larger questions implied by what you are doing. Indeed, editors are nearly unanimous in advising beginning journalists that the capacity to think analytically is as indispensable as any quality if you are to succeed at your craft. Whether you are covering a breaking story or writing a feature, or making your career in advertising or public relations or the trade press, what makes for good reporting remains the same. It is the person who writes with his or her audience firmly in mind and can see significance in the smallest of details who serves his or her audience.

The intense competition for the attention of readers forces reporters to write economically. That is what our authors urge you to do. Your editors will insist on it because that's what audiences insist on. Audiences are impatient in their search for significance. If they do not detect early on that you have something they absolutely need to know, they will not stay with you. Even if you have something they want, but do not state it well and quickly, they will not stay. So the burden is on you.

While gathering and writing news do not require the training of a brain surgeon, beginning journalists nevertheless are brain surgeons of a sort. Your business may not be to change minds, but you will change them. Every story will contain ideas that audiences embrace, reject, or ignore. Sometimes the information is received, but often it is not. And that may make the difference in the direction our nation is headed. That is why it is hard to find a career that requires more of the people who do it.

Think of that as you go through these chapters and read the essays that accompany them. News organizations will continue to place high priority on discovering what most interests the widest range of readers and viewers and in finding young men and women of intelligence and talent to write those stories. As you prepare for a career in journalism, have a high regard for the person who will be reading and hearing what you write. That is this text's primary message. Audiences can be trusted to make up their own minds with the information you give them if that information is as scrupulously sourced, as fairly balanced, as impartial, and as complete as you can make it. Our hope is that this text will help you develop the skills necessary in producing copy just like that, while preparing you for the challenges of responsibly reporting our world on the eve of the 21st Century.

Perspective...

THREE PIECES OF ADVICE

By SEN. PAUL SIMON, former United States Senator from Illinois and veteran journalist

Three major items of counsel I pass along to you:

The *first* advice to beginning journalists is not to become too cynical. When I was a young reporter, whiskey was the greater danger for reporters. I'm not suggesting that has totally disappeared, but the great danger today is cynicism. Reporters should be a little skeptical, but cynicism goes beyond that. The cynics aren't going to help build a better world; all they do is tear it down. They see everything wrong and nothing right and are unable to do or write about the constructive things that our society needs.

Second, focus on the important matters and not just what may have some current fascination. Just before writing this, I picked up a major newspaper in this country, which had a great deal of front-page coverage about O. J. Simpson's trial, and then back on the seventh page, I learned that Kim Il Sung, the dictator of North Korea, died. While the O. J. Simpson story has much appeal, and we can learn about human nature and ourselves from it, in terms of news value and importance to the world and importance to our future, the death of Kim Il Sung was infinitely more important.

I learned about the difference between what's important and gets covered when I was in the Illinois State Legislature many years ago. I received a telephone call from my political mentor, then U. S. Senator Paul Douglas. He asked me to introduce a resolution urging in the Illinois House of Representatives that the corn tassel be designated the official national flower.

Reflecting on his request during the day, more and more I felt uncomfortable offering such a trivial resolution; so that evening I called him and asked, "Are you sure you want me to introduce a resolution on the corn tassel, so that you can do it in the United States Senate?" He laughed and replied, "Just remember this, Paul. The substantial things you do in public life generally receive little coverage; the trivial receive the attention. You introduce your resolution; then I will introduce one in the United States Senate. Our names will be in every newspaper in the state. The resolutions will not pass, but no one will be angry with us. And you will have done something essential to survive in public life."

I learned something about both journalism and politics that evening!

Third, people understand issues as they understand the problems of people. A story about health care in its generalized terms is fine, but it becomes alive when you find someone in your community who can't get health care and faces overwhelming problems because of that. Then people understand the issue. There is not enough personalizing of many key issues.

A few other thoughts: I would advise a beginning or an aspiring journalist to be extremely careful on details. Be accurate. Be accurate. You've heard that before, and I reiterate it. I can't tell you how many times I have been misquoted. Only rarely has it been maliciously, but whether it was an intentional distortion or not, the net effect can sometimes be the same.

Learning another language would be helpful. We have too few American journalists who can travel to other countries and pick up information except through that small percentage of the population who speak English.

Finally, simply work hard. One of the best-known journalists in this country today is someone I regard as a person of unusual willingness to work hard. The brilliant journalist who does not work hard will always be surpassed by the average journalist who does.

I wish you the best.

2

HISTORY OF REPORTING

The tradition in news reporting has been objectivity—fairness, balance, impartiality. It is rooted in a deeply held faith that the American people can be trusted to make up their own minds, if given enough useful information by the press.

When Nicole Brown Simpson and Ronald Goldman were murdered in 1994, the news media provided intense coverage for millions who soaked up every detail. The double homicide was horrific enough, but when Simpson's ex-husband, sports personality O. J. Simpson, became the focus of the investigation, the case took on a fascination equaled by few cases in American crime. Add to that Simpson's flight along the freeways of Los Angeles and the preliminary hearing that led to his being bound over for trial—both viewed by millions on television—and the news media had a story that at once fascinated and appalled its audience. The wrongful death trial of 1996-1997 did little to diminish the media's enthusiasm.

In many ways, criticism of news media coverage makes concrete the findings of Rick Garlick's Gallup poll of public attitudes about the press. How can the press be considered credible and trustworthy when reporters often refuse to tell their audiences where the

BY MICHAEL BUCHHOLZ

Associate Professor of Journalism at Indiana State University, Dr. Buchholz is a former reporter for the Fort Worth *Star-Telegram*. He has taught at Oklahoma State and Texas A&M universities. He is the author of the chapter "The Penny Press, 1833-1861" in Sloan and Startt, *The Media in America*, and has served as editor of the *Intelligencer*, the newsletter of the American Journalism Historians Association.

facts in their news stories come from, especially when some of these "facts" turn out to be wrong? How can there be any respect for a business that trusts its readers and viewers so little? How can there be much regard for journalistic ethics when the audience can see— live and in living color—a distasteful portrait of the press in full pursuit of a story?

Journalistic techniques, including those on full view in the Simpson story, did not develop in a vacuum without reason. They are grounded in ideas about what the press should do in society and how it should do it. This chapter examines the development of those philosophies that have been used throughout American history to justify journalistic practice.

Reporters had been criticized for relying on anonymous sources, some of them wrong, in reporting a scandal that led to the resignation of President Richard Nixon in 1974. Nixon and the two administrations that preceded him had been bedeviled by an allegedly biased news media whose reporting, some were convinced, had lost the war in Vietnam. In the Jazz Age, tabloid newspapers submerged the nation in sensationalism with reports of gangsters, gun molls, and movie stars. And little more than twenty years earlier two New York publishers were accused of starting a war with Spain to keep the circulation of their yellow-tinged newspapers spiraling ever higher.

Many reporters, although sometimes accused of slanting the news, pride themselves on their objectivity. This generally means that they try—and expect the same of other reporters—to keep their opinions, biases, and prejudices out of their news reports. The theory behind this attitude is older than English-language journalism on the North American continent. It is based on the Enlightenment belief that people are rational and that they can discern the truth from a bedlam of competing voices. Printers in England and in the British colonies did not argue that writing should be unbiased. But they did argue that the press should be free, that everyone should be allowed to write and publish whatever he wanted without government restriction and censorship. Truth could then contend with falsehood in this open marketplace of ideas, and the good would drive out the bad. The British poet John Milton, later a government censor himself, stated the proposition effectively in his *Areopagitica* in 1644: "Though all the winds of doctrine were let loose to play upon the earth, so Truth be in the field, we do ingloriously, by licensing and prohibiting, to misdoubt her strength. Let her and Falsehood grapple: who ever knew Truth put to the worse in a free and open encounter?"

THE EARLY AMERICAN PRESS

British transplants on American soil brought this attitude with them. Benjamin Franklin stated the Enlightenment principle of printing neutrality in 1731. In "An Apology for Printers," published in his *Pennsylvania Gazette* in 1731, he wrote the following:

> Printers are educated in the Belief, that when Men differ in Opinion, both Sides ought equally to have the Advantage of being heard by the Publick; and that when Truth and Error have fair Play, the former is always an overmatch for the latter: Hence they chearfully serve all contending Writers that pay them well, without regarding on which side they are of the Question in Dispute.

Printers did not agree with everything they printed, Franklin wrote, yet many people assumed they did—and thus they managed to offend a number of their readers. He continued: "They print things full of Spleen and Animosity, with the utmost Calmness and Indifference, and without the least Ill-will to the Persons reflected on; who nevertheless unjustly think the Printer as much their Enemy as the Author, and join both together in their Resentment." He noted that if printers printed only that which offended no one, very little would get printed.

Many colonial printers adopted Franklin's attitude more as a trade strategy than as a matter of principle. To survive, they needed the support of all the members of their community and printed whatever they were paid to print. In times of political controversy, some avoided giving offense that might lose them business by refusing to print anything about the issue. But as the British colonies moved closer to revolution, it became tougher for printers to stay on the sidelines. Caught between those who were loyal to the Mother Country and those who felt the colonies should declare their independence, most printers eventually moved to one side or the other.

Thus partisanship in the press has had a long history in the United States. As political factions developed in the early years of the republic, so did the political press to support them. These newspapers did not have to avoid political controversy to survive; instead, they thrived on it. Neither did they have to open their columns to all manner of opinion. There was now enough business to support several newspapers, at least in the nation's larger cities. "Professions of impartiality I shall make none," wrote Federalist editor William Cobbett. "They are always useless and are besides perfect nonsense." Federalist John Fenno was blunt about supporting his party, which controlled the government when he wrote this in his *Gazette of the United States:*

> To hold up the people's own government, in a favorable point of light—and to impress just ideas of its administration by exhibiting FACTS, comprise the outline of the plan of this paper—and so long as the principles of the Constitution are held sacred, and the rights and liberties of the people are preserved inviolate, by *"the powers that be,"* it is the office of patriotism, by every exertion, to endear the GENERAL GOVERNMENT TO THE PEOPLE.

Editors and writers in the Federalist and Anti-Federalist/Republican newspapers attacked each other with abandon. In fact, the Federalists thought that the Anti-Federalist/Republican press was so partisan that it bordered on treason, and they passed a series of short-lived alien and sedition laws in an attempt to curb it. But the Republicans outlasted the Federalists, only to split into three factions themselves—each with its own newspapers—and usher in the nation's second party system.

THE PENNY PRESS

During the heyday of the partisan press, editors began separating opinion from news, sometimes labeling or signing articles of opinion, thus publishing what is considered to be the first true editorials. By the fourth decade of the 19th century, another important shift had occurred: newspapers emerged that were read for the news they contained, not for the political party or philosophy they supported. True, James Gordon Bennett's New York *Herald* was Democratic; Horace Greeley's New York *Tribune* was Whiggish; Henry Raymond's New York *Times* was Republican. But these newspapers and the first successful cheap daily, Benjamin Day's New York *Sun*, were read by a mass audience because of their emphasis on news and sometimes in spite of their editors' political proclivities.

Why the penny press developed in the 1830s is a matter of intense debate among historians even today. Some said it was just part of the natural development of newspapers. Others said that changes in technology—the development of new sources of newsprint; the invention of faster, steam-powered printing presses; the revolution in communication brought about by the railroads, the steamship and the telegraph—made the penny press possible. Still others said that increasing literacy rates produced a demand that penny press publishers were quick to recognize and satisfy. Others have argued that the penny press was a manifestation of a democratic market society in which an emerging middle class valued business enterprise and political independence.

Regardless of the cause, those who developed the penny press in New York between 1833 and 1861 recognized that there was money to be made by producing bright, lively, relatively non-political newspapers that would attract a mass of newly literate readers who did not like or could not afford the more expensive partisan newspapers. The resulting circulation figures—admittedly not subject to verification in those days—indicated that they were successful. Day, Bennett, Greeley, Raymond, and other editors like them in other large American cities continued the trend of separating news from opinion. James Parton, a journalist who was Greeley's contemporary and biographer, wrote in 1866:

> The prestige of the editorial is gone.... There are journalists who think the time is at hand for the abolition of editorials, and the concentration of the whole force of journalism upon presenting to the public the history and picture of the day. The time for this has not come and may never come; but our journalists already know that editorials neither make nor mar a daily paper, that they do not much influence the public mind, nor change many votes, and that the power and success of a newspaper depend wholly and absolutely upon its success in getting, and its skill in exhibiting the news.... The news is the point of rivalry; it is that for which 19/20ths of the people buy newspapers; it is that which constitutes the power and value of the daily press; it is that which determines the rank of every newspaper in every free country.

In place of a slavish devotion to political party, the penny newspapers gave their readers brightly written, relatively unbiased news grounded in sensational stories of crime and sex seasoned with strong dollops of human interest. Perhaps it became easier to do so as their editors discovered a source of income other than the political party—the advertiser. But the emphasis was coming to focus on news. Their editors also made clear that they thought that newspapers had a greater mission than the mere support of a partisan philosophy. They could be used to revitalize society. Bennett in the first issue of the *Herald* in 1835 said:

> I mean to make the Herald the great organ of social life, the prime element of civilization, the channel through which native talent, native genius, and native power may bubble up daily, as the pure sparkling liquid of the Congress fountain at Saratoga bubbles up from the centre of the earth, till it meets the rosy lips

of the fair. I shall mix together commerce and business, pure religion and morals, literature and poetry, the drama and dramatic purity, till the Herald shall outstrip everything in the conception of man.

Raymond said the *Times* would serve the public good regardless of which political party it helped or hurt. That meant that the *Times* would be conservative or radical as the situation demanded, not as the political philosophy of the current administration or of Raymond's own Republican Party might require. He wrote the following in the first issue of the *Times* in 1851:

We shall be *Conservative*, in all cases where we think Conservatism essential to the public good;—and we shall be *Radical*, in everything which may seem to us to require radical treatment and radical reform. We do not believe that *everything* in Society is either exactly right, or exactly wrong;—what is good we desire to preserve and improve;—what is evil, to exterminate, or reform.

Even outside the nation's newspaper capital, editors were expressing the same sentiments. Earlier in 1851, Samuel Bowles, the editor of the Springfield (Mass.) *Republican*, wrote:

The brilliant mission of the newspaper is not yet, and perhaps may never be, perfectly understood. It is, and is to be, the high priest of History, the vitalizer of Society, the world's great informer, the earth's high censor, the medium of public thought and opinion, and the circulating life blood of the whole human mind. It is the great enemy of tyrants, and the right arm of liberty, and is destined, more than any other agency, to melt and mould the jarring and contending nations of the world into that one great brotherhood which, through long centuries, has been the ideal of the Christian and the philanthropist. Its mission has just commenced. A few years more, and a great thought uttered within sight of the Atlantic, will rise with the morrow's sun and shine upon millions of minds by the side of the Pacific. The murmur of Asia's multitudes will be heard at our doors; and laden with the fruit of all human thought and action, the newspaper will be in every abode, the daily nourishment of every mind.

These ideals also served an economic purpose. People could be expected to buy a newspaper that claimed to represent their interests, and the resulting circulation—as Bennett and his competitors learned very early—could be used to attract advertisers.

Not all newspapers in the middle of the 19th century followed the lead of the penny press. A study by scholar Donald Lewis Shaw showed that the nation's newspapers in general were slow to adopt some of the changes made by their big-city brethren. He found that from 1820 to 1860 most newspapers still emphasized news of politics and economics instead of the more sensationalized fare that titillated readers of the penny press in New York. Nor did he find the brighter, breezier style of the penny press invading the columns of most other newspapers. He did note an increase in wire news from 1847 to 1860; and, in another study of newspapers in Wisconsin from 1852 to 1916, he observed that wire news about presidential campaigns tended to be relatively unbiased. An increase in wire news contributed to the trend of separating opinion from news.

Samuel F. B. Morse introduced the telegraph to an incredulous public in 1844, and it was only four years later that the forerunner of today's Associated Press, the Harbor News Association, was formed in New York City. Newspapers in New York and other cities already had seen the value of cooperative newsgathering and had used everything from carrier pigeons and pony expresses to news boats to gather the news quickly and cheaply. With the outbreak of war between the United States and Mexico over a border dispute in 1846, newspapers in the North faced a difficult and expensive task of covering military action that took place in Mexico, far beyond the southernmost telegraph lines. Most relied on newspapers in New Orleans to do the job. A study by historian Tom Reilly found the New Orleans press to be highly biased in favor of the American army and against the Mexicans, and stories in the New Orleans newspapers spread this bias throughout the country.

The New York wire service, though, over the years gradually removed most of the opinion from the stories it transmitted. This was in keeping with the penny press emphasis on news instead of views, and it also made good economic sense. The Associated Press, the name the wire service adopted in 1893, was made up of newspapers that were responsible for covering events in their areas and putting their stories on the wire for other newspapers to use. If the stories were politically slanted and contradicted a member's political philosophy, some members would not want to publish them. Wire service reports had a strong influence on the newspapers that used them. Local writing styles began to mirror the wire service reports, which adopted the summary lead and the inverted pyramid format because of the uncertainties of moving stories by telegraph during the Civil War. The neutrality of the wire service reports may have had a similar influence on the straight-news writing style that became more prominent toward the beginning of the 20th century.

THE LATE 19TH-CENTURY PRESS

As the old century was ending, the most influential figure in American journalism was Joseph Pulitzer, editor of the paper he bought from Jay Gould in 1883, the New York *World*. Pulitzer was not so much an innovator as a synthesizer. He managed to integrate many of the trends of late-19th century journalism into a single paper that was imitated in many ways by his major rival, William Randolph Hearst. Readers of the *World* reveled in Pulitzer's sensational reporting; followed his globe-trotting reporter Elizabeth Cochrane, writing as Nellie Bly, as she reported her travels around the world; and supported his crusades, like his fund-raising campaign for the donated Statue of Liberty. But they also found a strong commitment to public service in a newspaper that was dedicated, as Pulitzer expressed it in 1883, "to the cause of the people rather than that of purse-potentates... that will expose all fraud and sham, fight all public evils and abuses—that will serve and battle for the people with earnest sincerity."

Pulitzer desired influence. According to one of his biographers, W. A. Swanberg, he wanted to speak to the nation; he wanted to influence public policy. Unable to run for president himself because of his foreign birth, he wanted to do the next best thing, influence the election of a president. For that kind of influence, Pulitzer needed circulation. Once he attracted large numbers of readers to his paper with the lively, sensationalistic reporting of his staff, he could expose them to his editorial ideas, which emerged from what Swanberg called "the most earnest, powerful and efficient social conscience yet seen in journalism." Although Pulitzer's emphasis was on news, he knew that the newspaper should be more than a recorder of events. Fleshing out his philosophy of journalism in 1886, he wrote:

The newspaper that is true to its highest mission will concern itself with the things that *ought to happen tomorrow*, or next month, or next year, and will seek to make what ought to be come to pass. It is not enough to chronicle the life and thought of the people and to reflect their tone and temper. This is a most important service. But a paper which has the moral sense, the intellectual perception and the political independence to speak to the heart, the mind and the conscience of the people and tell them what they will feel that it is for their good to hear and to heed, can do more to benefit the country than can a hundred pulpits or a score of Governors—more than any one session of Congress, or any four-year President, or any party.

The highest mission of the press is to *render public service*. It does this by publishing the news and by speaking the truth fearlessly in regard to current events.

Scholar David Paul Nord saw Pulitzer doing in New York what Melville E. Stone had done in Chicago after founding the Chicago *Daily News* in 1875. Other daily newspapers in Chicago—such as the Chicago *Times* and the Chicago *Tribune*—were tied to the mid-19th century values of individualism and private property, Nord maintained. To a greater or lesser extent, Wilbur F. Storey of the *Times* and his nemesis, Joseph Medill of the *Tribune*, believed that most people should take care of themselves and that government mostly should leave private property alone to flourish or flounder according to the abilities or ineptitude of its owner. Their papers' content reflected their editorial values with an emphasis on news of government, politics, and business. Both tried to be all things to all people and printed a vast collection of stories about disparate events, each of which would interest at least one reader. Nord called it the "smorgasbord model," based on the idea that readers were individuals who had individual interests.

Stone and the *Daily News*, on the other hand, felt that individuals were not always responsible for their circumstances and that private property had an obligation to the community in which it operated. Editorially the newspaper urged action for the common good by charities, voluntary associations, and government. Stone saw readers as having common interests and tastes as part of a larger community, and thus he attempted to fill his newspaper with a smaller number of stories, most of which would be of interest to most of his readers. As the newspaper grew, it focused more and more on investigative reporting and crusading in the public interest. "It was neither the first popular nor the first modern newspaper in the city," Nord wrote. "But it was the first thoroughly urban one—that is, the first to articulate a vision of public community." The early penny papers editors were more like Medill and Storey, and Pulitzer was more like Stone in promoting his readers' common interests.

Thus editors like Pulitzer and Stone in New York, Chicago, and other cities helped to make public service a major component of the newspaper's reason for being. They knew of the penny papers' attempts to expose corruption and abuse in the 1830s and 1840s. They had witnessed the crusade of the New York *Times* and *Harper's Weekly* that brought down the grafters of the Tammany Hall political ring. And they conducted crusades of their own. The tradition was picked up by the muckrakers in the first two decades of the 20th century and by the investigative reporters of the 1960s and the Watergate era. It is reflected today in the news media's constant attempt to reveal corruption in public office and to help the less fortunate in society through charity work. It leads editors to emphasize that one of their reporters' greatest obligations is to their readers and viewers. It is a tradition that by necessity is tied closely to the news function. Yet it goes beyond the principle that the overriding purpose of newspapers is to provide news. The preeminence of news is a principle that has had many articulate advocates. One of them was Pulitzer's competitor Charles A. Dana, editor of the New York *Sun*. He emphasized in an 1888 lecture:

> The newspaper must be founded upon human nature. It must correspond to the wants of the people. It must furnish that sort of information which the people demand, or else it never can be successful. The first thing which an editor must look for is news. If the newspaper has not the news, it may have everything else, yet it will be comparatively unsuccessful; and by news I mean everything that occurs, everything which is of human interest, and which is of sufficient importance to arrest and absorb the attention of the public or of any considerable part of it. There is a great disposition in some quarters to say that the newspapers ought to limit the amount of news that they print; that certain kinds of news ought not to be published.... [B]ut I have always felt that whatever the Divine Providence permitted to occur I was not too proud to report....
>
> News is undoubtedly a great thing in a newspaper. A newspaper without news is no newspaper. The main function of a newspaper is to give the news, and tell you what has happened in the world, what events have occurred of all sorts, political, scientific, and nonsensical.

THE DEVELOPMENT OF OBJECTIVE REPORTING

In the 18th and 19th centuries, Enlightenment theory meant that people should be exposed to all sorts of ideas and opinions so they could decide for themselves what was true. By the beginning of the 20th century, the stuff of news stories was not ideas and opinions, but facts, and reporters felt that if they could provide their audiences with all the relevant facts, all the various sides of an issue, readers could decide for themselves what was true. The job of reporters, then, became one of gathering information and presenting it to their audiences. This 20th-century notion of objectivity—not all the views but all the facts—was described by journalist Walter Lippmann in his 1922 book, *Public Opinion*. Lippmann started with the proposition that everyone develops concepts of the world around him based on bias and prejudice. He called these "stereotypes," the pictures that everyone carries in his head. They may be true or false, but everyone uses them to make sense of a confusing, complicated reality. Lippmann wrote:

> For the most part we do not first see, and then define; we define first and then see. In the great booming, buzzing confusion of the outer world we pick out what our culture has already defined for us, and we tend to perceive that which we have picked out in the form stereotyped for us by our culture.

Using stereotypes is efficient because people do not have the time to examine anew everything they encounter, Lippmann said. Putting a person or a thing into a larger, general category lets people know instantly—based on their stereotypes—what to think and do about what they see. The danger is that people also use their stereotypes to judge. "The stereotypes are loaded with preference, suffused with affection or dislike, attached to fears, lusts, strong wishes, pride, hope," Lippmann wrote. "Whatever invokes the stereotype is judged with the appropriate sentiment."

Reporters can attempt to cover the news objectively, Lippmann said, but first they have to recognize their biases and prejudices, the pictures they carry in their heads. If they cannot recognize their stereotypes for what they are, they will see the world according to their preconceived notions and pass them on to their audience. If they can recognize them as mere opinions, they can treat them as scientists treat hypotheses, examine them in light of the facts they gather and the observations they make, and accept or reject them accordingly.

Once reporters recognize and overcome their prejudices, Lippmann said, they can begin to report objectively. But reporters also have to recognize that they cannot provide all the information that everyone needs to form an opinion on everything. News is not the same thing as truth—the former describes an event while the latter produces a picture of reality based on exposing hidden facts and showing the relationship among them. Reporters cannot observe everything and bring it to their audience. They must instead depend on sources they consider to be reliable and fashion the best picture of reality they can. They are forced, in other words, to depend upon what has been recorded for them by the institutions of society.

Objective reporting as it developed in the early part of the 20th century, then, attempted to avoid coloring the news with opinion by emphasizing observation and official sources. Reporters described what they saw at trials and city council meetings, unaware of how observable facts might not represent underlying reality, and they depended on prominent people to provide accurate information about what they knew. Overseas, the Associated Press forced its correspondents to report only what had happened, leaving out the background and context some of them could have supplied about European politics.

THE CALL FOR SOCIAL RESPONSIBILITY

The technique worked reasonably well in routine situations—car wrecks, death notices, the run of police news. But some stories were too complicated to cover this way, and traditional objectivity ended up misinforming the public. Reporting of the international negotiations before the outbreak of World War I told readers only what diplomats wanted them to know, and the start of hostilities in 1914 came as a shock to Americans who had been reading only the wire reports in their local newspapers. Objective reporting also made it difficult for Americans to understand the stock market crash in 1929 and the causes of the Great Depression that followed during the 1930s. The demand grew for more in-depth reporting about the economy, its woes, and the growth of government in response—a demand the news media began to meet in news magazines, books, newsletters, and expanding feature sections in newspapers. Reporters also began turning to sources inside and out of government to explain the Depression and developments in a number of other seldom-covered fields like labor relations and science. They began to recognize the problems that depending on official sources could cause for reporters, especially when they assumed that statements from such sources were automatically newsworthy. When followed to extremes, this narrow view of newsworthiness meant that reporters would accept uncritically and print whatever public officials told them. It mattered little whether the statement was true; the prominence of the source made it newsworthy.

The Commission on Freedom of the Press in 1947 argued for the "social responsibility" of the press. As described by scholar Theodore Peterson, the theory is based on the following assumptions:

> Freedom carries concomitant obligations; and the press, which enjoys a privileged position under our government, is obliged to be responsible to society for carrying out certain essential functions of mass communication in contemporary society. To the extent that the press recognizes its responsibilities and makes them the basis of operational policies, the libertarian system will satisfy

the needs of society. To the extent that the press does not assume its responsibilities, some other agency must see that the essential functions of mass communication are carried out.

In its main report, *A Free and Responsible Press*, the commission maintained that some of the premises that supported the traditional libertarian view of the press no longer held true. People no longer lived in small communities where they could test a variety of opinions face to face or observe everything that happened. In a complex society they necessarily depended on others to provide them with information, and the volume of information was becoming overwhelming. But while the news media were bombarding the public with more and more information, consolidation was shrinking the number of competing media voices. Those remaining had a new kind of responsibility to their audiences.

The commission thus outlined five requirements that a free society has of its press. The first would eventually have a major impact on how reporters did their job. The press, the commission said, must provide "a truthful, comprehensive, and intelligent account of the day's events in a context which gives them meaning." This means, first of all, that the press must tell the truth. Reporters, the commission said, are "the first link in the chain of responsibility" since they gather the news at its source. Thus,

[A reporter] must be careful and competent. He must estimate correctly which sources are most authoritative. He must prefer firsthand observation to hearsay. He must know what questions to ask, what things to observe, and which items to report. His employer has the duty of training him to do his work as it ought to be done.

Reporters and everyone else involved in the editorial product must try as much as possible to identify fact and opinion and separate one from the other, because the public could no longer do it alone. The commission also recognized that facts must be supplied with context, as it explained:

But modern conditions require greater effort than ever to make the distinction between fact and opinion. In a simpler order of society published accounts of events within the experience of the community could be compared with other sources of information. Today this is usually impossible. The account of an isolated fact, however accurate in itself, may be misleading and, in effect, untrue.

In other words, a story could be accurate in every detail but inaccurate and misleading in total impression if context is missing. The commission noted, "It is no longer enough to report *the fact* truthfully. It is now necessary to report *the truth about the fact.*"

The commission also said that the press must provide "a forum for the exchange of comment and criticism," project "a representative picture of the constituent groups in the society," present and clarify "the goals and values of the society," and provide "full access to the day's intelligence."

The press immediately attacked the report, partly because journalists perceived the commission as a group of ivory-tower intellectuals who had never spent a day as working reporters or editors. The press also thought that the commission's criticisms of its performance were too harsh. And some elements of the industry and the academic community were especially concerned with the commission's suggestion that someone or some agency outside of the industry might have to step in if the press could not fulfill its obligations to society on its own. However, hardly anyone in the media challenged the commission's basic contention that the press had a responsibility to society or the report's list of the press' functions in a modern democracy.

THE EMERGENCE OF INTERPRETATIVE REPORTING

What has emerged since the commission's work is the concept of interpretative reporting, one of the most important journalistic developments to come out of the 1930s and 1940s. As practiced by conscientious journalists, interpretative reporting involved adding one question—why?—to the catechism reporters were expected to follow in answering all the basic questions their audiences would have about an event: who, what, where, when, and how. In explaining the why of an event, reporters would try to explain what had led to the event over time and what the event might mean in the future. Reporters, of course, were not expected to speculate. They were expected to provide the explanation by interviewing a number of knowledgeable sources who could put the event in perspective. Erwin D. Canham, former editor of the *Christian Science Monitor*, said that if reporters quote a misleading statement, they should also report the balancing fact. Harry S. Ashmore, once the editor of the *Arkansas Gazette*, declared that reporters were not required to give equal space to both "saints" and "sinners," that "a set of indisputable facts does not necessarily add up to the whole truth." Reporters thus were able to go beyond the surface reporting of events by attempting to place them in context for their audience.

Although reporters continued to use the techniques of traditional objective journalism—observation and dependence upon official sources—through the 1960s and into the early 1970s, they also continued to add context to their stories. This suggested to some that the news media were becoming more critical of political authority, apparent in the increasingly critical attitude they saw the news media taking toward the conduct of the Vietnam War. It was America's first television war. Cascading into American living rooms were images of helicopter-borne assaults of American infantry, firefights that left bleeding GIs to be treated on camera by medics, and villages being burned to "save" them. Unlike the correspondents who had covered wars in the past, the corps of Vietnam War correspondents did not consider themselves part of the American team. They took seriously the idea that facts should be reported in a context that gave them meaning. When David Halberstam of the New York *Times* became convinced from what he learned in Vietnam that the U. S. military was wrong in some of its assumptions and was pursuing a faulty policy, he reported the problems. When the American military touted its success in bombing military targets in North Vietnam from high-altitude B-52s, Harrison Salisbury went to Hanoi and reported major bomb damage to non-military facilities. Seymour Hersh revealed that American troops had massacred hundreds of Vietnamese civilians in the village of My Lai. The American military called the reporting negative and unpatriotic, and some said it led to the nation's defeat in the Indochina war. If these critics were right, the news media had abandoned their 20th-century tradition of neutrality in favor of a muckraking form of advocacy journalism.

Scholar Daniel C. Hallin, however, studied television coverage of the Vietnam War and concluded that:

> The evidence does not suggest any dramatic shift in the basic ideology and news-gathering routines of American journalism. The routines of objective journalism—routines which are incompatible with an actively oppositional conception of the journalists' role—seem to have persisted more or less unchanged throughout the Vietnam period. The media continued, in particular, to rely heavily on official information and to avoid passing explicit judgment on official policy and statements.... The media were not inclined to favor opponents of administration policy, and... critical coverage in the latter part of the war did not extend to the political system or to basic consensus beliefs.

So why the perception of opposition? Hallin began his explanation by saying that journalists operate in three spheres. One he called the sphere of consensus wherein lie "those social objects not regarded by journalists and by most of the society as controversial." Outside that sphere is what Hallin called the sphere of legitimate controversy. "This is the region where objective journalism reigns supreme: here neutrality and balance are the prime journalistic virtues," he said. Beyond these is an area that Hallin left nameless, where "lie those political actors and views which journalists and the political mainstream of the society reject as unworthy of being heard."

In covering the Vietnam War, Hallin pointed out, the news media were covering two different stories—military action abroad and domestic dissent at home. As the opposition to the war grew at home, Hallin said, it moved from the radicals on the fringes of society into Congress and the electoral system. The criticism was coming more and more from those who journalists and the public considered to be legitimate spokesmen. "As this occurred the normal procedures of objective journalism produced increasing coverage of oppositional viewpoints," Hallin wrote. As the sphere of legitimate controversy expanded, he said, the sphere of consensus shrunk. "Stories that previously had been reported within a consensus framework came to be reported as controversies; subjects and points of view that had been beyond the pale in the early years came to be treated as legitimate news stories," he wrote. The change in coverage, he concluded, was "a reflection of and a response to a collapse of consensus—especially of elite consensus—on foreign policy."

The danger for reporters today lies in forgetting that interpretation is not the same as subjectivity, that a journalism degree and a news media job do not provide a license for reporters to masquerade their opinions and biases as facts or to weed out "facts" and opinions with which they disagree. Turning "social responsibility" into a right to limit the public's access to information only substitutes one form of control for another. The public's perception that the news media are attempting to become "information czars" may have led to the disenchantment represented in the Gallup poll cited in the preface of this book.

In the early 1980s, scholars George S. Hage, Everette E. Dennis, Arnold H. Ismach, and Stephen Hartgen declared:

> Journalistic excellence... combines devotion to the factuality of objective reporting *and* recognition of the need for interpretation. It rejects the ritual model of journalistic objectivity that grew

with the rise of the scientific method in the nineteenth century. That model, in its purest form, called for faithful recording of the observed event and suppression of the observer's prior knowledge of the subject.

Rejection of the pure objective model, however, doesn't mean approval of *subjective* reporting. Personal bias, unsupported assertions, and one-sided presentations have no place in news stories. The happy marriage of objectivity and interpretation demands factual observation along with a balanced presentation of pertinent background and contextual information.

These scholars describe a wedding between the best aspects of two reporting philosophies that have dominated almost half of American journalistic history. Reporters would continue to observe the events around them, reporting those of interest to their audiences and interpreting them by drawing on information and sources representing all perspectives. Reporters would also have to be honest and up-front, naming their sources so the audience can gauge the credibility of the information. Then, perhaps, the news media could regain some of the confidence they apparently have lost over the last generation.

Perspective...

WHAT AN HISTORIAN WISHES
BEGINNING JOURNALISTS KNEW ABOUT HISTORY

By STEPHEN VAUGHN, Professor of Journalism and Mass Communication at the University of Wisconsin—Madison

All journalists will use history whether they realize it or not. The question is whether they will use it intelligently. The person who is ignorant of history is at risk of being victimized by those who claim to know the lessons of the past.

History is perhaps most useful if thought of as a way of thinking about issues through time. It is the element of time that sets history apart from most other disciplines. The process of studying the past, making for a time a period of history our present, is often as valuable as the information we learn from our study. One emerges from this experience with a fresh perspective and the ability to look at contemporary issues in a more insightful fashion.

The intelligent use of the past involves understanding history's limitations. Most reporters have heard the admonition that "those who fail to remember the mistakes of the past are condemned to repeat them." But history rarely repeats itself. It does not lend itself to easy formulas; it is not a book of recipes. It is unlikely that studying the past will give us the ability to predict the future, although it does help us to anticipate what will occur in much the same way practice helps the musician or athlete perform better. Another way to think about history is to compare it to a light on the stern of a ship passing through the night. It does not cast much light on where the ship is headed, and yet it is the only light the ship has.

All stories that journalists cover have historical contexts, ones that usually go well beyond the recent past. The better the journalist's sense of history, the more likely he or she will report what is significant. Unfortunately, members of the media frequently discuss history in a shorthand that masks the complexity of the past and skews its meaning. For example, "the 1960s" is often invoked to bring to mind the civil rights, antiwar, and counterculture movements; or "the 1980s" is characterized as the decade of Reaganomics. Historical developments usually do not group themselves into tidy chronological categories. The roots of the civil rights movement trace to World War II and beyond. The seeds of Reagan's opposition to the welfare state were sown during the New Deal of the 1930s, if not during the 1920s.

It is difficult, if not impossible, to think about the present and future without reference to the past, and historical analogies are among the most effective and powerful ways to provide meaning. But historical analogies can easily be misapplied or manipulated. Hence the Gulf War was portrayed in terms of the Vietnam War, just as American involvement in Vietnam was justified in terms of the Munich analogy and the events leading up to World War II. Too often historical analogies are drawn only from the memories of the current generation. When journalists limit themselves in this way, they are imprisoning their readers in one time period. For historical analogies to give insight into present-day problems they should be drawn not merely from the present generation but from many generations. It is the journalist's challenge first to make the appropriate analogies and, second, to make them meaningful to the public.

Propagandists are especially adept at manipulating analogies. Indeed, the propagandist often distorts the meaning of history by selectively choosing information from the past that fits a preconceived view. Journalists should recognize the difference between this type of history and the work of writers who attempt to examine contemporary problems historically by studying the past on its own terms to the best of their ability.

All history, good or bad, involves interpretation because what we know of the past is not static or merely a collection of facts etched in stone. At least two histories exist—all those events that actually happened in the past, and what we can know of those events. Most of the past lies in the "black night of the utterly forgotten," and what we can know of past occurrences will always be incomplete. But as we expand our knowledge of what went before and as new questions are asked of the past, new interpretations arise.

3

THE NEWS OPERATION

Learning how to identify news, gather, and write it is but the first step into journalism. Different media, editors, and newsroom practices will modify your expectations and shape the kind of journalist you will become. This has been true historically; it is true today. In addition, there are the twin concerns of all journalism: to make money and to serve the reader. This chapter helps you to anticipate some of the pressures generated by those workplace realities.

The murder of Nicole Brown Simpson and Ronald Goldman in 1994 created a great media event. The coverage by print and electronic media raised several issues: free press and fair trial, tabloid journalism, and checkbook journalism. Important as these issues are, they are not the issues we will focus on in this chapter. Instead, we will look at how newsroom organization affects coverage of a high profile episode such as the O. J. Simpson case.

Four news operation practices stood out in the episode. In descending order of importance, they are these:

1. The distinctive strengths of each form of journalism—newspapers or television—were clearly shown.

BY TED C. SMYTHE
Professor Emeritus at California State University at Fullerton, Dr. Smythe is Distinguished Scholar in Residence at Sterling (Kansas) College. He is co-editor of *Readings in Mass Communication*, now in its ninth edition, and is a specialist on newsroom dynamics.

2. It was important for reporters to know court and police procedure.

3. Competitive pressures on reporters, especially on-air reporters, caused them to report events or make prejudicial statements which, under normal circumstances, might have been edited out of a final program.

4. Covering the story, until it moved to the courtroom, involved moving reporters and equipment over great distances rapidly and sometimes simultaneously. This aspect of the coverage demonstrated the need for journalistic teamwork.

It should be borne in mind as you read this chapter that no single news event can illustrate most of the newsroom operations we need to discuss, but this particular event, because it is fresh in the mind of most readers, should launch us into our discussion.

Let's briefly examine each operation and see how it has developed historically.

THE MEDIUM SHAPES THE PRODUCT

Following news of the murder, but before the district attorney decided to arraign Mr. Simpson, the Los Angeles *Times* and the Los Angeles *Daily News* had the most exclusives on the police department's developing case. The *Times* in particular was ahead of every other newspaper or television station in revealing the police findings and investigations. A news producer at one of the major television stations acknowledged it had been following the *Times'* lead each step of the way, because the paper had better sources inside the police department.

Newspapers having better sources is a natural outcome of television news practices which tend to downplay police tactics and procedures even while they play up on-the-scene reporting of murders and violent deaths. Tactics and procedures aren't visual, and television news producers are less interested in covering those subjects. TV stations often have fewer reporters covering the police department in a city as large as Los Angeles. Therefore, the reporters for the paper, who covered crime beyond the quick pictures available at the scene and the press conference, had established contacts with line investigators and prosecutors in ways denied to most television news reporters. This is one of the strengths of daily newspaper journalism. This, plus the space to tell a detailed story. Thus, the difference in coverage of police news is not a reflection on the quality of television news reporters so much as a natural outcome of contemporary television news.

As we all saw, however, television news offers unbeatable

coverage under certain circumstances. When Mr. Simpson and his close friend Al Cowlings fled the preliminary arraignment, and police finally located the escape car on a Southern California freeway, partly because local citizens, alerted by radio, reported its location, only television news could—and did—provide the coverage that held Americans riveted to their sets for several hours, until the fading light was finally too dim for even the sensitive cameras in the hovering helicopters. The cameras couldn't tell us that Mr. Simpson was in the car, but continuous radio contact with police assured us he was; so we were privy to information as it was being developed by the police. In fact, we felt we knew as much or more than some of the patrolmen as they followed the white Bronco. We learned of Mr. Simpson's desire to return to his house and to contact his mother. Even police at headquarters followed events on television. Only television could provide us with a grandstand seat in what we call "real time," that is, as the event takes place. Each news medium showed its particular strengths in those early days of the case.

This has been true historically. For well over a century newspapers had virtually no competition in providing news to the public. Magazines generally weren't news oriented and, in any case, tended to focus on national events when they did deal with "news." Competition was between newspapers in the same community—and there were numerous papers competing vigorously with each other, especially in the last third of the 19th century. It was radio, developing commercially in the 1920s, that offered newspapers their first taste of competition for news by a different medium. Radio's "immediacy"—the ability to be on the scene of an incident as it occur—could not be matched by the printed press. The press adjusted by providing more pictures and diagrams and more extensive coverage, something radio could not do. Newspapers had to concede most breaking news to radio as the medium developed its own news services.

It took many years after television developed for it to begin to provide the kinds of on-the-scene reporting that radio could. TV did use still and motion pictures (video came later) and, as a result, offered a different kind of competition to both newspapers and radio. Today, technology enables TV cameras to be set up in remote places, to be placed in helicopters or vans with the signals transmitted to pickup points. The signals then are relayed to television studios and retransmitted to a watching audience.

The result of television's advantages is that TV news today is a money maker for many stations. Early network programs were only fifteen minutes long; today local news programs in Los Angeles and other major cities may be two hours. When new management took over WHDH, Channel 7 in Boston in 1993, the station went from two hours of local news daily to six and one-half hours! It bought two "live-transmission trucks, expanded studio-production facilities, and hired handfuls of new reporters," according to the *Christian Science Monitor,* which is located in Boston. And the station began to earn money. TV news today is one of the reasons afternoon newspapers have been declining around the country. Television is a powerful competitive news medium by any definition.

REPORTERS MUST HAVE SPECIALIZED KNOWLEDGE

The Simpson case showed us that reporters need to know court and police procedures. This is but one element in a much larger principle: all reporters need to know the rules and procedures of any field on which they are reporting.

It was clear, especially in the first few days following the murders of Nicole Simpson and Ronald Goldman, that reporters and anchors were swimming in murky waters. Several times anchors accused the police of being lax in not keeping Mr. Simpson under surveillance, thus allowing him to flee and make his dash for freedom—or whatever he was doing. This accusation not only was unfair to the police; it also revealed a significant lack of knowledge on the part of those anchors who were making the charges. When a celebrity has a lawyer and that lawyer has the confidence of the police, as was true with Robert L. Shapiro, the police don't need to expend taxpayers' money by keeping the suspect under surveillance. In other words, not only were the anchors confusing the viewer, they were revealing their own ignorance.

Ignorance of court rules and practices on the part of the working press is something Shapiro commented on in an article he wrote for the National Association of Criminal Defense Lawyers, published more than a year before the Simpson case. Based on his experience with other celebrity cases, in which reporters who normally don't cover the police beat become involved in the story, he concluded that "most reporters couldn't tell you the difference between a preliminary hearing and a pretrial conference. They know little or nothing of how bail is posted and what the legal requirements are."

In this sense, the Simpson case is an excellent example of a problem in American journalism. Reporters often must cover subjects on which they are unprepared. This happened in the Gulf

War, when reporters who had never covered the military and didn't understand military culture or technology suddenly were reporting on military action. The questions some of them asked during press briefings were appalling to many viewers who were watching on C-SPAN (the cable industry-sponsored public affairs network). This was not true of all reporters, of course, for many had covered the Pentagon and military affairs for years. But so many unprepared correspondents were sent to the Gulf that it made the entire correspondent corps look incompetent.

There appears to be the same problem in covering business. A recent study by the Freedom Forum First Amendment Center at Vanderbilt University reported that business people feel that "[c]omplicated business stories are too often assigned to inexperienced reporters, who fail to understand the nuances of the stories." The recent economic recession resulted in cutbacks in business staffs on newspapers, which meant the remaining reporters didn't have time to do stories in depth. It was worse on television, the study claimed: "Coverage of business by local television is poor. And television has far fewer reporters skilled in the coverage of business than do newspapers."

The lack of experienced and knowledgeable reporters on many stories is a fundamental problem in journalism, one that has no easy solution. Thus, it is important that journalists learn as much as possible about the subjects on which they must report.

There is a myth in the business that a good police reporter can report on anything. It is a shorthand way of saying that the techniques used in covering a police beat could apply in all news gathering. This bromide was only partly true at any time historically, for some subjects require special knowledge or the reporter will make serious errors. That principle includes even the police beat, where the language of law is quite explicit and requires specific knowledge. Unfortunately, police reporting all too often is the beat on which reporters get their initial experience on the newspaper. A survey conducted a few years ago revealed that most newspapers outside of the metropolitan areas did not have experienced reporters on the police beat. As soon as reporters gained experience there, they often were assigned to a different beat.

In this, newspapers today differ substantially from fifty or a hundred years ago, when the police beat often was the domain of veteran crime reporters who stayed on the beat for years, becoming experts in their fields and knowing more than many of the policemen and detectives they covered. On major newspapers today some reporters covering courts and police have earned law degrees, though this is rare. The beat was—and is—an interesting one with interesting people and news.

This need for specialized knowledge affects TV reporters, too. But there is an additional problem affecting the TV reporter: coverage of police news focuses on the visual event rather than on police procedures or legal maneuvering. There are exceptions, of course, which usually occur during high-profile cases, such as that of the Menendez brothers, who were tried for killing their parents for profit, or O. J. Simpson. In such cases, television managers sometimes contract with specialists—former prosecuting attorneys or defense lawyers—to offer comment on courtroom events. The same thing happened during the Gulf War when networks hired military "experts" to comment on war plans and on combat itself. Newspapers seldom use such experts, though they may interview them for a story.

COMPETITIVE PRESSURES CAUSE ERRORS

While few journalists who cover the police beat are as experienced today as reporters were a hundred years ago, we have made some progress in the ethics of their practices. During and after the Yellow Journalism period at the turn of the century, police reporters often tried to *solve* crimes in an attempt to get exclusive stories or scoops. Some would steal or conceal evidence so they could beat even the police in solving the case, at which time their papers named the "guilty" party on the front page before the trial occurred. Today's reporters tend to rely upon official, if anonymous, sources for exclusives.

A fairly new practice in American journalism, though long used by England's sensational press, is checkbook journalism, which is the practice of paying a witness to a crime, for instance, for an exclusive story. In the Michael Jackson scandal and the Simpson case, syndicated television news programs such as *Current Affairs* and *Hard Copy* paid for exclusive stories from potential witnesses. So did national tabloid newspapers such as the *National Inquirer*. Such a practice may hurt the defendant in the public's eye and create difficulties in getting a fair trial, but it also may destroy the prosecutor's case since witnesses who get paid for their testimony by the media weaken their credibility on the witness stand.

Iain Calder, editor in chief of the *National Inquirer*, claims checkbook journalism was an unpopular thing to do in the early 1980s. "People would call us and say, 'This is awful journalism.' I think it's become more accepted," he told the Washington *Post*. "The younger journalists have grown up with the idea that television does it. '60 Minutes' has done it on occasion. The mainstream press has moved closer to the Inquirer."

When "everybody's doing it," the pressure on reporters and editors or news producers to get a story is enormous. One New York reporter flew to Bermuda in 1989 to interview Janet Culver, who had survived fourteen days at sea in a rubber raft. But the reporter couldn't get an interview because Ms. Culver had sold exclusive rights to her story to *People* magazine for $10,000. A *People* reporter had won the race to tie up the story under the victim's byline. The reporter who had been beaten opined, "If someone paid me 10 grand, I wouldn't talk either."

There have been times historically when newspapers bought stories from notable figures and syndicated them to other, noncompeting newspapers across the country. This happened in 1927 when Charles A. Lindbergh flew the Atlantic solo. The New York *Times* syndicated his story. In the 1970s *60 Minutes* paid former Richard Nixon aide H. R. Haldeman $25,000 for an interview and G. Gordon Liddy, Watergate burglar, $15,000. David Frost paid the former President himself $600,000 for a series of television interviews, which have been rebroadcast frequently. There have been other cases, but each differs from today in that witnesses were seldom paid for their stories of crime and sensationalism.

Which is not to say that early editors were pristine. Some editors did practice a kind of journalism that we would not accept today. They found witnesses or family members and then hid them in order to get exclusive stories. This tactic kept their story not only from competitors, but from the police as well! There appears to be none of that today. Court rules have changed so much—and the police are so much more professional—that journalists would come under severe criticism or face prosecution should they hide witnesses.

Competition also tempts editors or news producers to publish or broadcast news before it is verified. Howard Kurtz, media critic at the Washington *Post*, analyzed the early coverage of the Simpson case to determine how accurate it was. He wrote:

> [I]t is the errors, born of the inevitable rush to be first, to unearth some new tidbit to milk those ever-present anonymous sources who may or may not know what they are talking about, that have truly distinguished the Simpson coverage.... In today's supercharged news-media universe, it takes only one sighting of information streaking across the sky to prompt a thousand journalists to keep repeating the pseudo-fact until it hardens into news.

The problem is not new. Competition drives a lot of coverage. Newspaper reporters have always faced deadlines and, under the pressure of multiple-editions in the 1880s and after, faced the same pressures television and radio reporters face today: constant "up-dates" to a story. Even if the reporter didn't have new information, editors demanded new leads for each edition of the paper. Multiple-editions and extras have largely vanished from the scene today, but we see the same pressure in broadcast news. Reporters are asked—live, on camera—for the latest news. Woe to the reporter who responds, "Sorry, there's nothing new to report." Just as newspaper reporters were literally forced to come up with news—whether or not there was news—so TV journalists face the same dilemma on any continuing story.

Today, unfortunately, when all of the media cover a big story such as the Simpson case, newspapers also feel the pressure to respond with rumors because television can provide news first. So the effort to find a unique piece of news—an exclusive—also affects newspaper journalism.

We have learned from the history of journalism that such pressure results in incomplete reports and unchecked fact. When there isn't time, rumor becomes fact because so many papers and broadcasts are carrying it. Ron Kaye, the assistant managing editor of the Los Angeles *Daily News*, explained why his paper went with a story about an entrenching tool that supposedly was the murder weapon in the Simpson case. He told Kurtz that the "paper tries to avoid such misinformation but succumbed 'in the frenzy of dozens of half-facts and partial facts.'" Two Los Angeles *Times* reporters reviewed the Tonya Harding news coverage before the Winter Olympics had even started and concluded that "standards have all but vanished when it comes to passing along speculation and rumor as 'news.'"

Is there a solution to such problems? Yes, get at least two independent sources to verify the fact. Make sure the sources are reliable. Recognize you have incomplete information, and let that fact influence your report. Don't claim more than your information justifies, and leave personal opinion regarding motives to the editorial page. Let the editorial writers make jackasses of themselves. You have enough burdens as a reporter without adding that one. Remember, facts count. Since facts have different meanings in different contexts, though, it is the professional's job to assess and evaluate. These are principles of journalistic writing developed over many years. They are valid today.

Unfortunately, in real life the competitive pressures are enormous, and the terrible temptation to run with a rumor is understood only by those reporters who are covering the story. After all, the rumor might be right. And who wants to be beaten on a story? Only the thoroughly professional reporter *and* editor or news producer will have the courage and unshakable judgment to resist the temptation.

COVERING A STORY REQUIRES TEAMWORK

Although journalists think of themselves as individualists, they work in a highly structured industry which requires a great deal of cooperation from everyone. On a breaking story—that is, when either the event or information about the event continues to unfold over time—reporters are dispatched by editors or news producers to gather segments of the story. No reporter has all of the story; no reporter can, under deadline pressure, get all the pieces or have time to put them together in a coherent picture.

In journalism history we often relate stories of those reporters who traveled under horrendous conditions to the site of natural disasters where they gathered information from disparate sources, interviewed eyewitnesses, observed the scene themselves, then put this information into a coherent story which was sent via telegraph or train to the paper. We honor those individual reporters because they were remarkably durable, courageous and skillful. But those events do not reflect the way news generally is gathered and presented.

News presentation, whether in a newspaper or on television or radio, involves multiple players—news gatherers, writers, editors, graphics artists, etc. This is not a new phenomenon created by television. Newspapers have had writing specialists for over a century. Their responsibility was to take information telegraphed or phoned in from one or more reporters and craft it into a coherent picture. We have traditionally called them "rewrite men." Their function still exists on newspapers and in broadcasting. Today's news media are collaborative. Numerous people are responsible for helping reporters get their story into the paper or onto the air. In doing so, each person shapes the final story.

In television, a cameraperson usually tapes the action as the reporter delivers a "standup" (that is, speaks to the camera with the scene in the background). The video report usually is edited in the studio's facilities with sound or dialogue (voice over) added. (That is, the reporter narrates as scenes of the event appear on the screen. But we don't see the reporter during the narration.) Editors and news producers and others get involved in shaping the final news report.

Print reporters also have collaborators. On breaking stories, or investigative stories, several reporters might participate. Even when a reporter gathers all of the news and writes it for publication, the editor gets involved by seeking clarification, tightening the story, editing to avoid problems (such as bad taste or libel), or raising points that need to be pursued to complete the story.

In recent years a few dailies have experimented by changing news operations so that reporters edit their own stories—some even write the headlines—and thus save the cost of a copy editor on the editing desk. These experiments usually have failed, because reporters are simply too close to their stories either to edit well or to see where holes appear in a report.

Reporters might even collaborate with competitors today. A recent development in Virginia had the state's four leading dailies cooperating in an investigation of the financing of the state's system of higher education. Rosemary Armao, one of the two editors who headed the cooperative effort, summarized some of the problems in an article for *American Journalism Review*. She personally finds it difficult to tell reporters on her own paper that their work isn't good enough. This is her least "favorite part of editing." But it's worse when working with competitors. She said she is uneasy criticizing a reporter's work "when the reporter has never worked with you, has no reason to trust you, and fears losing face in what amounts to a writing contest with his peers across the state." Things got very tense when the writing teams submitted their drafts. But, despite some bickering and nightmares, the five-part, seventeen-article series was completed on deadline. It proved so successful that after a "non-compete" clause ran out, several newspapers worked together or planned to share projects in the future.

Admittedly this cooperative effort is unusual, but it illustrates that journalism changes and reporters and editors might even find themselves working with the competition on certain stories.

ORGANIZATIONAL PRACTICES THAT AFFECT YOU AS A REPORTER

As mentioned earlier in this chapter, no single news event illustrates all of the organizational issues that affect you as a reporter. The remainder of this chapter will examine the following issues: pay, working conditions, and service.

Pay

Fifty years ago many cub reporters worked from one to two years without pay just to get started in the business. Pay, except for experienced reporters, was low. Over the years this situation changed on major dailies, though even there the Newspaper Guild's top minimum salaries applied only to reporters with five or more years' experience. A study of twelve newspapers, ranging from the New York *Times* to the San Francisco *Chronicle,* East Coast to West Coast, showed a median annual reporter pay of $28,800 in 1982 and $44,500 in 1992. TV reporters earned about 25% more than their print counterparts. These figures are for the largest markets in the U. S., but most newspapers and television stations are located in other markets. Their pay levels are much lower. Pay affects job satisfaction. If a reporter cannot live on a beginning salary, it means he or she must depend upon support from family, delay marriage or rely upon a spouse's income, and otherwise find ways to augment salary. A few years ago Louis Peck interviewed journalists to get their view of the industry. His article, which appeared in the *Washington Journalism Review*, was entitled "Anger in the Newsroom." He offered several reasons for a general disenchantment he found, and pay was one of them. Small and medium-sized papers are affected the most by the dissatisfaction of their employees, since they often get graduates who can't crack the larger markets. The major papers generally have their pick of the crop.

Working Conditions

Pressures in the newsroom affect your job and your interest in your job. Journalists have always griped about their jobs. They always will. But Peck found that there were important changes occurring in newspapers that affect reporters and editors. Papers are undergoing change internally in order to prepare for the future—a future they do not yet recognize. Thus they are doing a lot of experimenting. Some newspapers emphasize short, pithy stories that are "relevant" to the reader with graphics to jazz up the page; others emphasize long, investigative pieces that help readers understand their environment, whether political or occupational. Still others are experimenting with ways of distributing papers directly to the consumer through electronic means—electronic distribution through data services. Where all of this will lead, no one knows. But most publishers and editors feel that the newspaper of the future will be quite different from the newspaper of the present.

This experimentation and change creates anxiety among journalists. A newcomer just learns the rules of the game when the rules are changed. This is unsettling.

What does change mean to you as a reporter or aspiring editor? It means what it has always meant: Opportunity, with a capital O. The reporter who is flexible and capable of adapting to change will win out in the end.

Editors are not immune to the pressures of the job. Carl Sessions Stepp, a former reporter and now senior editor of *American Journalism Review*, recently offered several methods for improving retention and quality of the editorial staff of newspapers:

- Hire more editors.
- Pay them better.
- Build in escape valves, such as forcing them to take vacations or rotating assignments.
- Develop flexible schedules, perhaps four ten-hour days a week.
- Select editors more carefully and train and support them.
- Allow editors to edit and to manage and innovate.
- Give them more control.
- Stress teamwork, especially in the daily news meeting.
- Offer praise for work well done.

It's the nature of the beast that journalism is a high stress job. It has been for more than two centuries. Daily deadlines—hourly or more frequently in the case of broadcasting—cannot be avoided, but the pressures can be reduced through enlightened planning on the part of managers. As a journalist, you need to evaluate everything you do in order to reduce the stress of the job. Working conditions do affect the final product—the news article or television news report.

Service

In this crass society, the idea of "service" often is ridiculed. By service I mean two things: to help others in society and to enjoy your work without having to apologize to anyone.

The news business, whether print or electronic, provides the public with information that people can use in making decisions. Those decisions may be on how to vote or for whom, how to improve job performance by using new techniques or equipment, or how to buy goods carefully and critically. These do not exhaust the possibilities, of course. One of the most important functions of the news media is to provide timely, useful, and accurate information or "news" for those readers or viewers who choose to use it. There are other functions, of course, such as entertainment, education, or guidance, but the news function is premier. Many journalists went into the business because they wanted to serve. This still is a viable reason.

Yet, there is another side to the business that attracts so many of us: the excitement of the job. Pete Hamill, columnist and once editor of the New York *Post* for five weeks before being fired, wrote that the screenwriters of the motion picture *The Paper* had produced solid reporting: "...they captured the obscene banter of news meetings—the energy and laughter of the game—and they understood the obsessed, *driven* quality of the tabloid professionals." Hamill recounted how people he has known, "reporters and editors, male and female, are often faced with the...dilemma [of choosing between spouse and job]. They always choose the paper." This, of course, is a price one should not pay—but it happens. Hamill was referring specifically to tabloid journalism, but the thrill of the game applies in all news gathering and producing.

One survey of journalists by the American Press Institute found that 80% to 85% of the respondents expected to be in the business four years later. They offered two reasons:

1. "What do you mean get out of it? It's what I do, and there's a lot of stuff that I love."

2. Many have their identity tied up "in being a journalist."

In a CBS *48 Hours* report on the New York *Daily News* one of the young reporters was followed as he gathered news for a story. His interview with the segment's producer was fun to watch because the young reporter was excited about reporting. The news business often is a game—a game in which one gets the news first, perhaps even is first in breaking an important story, and one's picture or name appears with the story. Our identity frequently is tied up in being journalists, and if we are doing a good job we should be proud of what we do.

It is this last point that needs elaboration. Sometimes, in the news business as in other businesses, one is asked to do something against one's personal beliefs. In the case of journalism it may be to write a story or produce a program that isn't justified by the facts. It doesn't happen very often, but when it does it is hard for a young reporter to refuse. Car payments, rent, and a host of other expenses need to be met—the job and its income are too important to toss over for principle.

What can a young reporter do? Put aside a "tithe" of each check into a savings account to be used for no other reason than to protect your integrity. Don't dip into it for a down payment on a house or a car. It's there so that when an editor or program producer harasses you or requires that you do something against your own beliefs, against your personal and/or professional concept of journalism—and you can't talk the editor out of it—you can tell the editor to "Get Lost" and walk out. Many young journalists have found such a fund gives them courage—and financial protection—to follow their own star with integrity, the most precious commodity in journalism. You may never receive a reward from journalism organizations because you've remained true to your beliefs, but you will have the satisfaction of knowing that your integrity couldn't be bought because you had to pay the bills.

Of course, first "know yourself." Then "to yourself be true."

Perspective...

WHAT A VETERAN EDITOR WISHES BEGINNING JOURNALISTS KNEW ABOUT THE NEWSPAPER BUSINESS

By RICHARD LIEFER, member of the Chicago *Tribune* editorial board and former Op-Ed Page editor

The first thing beginning journalists should know about the newspaper business is that it could well be different next year, if not next month.

The second thing to know is that the basic principles of information-gathering and dissemination at their core will remain the same.

Editors and reporters must be amenable to change because the proliferation of competing media has forced newspapers to become more dynamic.

Successful papers constantly evaluate their missions and methods. They are much more consumer- and service-oriented nowadays, much more inclined to question traditional news, advertising and marketing practices.

They are increasingly conscious of the need to play to their strengths, the most obvious of which are their marketing reach, the comprehensiveness of their news coverage and their ability to portray events, trends and personalities within a meaningful context.

What does all this imply for new journalists?

For one thing, newspaper journalists not already producing copy available to readers by means other than words-in-print will be doing so eventually. For another, they will be increasingly appreciative of the time and attention devoted to the packaging of news and feature stories in newspapers.

And as for content, it won't be enough for journalists to concern themselves only with who-what-where-when-and-how. An emphasis on the so-what?, already present, will grow as newspapers give priority to news analysis and commentary.

This could pose a problem for beginners, for they may be tempted to follow the new rules at the expense of time-tested but indispensable ones.

An editor's direction to amplify and explain can be a challenge, calling for critical thinking and polished writing. Yet it cannot become an excuse for slighting essential qualities and skills associated with sound reporting.

What are these?

Curiosity, of course. Incurious people belong in other occupations.

Also a certain degree of professional self-effacement which is not to be confused with a lack of prized reportorial assertiveness.

Such a mind-set helps the journalist stay focused on what's uppermost (the event, issue or profile subject at hand) and, as much as possible, keep his or her own ego out of the reporting of the facts.

It hardly needs saying that a journalist must get those facts right. Accuracy, though, involves more than pinning down names and dates. It includes understanding and highlighting what's significant (the wheat) and dispensing with the trivial (the chaff).

Finally, clear, compelling and thought-filled writing has to come into play. So does courageous but careful editing. The two are friends, not mortal enemies, as some newcomers seem to think.

Although newspaper writers are freer to experiment than they used to be, too often the results still create a nostalgic yearning for a return to the straitjacketed styles of yesterday. Remember that simple is better.

These, then, are a few of the basics that change does not change. They are the cherished tools of the trade which beginning and veteran journalists alike must continue to use for the sake of their own integrity and that of their craft.

4

A REPORTER'S PROFILE

Intellectual curiosity, the power of acute observation, and critical thinking characterize many of the best reporters. Students entering the profession should have a love of language, an affection for history, and a passion for truth-finding.

Reporters," said the actress Julia Roberts, "are like birds pecking at you," when she was interviewed on ABC's *Good Morning America* after her role in *The Paper*. She identified two types of reporters, however: reporters so bad she won't formulate opinions about them, and reporters who are committed to fact and accuracy.

Roberts was not the first critic to paste upon reporters the label of "pecking birds." The critics called a first-century journalist named Paul, the Apostle, a "babbler," *spermologos* in Greek, when he appeared in Athens among the philosophers to report about his findings in Israel. The Stoics and the Epicureans were referring to Paul with the term used for small birds that picked seeds from among the paving stones or men who hung around the markets

BY CHARLES MARLER
Dr. Marler is chairman of the Department of Journalism and Mass Communication at Abilene Christian University, where he was selected as University Teacher of the Year in 1987. He earned the Ph.D. in Journalism from the University of Missouri at Columbia and holds degrees in English and history. He has worked for the Abilene *Reporter-News* in Texas, in public relations for his university, as editor of the alumni magazine *Horizons*, and in the Freedom of Information Center at Missouri.

scavenging scraps—parasites, retailers of secondhand information, and eventually plagiarists.

"Many newspaper reporters...are lazy, careless, cynical and inclined toward exaggeration, speculation and sensationalism," writes David Shaw, Los Angeles *Times* media critic. "Worse, they often decide what their stories should say before they even begin their interviews and research." He came to this dim view in 1988 after he interviewed top American newspaper editors and other prominent journalists about their experiences as subjects of stories. "The painfully pinching shoe," Shaw says, "is often on the other foot."

In this chapter, the profile of good reporters is explored, beginning with the corollary proposition that young men and women should, if they can, avoid the reportorial craft. Only if they must, should they become reporters. Journalism needs only the brightest, the best—young men and women who are passionate about justice, truth, impartiality, and fairness—because the community needs a newspaper edited with these values. Babblers need not apply here.

CHARACTERISTICS AND ROLES OF GOOD REPORTERS

The genesis of the reporter lies in two magnificent processes—two adventures of the mind—two experiences invariably discovered in the intellectual lives of entry-level and veteran reporters. They possess a passion for reading, and they engage in critical, analytical thinking and writing. An insatiable curiosity leads them from book to book to book—and through other forms of the written word.

Reporter as Reader

A celebrated Texas journalist, Frank Grimes, described his reading as voracious and systematic, proceeding from author to author to author. He typically read the entire output of the Associated Press every day in addition to sundry magazines and other newspapers in his rigorous, never-ending educational regimen of accumulating knowledge about current events. Hostesses of the city who planned parties for the three local college presidents always invited Grimes because the trio of educators would gather around the journalist to listen and probe his knowledge of current events.

As in athletics where no substitute is found for speed, in journalism no substitute is found for reading. The day's intelligence, of course, forms the nucleus of the reporter's daily intake of information, and the journalist who is apathetic about current events is as rare as an albino dinosaur. Current event reading is a centerpiece in the reporter's lifestyle.

Reporter as Critical Thinker

The reader is building an on-line cerebral database ready for retrieval for all types of thinking, which can be described as cerebral aerobic exercises: memory, reverie, incubation, reflection, illumination, translation, reasoning from specific examples, reasoning from general principles, interpretation, analysis, synthesis, and verification. The benefits available through these cerebral aerobics are accessible only with a great deal of disciplined mental activity. The good reporter is adept at "newsthinking," as the journalist Bob Baker calls it, the ability to apply critical thinking to the problem of telling the story.

Ever the empiricist, the critical thinking reporter asks the basic what, who, why, when, how, and where questions of journalism and goes beyond, as suggested by writer Linda G. Barton. The reporter's profile includes an additional list of words he or she is adept at using: tell, recall, select, omit, label, define, compare, rephrase, contrast, illustrate, demonstrate, summarize, outline, show, explain, classify, develop, organize, identify, choose, inspect, categorize, assume, examine, distinguish, compile, discuss, theorize, elaborate, originate, suppose, test, change, predict, formulate, criticize, judge, recommend, prioritize, perceive, conclude, defend, evaluate, justify, and appraise. These and other words are the verb roots of the question repertoire of the thinking reporter who will discover the most accurate facets of the story and create the most reader appeal. Good reporters come not from the lineage of the couch vegetable but from the population of reading thinkers who were willing to pay the price to discipline the intellect. They discover the twin joys of reading and critical thinking.

Reporter as Interviewer and Observer

Promising reporters exhibit curiosity through reading, but they also possess two other characteristics: they are tenacious interviewers and quintessential observers. Curiosity in the reporter profile manifests itself through these four processes—reading, thinking, interviewing, and observing—which endow the reporter with a kind of hunger and restlessness for information. This unsated curiosity in experienced reporters is reigned in and made useful through "planning the content of the story," says Don Fry, a writing coach with Poynter Institute. The reporter, says

Fry, uses the Temporary Expert Test, in which curiosity drives the reporter—the temporary expert—to the formation of an initial list of questions, more questions, and finally answers to all the questions. Poise to handle the often confrontational nature of the interview in a productive manner is another requirement. At the observation level, journalist-historian Theodore H. White says, "...A young reporter in a war is best advised to get as close to the sound of guns as possible; the closer he gets to combat and the intight view of battle conditions, the more useful his dispatches." If the reporter, White says, writes about grand strategy from headquarters, the story will be left to the historians. When the reporter reasonably satisfies his or her curiosity, then comes the storytelling.

Reporter as Storyteller

An educated reporter who reads, thinks, and tells about small and large events in an accurate, interesting fashion can be characterized as a "storyteller," White's self-description in his *In Search of History*. Reading and thinking nurture the reporter's sense of storytelling—how to construct phrases, sentences, and paragraphs with style, fluidity, clarity, unity, and cogency to arrest the reader. A passion for reading leads the strong writer to discover cadence in poetry, plot in fiction, description in biography, the big picture in history, timeliness in the daily newspaper, and vocabulary from every storyteller and muse. The habit of reading—the intellectual labor and recreation of hundreds of hours—poises the reporter at the brink of a career as a storyteller.

Reporter as Writer

Close examination of this storyteller's profile reveals a love of the language, a fierce dedication to the notion that some words are better maps of territory than other words, a passion for clarity through concrete word choice, an addiction for active verbs, a fascination with origins of words, and a mastery of grammar, punctuation, and spelling. The reporter knows that the word "Longhorn" draws a more complete picture in the mind of the reader than the word "cow." This town crier flees from the cliché ("needle in a haystack"); the euphemism ("selected out" for "fired"); gobbledygook ("multi-faceted interface"); the obscure word ("eudaemonic"). But the same reporter knows that "egregious" is not "a type of lettuce" and can correctly and wisely use "ubiquitous," "sagacious," and "ambidextrous." The able reporter treasures words as some people collect baseball cards or Barbie dolls.

So why did the New York *Times* baseball writer Red Smith say writing is "a case of letting little drops of blood in search of the right word, the right pitch"? The reporter stamped with the legacy of Smith quickly discovers the logical fallacy in the mythical syllogism: "Writers use typewriters. I can use a typewriter. Therefore, I am a writer." The real reporter vows that he or she will write, rewrite, polish, and refine until the message in the mind of the reporter has its best chance of near duplication in the mind of the reader. Writing, the reporter discovers, sharpens the writer's thinking more thoroughly than any other verbal exercise of the intellect. Again and again, the reporter goes through the birthing pains of storytelling—seldom easy, usually painful, always exhilarating at the end.

Reporter as Historian

Another part of the nature of a reporter is an affinity for history. Some wags call journalism "history in a hurry," an observation with an element of truth. Theodore White tells a story about history's "interlock with journalism" and the "history in a hurry" phenomenon. He reported out of China about the 1937-38 Japanese invasion and a relief project that had served 25 million meals in refugee camps. His story to *Time* magazine was garbled in transmission, and history books still report that 25 million Chinese fled the invaders. Innately, the reporter is drawn to history, sensing that the artifact left by the eyewitness reporter is the stuff history is made of—episodic, primary records of contemporary life, people, events, ideas, and processes. The careful, meticulous reporter has aptitudes and training that process information much in the same way that the historian does, (a) testing all sources for credibility and (b) examining every statement and fact for its contextual meaning. The reporter's accounts then serve the contemporary reader, the historian, and the historian's audience equally well. The ideal reporter handles the episode with expertise equal to the historian's treatment on the grand scale.

Reporter as Scientist

If reporters are historians, then they also are scientists. The education of the reporter exposes him or her to the scientific method through the social and natural sciences. The reporter, to whom critical thinking is central, nourishes the scientist's neutrality and is able to confront biases honestly and ethically. He examines premises and unfounded assumptions for what they are.

Data leads the reporter—as opposed to the advocate, who is led by a cause. A straight-line pattern of thinking marks the reporter scientist, who abandons rabbit chasing when uncomfortable sources try to deflect the pursuit of truth and who rejects tangential data that would taint the story.

Reporter as Mathematician

Mathematics, too, obtrude into this picture. Buster Haas of the Dallas *Morning News* believes that top journalists have a common marker—strong mathematical abilities. In all likelihood the reporter accumulates more knowledge about logic from mathematics courses than from any other area of education. One of the all-time great managing editors, Carr Van Anda, who was a mathematical genius and a student of logic and science, is remembered for his handling of a story in the New York *Times* about one of Einstein's lectures in which Van Anda spotted an error in an equation.

Reporter as Educator

From the other liberal arts and sciences, the sound educational program leads the reporter through introductions to political science, sociology, economics, foreign language, psychology, philosophy, anthropology, art, music, law, communication theory, and ethics. In each of these areas, the reporter demonstrates some reasonable depth of knowledge and understanding. The curriculum of the effective, modern journalism school focuses the reporter in three ways: (a) grounding in the traditional liberal arts and sciences, (b) entry-level professional proficiency through writing and editing courses, and (c) newspaper experience on the campus paper on through a summer internship or both. Ideally, the reporter emerges as a professional with a base for a life of learning, excellent discourse skills, and effectiveness when faced with unresolved problems and issues.

A REPORTER'S ETHICS AND CREDIBILITY

Whether the reporter will be led by the data is a primary moral question, and the modern reporter faces at least as many, if not more, value-based dilemmas than in any other era of journalism. The thorough reporter on the eve of the 21st century is an ethicist. The literature of journalism reveals more concern about ethics than at any period in the history of U. S. journalism education and practice. This struggle over what is good and right with useful consequences is a philosophical and practical challenge in the life of the reporter, and the reporter who does not examine this realm is a proverbial loose cannon. Ethics is grander than a set of rules adopted by the reporter's newspaper. It begins with the awareness, examination, and growth of the reporter's internal value system. It progresses through the rejection of ends-justifies-means thinking. Ethical concerns confront the reporter in the most and least reflective moments with nuances, no-win situations, greater-good predicaments, and legal-ethical conflicts. An introduction to classical ethical theory, exploration of the range of arguments in applied journalism ethics, a continuing reading of ethics materials, and participation in ethical discourse on the job and in seminars are crucial in the reporter profile. Thoughtless, unprepared reporters can step onto the slippery slope in the name of ends-justifies-means or the greater-good without pricing the personal pain or cost in credibility.

Believability, in one sense, is all that the reporter and the newspaper have to sell to the reader; so credibility stands among the inner circle of important reporter characteristics. Aristotle's formula for credibility posed three questions: (a) What is the quality of character of the messenger? (b) Does the messenger have good sense? (c) Is the messenger interested in the public's welfare? The source of today typically says, "You may burn me once, but you will not burn me twice." The reader of today says, "You misspell my name today, and I never will trust you again." The reporter lives in a glass house; and the reading public, which is under the microscope of the reporter, does not tolerate a double standard. The result is that the education, the source relationship, the gatekeeping, the writing of the reporter are under the readers' microscopes; and inaccuracies, ethical lapses, and editorialization will damage, sometimes in terminal fashion, the reporter's credibility. When trust is wounded, the reporter's ability to serve the reader is limited.

Sometimes, readers might attack a reporter's credibility because the news that the community needs to know is embarrassing or uncomfortable to sources, subjects or readers. The media execute an essential role in the community as social critics, but readers fairly ask, "Who will criticize the critics?" This forces reporters to grapple with criticism and develop coping strategies, a tough assignment because few humans relish criticism. One coping style is cynicism, an ill advised pattern of life. Another is growing the imaginary thick epidermis, which may be nothing more than denial. The best is the development and articulation by the individual reporter of a clear understanding about and faith in the role and mission of journalism in society. The responsibility of the reporter, as Robert Bellah and his group of sociologists say about citizens in *The Good Society*, is to help one another pay attention. "What is happening? What is calling us to respond?" are the questions Bellah poses. Reporters help readers answer those questions. But Bellah's cautions can be translated to say that the readers of the community will listen only to the reporter whom they trust.

REPORTER AS WATCHDOG

The community watchdog function of the reporter frequently draws a peculiar kind of displeasure from politicians, incumbent public officials, and their supporters. The reporter discovers that the angry politician treats the media as if they were noisy yard-dogs rather than valued watchdogs. And the reporter must be certain not to adopt the attitude of a junkyard dog. A reporter must operate with a sense of the priceless value of the First Amendment and a society structured by the concept that governance is "of the people, for the people, by the people" with responsibility delegated to duly elected public officials. Whether a reporter possesses a passionate allegiance to the concept of the public's need to know is a central litmus test. Behind the First Amendment, the reporter knows, lies the Miltonian premise: "though all the winds of doctrine were let loose upon the earth, so Truth be in the field, we...misdoubt her strength. Let her and Falsehood grapple; who ever knew Truth put to the worse in a free and open encounter."

Truth, at the end of the film *Absence of Malice*, undergoes scrutiny. Sally Fields as reporter Megan Carter muses about her character's involvement with a source and a story that contributed to the suicide of a young woman. In her own paper's preparation for a follow-up story, she tells another reporter, "Just say we were involved." The reporter follows up, "That's true, isn't it?" Megan answers, "No. But it's accurate." In experience the reporter discovers a weakness in the Falsehood vs. Truth encounter. Sometimes the Truth must wait for history because of the episodic nature of journalism facts and truth. The reporter is a soul searcher who faces the reality that Truth is elusive. But the reporter should be honest, rigorous in the search for facts, unswerving in the pursuit of context of the facts, and fearful about the possibility that inaccuracies will appear under his or her byline. Experience teaches that mistakes will occur; so the reporter double-checks and, like the surveyor, triangulates to validate with as much precision as possible the accuracy of the account. The reporter is an accuracy fanatic.

Soul searching also enters the picture when the reporter encounters crime and accident victims and other tragic human conditions that raise the question of empathy vs. professionalism: "Am I a human being, or am I a reporter?" Reporters caught in these predicaments swing from empathy when one or a few people are involved to reflexive denial when they face trauma of unimaginable dimensions. Steve Fainaru of the Boston *Globe* wrote about how he coped after seeing the macabre conditions of Rwanda in 1994. A veteran disaster reporter had told him, "Don't let yourself think about them." Fainaru described his mental process: "But I have found it is not a conscious decision; the mind shuts off death occurring on this scale, so that life simply can go on."

A REPORTER'S PRESSURE

Stress management and a related process—time management—are central issues in the life of a reporter. Working in a deadline driven activity—essentially a plant that manufactures a product from scratch each day—produces positive and negative effects. "Stress is what we love about newspapers," writes Robert H. Giles, editor and publisher of the Detroit *News*. "The adrenaline that flows when we are on deadline or in the grip of a big story works like an injection, giving us a burst of energy to focus on the day's news." Deadline realities teach the reporter closure; the reporting and writing of a story is a practical, daily problem-solving exercise that disciplines the reporter.

Deadlines create dynamic tension, but stress management experts warn that repetitive, unrelieved exposure to stress produces fatigue, anxiety, depression, inability to sleep, hypertension, addiction, and other serious stress-related illnesses. The rugged individualist—the storied American who never depends upon another person, never asks for help, never concedes a problem, is always self-sufficient—runs the most risk in this environment. Fortunately, the at-risk reporter of today can find stress-and-time management seminars and counseling in every medium-to-large-size community.

A REPORTER'S PERSONALITY AND WORLD VIEWS

News media draw reporters from both extroverts and introverts—and their variations. The *extroverted* journalist probably prefers reporting about people and events, but the introverted reporter most likely gravitates to stories about ideas and processes. Generally, the extrovert craves the timely scoop, does terrific interviews and masterful observation, quickly grasps cause and effect, strongly endorses objective analysis, hates changes in routine, and may be a late adopter of technological change. On the other hand, the *introverted* reporter generally looks into patterns of events for clues to understanding; approaches decision-making from a subjective, values-based posture; absorbs without a quiver the need to rewrite a story because of late-breaking developments; and is an early adopter of technological changes. The mix of these two types of reporters and their variations—combined with the diversity of their strengths and contributions—makes for a dynamic newspaper and one of the most interesting societal units in today's world.

A common denominator between extroverted and introverted reporters is the ego, the reporters' need for reader, peer and self-recognition, a need which tends to require repetitive reinforcement. The gratification reporters gain comes from several sources, probably in this order of frequency: the benefits of operating where the action is, the byline, self-evaluations, source and reader feedback, newsroom peer evaluations, and winning of contests. The reporter's first byline probably is a defining experience in the life of every reporter. The nationally syndicated columnist James Kilpatrick says he as a boy became a professional the moment he received ten cents for a magazine piece. Reporters' credentials let them step into inner circles of every type in a community, and the boring day is rare. Some commentators have called reporters "action junkies," whose need for the freshest and most timely information provides a key gratification. However, the negative feedback caused by an insensitive or poorly prepared interview, grammar and spelling errors, factual errors, a misquote, poor control of context, misunderstandings of data, and other shortcomings can challenge the reporter's ego. The most galling "news media kiss-off," says Richard Clurman in *Beyond Malice*, is the knee-jerk response: "We stand by our story." Reporters must be careful not to let their ego get out of hand.

Personality type, education, and environment affect the reporter's *world view*—the values, beliefs, theories of history and life, and the nature of good and evil that drive his or her understanding of how the world works. Three reporters with different world views, declares Jerry Reed of the Abilene (Tex.) *Reporter-News,* can cover the same event and write three totally different, verifiable stories. Each reporter may lean to one or a combination of the theories of cause and effect: the Great Leader Theory, an Economic Theory, a Religion Theory, Natural Law, the Cyclical Theory, a Political Theory, the Progressive Theory or any of a number of other theories. Reporters' world views challenge their honesty, information gathering, critical thinking, and critical writing capabilities to the ultimate degree. The world view litmus test is: Does the story mirror the reporter's ego, the reporter's world view, or the reporter's data? If reporters honestly handle the analysis with integrity, they examine their biases, premises and assumptions with as much diligence as they weigh the data. A sign worth hanging at a reporter's desk is: "An unfounded assumption lies at the root of every error."

THE SUPERREPORTER

Reporters on the eve of the 21st century also confront the Infobahn, which raises new, exhilarating, and frightening realities. The age, as media CEO Robert Marbut predicted in the late 1970s, calls for the Superreporter—a Clark Kent with more earthbound skills than any journalist in history with perhaps the exception of the pre-industrial-age printer-editor, who also had control of every step of the production process. The "information superhighway," rather than destroying print, merely creates another gigantic, unprocessed information option from which reporters can seek raw data and archival resources. It also requires the art of synthesis. Leo Bogart, author of *The Age of Television* and *Preserving the Press,* writes: "People want information professionally picked, processed and interpreted. They want this done with understanding of the human dramas that mere facts disguise and distort. They want it done with literary style, through the use of language that evokes imagery and emotion. That is the job of journalism. The future of journalism and literature—like the past—largely remains with print on paper." But the technology of computer networks, pagination, and the Infobahn is affecting who will be the creme de la creme in reporting. The Superreporter will:

- Place ethical decision making at the forefront of his or her priorities
- Draw on a deep background in the liberal arts and sciences and specialized background in one or two fields
- Develop an affinity for the Infobahn and understand its "multidimensional universe" nature, as Bogart says, as opposed to the workings of a two-way highway
- Gather data effectively and efficiently in traditional ways and via the Infobahn
- Analyze and synthesize critically and equally well both verbal and statistical data
- Write accurately, clearly, and captivatingly
- Edit copy flawlessly
- Interpret or help interpret data into information graphics,

which are designed to organize and explain complex events, issues, and processes
- Understand more thoroughly than ever before the reportorial nature of photojournalism as a full partner to word-journalism
- Realize that computers have altered forever the one-step-at-a-time assembly line nature of newspaper editing and production
- Design pages that readers cannot lay aside and that will guide the reader in an exciting visual tour through the day's news.

The Superreporter's profile clearly is a clarion call to the brightest and best of all types among today's youth. "Montage," then, rather than "profile," may more helpfully describe this chapter about these complex figures. Reporters of each generation toil to discover and practice justice, truth, impartiality, and fairness in the peculiar context of their times—an eternal battle to get it right.

Perspective...

WHAT A VETERAN WISHES BEGINNING JOURNALISTS KNEW ABOUT WASHINGTON REPORTERS

By FORREST BOYD, Chief Political Correspondent for the Standard News Network, based in Washington. Mr. Boyd worked for Mutual Radio for thirteen years, eleven of those as the network's White House correspondent. He is the founder and president of International Media Services.

I am tempted to repeat the advice of a young Nixon aide who said during the Watergate hearings, "Don't come to Washington." The reason is that the journalistic sub-culture here is not so glamorous a life style as most people think, and the journalism practiced is not so pure and rewarding as the journalism books indicate.

While there are many fine, professional journalists in Washington, they for the most part get little recognition, and they work in an environment that can be very frustrating because they are not part of the elite "everybody knows" crowd.

Here's what you'll find in the "real" Washington:
- Cynicism.

The distrust and skepticism that existed before Watergate escalated to cynicism by the Watergate coverup and the admission by press secretary Ron Ziegler that previous statements were "inoperative." In other words, not true.

- Lack of respect.

Partly influenced by Watergate, but encouraged by scandals and ineptness of government officials, reporters have reached the point of respecting nobody and rejecting authority of all officials and institutions.

- Herd mentality.

Yes, it does exist. For the most part, the game played here is to make sure you have what everybody else has. There are several things that encourage that kind of reporting. First, radio and TV stations are demanding that their networks and bureaus get all the top stories. Don't miss anything.

Adding to the similarity is the fact that the networks and bureaus are reading the same "daybooks" of events. And for broadcasters, there is a system of news audio distribution known as WAND (Washington Audio News Distribution) and PAND (Presidential Audio News Distribution). If you subscribe to these services, good quality sound of the major stories, including all of the presidential speeches, comes right onto your newsroom. You don't have to send a reporter to cover.

Then, there's the increasing trend of covering stories by pool. The number of reporters and crews working in Washington has proliferated so much that, in many cases, reporting pools are assigned to cover, and they then make a report to the other reporters. All reporters rely on the pool reports.

- 4. The show-biz mentality.

I once heard a TV network correspondent remind a fellow correspondent: "Always keep in mind that TV news is show-biz." The trend to tabloid journalism, the search for the dramatic angle, and the competition for ratings contribute to this. There's a saying here that goes like this: "If it bleeds, it leads."

- 5. The gotcha syndrome.

The idea is not to get information, but to "get the President," or "get the congressman." Too many journalists have adopted Watergate investigators Woodward and Bernstein as models and are trying to be investigative reporters.

- 6. The confrontation method.

Talk shows and panel discussions need controversy in order to succeed. It's not a good program if people aren't shouting angrily at each other. Very few shows are trying to find common ground or something opposite sides can agree on.

These are just a few of the attitudes and practices you'll find in Washington. The Washington journalistic scene needs more good, solid, serious reporters and correspondents. Balance and a measure of respect need to be restored. If you have a thick skin, a sense of humor, and don't take yourself too seriously, then come to Washington and help us.

Perspective...

WHAT A VETERAN JOURNALIST THINKS ABOUT THE PERILS OF PUNDITRY

By STEPHEN ZEIGLER, an Associate Professor of journalism at Belmont University. He has worked for newspapers in Illinois and Arkansas.

The word "pundit" derives from Sanscrit for "Brahman," or "learned scholar." Today in America it refers to a very influential but controversial class of mass media opinion leaders who enjoy the luxury of sharing their views on topics of the day with an audience bigger than last century's powerful editorial leader Horace Greeley could have imagined.

The modern practice of punditry began between 1910-1920, partly as a compensatory response to the increased value placed on "objectivity" in news reporting. The patron saint is Walter Lippmann, who with 22 books, more than 4,000 editorial columns and nearly 300 articles for 50 magazines, won respect as one of the greatest political philosophers of modern times. His insights and prestige made him a powerful adviser to presidents and an actor, not just a reporter, in world affairs. He was offered, and turned down, the presidency of the University of North Carolina and an endowed chair at Harvard, and why not? With his editorial column "Today and Tomorrow" he had his own endowed chair of influence over history. At his peak, his power was said to be equal at least to that of a Speaker of the U.S. House of Representatives.

Lippmann saw the pundit as "doing what every sovereign citizen is supposed to do but has neither the time nor the interest to do for himself," that is, educate himself and others fully about public affairs. He would be a mediator of ideas, a go-between, educating the public about issues while explaining the operations and policies of government.

Lippmann's role as interpreter and teacher helped prepare

America for its role as a world leader. His example attracted young people of education and sophistication to journalism, two of whom, Joseph Alsop and James Reston, became especially influential in the decades after World War II. Both were advisers and social companions to John Kennedy. Alsop, in fact, helped persuade Kennedy to pick Lyndon Johnson as his running mate, helped him choose his cabinet, and lobbied hard and successfully, both publicly and privately, for presidential prosecution of the Cold and Vietnam wars.

And here we begin to see the weaknesses in Lippmann's theory of the journalist as pundit. First, no set of ethical guidelines has ever been developed for the practice of punditry, and not all pundits are trained in the canons of journalism. George Will is an ex-professor, William Safire a former political speechwriter, Charles Krauthammer a psychiatrist, John McLaughlin a Jesuit seminarian. All more or less set their own rules of practice.

Punditry's second weakness, a corollary of the first, is human frailty. Lippmann championed the principle of disinterestedness, but neither he nor Alsop nor Reston was immune to the vanities of social prestige. All were close enough to their sources to be guilty of conflicts of interest, and too often they allowed themselves to be unquestioning publicity agents for their sources.

Even greater conflicts grew with the rise of television punditry, which made celebrities of pundits, with all the attendant financial temptations.

George Will once said his column was important because it got him on TV talk shows, which got him on the lecture circuit. Indeed, many pundits appearing on shows like "This Week With David Brinkley," "The McLaughlin Group," and "Capitol Gang" receive thousands—often tens of thousands—of dollars per speech, and some are paid by commercial and political interests. *New Republic* writers Morton Kondracke and Fred Barnes spoke at a $75-a-plate dinner for American Express Platinum Card holders, William Safire at a reward dinner for American Express members with 300,000 frequent flier miles. Kondracke and columnist Rowland Evans were paid well to speak to a 1990 Republican Governors Conference. Many other pundits have grown wealthy selling their celebrity, as well.

Conflicts of interest have damaged popular esteem of journalists even as they encroached on journalistic values of independence and disinterestedness. George Will coached his friend Ronald Reagan for the 1980 presidential debate—and then declared Reagan the winner in his column. He also criticized the Clinton administration's plan to put tariffs on Japanese luxury cars, although his wife earned $200,000 to influence American commentators to attack the tariff. Will revealed neither conflict, nor apologized when they were exposed. Sam

Donaldson criticized farm subsidies without admitting his own substantial gains from sheep and mohair subsidies. Understandably, the public increasingly doubts pundits' credibility and by association that of all journalists.

Some say the rise of television punditry has debased the quality of political discourse itself. Celebrity pundits are expected to give expert analysis on a variety of topics, not all of which they know much about. Instead of reporting and analyzing current policies and issues, they are expected to predict the future, and usually they do so with all the accuracy of astrologers and bartenders.

Moreover, the entertainment demands of television require belligerence, oversimplification, polarization and intolerance. Think of "Crossfire." Or "The McLaughlin Group," which critic Eric Alterman has compared to a roller derby. Argument without complex reasoning, emphasis on *ad hominem* attacks and discord, grandstanding and showboating substitute for honest, enlightening public debate on substantial issues. Columnist Jack Germond said his lengthy stint with "The McLaughlin Group" was "a half-hour of being a dancing bear to make a better living."

Television, fame, money, hypocrisy ... the Lippmann ideal of the journalist-commentator as social educator may today be mortally wounded. There is a hopeful sign, however: many newspapers are starting to see their editorial pages more as coordinators of local discussion, through letters, boards of contributors and guest editorials from the community, than as purveyors of "expert" but elitist opinion from on high.

Lippmann's "trickle-down" theory of opinion leadership never discounted the value of community discussion of issues. It may be that in an information age, a trickle-down model underestimates the intelligence, knowledge and potential of the public. If so, the ideal of community participation in public policy debate, of Lippmann's "sovereign citizen" educated by the reasoning of ordinary citizens unconflicted by the temptations of celebrity punditry, may yet be approachable.

5

ETHICS OF REPORTING

There are certain basic principles of right and wrong. Given those principles, what should journalists do in their professional activities? There are few clear-cut answers, for few situations are without their ambiguities. But there are foundation principles which may be usefully employed in teasing answers out of the tangles of real-world problems. This chapter will introduce you to the fundamentals of ethical principles and to the subject known as "professional ethics."

Journalism as an American institution has taken quite a beating in public discourse in recent years. Polls indicate readers and viewers trust journalists about as much as they trust used-car dealers. A recent Gallup poll indicates fewer than a third of those surveyed had either "a great deal" or "quite a lot" of confidence in newspapers; more than half did in 1979. Only two percent believed that journalists had very high ethical standards; only one in five thought they had high standards. As recently as 1981, 30 percent thought they had high standards. Press critics— some serious and thoughtful, others merely loud—routinely

BY STEVEN R. KNOWLTON
Dr. Knowlton spent fifteen years as a newspaper reporter, editor, photographer, and owner at small weeklies, large dailies, and a major wire service before earning a doctorate in history from Washington University in St. Louis. An Associate Professor of Journalism at Hofstra University, he is the author or editor of three books, two of them on journalism ethics, and of numerous scholarly articles, book reviews, and op-ed pieces.

accuse the news media of a great number of shortcomings, among them greed, political bias, sensationalism, and the invasion of privacy.

While it is true that skepticism about journalistic behavior roughly mirrors decreasing confidence in other major institutions, it is nonetheless disturbing that the reading and viewing public has so little faith in its journalists. It is disturbing not just because journalists, like other people, like to be well thought of, but, far more importantly, because this doubt has profoundly important implications for our society and our governmental system.

The charges are serious, the stakes are high, and it is important that those entering the journalism profession be able to join in a thoughtful discussion and debate about what newspeople should do and why. It is also important to be able to recognize that some press criticism is nothing more than self-serving noise. Thirdly, it is important to realize that a free press in a democracy is bound absolutely—and inevitably guaranteed—to be often messy, sometimes impolite, and occasionally dead wrong. This is not to say that we should passively tolerate sloppy or irresponsible journalism, but to note that the price of fixing some of the problems may be higher than we are willing to pay.

The following introduction to journalism ethics is designed to provide enough historical and philosophical background to allow meaningful participation in the debates of substance and informed rejection of the self-serving and the mean-spirited. It is in two major parts. The first part deals with the branch of philosophy called *ethics*, or moral reasoning. The second part deals with *applied ethics*, or professional ethics. That is, given certain basic principles of right and wrong, what should journalists do? There are few clear-cut answers, for few situations are without their ambiguities. But there are foundation principles, which may be usefully employed in teasing answers out of the tangles of real-world problems.

A BACKGROUND ON ETHICS

To deal with first things first then: What is ethics? Ethical thinking is what you do when you ask what is right, what is good, what is obligatory in the sense of duty, and when you have logical reasons for the decision. An ethical code about right and wrong is, by definition, at once deeply personal and broadly societal. For an action to be considered ethical, the person doing it needs to believe in its moral worth, its rightness. Yet, each person is not at liberty to design a moral code wholly independent of the code of others in the culture. In this sense, ethics is something like law and something like convention. By superficial example: If most folks on the block turn down their stereos at 11 p.m., there is some obligation for you to do the same, even if on the other side of town the music runs all night.

It is important to distinguish between ethics and prudence, particularly because they have enough similarities that they are often confused. Prudence means looking out for your own self-interest in a practical way, while ethics always involves some principle beyond the self, something that pertains to the broader society or group. We may look for oncoming traffic before crossing the street, for example, not out of any particular moral principle, but based on a perfectly sound desire to avoid being hit by a car. Most of us drive the speed limit, or close to it, to avoid a speeding ticket. That's prudence, and there's nothing wrong with that.

However, we could argue the speed-limit case on moral grounds as well. Such an argument would probably note that, statistically, faster driving leads both to more accidents and to more serious ones; so to avoid harming others we should drive at or below the speed limit. We could also argue that all civilized societies depend upon members voluntarily obeying most rules. Any deliberate violation tears, even just a tiny bit, at the fabric of society. Also note that it is perfectly possible, and probably quite common, to adhere to a group's ethical code out of personal prudence. We may adhere to a convention or ethical code not because we particularly believe in it, but because it's not worth the trouble to fight it.

How, then, to determine an ethical code to live by, or which we should live by? In classical Greece, where the Western study of ethics began, the key to determining where the good lay was in the *telos*, or what was to come. Put most simply, morally the best choice was the one that would produce the most good. This outcome-based ethical reasoning was called *teleology*. There were important questions about knowing what the good was—whether it was happiness, as the hedonists had it, or excellence, as Aristotle argued—and about distribution of the good, but that's the core of the matter.

With the emergence of the Roman Catholic Church as a powerful institution in the Early Middle Ages, a different way of determining right and wrong came to hold sway. The church, the institution most involved in moral questions, determined morality through a series of rules, the *Thou shalts* and the *Thou shalt nots* of religious orthodoxy. This rule-based ethical theory is called *deontology*. Deontologists argue that behavior has moral weight in and of itself, independent of outcome. For centuries, deontologists in the West were virtually unchallenged in the ethics business. The church provided both the rules and the keys to ethical interpretation and understanding.

THE RISE OF RATIONALISM

Beginning with the Renaissance in the 15th century, however, people began to turn from the hereafter and more toward the here-and-now. One of the bedrock principles of the Renaissance, and the Protestant Reformation that accompanied it, was a belief in the power and worth of the human mind. This was a monumental change in the way people saw the world and saw themselves in it. The mind, people increasingly came to believe, could actually figure things out. From the Renaissance on, more analytical ways of thinking, with their origins in classical antiquity, increasingly challenged the spiritualism and mysticism of the churches.

This return to rationalism reached its zenith during the Enlightenment of the 18th century, an era in which the power of the rational mind was thought to be capable of solving literally all problems, figuring out all mysteries. To some, the human mind came to replace the power and mystery of an older god. To others, the realization of the astounding power of reason was proof anew of God's presence. But however people saw God's role in this new scheme of things, the most advanced minds of the West were increasingly convinced that humankind could eventually approach perfection through the power of the human intellect. There was less and less room in this world of intellectual confidence for rules-as-rules, for people blindly and willingly accepting the dictates of their forefathers, or their landlords, or their bishops, and devoting their best energies to trying to live by others' rules.

In the field of ethics, this confidence, fueled in part by emerging faith in science, prompted a return to the Greek notion of teleology to determine moral judgments. What was morally right and wrong, this thinking went, was not blind obedience to a set of rules, but based on a rational prediction of what certain behavior would produce. The greatest champions of this new way of thinking were Jeremy Bentham and his godson, John Stuart Mill. The name they used for their version of outcome-based ethical system was *utilitarianism*. The name is somewhat unfortunate, at least to contemporary ears, for the term seems to contain a sense of mere practicality or usefulness. But as Bentham and Mill defined it, utilitarianism means determining the most likely outcome of the various choices under consideration and then acting on the choice that will produce the greatest possible amount of good for the greatest number of people—what Mill called the "greatest happiness principle." As a philosophy, utilitarianism is consistent with the political notions of populism and democracy, for it insists that each person is as important as any other and that all are entitled to their fair share of the good.

The most common complaint about Mill's greatest happiness principle is that it specifically denies any sense of right or wrong independent of outcome. This disturbs utilitarianism's many critics, who have argued that pure utilitarianism could allow a government to condemn an innocent person if the execution would calm an outraged populace and stave off a murderous riot. This, the critics say, must be wrong, even if the greatest happiness principle seems to condone it.

For all of Mill's rationalism, it must be noted that his philosophy and most others eventually get to some sort of first principles, some ideas so fundamental that they cannot be proved empirically. Mill's belief in the innate sense of justice or fairness is one such important concept. Theologians, social scientists, and philosophers have looked for empirical proof, but it must be conceded that they have not found it. This raises the question: if the existence of morality cannot be proved, why bother with it at all? There are two answers. Neither may be fully compelling, but between them they cover most of the needed ground.

The first explanation, grounded in theology, may be satisfying for those who are themselves religious, plus those who may not be active church-goers, but who acknowledge theological or religious influences in their lives. While the world's great religions differ in rites and in details of deportment, all contain a core principle of concern for and kindness toward one's fellow human beings, some version of what is known to Christians as the Golden Rule.

PROFESSIONAL ETHICS

For those who deny not only all religion itself but also the moral worth of all religious teaching as well, there is a societal reason to behave ethically. For people to live in societies, and all of us do, those societies have to function. And a society functions only if most of its members voluntarily obey its rules, its ethical code of conduct. Take, for example, the very common societal dictum that people should tell the truth. It is not just that truth-telling is nice, or pleasant, or even illuminating. Far more importantly, it allows society to function. Here's why. Without communication between individuals, there is no community, nothing outside the individual to hold people together. And while we value, especially in the United States, our individualism, we also belong to groups, whose members communicate with each other. But they communicate with the clear understanding, stated or implicit, that most of the information passed back and forth will be true. Otherwise, the communication is pointless: we learn to rely only on ourselves; and any sense of society disappears, replaced by atomized individuals, bumping into one another at random and without purpose.

This presumption provides an answer to one fundamental question about what journalists should do: as the leading communicators in society, they should tell the truth. But what sort of truth? About whom? And what truths should they not tell?

POPULAR SOVEREIGNTY

To get even a partial answer to those questions, we have to look at the principle of government called popular sovereignty, which means that the people—the citizens, not the politicians and not the bureaucrats—are in ultimate charge of public affairs. This idea is rooted in the Enlightenment belief that, under the right circumstances, people are capable of running their own lives. This idea is a frontal assault on what had been the dominant theory of government for a thousand years, the so-called divine right of kings. This theory held that kings were selected by God to run their countries, eventually for the greater glory of God. The new theory held that human life was worth living and that human society was worth improving, for the sake of humans themselves and to glorify God. Enlightenment thinkers believed that if ordinary citizens could only know enough they could govern themselves.

The United States is a country built on popular sovereignty. The nation's founders were well aware that their political successors would be tempted, as governments everywhere are tempted, to try to amass power, to strip the people of their sovereignty; and they built powerful safeguards into the system to try to maintain the people's sovereignty. Among these, nothing was more important than the guarantee of a free press, of a free flow of information that the governors themselves could not control. Knowledge alone did not *guarantee* the success of their grand experiment in self-government—even the most devoted Enlightenment thinkers never made that claim—but rather made success *possible*. Since the founders believed a free flow of information was so important, and because they knew it would be under such assault, they tried to make the protection unambiguous. "Congress shall make no law," reads the First Amendment, "abridging...freedom of speech, or of the press...."

The founders were committed to the notion of democratic self-government and went to great lengths to allow journalists free access to information. As a result, there's not just the First Amendment, powerful and unprecedented as it is—there are also tax breaks, subsidies (such as cheap postage), and other perquisites designed to provide an environment in which a free press could flourish. The founders could not require that the press act in a certain way, to provide certain information, because the whole point of a free press was that the government could not control what the press did.

THE PRESS AND GOVERNMENT

This raises one of the longest-running debates in journalism: does the press have an obligation to cover government, to keep the sovereign people informed about what their hired employees, politicians, cops, bureaucrats, and the lot are up to? The dominant theory for roughly the first hundred years of American journalism was that it did not. The press was free to cover government if it so chose, but, by implication, it was equally free not to. This thinking, usually called the libertarian theory, holds that for press freedom to mean anything, it has to mean the freedom not to cover town council meetings or legislative hearings or anything else. If somebody could command coverage, such as the government or the citizenry, as in the ersatz claim of "the people's right to know," then the press was surely not free.

But in this century, a powerful counter-argument has arisen. It argues that Thomas Jefferson and James Madison and the others didn't create a free press just to let Larry Flynt put out *Hustler* magazine. There was a clear and important political point to the guarantees in the First Amendment. This theory, usually called the social responsibility theory of the press, says there is a positive obligation on the part of the press to be a watchdog over the affairs of public officials, because nobody else can or will and because democratic self-government depends upon it.

Here we have a classic ethical dilemma. The libertarians have a powerful case, but so do the social responsibility theorists. The very existence of tabloid newspapers, and their television counterparts with shows like *Hard Copy* and *Inside Edition*, is proof that no one can *make* journalists act responsibly, which is as it should be. But it also seems clear that other, more high-minded shows and publications take seriously the implied contract of social responsibility and try to bring to people the information they need to make rational decisions in governing their own lives. The debate is still going on. A reasonable resolution is that while there must not be any *legal* compulsion on journalists to write about or to ignore whatever they choose, there is a strong *moral* obligation to monitor and report thoroughly on government at all levels and other major institutions, private as well as public, which have a significant impact on the nation.

The debate over libertarianism vs. social responsibility got its most thorough airing in 1947 by a privately financed study group called the Hutchins Commission. The commission concluded that American citizens were entitled to have, and thus the press was morally obliged to provide, "a truthful, comprehensive, and intelligent account of the day's events in a context which gives them meaning."

That is a tall order, for it raises a number of questions without easy answers. The first is the notion of "truthful." The truth is an elusive beast, and more often than not one's view of the truth is deeply colored by one's stake in the story. A politician caught in, say, an extramarital affair may argue credibly that the affair has nothing to do with performance of public duties. Others, perhaps including the spouse, may believe the affair says something extremely important about the politician's trustworthiness, which surely is important in a political figure. The politician's children may see the matter as an entirely private pain that is none of the public's business. All are plausible arguments; and for the journalist, relying on a single "truth" is hardly satisfactory. Utilitarianism would suggest that if the personal shortcoming has a plausible connection to performance of public duties, the journalist is obliged to report it, doing as little harm to the family as possible, but refusing to let familial embarrassment kill the story.

OBJECTIVITY

This brings up the chronically vexing notion of objectivity. Probably no concept in journalism has been the subject of as much misunderstanding and abuse as this one. It is impossible to set the problem to rest with this chapter, but a few words about what it is and is not may help the debate along.

The notion of objectivity had its origins in the early decades of the 20th century, when the press, for a series of historical reasons, was subject to one of the recurring rounds of criticism from the public. To charges of intrusiveness and unfairness, thoughtful journalists, borrowing ideas from the scientific positivism so dominant at the time, came up with the notion of objectivity. If objectivity could be said to have a one-word synonym, it would be something on the order of "testable" in the sense of being empirically demonstrable. The social sciences had borrowed heavily from the hard sciences, and in the 1920s many leading intellects believed that journalism could bench-test ideas much as a chemist could analyze a new formula. Since then, the belief that ideas can be tested and proved or disproved in this way has been heavily discounted, but the underlying point of objectivity has not. That point was and is to get the story right, to be accurate in a mechanical sense, but to be truthful in a broader sense as well.

Today, a better synonym for "objective" might be "fair" or "impartial." In practical terms, it means that journalists covering a political rally should be aware of their own political views and should make sure those views do not creep into the story. It means that business writers should recognize their own financial holdings and not let the chance for personal gain influence the story. Many critics have argued that we can never fully remove ourselves from a scene or a situation and that true objectivity is therefore impossible. The critics are probably right, but journalists who conscientiously try to be honest and fair will probably do a better job than those who give up and no longer try at all.

The Hutchins Commission's report charged the nation's press with providing an account of the day's event's "in a context which gives them meaning." This call for context seems reasonable enough, and journalists have increasingly tried to provide it. But providing context makes the other, equally laudable, goal of objectivity, or fairness, much more difficult. Imagine a head-on collision on a country road. Most people would agree that certain details of this event should properly be included in an account of the mishap. The identities of both drivers and, probably, their passengers, would be included, along with road conditions and whether either or both drivers were impaired with drugs or alcohol. But if some of the passengers would find it particularly embarrassing to be placed in that car with that driver, they might argue to be left out of the story, particularly if they were uninjured. Or, what if one driver was nearly incoherent with grief at having just broken up with her boyfriend? Some people might see that detail as important in helping explain why the cars collided, but the ex-boyfriend might well object that he was being unfairly blamed for something over which he had no control. If the left-front wheel on one of the cars came off, that would certainly be worth mentioning. But what if the make and model of one of the cars had steering problems a year or so ago, resulting in a factory recall? Or, what if the steering problems were not serious enough to mandate a recall, but the manufacturer "voluntarily" offered to repair the steering mechanism on the cars? Is that the kind of context the Hutchins Commission wanted? Consumer groups might say yes, but the auto industry might argue otherwise. Now recognize that most stories of any consequence are vastly more complicated than an automobile accident, and the difficulty in providing a story's needed context becomes clear.

FAIRNESS AND PRIVACY

Whether we can prove its existence or not, that sense of justice Mill wrote of seems to be extremely strong. It is this sense of justice, or fairness, that underlies perhaps the greatest complaint lodged against contemporary journalists: that they invade people's privacy. Even as viewers hang onto every detail of Michael Jackson's involvement with young boys and of the grisly murder of O. J. Simpson's wife and her friend, we are repulsed by the intrusiveness of the reporters who bring us the details we find so fascinating. We believe that Jackson and Simpson don't *deserve* the prying cameras, or, if they do because of their actions, then the innocents of their stories certainly do not.

This presents a serious dilemma for a utilitarian with a rational faith in popular sovereignty but with a much harder-to-quantify sense of justice. How can journalists provide the sovereign people with all the information they need, or might need, to govern their own lives, without violating at least some people's perfectly reasonable right to privacy? The answer among most professional journalists is that they cannot. News is centered not on what individual newsmakers want in the newspaper and on the air, but on what the citizen-governors need in order to manage their lives. There is often a difference, and journalists argue that a good deal of important information would be cut off if individuals had effective veto power over what reporters printed and broadcast. It seems unavoidable that people are occasionally going to have things about them made public that they would rather remain private. It is the journalist's duty to recognize both the general good as well as the private harm that publication of certain information will produce.

A tentative answer often offered up by those arguing for privacy is to print some details, but withhold others. "Why did they have to print her name?" they ask. Or, "There was no need to put his picture in the paper." This is a serious point and well warrants an answer. Why, indeed, are people's names and other details of their lives included in a story? Arguing the case from the position of the greatest-happiness principle, what, if anything, outweighs the harm from embarrassment or worse that befalls a person who makes the news?

Most journalists believe in not inflicting harm without good cause. But there is often a good reason, indeed, a compelling one to print certain details over the wishes of the people most directly involved. The reason lies in the journalist's desire to make stories interesting and comprehensible to the readers and viewers. And what makes stories interesting and comprehensible? As any writer will quickly answer: people, not abstractions. One of the most effective ways to tell a story is by putting people in it, not thousands of people, not numbers of people, and certainly not percentages of populations, but individual people with names and physical descriptions and words coming from their mouths and expressions on their faces. The journalist often will have to weigh the harm done to an individual by pointing to the ostensible greater good that comes from telling an important story well. The weighing process may well depend on the seriousness of the harm done to the individual. If the harm is just embarrassment, it will not weigh as heavily as the potential for bodily harm.

LIBERTY AND FREEDOM

There is a parallel in the balance between liberty and security. If the American people were willing to pay the price, both in dollars and in loss of personal freedom, we could have much cleaner, safer streets and neighborhoods than we now have. We could learn from the small nation of Singapore, where an American teenager was caned for spraying graffiti and other minor acts of vandalism. Similarly, we could get most of the firearms off the street and close the pornographic bookstores. We could shoot unleashed dogs on sight. Similarly, we could change the rules about when and under what circumstances a single citizen or group of citizens could exercise veto power over a newspaper's right to print information. There is a cost to each of these moves, a cost in liberty, a value that the founding generation considered extremely important. In terms of reining in a runaway press, it could be done with regulations, or fines, or any number of other devices. But once so controlled, it would not be free to do the job for which it was created. Alan Barth, a former editorial writer for the Washington *Post*, put it this way: "If you want a watchdog to warn you of intruders, you must put up with a certain amount of mistaken barking.... [I]f you muzzle him and teach him to be decorous, you will find that he doesn't do the job for which you got him in the first place. Some extraneous barking is the price you must pay for service as a watchdog."

A major reason that a reporter barks when it turns out there's no need is the same reason that a real dog barks needlessly: There's a funny noise somewhere, and the watchdog begins to bark before checking out the source. News is a fiercely competitive business, with great value placed on getting the story first, before the other paper or station gets it. This leads to rushes to judgment—extra barking, if you will—that a more measured pace would avoid. Many embarrassing corrections could be avoided if everyone involved in the reporting, writing, and editing of a story took a little longer and double-checked everything again. But they don't; and mistakes happen, many of them attributable to excessive speed created by competitive pressures.

Yet, overall, competition is almost certainly a net plus for citizens. Journalists have limited energy, just like everyone else, and it is always easier to wait another day before finishing a story. But much news is like perishable fruit: It is good today but useless later. For citizens to retain the appropriate control over their hired and elected officials, they must know what those officials are planning to do before the plans are irrevocable. Inevitably, government officials planning actions that they know will be controversial would like to be as far along as possible before word gets out. Competition goes a long way toward overcoming both problems.

Technology has generally been speed's upper limit, the news engine's governor. In the 19th century, mail boats brought the latest news from Europe to the United States, meaning that the freshest Continental news was weeks old. James Gordon Bennett's New York *Herald* tried to shave precious minutes off the arrival time by sending small, fast "news boats" out to meet incoming ships and rush editions of the European papers back to the *Herald* offices before the ships lumbered into harbor with the same information for the less enterprising of the *Herald's* competitors. From the days of sail and then steam, each new technological development—railroad, telegraph, airplane, radio and so on—has reduced the time needed to get an account of a news event to readers (and now viewers).

The positive side of this shortening of delay is obvious, but there is also a serious negative to news in an infinite hurry. As technological developments make news delivery more efficient and more immediate, the time to think about a story gets shorter and shorter. And while a veteran journalist's ability to work in a hurry is truly impressive (many wire service reporters regularly never write their stories on a keyboard at all; they dictate completed prose from the field just from a few pages of hastily scribbled notes), thinking time is essential to make sense of complex issues. Remember: The point of journalism is not merely to provide isolated bits of information, so many factoids, as CNN calls them, good for little more than playing trivia games. Rather, journalism's essential function is to provide, in the words of the Hutchins Commission, an accounting of the day's events "in a context that gives them meaning." Meaningful context takes thought, and thought takes time. With modern communications equipment essentially taking the governor off the news engine, it is increasingly possible to speed into pointlessness, to deliver news in a frenetic jumble of sound and fury. No one is well served by that.

The latest development in this race for speed is the coming of age of the Internet and the World Wide Web. The Web holds much promise for good journalism but has potential for bad work as well. On the positive side, a reporter who used to have to drive to the library to look up a document is delighted to find that document on the Web in a tenth the time, with no problems finding a parking space. Computer-based analysis of databases can turn up injustices and corruption that in earlier generations remained buried in paper records effectively forever. And no longer do reporters, especially those at smaller outfits, have to endure the frustration common even a decade ago in finding that basic reference books were unavailable. Reference works are pouring online, and there's no reason to think the torrent will abate any time soon.

Excess speed is one of the dangers inherent in Web-based journalism, although television can already cover events live, that is, with a delay of exactly zero. More serious, probably, is the question of credibility. A famous cartoon from a few years ago showed two dogs sitting in front of a computer, one saying to the other, "On the Internet, no one knows you're a dog." In that vein, it is difficult to determine authenticity on the Web. One Web page can look like any other, although the reliability of their information may be staggeringly different. Many thoughtful critics have worried about credibility in this way: Is the site what it says it is? Is the E-mail really from the person listed as the sender? It is still early in the life of the Internet, but it seems most likely that the credibility problems of different Web sites will almost certainly sort themselves out in roughly the same way that the credibility of printed sources have done. If you log on to the New York *Times'* web site, you are more likely to get good information than if you log on to that of an unknown source. In time, the same forces that make a printed newspaper's masthead valuable will make a Website valuable as well. Experience and common sense and reportorial radar sensitive to dishonesty will always be valuable, however the information gets transmitted.

The more serious credibility problem, and the one that seems harder to solve, is associated with the increased belief among the citizenry that because of the Internet, readers and viewers may be able to do without journalists altogether, taking their information directly from Internet sources, unfiltered and unmediated by a reporter. The fact that anyone wants to bypass the reporting process altogether is a powerful condemnation of journalism, for it suggests that reporters are not perceived as honest and credible gatherers, distillers, and conveyers of information. Instead, it suggests that news professionals, either through ignorance or through malice, distort what they learn, passing along to the audience an inaccurate account of the events they cover. Before the Internet, it was wildly impractical for ordinary citizens to gather, digest, and take meaning from the many sources that provided most of our news. But Internet technology makes some of the gathering part relatively easy, leaving the reporter's essential role that of digesting and interpreting.

The danger is that in both business and political circles, disseminating disinformation is now a high art. Without trained journalists to sort out the nonsense and the fabrications, to point out the inconsistencies and the errors, an unwary public will ingest, and quite probably believe, all sorts of misinformation. The result of citizens getting their information directly, rather than through the journalistic filter, seems bound to be less understanding, rather than more, about important questions of public policy. Those who believe in the journalistic process may take some solace from the great likelihood that many readers and viewers will return to news outlets after they once see how difficult is the task of doing their own reporting. It remains for those in the news business to hasten their return by behaving honorably and re-earning the public trust.

It is important to recognize that there is no perfect journalism, because the demands on it go in different directions, and it is impossible to satisfy them all. One person might want full details of a robbery, in order to avoid unsafe streets and intersections. Another, worried about declining property values, might prefer just a few vague details. The arrested suspect would doubtless prefer nothing at all be said. One victim could want full-bore headline vengeance, while another would prefer a quiet time of internal healing before anything is said at all. A front page holds only so much information, and a 23-minute newscast can report on only so many stories. But even with limitless time and space, it would be impossible to tell each reader and viewer just what each one wants and may well need on a given day.

The popular sovereignty argument outlined above implies that those publishers taking advantage of First Amendment protections would publish political and other information useful to the body politic. It was a reasonable assumption at the time the First Amendment was adopted, for in the 18th century there was little reason other than politics to be in the information business.

Now, of course, there is, and that raises what for many is the toughest nut of all to crack: how to control the power of money. Beginning with the first press lords in the middle of the 19th century, money has been a formidable force to reckon with. As early as the 1830s, beginning with Benjamin Day and James Gordon Bennett, newspaper publishers realized that people would actually pay money for information, and if that information was fresh and interesting, lots of people would pay for it. People interested in politics would pay for political news, but there were far more people interested in sports, in theater, in crime and vice, in gossip; and these people would pay for information they found interesting, too. The economics were straightforward: ten people paying six cents apiece for a political newspaper do not generate as much revenue as a hundred, or a thousand, paying a penny or two for a paper that interested them.

INDIVIDUAL AUTONOMY
AND COMMUNAL RESPONSIBILITY

Politically and socially, much of the story of the last two centuries in the West, especially in the United States, has been the tension between individual autonomy and communal responsibility. Economically, individual autonomy has clearly been dominant. There is a long-standing and deeply cherished notion of rugged individualism in the American psyche. And while it is true that most Americans never hoisted axes onto their buckskin-clad shoulders and headed out across the mountains, the idea that we might remains a powerful vision. For many Americans, the Davy Crockett fantasy has played itself out in the world of finance as a justification of fierce economic competition.

How does this idea square with the more communal vision that is at the heart of a self-governing democracy? In brief, it does not. Because the government must, for very important reasons, leave the press alone, we can ask for no meaningful legislation or regulation to force the press to behave. So it is probable that there will always be barbarians at the gate or even in the publisher's office. Publishing became big business within fifty years of the founding of this nation; yet there is today a New York *Times*, a *News Hour with Jim Lehrer*, a Washington *Post*, and a *World News Tonight*, shows and papers that take their obligations as journalists seriously. As Barry Schwartz argues in *The Costs of Living*, most of us place high value on many things aside from money and resist putting everything in our lives into a pure profit-and-loss statement. Journalism is especially vulnerable to financial motives, because the financial rewards of charlatanism can be enormous and the government recourse is virtually non-existent. But journalism continues to attract people for whom maximum profit is not the only motive.

If journalists remember their proper role in this society based on ideals of democratic popular sovereignty, and if they approach their work thoughtfully and make decisions deliberately after thinking through the implications, we can probably ask for no more. People entering the news business should be forewarned that journalism is at least as much a calling as it is a job or a craft. And the readers and viewers—news consumers, in the modern parlance—are free, indeed, are obliged as well, to vote with their remote clickers and their quarters for the kind of journalism they prefer.

Perspective...

IF IT BLEEDS, IT LEADS

By HAROLD JACKSON, winner of the 1991 Pulitzer Prize for Editorial Writing while at the Birmingham (Ala.) *News*. Since 1994 he has been on the staff of the Baltimore *Sun*.

Mankind has always had a sort of twisted attraction to the misfortune of his neighbors: Say there's a house on fire down the street? Let's go see it! Somebody got hit by a car? Which way do we go?

But have we ever, as human beings, been as preoccupied with other people's bad luck as the American public is today? Newspapers read like police blotters, and "if it bleeds, it leads" has become the slogan of many television newscasts.

The public complains that it's tired of so much "bad" news. But you can believe that if today's papers and TV news shows weren't providing large enough audiences to see the ads and commercials that bring customers into the advertisers' stores, then we wouldn't be seeing and reading many of the stories that we are.

Too many in journalism today, it seems, have lost their sense of responsibility to tell stories that matter, not just stories that draw a crowd.

I recently spent ten months on a leave of absence from my job to serve as a Freedom Forum professional-in-residence at the University of Alabama. One visitor to a sophomore level news writing class I taught was David Hamilton, an assistant managing editor at *Newsday*.

One of the things Hamilton stressed was his personal desire to see the news media shun some of the blood and gore and frivolity and spend more time on stories that really matter.

Having heard Mr. Hamilton say that, I had to wonder what his reaction was a few weeks later when *Newsday* reportedly sent five reporters and at least that many photographers to cover the sentencing of Joey Buttafuoco to six months in jail for the statutory rape of Amy Fisher.

Newsday's editors knew that as trivial as the Amy Fisher/ Joey Buttafuoco story was, it is a story that satisfies the current appetite of the American public. From Michael Jackson to the Menendez brothers to Tonya Harding to O. J. Simpson, Americans appear far more interested in the surreal than they are concerned with the realities of subjects such as national health care or education reform.

Well, you've got to give the people what they want, don't you? At least that's the attitude of today's news media. Thus you see so-called legitimate news programs, the 5 o'clock newscasts, doing promos that piggyback on the topics featured on the most sensational and lurid programs on TV—your *Hard Copies* and *Current Affairs*, not to mention your *Oprahs* and *Geraldos* and *Sally Jessys*.

And the phenomenon isn't limited to television. Newspapers across this country are following the example of the sensationalist tabloids, going overboard with their coverage of tawdry stories reeking of innuendo while relegating the stories that really matter to insignificant amounts of space in which it is impossible to give the reader enough information to fully understand the complexities of that particular issue.

The aim of this least-common-denominator journalism is to provide stories that will in no way mentally challenge the reader, watcher or listener. This user-friendly journalism, designed to stimulate only the most basic instincts in man, and woman, is not only a disservice to the public; it is dangerous.

With this type of journalism, too many shortcuts are taken in reporting a story. Too many reporters and editors don't bother to consider the implications of what they write or depict in photographs.

They don't take time to explain to the reader all the possibilities behind the facts. They stoop to using code words to elicit certain reactions that will guarantee an audience or readers.

You would think the public would be raising the question of whether it's reading and seeing stories that really matter or only being fed enough titillation to keep it looking until the next commercial or full-page ad.

But the public's protests are feeble and infrequent. For the most part, as long as the public keeps buying from advertisers, the news media will wallow in the mud.

That means this sickness must be treated from within. Journalism needs more professionals in decision-making positions who subscribe to the belief that integrity means more than circulation. Newsrooms need more editors and reporters who know the importance of being fair as well as the importance of being objective.

Newsrooms need editors and reporters who don't take shortcuts when the truth is at stake—editors and reporters who would rather tell a story that matters and have it read by one person than tell a story that matters to no one and have it read or heard by thousands.

That's the challenge to the next generation, the challenge for the journalism school students now preparing themselves for careers in this profession.

Many of them already possess the attributes that would make them that type of reporter or editor. Their life experiences, even at a tender age, have made them appreciate the importance of being fair and of giving people information that is meaningful to them, not just entertaining.

These are the people journalism needs. They must stay focused. Those of us already in the business are depending on them to keep our future from becoming a mirror of our present.

Perspective...

ETHICS IN PHOTOJOURNALISM

By JIM R. MARTIN, former editor and publisher of *Bulletin Digest*, a religious monthly. His Ph.D. is from Southern Illinois University, Carbondale. He teaches journalism at David Lipscomb University.

There is a fine line between virtue and vice. Thrift is only a step away from stinginess. Generosity can become extravagance; courage often leads to recklessness. Lust is perverted love.

For journalists, the fine line separates the people's right to know from the public's desire to be entertained and titillated. The tension is seen in the Code of Ethics of the Society of Professional Journalists. The code states, "The public's right to know of events of public importance and interest is the overriding mission of the mass media." But the code also warns, "The media should not pander to morbid curiosity about details of vice and crime."

Responsible reporters will not withhold information people need, but neither will they be driven by the public's insatiable appetite for gossip. Photo editors must judge what the reader needs to see versus what the reader wants to see. "Giving the people what they want" may sell more papers, but it can turn virtue into vice.

The *Globe*, a supermarket tabloid, crossed the line when it published stolen crime-scene photos of six-year-old murder victim, JonBenet Ramsey, a strikingly beautiful child who had won several Little Miss beauty pageants including Little Miss Colorado of 1995.

About 2 p.m. the day after Christmas, 1996, millionaire computer executive John Ramsey discovered his daughter's body in the basement of the family's Boulder, Colorado, home. Her skull was fractured and her mouth had been sealed with duct tape before she was strangled with a nylon cord twisted tight around her neck with a wooden handle. Authorities later determined she had been sexually assaulted.

The public could not get enough of the story. It had all the elements of a made-for-TV movie: wealth, social standing, an elegant home, and a beautiful Little Miss beauty queen molested and murdered. It also had the strange twists of a television drama. The house showed no signs of forced entry. A ransom note had been written on a pad obtained inside the house demanding the oddly precise sum of $118,000. A "practice" ransom note also turned up. A 911 call from the Ramsey house was made three days before the murder, ostensibly by a guest trying to dial long-distance. The Ramseys hired their own investigator, a lawyer each, and a media consultant. They refused to be interviewed by police, who were also keeping a low profile.

Three weeks after the murder, with hoards of reporters still in Boulder waiting for any break in the case, the *Globe* ran front-page photos of the crime scene. The pictures, leaked from a photo lab that routinely processes Boulder County Coroner's Office photographs, showed a garrote—a cord-wrapped stick that might have been used to strangle JonBenet—and a rope dangling from one of her wrists.

The *Globe* was not alone in its poor taste. Many TV newscasts ran pictures of the tabloid's pictures, under the pretense of reporting on the *Globe's* bad behavior. Even though *Globe* editor Tony Frost defended his action, and TV news directors defended theirs, printing the photos served no useful purpose other than goading the public's morbid curiosity.

If journalists are to be virtuous, they should remember:

• Because pictures are so powerful, they have an impact beyond words. Some pictures needn't be published. The public has a right to know, but the newspaper has an obligation to show restraint.

• The news media must guard against invading people's privacy. A legal right to publish is not the same as a moral right.

• Ethical considerations are not meant to muzzle legitimate news stories or hinder publication of photos, but curiosity must be balanced by taste, dignity and compassion.

REPORTERS AND LEGAL ISSUES

Accuracy and fairness are essential elements for constructing good news stories. They are just as important for the journalist to avoid legal problems. Most legal problems can be avoided with care, attention to detail, and an appreciation of journalism ethics. No journalist can understand or utilize knowledge of legal problems without a thorough understanding and appreciation of the ethical standards that accompany them.

Reporters quickly grasp the importance of accuracy in gathering and writing information and making sure information is correct. The good reporter also finds several dependable sources to cover every side of the story. Editors demand copy that is balanced, hoping to leave no room for complaints that their newspapers or broadcast stations did a shoddy job of covering the story. Often editors point out to writers, especially young reporters, that such good reporting tactics not only produce quality copy, but help to avoid lawsuits and other legal problems.

There is no substitute for good reporting. Experienced re-

BY GENE WIGGINS
Dr. Wiggins, Professor of Journalism and Director of the School of Communication at the University of Southern Mississippi, is the author of a communications law book and has written numerous scholarly articles in the field of law.

porters know that hard work and attention to detail pay off in producing good copy. These veterans learned that good reporting produces "good reporters," at least in the eyes of the public and the sources these reporters use daily for information. Good character (what you think of yourself) and a good reputation (what your peers think of you) can be essential in reporting and in defending yourself and your employer in lawsuits. Libel lawsuits frequently turn on the reputation (dependability, accuracy, thoroughness) of the reporter. Problems in the other areas discussed in this chapter—invasion of privacy, free press-fair trial, confidentiality and shield laws, and even access to meetings and records— can be alleviated or avoided by reporters who are known to be dependable, ethical, and accurate.

PROBLEMS WITH LIBEL

In its simplest terms, libel (that is, written defamation) can be defined as disseminating false information that damages the reputation of a person or business. Perhaps the best working definition comes from Phelps and Hamilton's book *Libel*: Defamation is a communication that exposes a person to hatred, ridicule, or contempt, lowers him in the esteem of his fellows, causes him to be shunned, or injures him in his business or calling. Therefore, words, pictures, or drawings that place any business or living person in one of the categories listed above are likely defamatory. Carelessness causes most libel lawsuits, i.e., failure to check or cross-check information or simply to read carefully the words we write for more than one meaning. Lawsuits are usually filed against the corporation that owns the publication and the publisher since they can pay larger amounts in damages than the reporters can. However, anyone who played any role in printing or broadcasting a defamatory story may be added to the lawsuit.

THE ELEMENTS OF LIBEL

Before any lawsuit can succeed, five elements must be established. These elements include:

1. Publication
2. Identification
3. Defamation
4. Injury
5. Fault

The first two elements are fairly easy to prove. *Publication* occurs when a story is printed and the newspaper distributed. Some courts automatically presume publication in libel suits involving mass media. A person who claims to have been defamed must prove that the person in the story, picture, drawing, or other likeness is actually him or her. Persons may be *identified* by likeness or by name, including pen names or stage names. Even a description of an individual from which readers are likely to identify one person can be used for purposes of identification.

No one can win a libel suit simply because the information published is false. The false statements must damage a *reputation*, hurt someone in his business, or cause his friends to shun him. In other words, the false statements must carry some kind of sting that hurts the person mentioned in the story.

To prove the fourth element, *injury*, a plaintiff must show that he or she suffered some kind of damage such as personal humiliation or financial loss.

Fault, the newest element added to the libel equation, means a person bringing a libel suit must prove that the defendants did something that placed them at fault in publishing the material. The defendants must have acted in an irresponsible manner that resulted in the injury.

Public Persons

In the 1960s and 1970s, the Supreme Court of the United States made it more difficult for public persons to collect damages for defamation. In the 1964 case of *New York Times v. Sullivan*, the court ruled that *public officials*—persons on the public payroll who act in some capacity of authority—must prove *actual malice* to collect damages. To meet this stringent standard, a newspaper or broadcast station must have known the libelous statements printed or broadcast were either false or displayed a reckless disregard for the truth or falsity of the statements.

The court's rationale for such a difficult standard of proof for public officials was that these people not only place themselves in the public spotlight for approval or disapproval; they also have ready access to the mass media to level charges or refute accusations about their public performances.

A few years later the Supreme Court added *public figures* to the list of persons who must prove actual malice. A public figure is someone who thrusts himself into the center of an issue of public concern. In the 1974 case of *Gertz v. Welch*, the court declared there were two kinds of public figures—*all-purpose public figures* and *limited-purpose public figures*. Few persons fit the first category, but some examples of all-purpose public figures would be well-known politicians, entertainers, and sports figures. These individuals would have constant media attention and are recognized by virtually everyone. In a libel suit, all-purpose public figures would have few private areas in their lives.

Far more common is the limited public figure, a person who, for whatever reason, voluntarily stepped into the vortex of a specific public issue. That person would be considered a public figure only in connection with the public issue in which he or she is involved. Only in a libel case involving that issue would such a public figure have to prove actual malice.

Private Persons

In *Gertz*, the Supreme Court ruled that all persons must prove some kind of fault, including strictly private individuals who do not fit the categories of public official or public figure. The court declared that private persons much prove at least *negligence*, which is much easier to establish than actual malice. Many states define negligence as a lack of reasonable care. Simple carelessness fits into this category nicely, and the majority of libel cases arise due to carelessness in stories of little news value. Reporters seem to pay a great deal of attention to detail in the big, important news stories but frequently pay far less attention to less important ones.

Since the high court said in *Gertz* that everyone must prove some degree of fault, most states have adopted the suggested standard of negligence for private persons along with the mandated standard of actual malice for public persons. However, a handful of states, understanding the Supreme Court to say that a more stringent standard could be required of private persons, require them to prove a standard such as gross negligence or actual malice. Since libel law is essentially state law, reporters should be familiar with the laws of their states. Many newspapers and broadcast stations furnish such guidelines to reporters and editors. State press associations usually have such information available, and these groups frequently sponsor state-wide seminars to keep reporters up-to-date on libel and other legal problems.

DANGER AREAS FOR JOURNALISTS

Warning flags should always signal good journalists when writing about certain areas concerning people or businesses. Here are a few areas in which journalists should tread with caution:

1. Charges or claims concerning a person's personal habits or character:

- Claiming someone has a communicable disease that causes his friends to shun him
- Stating or implying someone is mentally unbalanced or insane
- Reporting a person is unfaithful to his or her spouse
- Reporting a person has a "drinking problem" or a "drug problem"

2. Charges or claims concerning the professional reputation of a person:
- Calling a lawyer a shyster or ambulance-chaser
- Referring to a physician as a quack
- Questioning a person's business practices

3. Charges or claims that a person has done something illegal:
- Reporting that a person is a criminal
- Reporting that a person or business is engaged in "shady" practices

These are only a few of the areas in which reporters should exercise extreme caution. In addition, problems frequently arise when referring to a person's sexual preference, when implying that a woman is unchaste, or even when making references to a person's marital status, claiming someone is divorced when he or she is not. Reporters frequently write about such topics; and good reporters verify, they document, they double-check, and above all they have good reasons for printing such material. If such a statement is true, if the reporter has substantial evidence of its truth, and if a plausible reason exists for printing or broadcasting the information, then and only then should the story be disseminated to a mass audience.

DEFENSES FOR LIBEL

Suppose your newspaper or broadcast station decides to disseminate a story that contains information that is potentially libelous. After much consideration, the decision is made that the public should know the information. What legal defenses exist to protect you and your employer from ruinous damages if a suit is brought? Three traditional defenses normally provide total protection. These are truth, qualified privilege, and another form of privilege called fair comment. A fourth defense, absence of actual malice, also offers great protection.

Truth

Employees of every reputable mass medium work hard to ensure the news they gather and report is accurate and true. But truth is not only an ideal; it is a defense that will provide complete protection for a mass medium. The problem is that truth is often difficult to determine. After all, in a libel suit, there are always two versions of the truth—the plaintiff's version and the defendant's version. Which version will the court believe? Editors and reporters must always keep in mind that what they are convinced is the truth may not be so easily proven in court. Witnesses who spoke in confidence may not be willing to go public in court. Perhaps only part of what you know about a person's illegal behavior can be proved.

A libel defendant must prove all of the elements that carried the sting of defamation are true, not part of them. If a plaintiff can show that some of the defamatory statements are false, you as a journalist are in deep trouble. Print or broadcast only what you can demonstrate in court is true. Document stories. Video or audio tapes can be invaluable in court. Creditable witnesses are needed. Even a reporter's notes can save a news medium from libel damages.

Qualified Privilege

The public has the right to receive information about the workings of government—courts, legislative bodies, executive and administrative agencies. Most proceedings in these bodies are privileged, and records of these proceedings carry the same protection. From this absolute privilege flows a protection for reporters known as qualified privilege, sometimes called "reporter's privilege." A reporter has the right to attend public proceedings and to inspect and copy records of these proceedings for publication.

As long as the report is fair (balanced) and is an accurate and true report or summary of the public proceeding, the news medium is fully protected from libel damages. For instance, much of what is said upon the witness stand in court is certainly defamatory, but the reporter is protected by privilege to report to the public what was said in court. However, the reporter must be sure to cover all the proceedings, not just the defamatory part. A one-sided account of a public proceeding can land a reporter in the libel hot seat.

Reporters must be aware of what kinds of records are covered by privilege in their states. Are complaints filed in a clerk's office protected? What about police records? In addition, veteran reporters know they must get their information from the record or proceeding itself, not from a government official standing on the courthouse or police station steps. This public official may be more than willing to provide you with a summary of what happened at a public meeting, but that official is doing you no favors if he or she gets part of the information wrong.

"But," a reporter cries, "that information given me by Police Chief Smith was published exactly as he said. My quotes are accurate." Sorry, no excuse. Remember, you can accurately quote the greatest lie ever told or the biggest mental lapse ever made by that person. Should that excuse you when a person later proves in court that Police Chief Smith was wrong? Will that take back the damage done? If you miss an important court case or city council meeting, get the information from the records, not from a well-intentioned but misinformed public servant. To summarize this point, you cannot claim that accurately quoting a defamatory statement should protect you from libel suits. By printing a defamatory quote, your publication is spreading the libel to a much larger audience.

Fair Comment

Thus far, we have discussed protections for statements of fact. What about opinion? Since truth or falsity plays no role in opinion, how far can a journalist go in expressing opinions on matters of public interest? Critics can make or break a Broadway play or a restaurant with a review or column. Courts have consistently ruled that any person or business placed voluntarily before the public for approval is fair game for comment. Entertainers, sports figures, writers (including journalists), restaurants, and many other persons or businesses are open for approval or disapproval by journalists.

However, a 1990 decision by the U. S. Supreme Court, *Milkovich v. Lorain Journal Co.*, has left many in the news media wondering just how far protection of opinion really goes. The court said that many opinion pieces carry factual connotations that may be proven false, and in such cases the Constitution would not afford protection. To state someone lied under oath carries the implication that the journalist had unreported information that would prove that person lied. This is not pure opinion, and thus not protected. Chief Justice William Rehnquist gave an example in *Milkovich* that he considered pure opinion: "In my opinion Mayor Jones shows his abysmal ignorance by accepting the teachings of Marx and Lenin." This pure opinion would be fully protected.

The Constitutional Defense of Sullivan

Many legal scholars consider the constitutional requirement for public persons to prove fault—actual malice, for public officials— a complete defense. This requirement from *New York Times v. Sullivan* works to protect the news media in libel suits, providing as it does that the plaintiff must prove recklessness—that is, that the publisher, editor, or reporter knew prior to publication that the defamatory material was false or displayed a reckless disregard for the truth. This is indeed a difficult burden to prove.

Other Defenses

Few other defenses provide complete protection from libel suits. Of course, consent would provide protection, but who in his right mind would grant such a thing? *Retractions* work to mitigate damages and frequently satisfy a potential plaintiff. The retraction should contain an apology and a correction of the facts, printed in approximately the same location and in the same type size as the original story. Be sincere and never view a retraction as something you are doing just to get of out trouble. If a news medium unjustly damages a person's reputation, a retraction is owed to that individual. Some states require that a person request a retraction before proceeding with a lawsuit.

INVASION OF PRIVACY

Laws governing the growing problem of invasion of privacy are relatively new compared to libel law, and many states are still developing their laws in this area. Legal experts have outlined four major legal wrongs that fall under the umbrella of invasion of privacy, and each of the areas has little similarity to the other three. The four areas are the following:

1. Appropriation
2. Intrusion
3. Publication of private and embarrassing matters
4. False light

Part of the problem in the area of invasion of privacy is that some states do not recognize all four areas as legitimate grounds for a lawsuit. For instance, Mississippi recognizes the first three areas, but the question of whether the state supreme court has recognized false light is being debated among lawyers and journalists. The court has not clarified its stand on false light.

Appropriation

Recognized in most states today, appropriation is taking the name or likeness of a person without permission and using it for commercial gain. The news media do not become entangled in many cases of appropriation. In most cases, acts of appropriation are so flagrant that no argument can be made that the act was a simple mistake. Occasionally situations arise in which the media personnel involved are not familiar with the law and intrude upon someone's privacy.

Courts established long ago that newspapers could republish old stories or photographs to show potential subscribers the kind of news and feature fare they could expect in that publication. Several years ago, a major newspaper published a page of photographs from the past, including a picture of a beautiful young woman basking in the sun near a lake. She was attired in a brief swimsuit. The woman objected to the use of her photograph. Attorneys for the newspaper unsuccessfully argued the paper had the right to publish the photograph to show readers examples of recent editions. However, the newspaper had sold the space, and small advertisements were placed all around the boxed area containing the photographs. The material was no longer a promotion of the newspaper, but a paid advertisement.

Intrusion

An average person generally thinks of invasion of privacy as the right to be let alone. This is a description of intrusion in a nutshell. When we intrude upon the solitude of an individual in a private location, we commit the legal wrong of intrusion. Reporters rarely step onto private property without permission, which is the only good defense for intrusion in most states. This is either the case, or they do not get caught. Whichever is the case, intrusion problems are rare. Journalists must remember that intrusion takes place when someone steps onto private property uninvited. No publication is necessary; the damage already has been done.

Private and Embarrassing Matters

To many journalists, the one onerous aspect of invasion of privacy is to be found in violation of the law for printing something that is true. Courts have long recognized that the American public has a wide variety of tastes and interests. Thus the news media have been given a wide latitude to publish many things of interest to the public even though someone may be embarrassed by the revelations. Since courts try to determine if a particular fact is newsworthy in deciding cases in this area of privacy, a court would first determine if the facts were indeed private (never before published or made available to the public). If so, then the court would ask the following two questions: (1) would the published material be offensive to a reasonable person, and (2) is the published material of legitimate public concern or interest?

Whom the story is about plays a major role in determining legitimate public interest. A person already in the public spotlight or even a person dragged involuntarily into the public spotlight may become a public figure who has far less privacy than a private person who has not become involved in any newsworthy event. The public-person doctrine under this area of invasion of privacy covers a wide scope of topics and can even cover a person who involuntarily becomes involved in a newsworthy event.

Years ago a young mother took her small children to a county fair. As she left the fun house, a fan blew her dress above her head. A photographer for the local newspaper snapped her picture, which was published the next day. Although her face was covered by the dress, many of the citizens in the small city knew who the woman was because they recognized the children. Even though the event occurred in a public place, the embarrassing photograph, when published, constituted an invasion of privacy.

Why did the photographer take the picture? Even more puzzling was why did some editor approve the publication of such material in a local newspaper? Was the event newsworthy? Of course, the answer is no. The results were embarrassment to the young mother and a lost lawsuit for the newspaper.

False Light

Placing a person in a false light is the one area of privacy that is akin to libel. False light cases are increasing yearly. When a news medium places someone in a false light, it makes the person appear to the public to be someone he or she is not. In other words, the public has a false impression about the person.

In the 1967 case of *Time v. Hill*, the U. S. Supreme Court ruled that the plaintiff would have to prove actual malice to prevail in a false light suit. The plaintiff must show the newspaper or broadcast station disseminated the information knowing that it was false or displayed a serious departure from the norms of good reporting. Most courts have followed this ruling and interpreted it to mean all persons, public and private, must prove actual malice. Still, some states have chosen to follow the standards in the *Gertz* libel case, making private plaintiffs prove something less stringent than actual malice. Know your state's laws concerning all the areas of invasion of privacy.

Fictionalization is a false light problem that journalists should never have to face. Yet, time and again, reporters yield to the temptation to "jazz" up a story, adding fabricated information to make the story more interesting. Years ago, a book about baseball pitcher Warren Spahn was published. The book, aimed at a young audience, contained numerous exaggerated feats. For instance, Spahn was portrayed as a war hero, which he was not, and a great deal of fictional dialogue was included. He sued. While the fictional material made Spahn look good, not bad, the law is aimed at protecting persons who are made to appear different than they really are. Spahn won his case. The same legal principles apply if the mass medium involved is a book, newspaper, magazine, or broadcast station. The solution to fictionalization is simple. If the facts gathered by the reporter do not warrant a story, then there is no story. Save the untrue material for the fiction books.

Reporters face tremendous legal and ethical questions in dealing with problems involving invasion of privacy. Questions of decency and fairness crop up frequently when reporters encounter situations that deal with private areas of a person's life. It is not unusual for reporters to face the question, "Do I write this because I have the right and privilege to do so?" A better question is, "Would the public be better off knowing this information, or am I writing it to titillate the interests of the reading public?"

CONFIDENTIALITY AND SHIELD LAWS

When reporters promise to keep sources' names confidential, they should keep the promise. However, before any journalist makes promises of confidentiality, he or she should think the request through completely. People request anonymity for many reasons. If someone holds a grudge, he might provide a reporter with the information to "get" the person he dislikes and still hide behind the screen of anonymity. Reporters should not allow themselves to be used as a tool of revenge. Rather than granting confidentiality, journalists should seek other sources who will provide the same information publicly. Another avenue to explore is to ask sources seeking anonymity if they would "go public" if the reporter should need them in a lawsuit. Taking a person's word that he or she will "go public" if needed can be risky. A written agreement to "go public" is much more desirable.

Using anonymous sources can lead to mistrust by the public. There is a widening perception that journalists make up sources. A news medium has no way of demonstrating to the public that its reports are credible if it uses significant numbers of unidentified sources. As the Gallup findings reported in this book demonstrate, fewer than half of all respondents felt journalists practiced high ethical standards. Citing reputable sources "on the record" and using multiple sources to verify information will help alleviate part of this mistrust by the public.

If as a journalist you determine that you need the information held by confidential sources, then you might agree to keep their names secret. But utilize other sources to verify the information. And be aware that in the past thirty years, reporters have gone to jail rather than reveal to a grand jury or judge the names of confidential sources. As a veteran journalism teacher was fond of telling his young student reporters, "Take a tour of your local jail before you get carried away with promises of confidentiality. Mom won't be there to wake you for breakfast."

In 1981 the Washington *Post* returned a Pulitzer Prize when it was discovered that the writer, Janet Cooke, had made up the winning story. Since then, the editors at the *Post* and many other newspapers insist upon knowing the identity of confidential sources. This is a sensible rule because then editors can help reporters make decisions about the reliability and credibility of the sources. Journalists then can decide if they should find alternative sources rather than be forced to break promises of confidentiality.

Breaking promises can have legal ramifications, too. The U. S. Supreme Court upheld a decision that awarded $200,000 to a political consultant who worked for a Republican gubernatorial candidate in Minnesota. In the 1991 case of *Cohen v. Cowles Media Co.*, the court said that the Constitution does not prohibit a person from collecting damages when a publication breaks a promise of confidentiality. Dan Cohen had informed two reporters from Minneapolis and St. Paul newspapers and a reporter from a local television station that he would give them information concerning a Democratic candidate for lieutenant governor who had been convicted of a misdemeanor. But Cohen demanded his identity be kept secret.

The television station decided that a conviction for shoplifting needles and thread by the candidate when she was eighteen years old was not a story. Editors of both newspapers independently decided that the "dirty trick" tactics of Cohen deserved exposure, and they revoked the promises made by both reporters to him. Cohen's offer of information was certainly intended to benefit his own political party, and the reporters should never have made a promise of anonymity. If the allegations were more serious, other sources—court records or witnesses willing to speak on the record—could have been found. These allegations were not worth a story. But once made, the promises amounted to a contract between the parties.

Shield Laws

Over half the states have laws that provide protection to reporters who use confidential sources. The laws are intended to protect sources, notes, audio outtakes, and video outtakes. Many shield laws are written so loosely that any judge who does not care for the shield law in his state can find loopholes. In addition, most laws protect reporters when they obtain the information second-hand. If a reporter actually views a crime being committed by the source, such as producing illegal drugs, the court likely would rule that the shield law provides no protection for the reporter.

William Farr, a reporter for the Los Angeles *Herald Examiner* and later the Los Angeles *Times*, spent a record forty-six days in jail for contempt of court after refusing to provide a California court his sources for controversial information he obtained while covering the Charles Manson murder trial. All trial participants—lawyers, witnesses, and others—were under a court order not to make public any information that could interfere with the fair administration of justice. Although Farr claimed that the reporters' privilege law of California protected him from revealing his sources, the appeals court upheld his conviction. The court based its ruling on the "inherent power" of courts to regulate court matters without interference from other branches of government. In this case, the court said no legislative act--including the shield law—could declare that certain actions do not constitute contempt. This was usurping a function of the courts, according to the appellate court.

For over twenty-five years, journalists and experts in freedom of expression have pushed Congress to pass a federal shield law, providing nation-wide protection for the news media and their employers. The major obstacle has been disagreement among journalists themselves about what kind of law is needed. Should the law provide qualified or absolute protection? Should it protect only newspapers and broadcast stations' reporters, or should it cover authors of books and free-lance writers? Congress will not act until some kind of consensus among those who seek the law has been achieved.

Many journalists feel the First Amendment provides complete protection, despite some court rulings to the contrary. Journalists who follow this line of thinking feel that any shield law passed by Congress would never be as protective as the First Amendment and could encourage Congress later to pass laws that would reduce certain press freedoms.

ACCESS TO RECORDS AND MEETINGS

A basic tenet of a democracy is openness in government. Public officials chosen by the people to take care of public business are expected to run their offices in an open manner. To evaluate a public official's performance, the people must have access to meetings and records of these officials and their offices. All fifty states have laws providing access to records and meetings, and Congress has passed federal laws giving the press and public access to certain records and meetings of executive and administrative bodies.

Congress passed an access law in 1966, but other, more recent laws have restricted access to certain kinds of information. Federal laws that provide access to information are the 1966 Freedom of Information Act (FOIA) and the 1976 Government in Sunshine Act. Laws that restrict access are the General Education Provisions Act and the Privacy Act, both passed in 1974, and several criminal records laws passed since 1968.

Freedom of Information Act

The FOIA provides access to the records of many federal agencies, unless the records fall under nine exemptions. Federal agencies covered by the act include offices in the executive branch and all the independent regulatory agencies like the Federal Communications Commission. The FOIA does not cover records of federal courts or Congress. The nine categories of exempted information include the following:

- National security information that has been properly classified
- Internal personnel rules and practices of an agency
- Information exempted by other federal statutes
- Privileged or confidential financial information or trade secrets
- Intra-agency or inter-agency communications
- Personnel and medical records that would invade one's privacy
- Certain law enforcement investigatory files
- Reports by agencies that regulate financial institutions
- Geological and geophysical data, including maps, mainly

concerning oil and gas wells

No presidential administration has looked upon the law with much favor since it was enacted. When employees of federal agencies know their superiors do not favor providing access to information, they frequently erect barriers to make it difficult for the press and public to obtain records. Often much of a document will be blacked out, with the agency using the excuse that the excluded information falls under one of the nine exempted categories. Also, exorbitant fees may be charged for the document search and copying, despite legal limitations on such fees. Many agencies fail to meet the ten-day deadline set by the FOIA for providing a response to any request, and employees of these agencies know that little or nothing will be done for failing to respond on time. Bureaucrats even attempt to erase paper trails by shredding documents. Many of these documents should be kept as required by law, since they are official documents of a particular agency.

Despite these barriers, the public makes hundreds of thousands of requests each year, and journalists are among those who use the law. Although using the law is not difficult, journalists must be familiar with its requirements. For instance, a request must clearly and narrowly specify the information sought. To become familiar with these requirements, journalists should obtain a copy of the booklet *How to Use the Federal FOI Act* for about $3. Write to FOI Service Center, 800 18th Street N.W., Washington, DC 20006.

Access and the Sunshine Act

The federal sunshine law provides access to meetings of more than fifty agencies and boards whose members are appointed by the president. The law excludes the legislative and judicial branches. Ten exemptions provide for closed meetings. The first nine exemptions are virtually the same as those under the FOIA. The tenth exemption covers matters when a federal agency is issuing a subpoena, participating in arbitration, or adjudicating a case. While little litigation has occurred under the sunshine law, compliance is not good. Some media law experts recommend the same kind of constant legal and media pressure that forced many government agencies to comply with the FOIA.

General Education Provisions Act and Privacy Act

These two 1974 laws limit the public's access to many records kept by public agencies. The education act is more commonly known as the *Buckley Amendment*. This law allows parents to see their children's records at all federally funded schools and educational agencies, but the same law prohibits the distribution of most personally identifiable information to unauthorized persons without permission of a student's parents. Little is lost by the public and the press under the provisions of this law. Occasionally, educational administrators fearful of violating the Buckley Amendment may withhold information not covered by the law.

The *Privacy Act* was intended to provide citizens access to records about themselves held by many federal agencies. At the same time, the law seeks to halt the abuse of such records by the federal government. Part of the law limits the dissemination of personally identifiable records of individuals without their permission. Records required to be public under the FOIA are not covered by the Privacy Act. Fearing possible conflicts between the two laws, however, many government agencies have withheld information from citizens, including members of the press.

Criminal History Laws

Numerous federal laws have been passed since 1968 that restrict the kinds of information that law enforcement agencies can release about individuals. Since local law enforcement agencies are connected to national computerized records to help them in their investigations, Congress became concerned about the possible misuse of these records. Laws were passed that restrict local agencies that use the national computerized records from making public most information about a person's criminal history, including non-convictions. Unless the information is related to a person currently being sought by police, journalists will not be provided with such material. The situation often presents a dilemma for the press, which faces the difficult problem of not making information public that would affect a person's right to a fair trial and, at the same time, keeping an eye on the conduct of the police and the courts.

STATE LAWS OF ACCESS

State open records and open meetings laws vary so much that only a few generalizations can be made about them. Some states, such as Florida and Tennessee, have strong access laws while others have laws so full of loopholes they provide little access for the public. A good law should begin with a declaration that openness is the policy of the state, and exceptions or exemptions to the law should be few.

State *open meetings laws* are written from one of two approaches. A state may declare that all meetings of public bodies are open, and then list the exceptions; or a state may list the public bodies or agencies in the state that must be open to the public. Most meetings laws provide for closed, or "executive," sessions, from which the public is excluded. Generally, records of these closed meetings are required to be made public within a specified time.

State *open records laws* generally permit anyone to inspect and copy public records, although some permit only citizens of the state to do so. Like meetings laws, these laws either declare all records open and list the exemptions, or they list all the records that are to be public. Courts have been more liberal than the legislatures in interpreting the laws, generally ruling that exemptions are to be construed narrowly.

Journalists, confronting problems at the state and local levels, frequently find their state access laws too weak to do them much good. Some of the major weaknesses of the laws are these:

- 1. Too many exemptions
- 2. Exclusion of branches of government (usually legislative and judicial)
- 3. Little or no penalties for violations of the law
- 4. No procedures for seeking relief other than the court

Journalists should be thoroughly familiar with the laws that govern access to public bodies and records. By knowing your legal rights, you will be in a better position to stand up and object when you feel a public body approves a closed meeting or denies you access to records. While lists of exemptions to meetings laws are long in many states, numerous state courts have declared that it is not sufficient for officials simply to cite one of these reasons to close a meeting. A public body must be more specific, rather than just stating it is entering an executive session under one of the areas of exemption such as "personnel matters," one of the favorite topics for such meetings.

Most journalists acknowledge there are some subjects that might be best discussed in closed sessions, but these subject areas are few. As one state supreme court declared: All statutory exceptions must be strictly construed against executive sessions. Just because the law allows a public body to enter a closed meeting to discuss a particular topic does not mean that body must do so.

FAIR TRIAL/FREE PRESS ISSUES

Three U. S. Supreme Court decisions in the 1980s did much to ensure open trials and pre-trial proceedings in criminal cases. In 1980, the court declared in *Richmond Newspapers, Inc. v. Virginia* that trials should be open to the press and public unless there was some overriding interest clearly spelled out in a court's findings. In two California cases, referred to as "Press-Enterprise I" and "Press Enterprise II" because the names of the cases were the same (*Press Enterprise v. Riverside County Superior Court*), the high court declared that pre-trial proceedings should be open. In the 1984 "Press-Enterprise I" decision, the court said jury proceedings should be open and implied that such proceedings are part of the trial itself. In 1986, the court said in "Press-Enterprise II" that all pre-trial proceedings should be presumed open. In both cases, the Supreme Court left open the possibility of closing portions of proceedings if a court deemed it necessary and if no reasonable alternatives to closure could be found.

The problem of massive publicity, especially before a trial begins, is a critical one since it can damage a defendant's right to receive a fair trial. Journalists must be vigilant to ensure that what is made public will not endanger the right to a fair trial, a right that is just as precious as the right to a free press.

Appeals courts have been reluctant to approve restrictive orders, known as *gag orders* by journalists, on the news media. The First Amendment has presented a virtually insurmountable barrier to silencing the press in covering legal proceedings. However, judges can and frequently do use orders to silence trial participants. When everyone connected with a case is forbidden to talk to the press under threat of contempt of court, the press can have a difficult time finding information about a trial. Journalists must remember that while the judge usually cannot "gag" the press, the court will seek ways to ensure that a defendant, especially a famous or notorious person, can get a fair trial.

A new problem in the fair trial/free press dilemma is large payments to actual or potential witnesses in upcoming trials. Several witnesses involved in the pre-trial hearings of the O. J. Simpson case received substantial payments from national news organizations for their stories before they were to appear on the witness stand. Did these witnesses compromise their credibility by accepting payments? Was the right to a fair trial damaged by the efforts of a few media organizations to get exclusive stories?

LAW AND RESPONSIBILITY

If young journalists learn anything from law chapters, press seminars on legal issues, or from veteran editors and reporters, it should be that most legal problems can be avoided with care, attention to detail, and an appreciation of journalism ethics. It is no accident that the chapter on ethics in this book immediately precedes this chapter on legal issues. No journalist can understand or utilize knowledge of legal problems without a thorough understanding and appreciation of the ethical standards that accompany them. The two areas are inseparable.

A concerned journalist is one who takes the time to learn the laws of his or her state. Laws that restrict or grant access to public information are so different from state to state that it is essential for a reporter to stay abreast of the law. A basic understanding of the libel and invasion of privacy laws of a reporter's state is necessary, along with guidelines from the state press association or bar association on how best to avoid such problems.

Journalists, young and old, must never forget the responsibilities of the press to its reading, listening, and viewing audience. Far too often, journalists yell loudly for the rights and privileges of the press, overlooking the obligation a free press has to the American people. Full and open discussion is essential to a free society, but not every bit of interesting or titillating information is needed by the public to function in a democracy. When the publication of any information endangers a citizen's reputation, right to a fair trial, or right to be let alone, journalists must pause to decide if that information is needed by the public. If not, some other overriding interest should be present before a news medium assumes the awesome responsibility of destroying reputations, humiliating someone, or endangering the right to a fair trial.

Perspective...

WHAT A SPECIALIST IN MASS MEDIA LAW WISHES BEGINNING JOURNALISTS KNEW ABOUT THE LAW

By RICHARD F. HIXSON, who teaches communication law and journalism history at Rutgers University

I would of course start with the United States Constitution, instructing beginning journalists in the theories behind freedom of speech and the press. I would do this with the help of the late Harry Kalven,

First Amendment scholar and teacher, who once noted the paradox that speech, although highly prized, enjoys its great protection in part because it is so often of no concern to anyone. "To an almost alarming degree," Professor Kalven said, "tolerance depends not on principle but on indifference" (Harry Kalven, *A Worthy Tradition: Freedom of Speech in America* [New York, 1989]). Why then are we ever moved to try to limit speech? Or, as I ask my students every semester, why is the First Amendment always threatened?

Religion is a major motivator, but so are patriotism, public taste, and political action, each of which, at one time or another, has provided the raison d'etre for attempts at censorship. While efforts to stymie debate usually fail in the long run, they reappear, like the phoenix, because, as Justice Owen J. Roberts opined in 1940, religious faith and political belief create sharp differences: "The tenets of one man may seem the rankest error to his neighbor" (*Cantwell v. Connecticut*, 310 U. S. 296 [1940]). And when the Supreme Court early confronted efforts to improve forcibly the public's taste in entertainment, Justice Stanley Reed rephrased the same democratic principle: "What is one man's amusement, teaches another's doctrine" (*Winters v. New York*, 333 U. S. 507 [1948]).

In 1971, Justice John Marshall Harlan, for whom the reach of federal censorship posed real threats to free expression, said that it was "plainly untenable" for the government to eliminate certain language to prevent reaction to its display. After all, Harlan observed, expression was intended to serve "emotive" as well as "cognitive" functions, and "one man's vulgarity [was] another's lyric." It was precisely because government officials could not make "principled distinctions" of that sort "that the Constitution [left] matters of taste and style so largely to the individual." There was the risk, he added, that government censorship of particular words could become a "convenient guise for banning the expression of unpopular ideas" (*Cohen v. California*, 403 U. S. 15 [1971]).The opinion, one of Justice Harlan's last, exemplifies, in Professor Kalven's view, the best of the judicial tradition regarding the First Amendment.

Justice William J. Brennan Jr. said in 1964 in the landmark *New York Times* libel decision that cases involving the mass media must be considered against the background of a "profound national commitment to the principle that debate on public issues should be uninhibited, robust, and wide open, and that may well include vehement, caustic, and sometimes unpleasantly sharp attacks on government and public officials" (*New York Times v. Sullivan*, 376 U. S. 254 [1964]). I would want beginning journalists to study *New York Times v. Sullivan*, in which Justice Brennan led a unanimous Supreme Court to impose a significant restriction on the power of government to penalize libelous comments about public officials. The Court held that a public official suing a news organization for defamation would not only have to prove falsity and injury to collect damages. That official must also demonstrate actual malice, that is, "knowing falsehood or reckless disregard as to truth or falsity." Evidence of actual malice would have to be of "convincing clarity." Private persons not involved in public events would also have to carry the burden of proof in libel suits under *New York Times*.

But I would also want beginning journalists to understand the uneven playing field that these decisions created, including, ten years later, *Gertz v. Welch*, when the Court exempted private persons who become involved involuntarily in matters of public interest from the *New York Times* standard of actual malice. I would also encourage beginning journalists to read Donald M. Gillmor's *Power, Publicity and the Abuse of Libel Law* (1991). Gillmor believes, as Justice Louis Brandeis advocated long ago, that the ultimate remedy against falsehoods and fallacies is more speech, not enforced silence. (*Whitney v. California*, 274 U. S. 357 [1927]). By allowing only private persons and involuntary public figures to sue for defamation, the limits on speech are reduced and the freedom to speak is expanded.

7

SOURCES
OF INFORMATION

A story is only as good as the quality of information in it. Even great writing cannot hide poor reporting.

Every reporter faces the temptation to write evasively around a missing fact, to skip the extra interview, to get a quick quote over the phone instead of being there, and to let one's own interpretations of events replace those of expert sources. Don't do it. These are terrible habits to develop.

Instead, dig after that elusive fact, track down the logical source, and gather more information than seems necessary. Two reporters get the same news release from a community group expressing outrage at escalating apartment rates. One reporter makes some phone calls and turns in a six-paragraph story that appears on page 7. The other visits apartment complexes, talks to college students about the apartment hunt, gathers real numbers on local supply and demand, uses a computer database to compare local rates with national trends, and turns in a fascinating story that makes page 1. The difference? The second one was a real reporter. The dividing line between an excellent story and a mediocre one typically is the depth and quality of the information gath-

BY PAUL PARSONS
Dr. Parsons is Associate Director of the School of Journalism and Mass Communications at Kansas State University. Before becoming a teacher, he worked ten years with a state-wide daily in Arkansas, United Press International, and the Associated Press.

ered.

Good reporters rely on observation (what they see), interviews (who they talk to), and research (backgrounding a topic) as their primary sources of information.

At 2 o'clock one September morning, an Air Force maintenance team wearing white protective suits and breathing packs walked toward a nuclear missile silo in Arkansas and disappeared into the darkness. The underground silo had a leak. An hour later, an explosion and shock wave knocked to the ground the sleepy reporters being detained a quarter mile away. A huge orange and black cloud poured from the silo. By being there, a reporter captured this eyewitness account:

I found an airman dressed in the white garb. He was leaning against a truck crying "Oh my God. Oh my God. Please let them be alive!"

Arriving in [the nearby town of] Damascus, we found everything in a state of pandemonium. The Air Force was nowhere in evidence, but several quick-acting state troopers began the evacuation of the small town.

It was a startled and confused populace that came to their front doors on hearing the sirens and roof-mounted loudspeakers call for the immediate evacuation of the town. In little more than an hour, Damascus was a ghost town with only dogs, cats and policemen remaining.

A local radio station immediately called the Associated Press in Little Rock, which operates twenty-four hours a day, seven days a week. Within minutes, a sketchy story based on eyewitness accounts had been transmitted nationwide. Now the hard part began—bringing detail and context to the story. It would require continued observation, interviews with knowledgeable sources, and good backgrounding.

AP headquarters in New York queried: What happened to the nuclear warhead? Good question. The silo had housed a 103-foot intercontinental ballistic missile capable of delivering the nation's largest hydrogen bomb to a target 6,300 miles away. Military radio transmissions revealed that the Air Force had no idea where the bomb was. Hours later, it was found in a grassy field, dented but not detonated.

As the AP reporter at the scene, I slept in my compact car and ate cheese crackers for thirty-six hours while covering the dramatic search, discovery, and transporting of the damaged nuclear warhead to Texas in a convoy of eight military vehicles and two helicopters.

Interviews helped fill many of the missing pieces of the story. The leak occurred when a maintenance worker accidentally dropped a three-pound socket wrench that plunged seventy feet and punctured a first-stage thrust mount. Military officers confirmed that two crew members had died while they were scrambling to exit the leaking silo. An Air Force sergeant who conducted the evacuation of nearby Damascus said he encountered belligerent residents: "Most of it was confusion and fear. If you wake someone up at 3 a.m. and you have a [gas] mask on, you can't expect them to welcome you."

Meanwhile, the AP office was gathering valuable background research on this particular type of missile and its history of accidents. The missile's thrust was equal to that of 46,000 automobiles. It carried a twenty-four-megaton warhead—many times the power of the bomb dropped on Hiroshima—at a speed of 18,000 miles an hour. Another of the underground silos had blown up in Kansas two years before. This was the second time that Damascus had been evacuated because of a silo problem.

On Sunday, wanting more humanity and less technicality, I went to a church service in Damascus and filed this story:

> The Air Force was criticized for its secrecy and God was praised for his mercy Sunday in services at the First Baptist Church in Damascus.
>
> Following the singing of "Rescue the Perishing," the Rev. Tommy Hall said the residents around the silo deserve to know if "imminent danger" exists as a result of the blast that catapulted a nuclear warhead several hundred feet from the silo.
>
> "We don't want secrets revealed to us," he said. "All we want is the truth. Jesus said, 'Ye shall know the truth, and the truth shall make you free.'"

Journalism, like religion, is in pursuit of truth. As the Freedom Forum Media Studies Center at Columbia University put it: "The highest aim of both religion and journalism is to set people free with the truth. Religion seeks to liberate people with God's truth. Journalism, with more earthly aspirations, strives to free people by informing them about the daily truth of the world in which they live." Truth-telling, then, is the mission of the journalist.

Observation, interviews, and *research* are the reporter's primary tools in the pursuit of truth. All three tools may be employed in the same story. A reporter may observe state legislators fiercely debating the death penalty, noting the enthusiasm of a new state senator who keeps shouting "Remember the victims!" By researching state prison records, the reporter compiles a list of death-row inmates and notices that the latest occupant had kidnapped and killed the daughter of the high school principal in the senator's hometown. With that research, the reporter interviews the senator and learns of the community's continuing grief and intense lobbying in favor of the death penalty. The issue, then, is more than philosophical. Like most issues, it has a personal dimension. In the end, readers have that debate placed in a practical and more meaningful context.

OBSERVATION

The most exciting journalism is eyewitness journalism. Tell what you see, honestly and fairly. Just as eyewitness testimony carries great weight in a trial, eyewitness reporting offers the writer great credibility. If you were at City Hall when the mayor angrily shoved a city councilman against the wall, you can report it with confidence as an observer. If you were at the airfield when family members greeted American soldiers returning from abroad, you can write with certainty of the joyous moment. Because you are human, some distortion is inevitable as you observe. The best guard against distortion is an awareness of your own propensity to see what you want to see.

As a summer intern, full of enthusiasm and empty of experience, I watched a bank robbery suspect pull out a razor blade and slice his neck in the courtroom. My copious trial notes meant nothing now. I was an eyewitness to a newsworthy event. My editor barked at me to "make the reader see." So the story was full of detail:

> Brinkley was leaning back in his chair, his right arm hanging limp. A law clerk shouted "Call a nurse!" while holding a handkerchief to the bleeding neck. Brinkley, his shirt unbuttoned, was laid on the floor and a seat cushion was propped behind his head. Placed on a stretcher by four men, his eyes were open and blinking as he was wheeled to an ambulance.

My editor taught me a lesson that day. When I wrote of it as an attempted suicide, the editor deleted that interpretation from my story. The next day, in a follow-up, doctors said the suspect had sliced his neck in a way that posed no danger to his life. His motive, they said, evidently was to delay the trial, not to commit suicide. To be in the truth-telling business, then, I learned to show what happened, not interpret what happened.

Reporters are natural observers because of their natural curiosity for detail. In a story of bigger magnitude than some neck-slicing bank robber, hundreds of reporters poured into Cape Canaveral expecting to write a story about pride and achievement as the space shuttle Challenger carried schoolteacher Christa McAuliffe on her way into space and into the history books. Reporters were in the bleachers, not far from her parents. Even though we know what happened, this simple story, written by the Miami *Herald*'s Martin Merzer, shows the emotional power of observation:

So they stood in the sunshine Tuesday, Ed and Grace Corrigan, arm in arm in the bleachers at Cape Canaveral, and they watched in triumph. And then in disbelief. And then in horror.

Something terrible had happened. And now, a NASA official was making his way to them. He was walking up the bleachers, slowly, row by row. And with every step, he was sealing their fate.

Finally, he arrived, as they knew he must. "The vehicle has exploded," he said. Mrs. Corrigan looked back at him, and after a moment, she could find only these words, an echo really:

"The vehicle has exploded?"

The man nodded, and he was silent.

It was unthinkable. It was impossible. There were backup systems for backup systems.... Yet it happened, in full view of millions of Americans, many of them impressionable schoolchildren. The shuttle and its precious human cargo were gone, incinerated in a fireball, debris raining into the Atlantic.

The Challenger story, of course, had natural drama and emotion. Not every story makes the heart beat faster. A city commission story is designed to tell readers what their elected officials are doing. The topics may be as dry as a residential rezoning and as technical as a federal grant application. But readers appreciate detail. It's important to be at the commission meeting so the reporter can see what occurred, not rely on someone else's version of what was important.

Good reporting means showing, not telling. To say the city commissioner "was angry" tells; to say the commissioner "slammed his fist on the table" shows. By showing, the reporter bridges the gap between the observation and the audience. As Mark Twain once explained: "Don't say the old lady screamed. Bring her on. Let her scream."

Obviously, take notes. Don't count on memory to recall the colors on the clown's face, the make of the gun found in the alley, or the witty phrase uttered by the soprano who lost her voice. Memories are fleeting. Notes aren't. Good reporters are good scribblers, jotting down detail that may find its way into the story. Only by detail does the reporter give a story its authenticity, its specificity that readers crave, and its meaningful color that brings a story alive and helps the reader see. Detail adds to the immediacy and impact of a story.

INTERVIEWS

All reporters rely on other people for information, by necessity. The reporters weren't present when the car slid off the icy bridge; so they rely on those who came to the scene to investigate the crash. They weren't in the emergency room when the doctor performed a life-saving operation; so they interview those who witnessed it. They weren't in the coach's office when his assistant handed the recruit a wad of $100 bills; so they talk to the athlete who says it happened and to the coach who says it didn't.

And that's the problem with interviews. Unlike eyewitness observation or research, interviews involve talking with people. People may lie. They may forget. They may change their story. They may have hidden agendas. They may tell a reporter what they think the reporter wants to hear. They may have friends they want to protect, or enemies they want to hurt. They even may deny what they once said. Like secondhand smoke, reporters should beware of secondhand information. Treat the information cautiously and with skepticism. Look for ways to confirm what people say. Just because a person states a fact doesn't make it true. Still, this very human and fallible dimension of reporting gives journalism its life and zest.

Part of the pleasure of reporting is the gathering of people's opinions. Although facts can be provably true or false, an opinion cannot be. There is no such thing as a false opinion. If one caller to a talk-radio show refers to Rush Limbaugh as an idiot, and another sarcastically asks why President Clinton jogs every morning but never seems to lose weight, the reporter can truthfully cite these as examples of talk-radio. This is opinion and sarcasm, not refutable fact. No need to ask Rush for rebuttal, or to call the White House in futility for the President's current weight (although the brash reporter might do this just to see what happens).

Whether the interview is for fact or opinion, select the best sources. Turn to those whose expertise adds credibility to the story. Interview the cop at the scene, not the police dispatcher. Interview the people whose homes will be torn down to make way for a new mall. Talk to those who best know the facts and to those most directly affected by the story. The beatitudes do not include "Blessed are the shy."

When a fuzzy-cheeked Bill Clinton was elected governor of Arkansas at the age of thirty-two, a number of reporters sat around speculating just how far his ambitions might take him. My editor said, "Ask him." My first question in our first interview was "Governor, do you want to be President someday?" An amused smile formed on his face, and he answered in that gravelly voice, "Yes, I think I do." From that point, we talked of what he wanted to accomplish as governor of a small state that would put him in position someday to become President of the United States. Do not shy away from the obvious question. Although more experienced politicians might wisely have dodged the question, people being interviewed have a tendency to want to speak truthfully. Ask them direct questions that will get at the truth.

Because reporters ask the questions and sources give the answers, a news story must properly link the information with the source through attribution. With many major dailies providing sources for only 25% of the information in their stories—and broadcast journalism doing even worse—reporters need to recognize the importance of carefully attributed information in building evidence that drives a story.

News agencies are a beacon in illuminating the value of careful attribution in writing a news story. In the late 1700s and early 1800s, America's newspapers were highly partisan. They did not seek fairness or balance, and readers knew that a particular newspaper would attack Thomas Jefferson while another would revere him. An evolution in reporting came with the rise of the Associated Press and its ancestors. Because the AP didn't want to offend either a Democratic or Republican newspaper, the news report was deliberately neutral, with information attributed to the source. This concept of neutral reporting soon became the ideal for the mainstream media.

The rule is simple: attribute information whenever readers might have cause to wonder about its source. This includes all quotations, of course, and any information whose accuracy could reasonably be doubted. Undisputed facts need no attribution. If a tornado struck the city, say so. But if a resident reports seeing the twister suck two children out of a mobile home, and no one else saw it, attribute the information so that readers may judge the credibility of the source for themselves.

By connecting a piece of information to someone's name, the

reporter provides a mechanism to verify the information's truth or falsity. Now, sometimes a source's identity needs to be protected. If a public employee wants to reveal an illegal practice without risking job loss through public identification, then the reporter may agree to keep the source's identity confidential. Without such an agreement, the source may choose to stay quiet. Reporters, though, should be slow to grant confidentiality. Consider the motives of the source who requests anonymity. Any potential loss of information must be balanced against the gradual erosion of credibility that results from the practice of feeding audiences information without verifiable attribution.

RESEARCH

Because reporters are in the truth-telling business, physical sources can serve as reality checks for what human sources say.

Example: A mayor seeking re-election pledges a crackdown on pornography. By reviewing newspaper stories of the mayor's first campaign, the reporter discovers an identical pledge four years ago, although nothing happened. This research will place the mayor's latest campaign promise in perspective and will let voters decide if the mayor means it this time.

Information for backgrounding a story can be harvested from libraries, public records, reference publications, computer databases, and other physical sources.

If assigned to do a story on student drinking habits, don't settle for observing local watering holes and interviewing bartenders. Think first of backgrounding the story. Here are possibilities:

- *Newsroom files.* While looking through the "Alcohol" file in your newsroom morgue (a library where old stories are reverently buried), you discover that the university banned beer and alcohol in dormitory rooms five years ago. This story begs for a reality update.
- *City directories.* You decide to talk with members of a certain off-campus fraternity about their weekend keg parties. To get the neighborhood's perspective, you want to talk with residents who live on either side of the fraternity house. Rather than ringing doorbells hoping to find someone at home who will talk, you can look up the addresses in the city directory and learn the names, occupations, and family members, plus the telephone numbers in order to call for interviews.
- *Reference books.* A statistical almanac tells you that the average person under age twenty-five spends $311.92 a year on alco-

holic beverages. An encyclopedia reports that the average American consumes twenty-four gallons of beer each year.

• *Government publications.* Curious about alcohol use among entering college freshmen, you find a survey sponsored by the National Institute on Drug Abuse that reports 88% of high school seniors have tried alcohol at least once. But this percentage has been steadily dropping the past decade.

• *Reader indexes.* A quick check at the library turns up a New York *Times* article on how campuses are reporting an increase in alcohol-related sexual assaults. You'll want to check the alcohol-and-assault angle with local campus counselors.

• *State open records laws.* If campus police refuse to provide information about student disciplinary actions resulting from alcohol abuse on campus, state law may require that the records be opened for public scrutiny.

By engaging in such research techniques in conjunction with observation and interviews, a nebulous story assignment can be transformed into a major work that commands reader interest because of its depth and specificity.

Whenever possible, good reporters do their homework before talking with sources. The more facts brought to an interview, the less the reporter must rely on the source's particular version of truth. The tobacco lobbyist who authoritatively dismisses the danger of secondhand smoke cannot so easily dismiss the scientific data that a reporter brings to the interview.

In reporting the rundown condition of America's national parks, Jeff Taylor and Jake Thompson of the Kansas City *Star* scrutinized thousands of documents while interviewing more than 200 people for their award-winning series. The paper trail created specificity for the interviews. After first documenting in excruciating detail the dilapidated condition of Yosemite, Big Bend, the Grand Canyon, and other national parks, the two reporters called members of Congress. "We'd call these people and ask 'Who did this?' And we'd get silence on the line," Taylor said. Their research revealed that Congress routinely appropriates money for popular new projects in the national parks rather than providing money for repairing potholes in Yosemite's roads or cleaning up radioactive pollution in a Grand Canyon mine.

Reporters themselves need a deep reservoir of general knowledge. When I was a journalism student at Baylor University, Professor David McHam told us that journalists need to know at least a little about a lot because they will be interviewing people who know a lot about a little. News sources are experts on the specific topics they are talking about. A reporter may interview a doctor about cholesterol levels one day, report on a criminal trial the next day, and cover a speech by a Chinese diplomat the following day. If the reporter doesn't know at least a little about a lot, all three stories will be noticeably shallow.

The reporter, of course, cannot be an expert in medicine, law, and diplomacy. That's why experts are the reporter's sources. But when the doctor talks of "good" and "bad" cholesterol, the interview will go much better if the reporter is not a complete ignoramus on the subject. When a witness pleads "Fifth Amendment," a reporter shouldn't look around the courtroom in confusion. When the speaker refers to the need for more "ping-pong diplomacy," a reporter who knows history will recognize the reference to the use of sport to start exchanges between China and the United States in the early 1970s.

Good reporters have a storehouse of knowledge. They must know the workings of the political system, they must know common police procedures for making arrests, they must know what *Roe v. Wade* is—and they know they do not have enough time before their next deadline to understand a topic unless they already know something about it.

SURFACE INFORMATION

Pat, a TV reporter fresh out of journalism school, starts the day by covering a news conference where a stack of utility bills is set on fire. A community group is angry at a proposed utility rate increase, and the fire is designed as a visual grabber for the cameras. Pat returns to the office and goes through the day's mail, finding a news release about a blood shortage. She arranges by phone for an on-site interview at the Red Cross, with film of volunteers giving blood. Because it's a slow news day, Pat is told that a no-name candidate for governor has a rally on the Capitol steps planned for 4 o'clock. Pat makes an appearance, along with only fifteen supporters.

Pat has been on a Jungle Safari ride all day, following the tracks laid out for her and recording the events as they happen, such as getting snapshots from the train of the monkeys screeching and the alligators snapping their jaws. The audience will get the message that the local station is everywhere covering the news. But Pat's entire workday has been determined by events of other people's doing. The news conference, the press release, the political rally—all are surface events that use the news media to influence public opinion. Each of these events is legitimate news, but Pat has been a willing tool of these public relations efforts.

The conclusion is not that Pat should avoid these stories, but that she should dig deeper than surface events to uncover truth.

Journalists must develop a critical sense of the use and abuse of information and must recognize that all surface information communicates some particular person's or agency's point of view. The critical skill is knowing how to use such information without being used *by* it.

Sure, the burning pile of utility bills is a good visual. But Pat should do some research to determine if the community group's gripes are valid and, if they are, find out why utility rates are escalating. Pat can find out if blood shortages are cyclical and if shortages have been worse since the public became alarmed about the transmission of AIDS through needles and the blood supply. Pat certainly should air some of the no-name candidate's speech. But she also should directly ask him if his campaign has a chance when only fifteen people bother to show up at his rally. To be a real reporter, Pat must dig below the surface information conveniently provided for her.

Big-city newsrooms are inundated with mail. Secretaries slit open envelopes and stack the news releases for an editor's scrutiny whenever the pace slows. Here's one from a community college listing honor roll students. Is it worth a story? Here's one from Mothers Against Drunk Driving, announcing an upcoming meeting. Put it in the futures calendar. Here's another from a local radio station, plugging its new format. Toss it. Some days the editor really just wants to toss the whole stack.

A 1994 survey by *Media Relations Insider* showed that 92.8% of mail to journalists was discarded, with a third of that not even opened. The survey suggests colossal disregard in the newsroom for public relations news releases—but not complete disregard. Roughly one out of every dozen news releases finds a receptive reader in the newsroom and serves as the impetus for a news story. A reporter, though, should never convert a PR release directly into a news story. Instead, use the mail as foundational material to gather independent information from sources.

In a book on the public relations industry, Jeff and Marie Blyskal estimate that 40% to 50% of all published news stories originate from PR contexts. The published stories may be spin-offs from news releases, or coverage of political rallies, or the publishing of school lunches for the week. Other source-originated material includes obituaries provided by funeral homes, a list of dogs awaiting adoption at the animal shelter, and the daily crime report compiled by the police department.

Let's not be critical of surface information. It serves an important function by informing people of what is happening in their community. But a news report consisting solely of surface information would be like eating celery all day. You crunch and crunch—but eventually want something more substantive.

Think of reporting as an archeological dig. The mounds of dirt on the surface offer the hope of discovery below. But digging away the surface layer is only the first step. The treasure comes the deeper a person digs.

COMPUTER-ASSISTED REPORTING

The computer is an ideal archeological tool for reporters in the 1990s. It can put reporters in touch with a fascinating variety of human sources of information. It can provide news reports, corporate records, or the texts of government documents. And it can analyze mounds of public records and other data, helping the reporter to see the big picture.

The Poynter Institute for Media Studies calls computer databases "the dynamite of the information explosion." In tapping database services, reporters can browse through electronic libraries of data compiled from newspapers, magazines, government documents, directories, and a host of other sources. This information flow is one-way and designed for rapid retrieval.

For the reporter, the information may be a transcript of ABC's *20/20* newsmagazine (Burrell's Broadcast Database) or a new Supreme Court decision (Westlaw). It could be Hollywood Hotline (Delphi) or Congressional Quarterly (Washington Alert). Hundreds of magazines and newspapers are now on-line and indexed each day, ranging from *Consumer Reports* to the *Salt Lake Tribune*. Reference books and directories are more up-to-date in database versions than in published versions. Virtually every city in America now uses computers to store information that is open to public scrutiny. In addition, information from more than 300 federal agencies is in government document databases, including the full text of Securities and Exchange Commission filings that regulate financial matters. As in the past, it's still wise to "follow the money" in pursuing a story. But instead of a "paper trail," the reporter may need to follow an electronic trail.

In the 1990s, reporters increasingly have turned to computer bulletin boards as interactive sources for information. The Journalism Forum on the Internet lets people exchange information and start arguments. They fuss about sensational media coverage. An economics writer for an Italian newspaper finds a journalistic pen pal. Some on-line reporters begin a long-distance discussion on the origin of the —30— symbol to designate the end of a news story. Private bulletin boards also are popular. Through a bulletin board called The Pressroom, accredited White House journalists can obtain the President's daily schedule, photographers dominate the classified ad forum with items about camera equipment, and Washington journalists can exchange ideas privately with other journalists, one-to-one through electronic mail (e-mail) or in small groups.

Another concept is ProfNet, which brings together reporters in need of expert sources with university professors who can provide that expertise. Twice a day, a dozen or more requests for expert sources are delivered on ProfNet to hundreds of colleges and universities. Public information officers at each institution distribute these requests to professors. Here are three ProfNet examples from a single day in summer 1996:

The Ventura County Star seeks leads today on experts who can discuss free speech on the Internet. A local school has adopted "appropriate use" policies for its Internet users, to prevent students from sending hate messages and downloading pornography. Is this a good thing? Phone or e-mail me today at....

I am a writer with Newsday in New York. I am doing extensive research on the Nazi occupation of Czechoslovakia during World War II. Specifically, I want to focus on the Heydrich assassination and the destruction of Lidice. I'd appreciate some advice on how best to find German records, if they exist. My e-mail address is....

I'm a features reporter at the Boston Herald. I'm writing a story on the impact of false rape charges and why some women might make false accusations. This might also involve research on how rape cases are handled within the judicial system. I'll be working on this through next Monday. You may call me at....

Professors at Harvard, Stanford, and other elite universities are standard sources of information for journalists from leading media such as NBC News and the New York *Times.* They already feed one another. But ProfNet widens this sphere.

"ProfNet is treated like a phone call from a media outlet. It gets immediate priority," said Cheryl May, news services director at Kansas State University. She noted a recent request from CNN for professorial assistance. "Believe me, when we see those three little letters, we're going to hustle to fulfill that request."

ProfNet has extended reporting at local news outlets to a national scale. A Chicago radio station needed experts to talk about the future of America's big cities. The South Bend, Indiana, newspaper needed experts in food canning. A company producing a show for ABC News needed experts to discuss vigilantism on a national scale. A freelance writer for *Animals* magazine needed experts to talk about how children cope with the loss of their pets.

"ProfNet has made my life much simpler," said freelancer Brad Swift. For the pet-loss article, he received more responses within forty-eight hours than he could use, ranging from Auburn to Albany and from Florida State to a professor in Canada.

In the newsroom, then, the computer helps reporters background their stories through one-way data retrieval and helps them to discuss issues with other journalists and to locate expert sources through two-way bulletin boards.

But the computer also is dramatically changing the news product by allowing for journalistic analysis of data. The Providence *Journal-Bulletin* won a Pulitzer Prize for an early example of a computer-assisted news story. When three Rhode Island children were killed in separate school-bus accidents in 1985, the newspaper compared its list of bus-driver licenses to a computer search of state traffic violations. The cross-indexing showed that some bus drivers had been ticketed as many as twenty times during a three-year period. This information, coupled with a computer search of criminal convictions, showed that several drivers of school buses had even been convicted of drug dealing.

"These were people who shouldn't have been allowed to ride a bicycle," reporter Elliot Jaspin told the *Wall Street Journal*. "Without a computer, this story couldn't have been done."

Tom Koch of the European Journalism Centre makes this point about the value of computer-assisted research:

When a physician says at an inquest that a death in his office "was simply a one-in-a-million unfortunate occurrence," reporters can say, "Actually, it was one in at least 135 deaths, and in every case where those deaths have been reviewed, the physician has been held responsible. So, et tu, Jack?" Read all about it. Watch them sweat!

Traditional reporters can rarely do this, Koch said, because they don't have the knowledge or the background to call a politician's or an expert's bluff. He wrote in *Quill* magazine that traditional reporters often do not have data to allow them to say: "All available evidence proves 'x' is right and 'y' is not. You lie." But with computers, they may be able to get that evidence.

Of course, finding sources and researching stories can be done without the computer, just as a person still can write on a manual typewriter and do algebraic formulas by hand. The computer does add expense and time to the task of reporting and certainly is not necessary in covering all stories. But the computer can be a powerful reporting tool in the journalistic quiver.

Nora Paul offers this illustration in the Poynter Institute's 1994 guide to on-line information titled *Computer Assisted Research*, which offers reporters a central listing of available databases and a brief description of what each one contains:

> You're in a restaurant and notice a dish full of candy beside the cash register. Attached is a coin box and a sign that says "Hugs, Not Drugs" and asks for your support. The sponsoring organization mentioned is the National Awareness Foundation. You're curious: What is this National Awareness Foundation? Is it legitimate? Where does the money go?

> Back in the newsroom, you start with Dialog, which accesses the databases for the *Encyclopedia of Associations* and for the *Foundation Directory*. There's no listing for the National Awareness Foundation, which seems odd. So you decide to see if anyone else has written about this organization. You access a database that covers more than forty newspapers. Sure enough, you find articles in the Fort Lauderdale *Sun Sentinel* and a few other newspapers about fund-raising events sponsored by the National Awareness Foundation. Most are positive, PR-styled articles. But one article warns consumers about contributing to mystery organizations and lists NAF as a questionable charity. The article describes NAF as nonprofit but not tax exempt. For financial information or a company profile, you turn to the *American Business Directory*. It gives the names and Florida addresses of the two foundation directors.

> By using Compuserve, you plug into the Florida secretary of state's database and discover that the foundation was incorporated but later involuntarily dissolved. Could the foundation have incorporated elsewhere? A search of other state files through Mead Data Central finds incorporation records in Maryland and California.

> You're a bit stumped about how to check out whether a charity is legitimate. You log onto the Journalism Forum via Compuserve and ask your colleagues. The next day, you have three responses. One says that state attorney general offices often have a charities

division that monitors nonprofit agencies. Another recalls an article on this topic in the *Investigative Reporters and Editors Journal* and gives you the phone number for the IRE morgue. The third mentions the National Charities Information Bureau, which you hadn't heard of before. Thanks to computer-assisted research, you now have some good advice and information and are ready to do some traditional reporting.

"Remember, the information you get from computer-assisted research is a complement to reporting, not a replacement," declares Nora Paul of the Poynter Institute. "In fact, the ease with which you can find information and the amount of information that can be retrieved can make the reporting task more complicated."

But it does provide greater depth and richness to the reporting.

A BODY OF SOURCES
Sources of information these days are plentiful. In fact, I think of body parts when contemplating the practice of reporting. Just as a reporter needs a *nose* for news and must keep an *ear* to the ground, so should a reporter use the *eyes* to observe, the *tongue* to interview, and the *fingers* to research. The *feet* get used a lot, too. And with the computer, a reporter can spend hours sitting on his....

Well, the point is, reporting is a mentally and often physically active process.

Besides news releases, political rallies, and other surface information that inundate the typical reporter, other sources include:

• *Wire-service stories*. Keep a lookout for stories that naturally have a local angle. If the Federal Reserve Board in Washington raises the discount rate, then a reporter ought to call local bankers and ask about the impact this eventually will have on interest rates for families wanting to buy a house in town.

• *Your own news coverage*. I worked with a reporter who was good at seeing linkages between stories. One day, after a Sunday morning house robbery, he asked the police if the victim happened to be a preacher. Yes, he learned. The reporter had noticed that a previous Sunday morning robbery victim also had been a preacher. By looking into crimes of previous weeks, he discovered that five preachers' homes had been robbed on Sunday mornings in the past year, with robbers assuming the homeowner would be in the pulpit at a certain hour. The story came about because of a reporter's observation of facts.

• *Solicited comment*. Washington *Post* readers are invited in a house ad to call the newspaper and share their investment strategies. This way, the reporter doesn't have to dig for sources; the sources voluntarily come to the newspaper.

• *Insatiable curiosity.* While reading a report about radiation experiments on animals, Eileen Welsome of the Albuquerque *Tribune* came across a footnote about human patients who were injected with plutonium during the early years of the atomic age. "I came back to the office very excited," she remembers. "The city editor told me, 'Well, that's a great story, but we hired you to be the neighborhood reporter.'" Welsome began collecting documents on her own time and filed Freedom of Information requests with the Department of Energy. Years passed. Eventually, she learned the names of patients injected with plutonium during the 1940s, apparently without their consent. Her series won a 1994 Sigma Delta Chi excellence in reporting award.

Reporting is a surveillance of society, discovering what has happened or is happening and how best to communicate those happenings to the public. Journalism is fact-based because facts help readers draw conclusions on their own.

A good news story starts with information, not language. Too many stories are *written* instead of *reported*. They are created through rhetorical skill instead of through reportorial skill. All writers need raw material—specific, accurate pieces of information from which to construct a story with a pattern of concrete detail.

Perspective...

COMPUTER-ASSISTED REPORTING

By STEVEN S. ROSS, Associate Professor for Professional Practice in the Graduate School of Journalism at Columbia University, is also an environmental activist and past president of the New Jersey environmental lobby. He is a frequent contributor to magazines and books.

For me, computer-assisted reporting (CAR) has two paths. By far the biggest highway runs by "data town." Journalists can find so much information online that they may be tempted to do less original reporting. At the same time, journalists have increasing difficulty judging the veracity of online sources. It is easy for sources to masquerade.

Sources may change their mind on issues, too. Thus, the careful journalist will take extra time to track down sources by phone, or for an in-person meeting, even if most of the interviewing is done by computer, or involves reuse of "old" quotes found on web sites, newsgroups, LISTSERVs or text databases such as NEXIS.

The road less traveled by CAR practitioners is the analytical trail. Using spreadsheets and databases, a reporter with some logical sense and perhaps a little math savvy can "create" new information, new slants on stories, starting only with material already public.

It is not wise to let the paths diverge too far apart. Sometimes, as I will explain later, it may be necessary. But journalists must try harder to find live sources to explain and authenticate data they find online. You will find that CAR, well done, creates more questions than it answers.

Most large companies, for instance, publish financial data on their web sites. What if you go to the web site of a large company, check out the annual report section, and find a five-year summary that shows a decline in the number of U.S.-based employees while indicating a rise in overseas workers hired by the firm? Why call the company for comment? Aren't you just using its data, perhaps putting it into a more comprehensible format?

Well, if you call the company's PR department, you might be supplied with verifiable data showing that the drop in U.S. employment was due to the sale of a U.S.-based division, and no one was actually laid off in the U.S.. You may also find that the rise in overseas employment was due to purchase of an international firm. Maybe you can still question the company's motives in investing more overseas than in the U.S. But the tone of the story will differ from what would be obtained from raw data alone. And even if the "live" interview confirms your worst suspicions, won't the final story be more credible if you make the call?

Federal Election Commission data is notoriously error-prone, but journalists often report the results of searches in the FEC database, without verification. It's federal data, isn't it? Because it is official, citing it cannot lead to your being charged with libel, can it? No, you are protected as a journalist in those circumstances. But being legally correct is not the same as being ethically correct.

At Columbia University, I show students FEC data that records one contributor making three $1,000 contributions to a candidate for the U.S. Senate. At most, only two contributions of that size would be legal (one for the primary campaign and one for the general election). That particular information was once responsible for a broadcast story that ran like this (only the contributor's name has been changed):

"John Smith, well known Scarsdale financier, has apparently violated Federal election laws. An exclusive Eyewitness News examination of campaign contribution data reveals that Smith donated $3,000 to Senator Pat Moynihan's last Senatorial race. That's $1,000 over the limit. Mr. Smith was unavailable for comment."

Turned out that only one phone call was made, to his business office after the office had closed for the day. Our students, following up on the story, found that the contributions were indeed legal. One had been made by Smith's wife, using a check drawn on their joint account. Both names were printed on the check, and her signature was not clear (whose is?). So Moynihan's volunteer campaign workers had mis-recorded the check. Students obtained faxed copies of the original checks, free, from the FEC.

CAR can also be used to ply information out of a recalcitrant source. In May 1995, a story of mine was published by *New York Magazine* on the city's use of untested, possibly unsafe lightweight subway wheels. "Light" is a relative term—the new wheels weigh 700 pounds each; a conventional wheel weighs 800. There are eight wheels on each subway car. I had worked on the story, in spurts, for almost six months. A key point involved claims by subway technical personnel that each pound of weight reduction saved a dollar a year in electricity costs for running the subway. Thus, although the new wheels cost more, they would save a great deal of money.

For four months, I badgered subway officials to send me their calculations. The best I could get was that the dollar per pound savings was "a rule of thumb." When it comes to money, I trust spreadsheets more than I trust body parts. Using a technique called "reporting," I found out how much electricity was used to run the trains (the subway system gets its juice from a public agency, the Power Authority of the State of New York, PASNY) and calculated an upper limit on savings. I'm a physicist by training; so I did the calculation myself. But any freshman engineering student could have done the same thing if a journalist asked.

Turned out that the maximum savings was 20 cents per pound. The wheels would not be cost-effective! Only when I sent a copy of my calculations to the subway officials did I get a confirmation, on the record, that I was correct.

8

NEWS GATHERING TECHNIQUES

Gathering information for dissemination as news is challenging. It begins with thinking through a story from start to finish before starting the reporting. Thinking through the story helps focus the idea, which leads to focused reporting and focused writing. Always remember that reporting is not practiced in a vacuum. Respectability, responsibility, and reporting go hand-in-hand, although reporters don't always seem to think so. To improve the image of journalism and to maintain the respectability of the institution, reporters must exercise greater responsibility as they report on the news of the day. They can no longer take an indifferent attitude toward the impact of the stories they report. This does not mean reporters should be less aggressive, but rather they should be as responsible in their jobs as they demand other public servants to be. They can do so by putting the concepts of fairness, accuracy, and public service first. When reporters keep their purpose in mind—to serve the public—they should be able to help restore public credibility to their craft.

BY KENNETH CAMPBELL
Associate Professor of Journalism at the University of South Carolina, Dr. Campbell is a former reporter with the Miami *Herald*, Greensboro *News and Record*, and the Niagara Falls *Gazette*. He holds the Ph.D. in mass communications research from the University of North Carolina.

Responsible and purposeful reporting is the solid foundation of quality journalism in a democratic society. If journalism is to remain a respectable institution, one that is both credible and effective, reporters must lead the way. Even though effective journalism exposes wrongdoing, promotes fairness and justice, and offers solutions to problems, the latest national polls show that journalists are ranked down there with used-car salespersons and politicians on the credibility scale. It is troubling images like that of the snooping reporter encamped outside someone's house or dogging a person in public, and the refusal of journalists to admit mistakes when they make them, that perpetuate this negative perception. The growing public disillusionment over journalistic ethics and professionalism severely hurts journalistic credibility. Reporters have an obligation to gather information, but that obligation carries something reporters don't always like to own up to—responsibility.

PHILOSOPHY, PURPOSE, AND PROTECTION

Journalism, free speech advocates like to say, is the only profession singled out for protection in the U. S. Constitution. What the advocates don't like to say, it seems, is that journalistic reporting and expression are protected for a reason. The reason is not free speech for the sake of free speech. It is useful to turn to the legal history of the First Amendment, which protects freedom of speech and the press, to gain an understanding of journalism in the United States. The governments in both medieval England and the early American colonies instituted a system of licensing to restrain the power of the printing press to influence public opinion. When the public rebelled against the licensing systems, the restraints were allowed to die, but governments then turned to seditious libel laws to keep the presses from being used to criticize the government in power. However, despite the restraints, there were always groups of people in each society masterfully circumventing, or outright flaunting, the government restrictions in order to bring information and opinions to the public. It was in this spirit of informing the public on politics and other public matters that the First Amendment was ratified in 1791, stating: "Congress shall make no law... abridging the freedom of speech, or of the press."

The U. S. Supreme Court's interpretation of the First Amendment has given reporters guidelines for doing their job. The Court has emphatically stated that the First Amendment protects expression that promotes "uninhibited, robust, and wide-open" debate on public issues. The view, stated by Justice Brennan in the *New*

York Times v. Sullivan landmark libel case in 1964, provided the rationale for the Court's protection of facts, unintentional falsehoods, and fact-based opinions in the public arena. The Court is so committed to the principle of aggressive public debate that it does not always require responsible reporting. When persons in the public's eye are involved with public issues, the Court permits sloppy reporting at times. Therefore, it is up to journalists to establish and maintain their own high standards.

Too often students and journalists seem to ignore or to be unaware of the public trust that is inherent in their job. While newspapering is a profit-making business, the news side is also a public service. Reporting is not done for the sake of the exercise. It is an essential part of the practice of journalism, and journalism is protected because it is vital to an effective democracy. Journalists are entrusted by the public to report on major institutions and their players and to portray an accurate picture of life in the community. Because of these surveillance and informational functions, reporting is not to be taken lightly.

OBJECTIVITY VS. FAIRNESS AND ACCURACY

Traditionally, we have thought of newspaper reporting as an objective enterprise. That is, an objective-minded reporter "selectively" gathers information for a story, then writes that story in an objective or balanced fashion. This concept has two problems. One, by its very nature reporting is not an objective enterprise. Reporting is subjective. All of us, no matter who we are, carry "baggage" into the reporting of a story. It doesn't matter where we are taught reporting skills, or by whom; *who* we are does matter when we develop a story idea or report a story. That's not necessarily bad. If who we are does not matter, then why all the push for diversity in the newsrooms? It took the presence of people of color and women in the newsroom to improve the accuracy of how they are covered in the newspaper, and we still have a long way to go. Accuracy is more important than objectivity.

The second problem with objective reporting is that it suggests balance. And balance suggests equal weight. This can result in an undeserving side getting as much space in a story as one that clearly has something to say. In such cases, reporters can find themselves filling space with unnecessary detail or gratuitous quotations just to fill up space and give a side its due. Good reporting does not mean unlimited opportunity for sources to talk, or that everybody who has something to say on an issue says it. Rather it means that everything worth being said on the issue is said. Students are sometimes surprised when an instructor slices their story by one-third to one-half. Usually, the instructor is only cutting out unneeded quotations or minor detail or information that is not directly related to the focus of the story. When asked to recall what has been cut out, the student often comes up empty. The readers wouldn't remember either; so why force them to read it? Reporters are not stenographers who take down and regurgitate everything that is said. Reporters make judgments about what is newsworthy or what is needed for context. Reporters synthesize and evaluate information, keep what is needed, and store the rest away. It is an awesome power and a powerful responsibility to be fair and accurate.

How do you determine what to keep and what to throw away? It is not easy. The value of each piece of information is relative to the most important information you have. You determine the value by public interest in the information, its possible impact, and its importance to readers. When the impact and importance are less clear, you give more weight to other factors such as what the source of the information has to gain from releasing it and who or what will benefit or be hurt by the information. Always remember the focus of the story, too. Information that is newsworthy, but not directly related to the focus of your story, should be saved for another story. When you completely think through a story before you begin reporting, you are likely to do a better job keeping focus. Also remember that when you've finished reporting, it is always better to have information you can strike from your notes than to have unanswered questions.

With so many judgments to make, reporters should be guided by the concepts of *fairness, accuracy*, and *public service*. Reporting is not a social science where people are programmed or scripted to go through the same motions and to ask the same questions. And even if reporters were to ask the same questions, it is unlikely they would get the same answers although the substance of the answers might be similar. More than anything, reporting is *critical thinking*.

Reporters must think first, and while thinking they must make decisions about what the story is and how to report it. Reporters practice their craft with a healthy skepticism, but that does not mean an unhealthy cynicism. Reporters must always raise questions, yet also know when it's time to stop raising questions and to start weeding the good information from the bad. It's a never-ending process until the story is written, and even then it's not unusual for the reporter to startle a dinner guest or wake up in the middle of the night with the realization that another question could have been asked or that something in the story could have been said differently.

As long as reporters are guided by the concepts of fairness, accuracy, and public service, they will do a good job. Not every story is a potential award-winning piece. Most stories are not, but they should be treated like they are. No story is unimportant. Reporters should always keep in mind that they are informing the public and that every bit of information could be important to someone. As a guiding principle, fairness requires reporters to think critically rather than act as empty vessels waiting to be filled with information. Reporters have to evaluate information as they receive it, then formulate new questions. Information must be accurate not only in individual facts and details, but in painting the broader picture. Readers will not trust newspapers with big details if the papers cannot get the small details right. But neither will readers trust reporters with small details if the reporters do not get the big picture right. The importance of the concepts of fairness and accuracy for journalists should be heightened by the concept of public service. Fairness and accuracy become paramount if reporters remember their job is to serve the public, not just to get the big story. Reporters must always keep their public responsibility in mind, a responsibility as great as that of politicians or other public servants, perhaps even greater since the check on government—reporters—rarely subjects reporters to the same scrutiny.

IDEAS AND FOCUS

Reporting is more than the gathering of information. It is gathering newsworthy information in a focused, skillful, purposeful way.

The biggest problem that students have with putting a story together is lack of *focus*. It is the biggest problem because it is the most frequent one and it comes first in the process of thinking through a story. If reporters overcome this problem at the outset, they help to avoid other problems later. It is not uncommon for a student to propose a story on the homeless, drugs, battered women, teen-age pregnancy, or migrant workers or on some prominent political issue either locally or nationally such as crime or health care. But ask yourself, "Why is this news now?" Is homelessness a story *now* because the number of homeless people locally has gone up or a shelter is opening or closing? Are drugs a story because there is new evidence they are spreading to the younger population, or not only students but teachers are found carrying drugs at school? I often ask students, "Why would someone want to read this story?" "What will readers find out from this story that they did not already know?" or "Would you read this story if you hadn't written it?" We know that there are battered women, pregnant teen-agers, and migrant workers; so that's not news. But it would be news if an official report were just issued indicating that the number of battered women, pregnant teen-agers, or migrant workers is significantly increasing or decreasing, or if a program serving one of these groups, especially a program that's effective, were running out of funds or just being eliminated.

To further help focus stories, I ask students to *write a possible lead* based on what they anticipate finding during the reporting. In many ways, the anticipated lead is the ultimate focus. Anything that is not directly related to the lead should not be in the story. Thus, information in a story first of all should buttress the lead, then provide necessary details to flesh out the story. Although reporters should always anticipate what they will find when they do the reporting, reporters must remain open-minded through the process. The anticipated lead is for direction only. If in their reporting, reporters find a better story, or find that the anticipated lead does not work—which can often be the case—the story should change accordingly. Another possible lead should be written at this point so the reporter will continue to have direction.

Also a part of focusing a story is *identifying sources* for the story and determining what information the different sources can provide. Sources are primarily paper and people. Sometimes when reporters dream up their story ideas, they are assuming they can get information that is not available to them. The information might not be available because it does not exist, or it is part of a private file or a closed public file, or it cannot be gathered from the different sources by the reporting deadline. Being aware of what information is and is not available can help reporters focus their stories. Time spent focusing a story prior to reporting can save enormous unnecessary work during the reporting process and can help the reporter spend even more time gathering and evaluating relevant information.

REPORTING

Doing a good job focusing the story will pay off when it's time to report and write the story. Whether it is a routine police, meeting or speech story, an exposé or a feature, the best-written journalistic story is the best-reported story. Reporting separates journalism from fiction and other nonfiction writing. Reporting not only establishes a factual basis for the story; it also involves evaluating and fairly presenting the facts. Thus, how a story should be reported, including what information the reporter is likely to find and who the sources are, should be a part of the initial thinking of a story. It will help determine how the story should be organized and written.

Reporting Begins with Thinking

Reporters must be open-minded—but an open mind does not mean an empty mind. A good reporter will be able to anticipate, or might even know, much of the information he or she will get from the sources that will be used in the story prior to interviewing those sources. Reporters should spend some time—keeping the deadline in mind—gathering information on which to base their reporting. Some call this concept backgrounding or pre-reporting. Perhaps it is best to just consider it a part of the reporting process. Too many students take an unfocused story idea and run to the telephone to call that first source. When the source agrees to answer a few questions on the spot, the student is delighted and begins firing soft questions that elicit information but no news. Or, if the first source is not in, the student talks to anyone who will talk, or the student begins a phone watch hoping the source will call back and essentially give the story a story. That's not reporting.

The reporter must come to a story knowing something, even if it is just how to think—preferably, how to think critically. The reporter should think the story through even before sharing the idea with an editor or colleague. Not only does this help the reporter assess the quality of the story idea; it also helps focus the story as well as identify sources. While reporters and their editors determine what information goes into a story, sources determine what information reporters and editors will have to choose from. Sources, in effect, can determine what the story will be. You can't write what you don't have, and sources determine what you will have. That is why the selection of sources for a story is vitally important.

There are three methods of gathering information—*interviewing, reading,* and *observing*. The best stories combine different sources and methods of gathering information.

Beginning reporters should always remember that the concept of journalism in the United States is to give the reader the best factual information possible in the proper context, then let the readers come to their own conclusion about what the truth is. This does not preclude the reporter from helping the reader understand the story or issue by explaining or interpreting the facts, which can include the reporter suggesting conclusions based on the factual information reported. Reporters must remember, however, that their job is not to knock the reader over the head with what the reporters consider to be truth. That should be left for editorials, columns, or letters to the editor. On the news pages, readers have a right to figure out truth for themselves.

Like everybody else, journalists often do not know what the truth is. Take any controversial issue, be it abortion, affirmative action, the Iran-Contra or the Whitewater scandal, or criminal and civil trials of O. J. Simpson. Look at the police beating of motorist Rodney King, captured live on video tape. Despite the video showing officers striking King, a jury found the police officers not guilty. Do we know the truth? Is the truth a set of facts, and if so, how exhaustive must the facts be? Or is the truth a conclusion derived from a set of facts, and if so, whose conclusion, the reporter's, the individual reader's, or that of a leader, whether elected or self-appointed? Or is the truth the voice that screams the loudest and gets the most attention. Or is the truth simply the view of the majority? In *On Liberty* in 1859, John Stuart Mill contended that people do not necessarily know when they have attained truth. Thus, he gave four reasons why free expression is valuable—reasons that support fairness in reporting:

First, opinions that people hold might be false; therefore, opinions that the people have not received might be true.

Second, true opinions are strengthened in a conflict with opposite opinions.

Third, the meaning of opinion is established in debate.

Fourth, instead of one opinion being true and another false, opinions may share the truth between them.

Reporters provide the facts and, when necessary, an explanation of those facts. Readers determine the truth.

POLICE, SPEECH, AND MEETING STORIES

Routine police, speech, and meeting stories tend to be the fare of inexperienced reporters. If you do not like covering these hard news stories, strongly reconsider whether you want to go into newspaper journalism. The majority of newspaper reporters will see plenty of these stories during their first few years, if not longer.

Police Stories

The rationale for starting you out on police stories is that you learn the value of accuracy and tight news writing. It does seem odd that to learn accuracy rookies are put on the stories most likely to draw a libel suit if a mistake is made. Perhaps there is something accurate about the suspicion among cub reporters that they really get the police beat because no one else wants it.

Covering the police beat is probably the most routine of all beats. It calls for daily checks of the police reports and writing stories about the most significant of the incidents. Small papers often require the reporter to write something each day from the police records, while larger papers only report serious crimes such as a slaying unless a less serious crime includes some sort of twist that makes for an unusual story. Reporters generally stick to the facts on the police reports and whatever else they can get from the notoriously tight-lipped law enforcement officers. The more serious the crimes, the more the reporter tries to flesh out the story by talking to law enforcement officers and victims, or in the case of a slaying, family members and friends of the victim. Experienced police beat reporters have learned to find the stories of personal tragedy or triumph behind the police reports—the story of the convenience store clerk who foiled a robbery attempt, the shooting victim who survived a near-fatal wound, or the ordeal of parents who donated a kidney from the body of their teen-ager killed in an automobile accident while coming home from the high school prom.

Meeting Stories

Covering meetings and speeches is different from covering routine police beat stories because meetings and speeches are live. You must sit through them and observe what is taking place to cover them adequately. To properly report on and convey the meaning of the actions taken, you must understand what kind of body or organization is meeting. Is it an advisory group such as a commission, a policy-making body such as an elected council, or some other body with lots of power or no power? Are its decisions final? You should also know who the top administrator is and what that person's responsibilities are. The person may be an executive director, a city or county manager, or a superintendent. The administrator's job is to carry out the policy set by the board, to run the agency or governmental unit. Always know the agenda for a meeting, and, if possible, talk with the chairperson of the body, the top staff person, a public information spokesperson, and/or your best source about what is expected to happen at the meeting.

No matter what kind of group it is that is meeting, the story is "what happened" or "what action was taken." If, of course, some action was expected to be taken and it was not, then the story might be the action not taken and why. The biggest problems in covering a meeting are following the parliamentary procedure and keeping up with who says what. The solution is understanding the body you are covering and knowing the players. If you know the body, you know what action can and cannot be taken, and if you know the players, you know what they are likely to say and do.

It is also important to know the players because meeting stories should be people stories. After all, it is people who take action, not a board. There are obvious people sources that can be a part of the meeting story. Always be aware of the chairperson's vote and comments and always be aware of the person who made the motion. If the action is controversial, the person making the motion becomes important for the story. So do the board members who vote in opposition.

Reporters should always take notes, including comments that can be used as quotations, during the meeting. If time permits, though, much of the reporting can be done before or after the meeting. I like to accompany my beginning reporting students to their first council or school board meeting. Although we arrive early, invariably they go into the meeting room and sit down. I get them up one by one and tell them that at the very least they should introduce themselves to the board members. That helps because usually the students have to talk to board members after the meeting. Covering a meeting is more than recording official action of a board.

Speech Stories

Speeches are different from meetings because no action is taken; the focus is on what the speaker said. When possible, get a copy of the speech beforehand. However, it's the lazy reporter who just listens to a speech and then repeats what was said in a story. Reporters should challenge the speaker in an interview after the speech or seek out other sides if the speaker addresses a controversial issue. The reporting should not be limited to the few minutes a speaker speaks.

When reporting the story, you should listen for the speaker's theme at the beginning. If there is no hard information, the theme often becomes the focus of the story. Reporters should also listen for points of emphasis, whether it is when the speaker raises his or her voice, or when the speaker lists points by number. Sometimes, audience applause helps you decide what's important. (But be on guard against orchestrated applause.) Since a speech story is what a speaker says, if the speech is good the story should be peppered with good quotations and, if possible, anecdotes from the speech. But a story should not be a transcript of the speech. Finally, the story should almost never be written in the order the speech was given because speakers often save the best for last. Why would a speaker give an audience the most important thing he or she has to say and then watch them lose interest? So, since the news is likely to be closer to the end of the speech than the beginning, the reporter must stay alert throughout.

INTERVIEWING

An essential part of reporting is interviewing. As a beginning student journalist, I was terrified at the thought of having to interview someone, and even more terrified when I arrived at my first off-campus interview. When I was growing up in rural North Carolina, I did not have the opportunity to talk to doctors, lawyers, community leaders, politicians, and other people of official importance. The biggest people in my world were teachers and preachers. And I didn't talk to them, either; I just admired and respected them. So, interviewing officials was a huge step for me. I knew how to interview, but knowing how to interview is only the beginning. Getting it in my head that these people either wanted to talk to me, needed to talk to me, or had to talk to me was a long bridge I had to cross. I did so by understanding—if only for convenience's sake then—that I represented my student newspaper, the university, and theoretically the public; therefore, I was somebody to be talked to. Many beginning student journalists begin their quest with a level of confidence that I did not have; unfortunately, too many begin with an air of overconfidence that stunts rather than improves their reporting. Once I gained the confidence that I had a right to interview people for stories, interviewing itself was relatively easy.

When you think about it, all of us have been conducting interviews much of our lives. When you miss your favorite soap opera or ballgame, you ask a friend about it. If you want the friend to decide what he or she thinks is important to tell you, you ask a general, or open-ended, question like "what happened?" The more you want to know, the more questions you ask. Sometimes, instead of asking questions, you react to what you've been told with emotion and/or gestures, which, of course, elicit more detail. If there is specific information you want, you ask a narrow, or closed-ended, question to get it. "Did she keep her promise?" or "How many strikeouts were there?" We've all interviewed strangers, too. If you are at the back of the audience and the people in front start laughing, you have no qualms about turning to a person next to you who is laughing and asking "what happened?" or "What did she say?" The best interview is a conversation, not a series of sharply worded questions designed to elicit only the answers you want.

Interviewing ranges from talking to high government officials, top business executives, and celebrities to talking to ordinary people. Reporters should not lose sight of the fact that they are interviewing real people and that all people have honest feelings and emotions (until proven otherwise). People who are involved in corruption are real people; so are the homeless. Treat them like you would treat the upstanding pillar of the community—with respect. Always put yourself in that person's shoes, and ask how you would want to be treated. Or better yet, ask yourself how you would treat that person if the person were a member of your family or a close friend. Be assertive, be aggressive, whatever it takes, but do so with respect and courtesy. Reporters should also remember that some people have little or no experience dealing with the news media. Most of the time, these people, especially if they are not in a public office, have no obligation to talk to the media. Reporters should be considerate of such persons and give them the opportunity to adjust to this moment in the sun.

A variety of techniques can help you conduct effective interviews:

• Watching good interview news programs on television, such as *The Newshour with Jim Lehrer* and *Nightline*, can help. Observe the tactics the hosts use. Jim Lehrer is excellent at maintaining a casual but authoritative tone in interviews as he coaxes guests into breaking down their information so the mass audience can understand it. Too many officials and experts like to use jargon that communicates to their colleagues, but not to the general public.

• Nothing beats being prepared for an interview. When possible, get the basic facts prior to an interview. Such information could be available from office handouts or press releases, a resumé, or a conversation with another source. Preparedness allows you to go into an interview knowing whether it will be confrontational or easygoing; it allows you to know whether you can begin the interview with light chatter or if you need to get down to business the moment you arrive or get the person on the phone.

• Unless you have a strategic reason for surprising a source, you should always call and try to schedule your interview.

• Always be prepared for the source who says, "I won't have time later; ask your questions now."

• Beginning student journalists should always prepare a list of questions when focusing the story idea. Persons who are experienced at being interviewed can easily gain control of a interview with vague or rambling responses that do not address the question, or by asking the reporter questions, which might catch the reporter off guard. Persons who are not experienced at being interviewed can unintentionally get the reporter off track by failing to understand the process and wanting to restate answers, or wanting to take back things they've said or allowing the interview to be frequently interrupted. Reporters who have written questions to guide them can stay focused by following the questions.

• While a list of questions is the best approach for beginning student journalists, an alternative would be to outline the interview so that you will have an idea of categories of information to cover. A list of questions or an outline also makes it easier to have something to glance back over at the end of the interview to make sure you've covered everything you wanted to cover.

• In general, you should plan to get to work immediately after shaking hands or introducing yourself on the phone. You state your purpose for the interview, make it clear the interview is on-the-record, and then begin. (Feature story interviews, however, can be more casual and might begin with chatter about something you have observed or about something that has nothing to do with the story.)

• As a general rule, questions in news story interviews tend to get specific earlier in the interview than would questions in feature story interviews. Time often controls an interview. The shorter the interview, the more quickly you ask the most important questions.

• Nothing's more important in an interview than active listening. You must show interest in what the source is saying, even if it is not interesting. Do not be so obsessed with note-taking that you do not hear and understand what is being said. While you should avoid indicating agreement with the source, body language such as nodding your head or looking the source in the eye or an occasional phrase such as "I see" or even a grunt will tell the source that you are paying attention.

• As much as possible, allow the source to finish responses to your questions. If you must interrupt because the source is intentionally not answering the question, rambling, or being long-winded, always be polite. A simple "excuse me, but..." will help soften the interruption.

• Sometimes, the source will ask you questions, but you should remember that you are not the one being interviewed. Don't answer, if your response would indicate bias that would taint your story. Also, an interview is not a debate. You are seeking information for the reader. If the reader wanted your opinions, you wouldn't be interviewing someone else; someone would be interviewing you.

• However, you should not be reluctant to challenge what the source says if it is inconsistent with other information you have or something the source said earlier.

• Each interview can be so different, and no matter how well you plan the interview, it can change depending on the mood of the source or the answer to the first question. Even if you anticipated the answer, it could be one of several that you anticipated, and therefore you have to adjust your approach accordingly.

• As a general rule everything said is on-the-record. Many newspapers have a policy on when to go off-the-record and when anonymous sources may be used. Generally, do not go off-the-record unless you absolutely have to, and do not promise anonymity to a source. If you have to go off-the-record, and your newspaper's policy allows you to do so, make sure you and the source understand the ground rules. For example, make sure you understand whether you can use the information as long as you do not attribute it to the source, or whether you can't use the information at all, even if you should later find it out from another source.

• You get out of an interview the same way you get into it. You are polite and courteous. You tell the source that you have asked all of your questions, but before you close the interview you would like to know if there is another question that should have been asked or if the source would like to say something else. This often provides additional information or a good quotation.

• When the interview is over, you thank the source for the information and time. You might also ask for permission to call back if you need more information or need to clarify something.

SPOKESPERSONS AS SOURCES

Sourcing a story should not be limited to nor should it exclude the spokespersons that organizations, public agencies, and businesses put out front for the media to use. You should not automatically assume that spokespersons are distorting the truth or are holding back information. In fact, spokespersons should be used because they are knowledgeable about their group or agency. The job of the reporter is to go beyond them. Readers should hear from the actual source of the action or information whenever possible. Spokespersons should help you understand what is going on, then help you to get to the original source, be it a head of government, top executive of a company, or a lower-level employee. If you cannot get beyond the spokesperson, try to have the spokesperson take your questions to the person and get them answered in that person's words. Don't rely on spokespersons to do your reporting, but don't let them hinder you either.

Reporters must understand that official spokespersons have a job to do; and that job, in general, is to put their organization or their side of an issue in the most favorable light. When developed with mutual understanding, the relationship between an official spokesperson (or any source) and a reporter can be beneficial. Each needs the other. Reporters might have to print some positive newsworthy stories, such as employee promotions or company contributions to local charities, fed to them by a public relations source in order to have access to the source and the source's resources when a not-so-positive story comes along. The reporter might have to attend official occasions, such as dinners and receptions, where there is no news in order to have a rapport with the source when there is news. To go knocking on a source's door, public spokesperson or otherwise, only when there is bad news is not good reporting. Reporters must get their editors to understand this. Most editors tell you, the reporter, they want you to cultivate sources but seldom give you time to do it. Editors, especially at small newspapers, tend to want a story from every occasion you attend or every visit you make to a source. Developing sources takes more than just seeing them at meetings or contacting them when you want a quotation or piece of information.

NOTE TAKING

Having a focus during the note-taking stage helps the reporter take notes selectively, which in turn helps the reporter keep the focus when writing the story. While taking notes selectively helps cut down on the writing, each reporter has to develop his or her own system for taking notes in order to get enough information. Some reporters use formal shorthand, although transcribing it can be time-consuming. Most reporters develop their own shorthand. They often drop articles and prepositions when taking notes because they can be easily filled in later. Symbols can be used for some words, and capital letters and shortened versions of words can be used, especially names or words that appear frequently. All that needs to be taken down verbatim are statements that might be used as a quotation in a story, or numerical information. In general, a short quotation will stick with you long enough for you to write it down if you do so immediately. It helps to put an asterisk in the margin by information that needs to be checked or followed up on during the interview. You can also use symbols such as asterisks, checks, or numbers to order information so that when you get back to the newsroom you do not have to determine the importance of information all over again.

Accuracy in Notes

Whatever your approach is, *always emphasize accuracy*. During an interview, for example, you can ask the source to repeat a statement or explanation, stressing that you want to make sure you write it down accurately because of its importance. Or you can ask a question similar to the one previously asked hoping it will get you essentially the same answer. You preface such a question with a phrase such as "let me make sure I understand this." Or you can ask a follow-up question that keeps the source talking. Your purpose is to write down what has already been said, or to take better notes this time since you will be familiar with what the source is going to say.

Active Listening

It is always a mistake to start writing with the first word and to keep writing intensely until the interview, speech, or meeting is finished. You should *listen first*, then take notes when the information warrants it. You can sometimes judge whether something is worth writing down by body language of the interview subject or the reaction of the audience or members of the board or group you are covering. The interview subject might clear his or her throat before saying something with emphasis, or use hand or facial gestures that indicate some information is more important than other information.

Also remember that when an interview or a meeting or speech is over, the reporting isn't. The information you collect as you chat at the end of the interview or are escorted to the door is a part of your reporting. Similarly, you frequently have the opportunity to quickly interview board members or the speaker before you rush back to the newsroom to write your story. You should know ahead of time whether this is possible since the speaker could have a plane to catch.

Note taking raises the issue of whether to use a *tape recorder*. Interviews for long profiles or features call for tape recorders as long as the source(s) would not be inhibited from talking freely. So do interviews for controversial stories, where taping protects both sides. In fact, these days sources in controversial stories often record the interview for their protection. Always clear taping ahead of time. Do not arrive at the interview with a tape recorder without prior approval.

WRITING STORIES

How to write journalistic stories is focused on elsewhere in this book. But to complete the reporting process introduced earlier in this chapter—focus, reporting, and writing—following are two examples of stories that are well-written in large part because they were well-reported. Each story represents the complete reporting process.

Example: Hurricane Hugo

When Hurricane Hugo was headed for the South Carolina coast in September 1989, we gave students in our newspaper practicum the opportunity to cover the story live. Two reporters and two photographers took us up on the offer. Another professor, Keith Kenney, and I accompanied the students to the office of the *Post and Courier* in Charleston, driving through heavy rain much of the two-hour trip. When we arrived, the students were allowed to go out with the newspaper's photographers and reporters until it was too dangerous for anyone to be outside.

The entrance to the newspaper was boarded up, and we went to the newsroom to wait for the hurricane to hit. The first side of the hurricane arrived right on schedule about midnight. While the eye of the hurricane passed over—there is complete calm in the eye—many of us in the newsroom scurried outside to get a glimpse of the damage. It was already devastating. After about 20 minutes, we rushed back in as we felt the winds whipping up and knew the other side of the hurricane was coming ashore.

When daylight arrived, the question for the reporters was "what story do we write?" We were so stunned by the devastation we weren't quite sure which of the many stories to report. We wanted a story that would show we were in Charleston for the hurricane; so we decided to walk through some neighborhoods near the newspaper and talk to residents. After only a couple of casual interviews, the students found their story and their focus—people who stayed home to face the storm despite the danger. The students then began seeking out these persons and asking them why they stayed, what they experienced through the night, and what kind of damage was done to their house. The students waded through flooded streets and sidewalks and carefully made a path around fallen trees, tree limbs, and wires to get to the battered porches of the victims. We also decided that this would be a people story. We would not be concerned with city-wide damage totals, official comments about the danger the residents put themselves in, or other official response. We wanted the people to tell their experiences. The story, written by Nancy Jo Thomason and Kelly S. Marshall, appeared in our practicum newspaper, *The Carolina Reporter*. It began as follows:

> The upper floors of Charleston's East Side homes became fragile shelters for people who wouldn't, or couldn't, flee Hurricane Hugo.
>
> The storm, which hit around midnight Thursday, took many residents by surprise—and left some of them with shaken confidence in their ability to survive another hurricane at home.
>
> "Oh, my house, it was a rockin' and a rockin'," said Debra Milligan, who lives in a three-story wooden house on America Street. She pointed to her house as she stood on the street talking to neighbors among the broken limbs, boards and other debris blown by the storm. "I was prayin', because the house down there, it just went down the street like it was nothin'.
>
> "I thought we could stand it, but next time they tell me to go, I'm goin'!"
>
> Milligan said Hugo shattered her windows and toppled her trees, but she was fortunate her house was still standing. Some of her neighbors weren't so lucky.

Example: Negro Baseball League

Sometimes the story you envision is not the one you end up with; sometimes it's better. Wayne Washington had that experience with a story he wrote as a sportswriter for the *Mercury News* in San Jose, California, where he began his career. Washington was reporting a story on the suspension of a coach who had verbally abused an umpire, when he learned from the players that the umpire might have played baseball in the old segregated Negro Leagues. So after he finished the story on the coach's suspension, he pursued a story on the umpire, Roosevelt Kelly, only to find out that Kelly really had not played in the league. But fortunately, Kelly told Washington that a friend of his had, and the friend was Willie Mays. His team was the Kansas City Monarchs. This was an even better story because of the name recognition—the legendary Willie Mays had played part of his career for the San Francisco Giants, some forty miles north of San Jose. Washington explains how he approached the story:

"At first, I had trouble finding Mays," Washington recalled. "Kelly said he hadn't been in touch with him in a long time. He didn't have a telephone number. He only knew that he lived in Oakland. So, I got out the Oakland phone book and wrote down all the numbers of people listed under William, W. or Willie Mays.

There were five of them, and I called them all. The first four were wrong numbers. And I couldn't get an answer at the fifth.

"...Finally, a woman answered and told me that Willie Mays did live there and that he was indeed the Willie Mays who had played for the Kansas City Monarchs.

"I wanted to talk to Mays, but she told me he didn't want to talk on the phone. She gave me the address and told me to stop by. My editors cleared out time for me to work on the story, and I went to visit Mays.... He took me into his home and showed me old photographs of him during his brief playing days [with the Monarchs]. He told me stories about how he was teased by the other players because of his short stature. Then, as if I couldn't tell by the tenor of his voice and the look in his eyes, he told me how much he loved baseball and how he wished he could have joined a professional team in California when he moved his family there.

"The only baseball team available for him to play on was the Oakland Larks, he said. I hadn't heard of the Larks before. As he explained that the Larks were a black team, the most solid franchise of a black baseball league a man named Ed Harris formed, I became convinced that my story had changed yet again.... I called Harris and interviewed him. His story was even more compelling than Mays'. I decided that he would be the center of the story because his life was the league. This will be more than just a baseball story, I thought.

"I knew I needed facts. I needed to know more about what life was like for blacks in the 1940s, when the league was started. I needed to know more about the Larks, more about how the league was established, more about its star players. And most importantly, I needed to know about the hopes the men who played in the league pinned on it. To get background information, I made trips to the Oakland Public Library at least twice a week for several weeks. I scanned through old Census Bureau statistics, books on baseball, the Negro Leagues and racism in sports. One of my better sources of information, though, was old newspapers on microfilm. I read through many of the sports sections of the Oakland *Tribune* from the early 1940s. There, buried in the briefs on the inside pages, I found valuable information on the early days of the league and its main draw, the Larks. These bits of information were essential because, though I believed most of what I heard from Harris and Mays about the league, I needed some kind of independent verification. That's just what the sports briefs provided.

"Once I had verification and background information, all that was left were the interviews. Getting telephone numbers and tracking down old players again was tough. But Harris' memories were clear. I usually visited him before each trip to the library. He gave me telephone numbers of people I needed to talk to or of people who knew how to reach the people I needed to talk to. In addition to helping me get in touch with people, Harris' garage was stuffed with boxes of information on the league. He had correspondence from league backers and from people who handled booking for teams in the league. Harris' documents, the newspaper microfilm and the dozens of interviews I conducted were enough to produce the story.

"The experience was far more rewarding than even I thought it would be. I helped educate readers about a league few knew about. I moved the cherished memories of a few proud black men from the inside pages of 50-year-old newspapers to the cover of the sports section. And throughout the process, I never knew just how much I learned about sports, history and reporting."

Washington wrote a two-part series for the San Jose *Mercury News* that was a finalist for the National Association of Black Journalist's Best Feature Story Award. The first story began:

If he played baseball today, America would know who Johnny Allen is.

His confident voice and his fluid play would be fixed on America's consciousness. But Johnny Allen doesn't play today.

At 72, he is just another old and unknown man who will watch and listen from his home in Berkeley as spring training unfolds these next few weeks.

As with many others, he was the wrong color at the wrong time. He played a sport no darker than its ball and lived too far from the leagues that would give him a chance.

Allen and many other top-notch players toiled in the short-lived West Coast Baseball Association or on semipro barnstorming teams along the coast, but little has been told about their story.

All black West Coast semipro baseball is not forgotten; for it never was known to most people, even during these weeks of Black History Month, when the trampled and misunderstood history of black America is in the spotlight.

So as the onset of a new season calls to mind memories of Willie Mays and Joe DiMaggio, few people can or care to remember that Allen and his peers couldn't play major Negro league baseball because the black leagues' westernmost team was in Kansas City, Mo. Most know only that blacks could not be major leaguers until Jackie Robinson broke the color line in

1947.

A museum in Kansas City, open to the public in 1992, soon will give Americans a firsthand look at Negro league baseball, the scar that lines the smooth tissue of the national pastime. But the untold story is underneath that ugly scar, underneath the stats and stories of Negro leaguers....

Washington did an excellent job in his story of putting the emphasis on people, even though he spent a considerable amount of time poring over dusty old newspapers and other documents to report his story. But he recognized that it was a people story.

Perspective...

THE NEED FOR COMPASSION

By MARK O. HATFIELD, former United States Senator and governor of Oregon. A deeply religious man, he has championed increased funding of social service programs to address what he calls "the desperate human needs in our midst."

Before deciding to campaign for public office, politicians must consider their motivations. They have to ask: are they running to help others? To improve the human condition? To bolster their own ego with victory?

Public servants, like journalists, must continually assess and reassess their motivations. The key to both professions is the ability to work with people.

That is why beginning journalists need to ask themselves a fundamental question: do you like people?

If the answer to this question is "no," aspiring journalists need to stop and think about their reasons for pursuing the profession. Empathy for people is usually reflected in the writings and the "angles" the journalist pursues. Only after an aspiring journalist is grounded with a compassion for people can he or she begin a successful career.

The most disturbing aspect of journalism today is the tendency to pursue stories that seek to destroy. Some of the greatest reporters of our time—Walter Lippmann, Edward Murrow, and others—were never out to get people. They had a sense of history. They were recording events of the day for history; they believed in that purpose, and they let it drive their work.

Reporting on national political life today is a double-edged sword. Journalists are charged with developing a comprehensive and balanced assessment of the issue. But there is rarely enough time or space to tell the whole story. The burden is on the journalist to dig deep, get the whole story, and present it fairly in the space or time provided. It is a difficult and daunting task, but the nature of politics demands it.

Journalists also need to resist the tendency to become lazy. It is easy to be victimized by slick political message-making and fall victim to the sound-byte of the day. Remember that substance and style are two different things, and the task of the journalist is to recognize the difference.

Journalists cannot and should not let ego drive their reporting. The thought of a front page "exclusive" sometimes gets in the way of balanced reporting. Know why you are pursuing a particular angle and look beyond the easy, quick-fix solution that might make a splashy headline but fails to tell the real story.

Like political figures, journalists need to recognize that initial impressions can be wrong. Question statements of "fact" from interest groups, from politicians. Ask opposing sides. Explore.

Political life is complex—the people, the process, the day-to-day events. It looks easy, but the job of a journalist is to read between the lines to convey to readers what really happened.

Daniel Boorstin, former Librarian of Congress, once wrote: "The obstacle to discovery is the illusion of knowledge."

Remember, there is always another angle.

Journalists should put themselves in the position of politicians. Don't presume to know everything about a public official just because he or she is in the national limelight. Seek to understand them, bearing in mind the human side of every politician. They are people too. They have families. They are entitled to a degree of privacy in their lives. Be considerate; it's an approach that will yield far more information than an aggressive in-your-face style will bring.

Few careers could be more thrilling than journalism. It is a mission of exploration; it is a lifelong education. Journalists, however, like politicians, should be encouraged to continually assess the reasons behind their actions. People are the lifeblood of their work. Let your compassion be your guide.

COVERING STANDARD STORY TYPES

Reporters work from events and construct stories based on the news values in those events. They follow their thinking through and discuss their thoughts with editors until they decide whether the story is hard news or soft news. Then they decide how to collect all the information they need and how to do the story fairly. They might write a hard news story, a feature, short "brite," or a complex analysis. Whatever they eventually do, the story will be based on the thinking they apply as much as it will be on the writing they do.

Reporting is a constant sifting of facts and ideas, and it is problem solving in its greatest form. In this chapter, the broad categorie of story types will be discussed. There are many varia-

BY SARA STONE AND DOUG FERDON

Dr. Stone is Professor of Journalism at Baylor University, where she teaches reporting, media law and ethics, and school publications advising. She has experience as both a print and a broadcast journalist. A former member of the national board of directors of the Society of Professional Journalists, she holds a Ph.D. from the University of Tennessee.

Dr. Ferdon is Associate Professor of Journalism at Baylor University, where he teaches editing and mass communication classes. He was editor of the *Korea Weekly* during his military service and a reporter in Florida before entering academia. He earned a Ph.D. from the University of North Texas.

tions to stories. When there is a great deal of information, more than one story will be written. A fire might involve (1) heroic action, often a feature story; (2) crime, a police story; and, of course, (3) the fire story itself. Reporters must categorize information and find a plan of action that will help present the story.

THE PROCEDURE

The procedure to use in determining the approach to any story may be broken into four parts:

- 1. Determine whether an event is newsworthy. Check for the news values of conflict, consequence, prominence, timeliness, proximity, and human interest.
- 2. Determine what type of story it will be, hard or soft.
- 3. Determine how a reporter is to find the facts. Are the sources officials, records, witnesses, or experts?
- 4. Determine how a reporter can check for objectivity. Check for personal bias, for truth, and for balance and fairness— then recheck each fact.

Is It Newsworthy?

News overwhelmingly starts with events. An accident is an event, an unplanned event. A speech is an event, a planned event. Each event may or may not be news, and the first step for a reporter covering a beat or an assignment from an editor is to determine the news value. The values associated with news include conflict, consequence, prominence, timeliness, proximity, and human interest.

Conflict in its greatest form is war and in its endless variations usually means argument or debate.

Consequence is the effect an event has on the status quo in at least a good portion of a community. An example would be when a bond issue on a proposed new school either passes or fails.

Prominence involves people who are well known within a community. Many of their actions are newsworthy. Politicians, millionaires, celebrities—all are examples of prominent persons. Ordinary people, especially victims, often become prominent, too. For instance, when "Baby Jessica" fell into a well in Midland, Texas, she became a household name. Likewise, Ryan White, a young hemophiliac, became a nationwide symbol of the tragedy of AIDS when he contracted the disease during a blood transfusion.

Timeliness must combine with one of the other news elements to become news. A story is timely when reported as quickly as possible; consumers want to know about things affecting them now.

Proximity (localizing) is another factor that affects news decisions. If a baseball player hits a home run in Cleveland but grew up in an area ten states away, chances are his hometown media will give the story good play, too. If a decision on taxes is reached in Washington, D. C., media outlets across the country will attempt to explain the decision in terms of how it will affect communities in their specific geographic location.

At the local level, the other news elements determine whether or not a story will be used. Timeliness and proximity, however, are often the deciding factors.

Human interest is found in the unusual or the beautiful or the bizarre or combinations of the three. Human interest stories are good news stories, too. They are often soft news, feature news. To cite an example: A man in England entered a contest for "The Most Beautiful Legs." This wasn't a classic news story, but it did have human interest. People want to see and read those types of stories.

Which Type of Story Is It, Hard or Soft?

In general, news can be broken into two broad categories: *hard news* and *soft news*.

Hard news is breaking news, with each new or developing piece of information pounced on by reporters. Breaking news is fires and accidents and bank robberies. Readers and viewers want to know the facts, and they want to know them quickly.

Hard news depicts facts. The six basic questions of hard news are who, what, when, where, why, and how. The key structure to the hard news story over the years has been the inverted pyramid with a summary lead on top emphasizing the major elements of the six basic questions. Timeliness and proximity are crucial to hard news.

Soft news appears in two big areas: analysis stories and feature stories.

Analysis stories include both investigative and interpretive stories. Although they really belong more to the hard news category, they de-emphasize one major news element: timeliness. Analysis stories also go beyond mere facts: they examine, explain, and analyze. They tell in detail the why, what, and how of a story.

Features emphasize emotions. They look at the human element in a story. A typical feature is a personality profile that provides insights from a person's philosophy into why he or she be-a lawyer and is committed to working for the poor. A feature ϊilt upon the storytelling concept. Features use facts to illustrate and to provide examples and opinion and narrative to create a mood.

Before reporters go out to cover stories, it is helpful if they know whether they are covering a hard news or soft news story. Why? The importance for beginning journalists lies in being able to *anticipate* how to cover the story and, once that is done, how to write the story. The greater the logic of the anticipation, the more likely the reporter will be to make the right choices in information gathering and later in organizing that material. For instance, if the reporter is covering a breaking conflict story, he or she knows before leaving the office that background information is needed on who the principal protagonists are, what divides them, who's winning, what the stakes are, and what difference the story makes for the reader or viewer. The reporter knows how to recognize and approach the next story, and the next and the next.

How Do Reporters Get the Facts?

Finding facts and sifting for truth and fairness to write a story are at the heart of the news story. Most organizations such as police departments, hospitals, schools, and businesses have a public relations representative. A good reporter knows to contact that person. A reporter covering the police beat knows to frequently contact the dispatcher at the police and fire departments. Dispatchers can provide information on any call received at the station.

To prepare for an unplanned event such as a robbery, reporters must know how to interview policemen on the spot and how to check records at the police station and the courthouse. There is a protocol with most stories that gives reporters access to events and to individuals. No one, however, usually tells reporters the protocol without their asking, and sometimes asking several times. Competitors and officials do not always volunteer information. Reporters will find they must ask and read and learn on their own initiative.

Rechecking facts and balancing a story by seeking others to interview are important, too; and examining government publications, reading stories done previously by a media outlet, and simply asking enough questions of witnesses are some of the methods used to construct an honest story. Computer databases also carry information that is readily available.

Veteran journalist Bob Sablatura, an investigative reporter for the Houston *Chronicle*, uses both his computer and the Internet on a daily basis to research and develop stories. According to Sablatura:

"Journalists in ever-increasing numbers are turning to their computers to help them do their jobs. Less than a decade ago, computer-assisted reporting meant dealing with bulky nine-track tapes and huge, mysterious main-frame computers. The development of inexpensive, powerful personal computers has changed all that, bringing computer-assisted reporting within the reach of even the smallest newsroom. Reporters today are using spreadsheet and database programs to analyze city budgets, track campaign contributions and expenditures, examine lending practices in their community, and monitor the criminal justice system, to name just a few. The use of the computer as a reporting tool has also begun to change the way information is gathered, as more and more government information is being released in electronic form. Many states have amended their open-records laws to allow greater access to information stored in government computers.

"The advent of the Internet computer network has also opened up avenues of research unheard of just a few years ago. Reporters today have access to information contained in hundreds of thousands of Internet-linked computers around the world. Through the use of powerful research engines operating on the World Wide Web, journalists can search for information on specific topics, locate knowledgeable sources and track individuals involved in news events. Through the use of electronic mail, known commonly as E-mail, journalists can instantly communicate with sources and exchange research materials and information. Many of the nation's largest newspapers have also begun publishing electronic editions over the Internet, and most allow access to their archives of previously published news stories. This has created a huge collective electronic library that can be tapped by any journalist searching for background materials on any given subject.

"The online journalism community has responded with a support system to aid reporters conducting research on the Internet. Many web sites offer resources and information geared largely for reporters. The Reporters Network (http://www. reporters.net) provides free E-mail services for reporters and a media directory of online journalists, while the National Freedom of Information Coalition (http://www.reporters.net/ nfoic) has launched a web site publishing details of all fifty states' FOI laws. The Society of Professional Journalists (http://www. spj.org) and Investigative Reporters and Editors (http://www. ire.org) both maintain active E-mail discussion lists for journalists to debate issues relating to the news-gathering process. In addition, hundreds of individuals and organizations have developed resource pages to help journalists locate everything from public securities filings to government-maintained pet databases."

How Do Reporters Check for Objectivity?

After determining newsworthiness, deciding what type of story, hard or soft, and checking and rechecking for facts, reporters should make one more check as they construct stories, a check for bias. In journalism, the counter to bias is usually called objectivity, and it means balancing the story.

Step one is to attempt to *eliminate personal bias*. If a reporter decides he or she likes someone or doesn't like someone, it is best for the reporter to consider, in collaboration with an editor, withdrawing from the story.

The second step is to *search for truth from sources*. People often do not remember, or they only admit to certain memories. Checking and rechecking even routine information is the key to overcoming source bias. Calling back a source to recheck a fact or a direct quotation is a great idea in most circumstances. It does not mean reading the entire story to that person, but it may mean reading a few important paragraphs. Reading documents is also important. If a source quotes a public record, a reporter should try his or her best to read that record.

The final step in a quick objectivity check is to *seek balance*. Reporters should continually search for those sources—pro and con, for and against—different from the main ones. A speech story, for example, will present the speaker's perspective. If the idea presented is controversial, then the reporter should take steps to find out how authentic the view is among the most knowledgeable people in that particular area and to balance the story with voices from the other sides of the issue.

The basic steps reporters take will then prepare them to decide on what kind of story to write. The story becomes a hard news story about a fire, or it becomes a soft news story about a hero. A weather story may become a story about property loss, and the reporter will then spend as much time with insurance adjusters as with the fire department.

STORY TYPES

Stories can be divided into three main types: those involving agencies, cultures, and planned events.

Agencies include government organizations such as the police, the court house, city hall, the local school district, and federal agencies such as the FBI, Environmental Protection Agency, the Interstate Commerce Commission, etc.

Cultures are more complex. There is a business culture, a sports culture, and cultures for religion, art, and politics. Even death is a culture. Obituaries are handled by the funeral home, the church or the synagogue, but they can be affected by a government agency, such as the coroner's office. Personality news falls under culture. Personalities and celebrities are being cultivated by the modern mass media as never before as circulation-stimulating devices. O. J. Simpson, Michael Jackson, Princess Di, and Sarah Ferguson are all examples of personalities who emanate from our various cultures. They are fodder for stories with little real relevance beyond the personality profiles the press attaches to them.

Planned events include press conferences, speeches, and meetings. Both agencies and the different cultures sponsor them. A press conference might become more important by what is left out than what is said, and a reporter should be prepared to ask follow-ups.

Agencies

Eventually, a reporter must make decisions on story organization, and this section of the chapter attempts to provide strategies for doing so. Objectivity, for instance, differs in stories. Quoting accurately from a court record and attributing the words to that record may be all that is needed in a trial, but in a business deal, company executives, laborers, stockholders, and customers may all have different positions on the outcome.

Police

Conflict is one of the major news elements in police reporting. Because of the nature of law and law-breaking involved, one of the main objectives for a reporter assigned to cover the police beat is to be wary of the "friendliness snare." To get good stories, perhaps even to be invited along on a drug bust, a reporter should be friendly. Danger comes, however, when the reporter becomes too close to his or her sources. Police officers are not above using newspaper reporters to their advantage. It is important for reporters to remember that defendants have rights, and journalists should try to balance each story.

Reporters need to know the exact status of a person who is in some way "connected" to a crime. The person's status determines how he or she is referred to in a story. Police may question a witness, arrest a suspect, charge a suspect, or have the suspect face a preliminary hearing when charges become official and bond is set. A savvy reporter knows not to use a person's name until he or she has been *charged* with a crime. (Some conservative editors won't allow a suspect's name to be used until after the preliminary hearing or arraignment.) Irrevocable damage can be done to an innocent person falsely or prematurely reported to be connected to a crime.

In addition, a reporter should carefully evaluate statements made by police at the scene. This is particularly true when identification may be given in advance of charges being brought. Litigation can result from damaging someone through premature disclosure of information that is not in the public domain. Such disclosure has three potential consequences: the innocent person's reputation may be destroyed; the news organization may suffer financially; and the reporter's credibility, news judgment, and self-esteem may be damaged.

Trouble on a police story often comes from using names that should be eliminated, such as the name of a juvenile or a rape victim. Other pitfalls for the reporter include using the wrong name, using poor attribution, and speculating on information.

The reporter should try to have notes on what he or she sees, what the officers say and do, what witnesses say, and what is recorded on the report written by the officers.

A fundamental requirement of police reporting is to check the offense reports several times each day. Police use the reports to record criminal activity and arrests. The arresting officer files the initial offense report. A reporter must find out what information is available and when it is available. Legal access to the reports differs from state to state and from police department to police department in practice, but there are generally four things to which reporters are entitled. These include (1) identification of the suspect by age, address, and occupation; (2) the charge; (3) names of arresting officers and agencies; and (4) the time, date, and place of the arrest.

Talking to the investigating detectives is also important. The detective on duty can provide valuable information. Larger departments have a media liaison officer, and it is important for a reporter to cultivate a solid working relationship with that officer.

Courts
Courthouse coverage will be either criminal or civil in nature. Step one is to identify which type of proceeding is to be covered. Step two is to know courthouse vocabulary. It is essential that the

reporter translate legalese into language that the average person can understand.

Testimony in court, for both criminal and civil trials, is privileged information. Reporters may use any information presented in court. Danger rises in failing to use careful attribution. It is important to use such terms as "In court testimony, she said," because it shows the reporter was not getting the information outside the courtroom.

Reporters assigned to cover courts should check lawsuits filed in the United States District Clerk's office and check with the United States Attorney's office. They should then go to the courthouse and check the docket sheet for that day; it lists hearings and trials to take place before a judge in a courtroom. If any of the cases has one or more tangible news values present (prominence, consequence, human interest), then the reporter should go to the courtroom and cover the proceedings.

Other sides of the story are important, too. Balance, research, and careful attribution, combined with defining terms explicitly and explaining them to the readers, are the fundamentals of sound court reporting.

Government

The basic four levels of government are city, county, state, and federal, each of which has offices in any medium-sized city and above. Each government branch will have a legislative, executive, and judicial branch.

Financial stories dominate much of government. Revenues and expenses consisting of bond issues, taxes, and bills from services such as city water are big issues.

An important point for a reporter covering government is to make sure he or she represents all the people. The poor need an advocate; so do the elderly and the young. A reporter's duty covering government is to make sure that stories are balanced and clear. Careful explaining of complex issues—perspective—is necessary for a government reporter.

Government reporters must handle one other major concern. In a political campaign there sometimes is a maverick who does not gain many votes but who has something valuable to say. How much coverage to give that person is always a dilemma. Another maverick is the person who writes frequent letters to the editor of the newspaper. If that person has something valuable to say, his or her views might be worth a story. A third maverick is the person who goes to city council meetings and asks questions or seeks the floor for statements. Many of these folks are simply blowing their own horn, trying to get attention. But some have legitimate complaints, and reporters should continually evaluate their messages for news content.

Covering government also means dealing with the laws guaranteeing public access to meetings and records. Reporters should make contact with the state press association and get information on access and the various problems they might encounter in serving the public.

Disasters
Disasters can come from natural elements like tornadoes or floods or from technological breakdowns like a gas line explosion. One of the most common disasters is a fire, which can come from natural occurrences or from product failure or even simple human error—or human intention. Major accidents, such as airplane crashes, are other disasters. In each case, officials, victims, and witnesses can provide information.

Fires
Fire stories are newsworthy once the fire reaches a certain level of property damage or if there is an injury to a person. The fire's location, the names of those involved, the value of the property damaged or destroyed, the time the fire started, how it was started, and how and when it was controlled are the factual elements that each fire story must include.

The original story is usually considered hard news, although there is often a sidebar feature on a person who helped another escape or on the heroic action of a firefighter. Because of the human elements in a fire story, a reporter should always look for a feature, too. It is important to be sensitive to victims, though, because the hero might feel great but the victim might feel vulnerable. A reporter should be sensitive to those in distress. Make sure any interview legitimately advances the story for the public and is not simply conducted for the shock value of the emotions conveyed. An ethical reporter always conducts a mental balancing act between the public's right to know and an individual's right to privacy.

Covering a fire can be difficult because the fire has to be put out before officials have time to talk. Sometimes access to the fire location is limited and investigation results come much later. A reporter should talk to firefighters, the fire marshal, witnesses, and victims at the scene. The reporter should be alert to fire safety codes, arson, carelessness, and other occurrences. Similar fires might indicate a pattern of criminal activity.

Thinking about the consequences of a fire, interviewing sources, double-checking official reports, talking to insurance agents who have to pay the costs, and looking for changes in city fire codes and procedures are some of the follow-up actions a good reporter will do. Beyond accurately reporting what happened at the fire, the why and how of the details should be considered. The good reporter knows that a fire story is not always over when the flames are extinguished.

Weather

Glancing at a newspaper or simply listening to a radio news show will demonstrate the importance of weather. Hurricanes, tornadoes, and floods are all weather stories. So are the four inches of rain that fell in the morning or the snowstorm developing in the afternoon.

Weather presents one main problem for a reporter: predictions. If a bad storm is on the horizon, and the television is running a story reporting that a "tornado watch" is in effect until 8 p.m., what does that mean? It means a tornado is possible. A tornado warning, on the other hand, means a weather observer or a weather instrument has detected a tornado and people in that vicinity are being urged to take immediate precautions. The conscientious reporter will try to check and double-check any reports on weather conditions. Occasionally, reports of a funnel cloud are simply rumors that cannot be substantiated. In fact, even officials such as police officers are not immune to reporting rumors, thus lending authenticity to non-credible information. The problem for the reporter is that readers and viewers will remember that the news was wrong, not that the information came from a police officer with a "better safe than sorry" attitude. A reporter too eager to get the story first and beat the competition, even if it means putting unsubstantiated information before the public, risks violating the social responsibility of the media to "get it right." Accuracy is the greatest and most important ingredient in the news mix.

Cultures

Government agencies are involved whenever a case becomes extreme. A murder is a death and can be covered as an obituary; but it is also a major news story, and the news elements in it will bring the police and the courts into the story. Nevertheless, certain areas are more often noted for their cultural significance rather than their political impact. Babies being born are a strong cultural influence, too, and are the natural contrast to the deaths of others. A dance group, an artist, and a rock star are parts of the entertainment culture. There is obviously a strong business culture, religion influences the majority of lives, sports entertains, and politics affects all people. In each of these areas, deciding whether a story is hard news, with a focus on the who, what, and when, or soft news, with a focus on the why and how—or whether it is both—is important. Knowing whether a story is hard or soft has implications for how the reporter covers and writes a news story. Examples from deaths, sports, and religion are explained below.

Deaths

Deaths can be categorized two ways: violent and nonviolent. Violent deaths are hard news stories and are often front-page news. Americans have a fascination, unlike many other cultures in the West, with violent death. Consequently, reporters and editors place a high news value on violent deaths, and particularly in naming those who have died violent deaths. Many Europeans think of this as an invasion of privacy or exploiting the tragedy of families. However, the "public's right to know" is and has been behind American journalistic decision-making since the earliest days of this country. Reasonable journalistic cause is a phrase that guides reporters, and openness is the rule. Bigger flaps are caused by suppression of news than by over-reporting. Both bring criticism to reporters, but the charge of suppression of news is worse. The key in a news decision is the "public" nature (the where, why, and how) in which the violent death occurred. Investigation and adjudication of a murder are handled by government agencies: the police, coroner's office, and the courts. Information on deaths in a tornado is handled by various government agencies. The funeral can be a major news story, too.

Nonviolent deaths are seldom front-page news, unless the person dying has achieved prominence. These deaths are handled by churches, synagogues, and funeral homes; and the reporting of them comes from the death report. Newspapers call the stories *obituaries*.

Newspapers often employ obituary clerks to obtain information. Most information comes from the funeral home and is recorded on standard forms. Some forms start with the name, funeral home, and burial information. Others begin with name, cause of death, and affiliations. While the basic formats for reporting an obituary can vary with newspapers, looking at news values and objectivity are standard practices for the reporter to determine important story considerations.

Sensitivity is a factor in how the obituary is written. A shooting or death from injuries suffered in an accident will be reported as such, but often a newspaper may use a euphemistic term such as "a long illness" instead of the name of the actual illness in describing the cause of death. In some states the cause of death is not a public record. How the cause of death is reported is a matter of policy for each individual news organization. Some always list the cause of death, others never. Often that determination is made by a publisher or station owner's perception of the public's right to know vs. privacy considerations for survivors. The decision often is influenced by a person's own feelings about perceived social stigmas about dying from certain diseases. The word cancer once was not spoken above a whisper. The same was true of AIDS. The size and geographic location of a community often determine the amount of information reported about the cause of death.

Suicides can present problems. Family members often are embarrassed by disclosure, and newspapers worry about describing how a person committed suicide. Publishers do not want to feel responsible for copycat suicides. Again, the determination on whether to report that a death was caused by suicide is often made at the very top of the news organization hierarchy—rarely by the reporters or obit clerk.

In writing obituaries, reporters must always remember to check and double-check facts. Calling family members is sensitive but often essential. Hoaxes are common on fortieth birthdays and other occasions, and reporters must be aware of the occasional need for verification that a death occurred.

Sports

Sports reporting has become one of the most important and popular news areas. A boom is occurring in the growth of sports personality news. Whether in newspapers or on broadcast stations, consumers want to know how teams or, sometimes more importantly, how individuals fared. But, despite the large human interest emphasis, many sports stories today are measured by the "newsvalue" yardstick applied to non-sports stories. A reporter needs specialized knowledge to write adequately about the high salaries of professionals, the tax burdens of cities wanting to attract a lucrative professional franchise, the conflict apparent in drug use, the boom in college sports, and the questions of fairness to minority athletes and to women. There are more sports stories on the front pages of newspapers, and there are more sports stories leading television newscasts now than ever before.

Therefore, a sports reporter should consider several factors when looking at sports coverage. In a university setting, for example, a reporter should consider traditional game coverage for stories and traditional features on athletes. But there are news values inherent in a university's entire sports program, too. The objective reporter will look at how much space is provided in the newspaper or television station for coverage of all sports. He or she will look at the graduation rates of athletes and how money is distributed among athletic programs.

In covering a game, the reporter should remember that the results of the game are basically hard news. A good sports reporter also should remember that a reader or viewer probably has seen the game already, or its highlights, and knows the outcome. Therefore, the tendency should be to emphasize explanation, the why of the game or contest, through interviews with key participants. A reporter's opinions should not intrude into the story. Soft news abounds around athletic programs; and a reporter should look not only for news, but also for stories that uplift the human spirit.

A reporter should also consider the "homer" factor. Is the reporter a cheerleader for the home team? If so, he or she has abandoned balance, fairness, and impartiality. It is not the reporter's job to be a friend or a public relations promoter. The reporter should be willing to take the risk of alienating sports personalities—coaches, players, owners, college presidents, fans, or others—if the public should know about a story.

The same criteria of objectivity should be used on all pages of a newspaper. Unfortunately, that is not true everywhere. Some publishers choose to use their "Neighborhood" or "Travel" or "Business" or "Sports" pages and sections as little more than a place to print warmed-over press releases, real fluff that advances someone's cause but not necessarily the reader's. Public relations masquerading as news is not good journalism.

Religion

Religion pages have been in daily newspapers since the last century. Until recently, however, not many reporters were assigned the religion beat. It might seem that religious news is not common except for the "Religion Page" on Saturdays, but interest in religion frequently is behind major stories.

Religious leaders are involved with business, education, politics, popular culture, and morality. Religions run schools, and religious leaders engage in politics.

Lack of objectivity, however, is a major obstacle in religion stories. First, a reporter has to overcome personal bias. Recent surveys show that most reporters have hardly any religious commitment, and coverage of religion tends to be negative. Reporters should gather all of the information and quote those participating accurately. They should follow religiously (pun intended) each step of solid reporting. They should be alert to the question of who represents the sides in a story. Does that include the atheist? A Methodist, if the story is about the Pope? Reporters should not accept at face value the proclamations of religious leaders any more than they would a politician; religious leaders have deceived the public, too. Yet, reporters should treat religion with great sensitivity. Belief is not only strong; it is, in fact, the basis of conduct for many people's lives. It is the central fact of the believer's life and should be treated with care.

Planned Events

Press conferences, meetings, and speeches are planned events; and normally their news value is related to consequence, prominence, and proximity. These planned events overlap all of news reporting. Mayors hold press conferences; so do dancers and quarterbacks.

The overall strategy of covering one of these events often follows a format: a press release arrives in the newsroom; and from it a reporter writes a brief, a short story that outlines the basic message of the event and identifies the speaker or speakers.

The reporter may then do a feature before the event if the editor believes the story has news value.

The speech or meeting is then covered, and a story is written about it. Afterward, an analysis story may be written about the contents of the event or the consequences or possible consequences.

These events are planned news, and some of them are simply to gain publicity for an idea or plan of action that a person or group wants to promote. Many political rallies or appearances fall in this category. Government meetings, of course, are required by law and often produce news that has a good deal of consequence. Even long-winded county commission meetings may have consequences that aren't readily apparent during the meeting.

At all of these events there are three things a reporter needs to monitor: the speaker(s), the speech itself, and the audience. For instance, a person who disrupts a meeting by protesting may be an important part of the event. Evaluating only the speaker can be a mistake at any public event.

Press Conferences

Many press conferences are called to help manage news. Reporters have to judge how much news value is present and how much of the conference the competition is likely to cover. If a television station gives a politician coverage, then the other media will likely follow suit. The importance of evaluating the news value of a story cannot be emphasized enough. While it is human to measure one's own actions by the competition, that should not be a journalist's yardstick for determining whether something is newsworthy.

Good reporters should mentally ask themselves these questions before writing: Is this topic relevant to the public? Is it significant? Does it tell the reader/viewer/listener something they don't already know? A reporter needs to have a wide range of knowledge to be able to intelligently evaluate or analyze the newsworthiness of a press conference or speech. Where does a reporter get all that knowledge? Some comes from having taken a broad range of liberal arts coursework in college. Some comes from being a voracious reader. The rest, especially for a rookie, comes from using the morgue, listening to other reporters and editors, and not being afraid to ask questions *before* covering a story. Reporters who have done their homework should have a pretty good idea of what to come *looking for* in a speech, news conference, or meeting. A feel can be developed for knowing what threshold must be crossed to make the story news (which takes us back to weighing news values).

Good reporters will even discover that the story can be written in part, or at least backgrounded, before they get to the scene since it is often difficult to write an entire story and meet a deadline after an event. Preparation is the key to good news coverage. Reporters who have done their homework and increased their knowledge base can go on even the toughest of assignments knowing that they can provide context and explanation for what happened at the news event rather than just taking dictation and writing the most superficial of stories.

Speeches

Speeches are presented with a point of view. To cite an example, a speaker may quote another person. Before giving that quote authenticity, a good reporter verifies the quote from the original source before using it. Speakers do not often use verbatim quotes. They pick and choose what they want.

If a speaker says something controversial, a reporter should clearly attribute it to the person and then should ask a follow-up question after the speech if possible.

Meetings

Meetings are often long and sometimes confusing. The main objective for a reporter is to verify and clarify all material. Asking follow-up questions, calling participants afterward, and rechecking information are all important.

There may be several items on a meeting agenda, and a reporter must evaluate whether to do one story or more. Obviously, conflict will produce a story, but it might not be the story that has the greatest consequence in the long run.

Perspective...

WHAT A FORMER WIRE SERVICE REPORTER WISHES BEGINNING JOURNALISTS KNEW ABOUT JOURNALISM

By EDMUND LAWLER, instructor in the Department of Communication at DePaul University. Mr. Lawler was a reporter for the Associated Press and The City News Bureau of Chicago and a reporter and editor for newspapers in Indianapolis, Phoenix, Santa Barbara and Tucson.

Young journalists must know that news is a moving target. Scriveners and stenographers need not apply as the race is to the swift and the street-smart.

News can be chaotic as it breaks out on multiple fronts and presents varying shades of truth. It must be collected through a cacophony of voices, each with its own perspective that must be instantly evaluated and balanced.

Some voices may choose to remain silent for reasons ranging from simply being too busy to talk, to distrust of the press, to fear for their job. Reports are unavailable. Offices are closed. Next of kin have yet to be notified. And the clock is ticking.

The journalists who can negotiate the white-water ride of news gathering will find their work leading the page. Journalists who content themselves with the low-hanging fruit of news releases, routine meeting and speech coverage and police blotter items will find their careers and stories going nowhere.

Here's my advice for a cub reporter:

• 1. *Get it right.* This is the price of admission. Check and double-check every detail that will go into the story. Don't be shy about calling the source again if there's the slightest doubt. Because a wire service story can appear in dozens, possibly hundreds, of news outlets, an inaccuracy will be repeated dozens, possibly hundreds of times.

Once is bad enough.

- 2. *Get it balanced*. Because news is often about conflict, there are at least two sides that need to be presented in the story. Both perspectives must be presented in the same news cycle.

- 3. *Get it first*. Hockey great Wayne Gretzky attributes his success to going where the puck will *be*, not where it *is*. Reporters who know their beats can often anticipate the issues that will become news. They take the initiative to set the agenda. When news breaks, they're ahead of the game because they know the right sources.

- 4. *Get it better*. Good reporters don't settle for the superficial. They provide the context and the details that no one else has. They are tireless in their efforts to collect the information.

- 5. *Get it organized*. It starts with a lead that is tight and bright. Well-sourced and well-documented copy flows logically from there.

Young journalists who have mastered those five requirements, I've found, possess several qualities, including:

- 1. *Curiosity*. They see the world, their city, their beat through a fresh perspective. They take nothing for granted. They're capable of thinking critically.

- 2. *Charm*. While they will make sources uncomfortable at times with their sharp-edged questions, young journalists must have the social skills to build a stable of reliable sources.

- 3. *Coachability*. The young journalist who resists advice or criticism from an editor or a more-experienced colleague is missing an opportunity. It pays to listen.

What am I looking for in a young journalist? That's simple: A good reporter who can write.

10

REPORTING THE WORLD ABOUT YOU

One of the best ways you as a reporter can assure that you do your job well is to develop a knowledge and understanding of those topics you will be reporting on.

Audience surveys show a deepening public perception that journalists do not take seriously enough the interests of the audience. One of the most long-lived and continuing criticisms of journalists is that they are superficial in their understanding of issues. The result of superficial knowledge is shallowness in explaining topics and even errors in elementary facts.

If you wish to do your job as a reporter well, you must take seriously the principle that journalists need to understand the world about them. Try to become a well-educated, knowledgeable person. Begin doing that while you are still a student. One of the things you can do is to take classes in such areas as business, political science, economics, religion, and history that will help you to understand the various subjects you will be covering as a professional reporter. Continued reading and self-education should become one of your lifetime pursuits. Always strive for depth of understanding. Be wary of the limits of your knowledge. Journalism will require more of your mind than you can imagine. So prepare yourself.

To give you a broader perspective than you might get simply from talking with other journalists, *The Responsible Reporter* solicited essays from specialists on various constituencies that are

,ented in and served by the news media. Beginning re-
;s need to be sensitive to the reasonable expectations of read-
,nd must make sure they responsibly represent the world to
their readers.

REPORTING THE PROBLEMS
OF THE AMERICAN CITY

By PATRICIA BRADLEY, a former editor and television reporter, now director of Temple University's American Studies Program

This is a nation that has not valued its cities. In the American
Revolution, London became a Patriot metaphor for corruption and
our Revolutionary ideology promoted the idea that America's
virtue was imbedded in its countryside. In our early years Jefferson's yeoman farmer became the embodiment of the national values of independence found in space and land. The yeoman
farmer was reincarnated into the cowboy and even the pioneer
woman. However, such a connection between space, land and
virtue—the American holy trinity—left out, of course, the city.

The role of the city was to be the dark side, the contrast to the
virtues of what lay outside its boundaries. It became a place to
promote private interests, to "make it" and move on. Even its
wealthy inhabitants used it only when necessary. As the suburbs
became the place for respectability, the city found itself providing
a gateway for immigrants, but home only for those who apparently
lacked the ability and the virtue to make it further. Not surprisingly, our heroes have not been city dwellers. Our most memorable presidents, whether George Washington, Andrew Jackson,
Abraham Lincoln, or the cinematic westerner Ronald Reagan,
have been framed by their connection to a rural landscape, not a
city one.

The easiest role for the journalist is to go along with the national myth by interpreting the city only in terms of depravity and
corruption. Such a course will be a comfortable place for readers—
supporting the decision of suburbanites to avoid the city at all
costs, encouraging well-to-do city dwellers to insulate themselves
further into private cocoons. Such an approach will also be most
beneficial to the reporter—after all, journalistic prizes are given
to such investigations. Nor is reporting under such a model de-
terred by most American journalistic education, influenced as it
is by schools located in what is often referred to—in that most
telling phrase—as "America's heartland."

But despite all these considerable pressures, I urge the reporter to examine the easy characterizations of the American city. Easy characterizations, like any stereotype, promote dismissal of the subject, the last thing a journalist should want. Indeed, the journalist assumes that exposure of a problem will necessarily lead to its correction. But when news consumers have only seen the city characterized in negative ways, the tendency, not surprisingly, is to seek distance from problems that must seem permanent and unsolvable.

What we think of as the traditional American city lumbered from the nineteenth century as an industrial behemoth. Given the myth of agrarian virtue, it is not surprising that the city was not able to translate industrial wealth into a permanent base. Yet, despite the present difficulties of the city, success is still defined by achievement based on city standards. Creativity flourishes in a city (despite another national myth that creativity exists alone, preferably in an attic room) because a living city is a place of exchange for many mediums. Creativity is the essence of the city—the synthesis of the complexity, compromise and confrontation that are the city's sun, air and water. It is our "product," one in which we all share, whether its nurturing ground is acknowledged or not.

I call on new journalists to look on the city not as the enemy, to be cordoned off and shunned, as if that contrast will better prove the virtue of the other kinds of American life. The American city belongs to us all—the city streets are as much the blood and bones of the country as cornfields, shopping malls, deserts, mountains and all the other communities of the nation. This is our land—all of it—and we need to be respectful of every square inch.

RESPONSIBILITIES OF THE COMMUNITY REPORTER

by MARTY THARP, Associate Professor in the Department of Journalism and Technical Communication at Colorado State University. She began teaching in 1985 after a newspaper career that began in 1955. She was managing editor of a suburban twice-weekly community newspaper, *The Littleton Independent*, a reporter for the *Ann Arbor News* and the *Pueblo* (Colo.) *Chieftain*, feature writer for *The Denver Post*, and research assistant for the Los Angeles *Times*, Denver Bureau. She teaches media management, public affairs reporting and coordinates the CSU journalism internship program.

Assuming that journalism students today are preparing for news careers and that they want jobs when they graduate, my advice is: Think small: small town and small papers. The obvious drawbacks are that young people may need to adjust to small-town life, the pay may not be good, and the variety of entertainment limited. But the advantages far outweigh the disadvantages.

That's not to imply that students aren't capable of being big city reporters—eventually. It's simply the reality of numbers. Of the more than 1,500 daily newspapers in the country, more than 84 percent are newspapers with circulations of 50,000 or less. An additional 7,000 weekly newspapers serve tiny towns or suburbs. Usually those newspapers have small staffs. A reasonable amount of turnover can be expected as more experienced reporters move to larger, better paying newspapers. From time to time there will be openings for solid, well-trained reporters capable of handling a variety of demanding assignments.

The responsibilities of the small-town reporter are enormous.

This is where democracy begins—where the local citizens read about what the city council is doing and where citizens take part in the discussions and decisions. They can't do that unless they have good, solid information provided by an objective, professional reporter.

The variety of experience sets a solid base for the rest of a reporter's career. At a small daily the reporter may be assigned to cover education and cops, implying that as beginner's assignments, these are easy beats. Well forget that. They're tough beats requiring an understanding of how government works and how citizens are affected by the decisions made by their elected officials. For example, the education reporter will learn more than simply how to report on schools. He or she will learn about politics, budgets, the power structure, the election process, and how the community functions. That knowledge will be valuable on any future assignment. The variety of issues relating to educating students is limited only by the reporter's imagination.

The cops beat is another assignment often given to the newest reporter, but it's more than reporting car crashes. It involves understanding and reporting community attitudes toward youth, crime, gangs, personal property and personal safety. Nothing is more important to a person than a sense of well-being that comes from living without fear in a community. Keeping on top of these issues will take a great deal of common sense, hard work and good contacts.

The ideal small-town daily reporter will be a journalism graduate with a solid understanding of how local government works and an appreciation of individuals. That reporter will know how to seek out and develop a variety of sources.

This ideal reporter may not yet be a polished writer. A good editor can improve the beginning reporter's writing, can clean up a sentence or spark up a lead. But the editor has to rely upon the reporter to ask the right questions, figure out who is affected, and search out a variety of sources to give the readers the true picture. That takes skill!

Journalists will never work harder than at a small daily, but the responsibility and satisfaction in knowing that what they do is part of what keeps democracy working will be the reward. And, they'll make life-long friends in small towns. They may even like the small town quality of life enough to want to stay. They wouldn't be making a mistake.

CONNECTING WITH YOUR COMMUNITY

By LINDA FIBICH, director of the Annapolis Bureau of Capital News Service, an intensive public affairs reporting program at the University of Maryland at College Park. Her articles critiquing press performance have appeared in leading periodicals in the field. She has worked for the Dallas *Times Herald* and her hometown newspaper, the Milwaukee *Journal*, where she rose from general assignment reporter to assistant managing editor.

If you're lucky, your first reporting job will be in your home town.

A story done in some new place is an end in itself. You write it because an editor told you to, and the impression you want to make is on the boss, not the reader. But undertake the same in the neighborhood where you grew up, and your audience grows—if only by a factor of Aunt Martha and Uncle Joe. Get something wrong, you suffer not only your embarrassment but theirs.

There is a complex connection between newspapers and their communities.

Every time we commit words to print in the name of local news, we shape readers' image of home. If the image is out of kilter with reality, our credibility suffers.

The more we tarnish our credibility with careless or irrelevant reporting, the tougher it becomes to reconnect with the skeptical community. And if readers doubt our authority in our own back yards, what trust can they put in our coverage of distant events?

And so we need Aunt Martha and Uncle Joe to remind us of where we came from and where we'll go back come quittin' time.

Report the city of your roots, and its residents will offer advice without being asked. Report a town you know more as media market than community, and you'll have to coax information from them. Either way, make the connection and renew it often.

Here, gleaned from my 17 years as a reporter and editor in four cities, are a half-dozen suggested routes home:

1. Answer the phones in your newsroom, especially when people get their papers. You'll hear more complaints than praise, but there's no more concentrated way to learn what's on readers' minds.

2. Get off the freeways and onto the surface streets. When you can, take a bus or bicycle to work. You'll find stories closer to readers' lives if you travel closer to the ground.

3. Go to a community association, PTA meeting or Little League game in a neighborhood other than your own. Regard it as an investment in source development, the same as you'd make by courting the secretaries at city hall. Tell them where you work, and measure their reactions.

4. When you cover a crime, an accident or a disaster, consider what goes on after you close your notebook and pocket your pen. Describe the setting, but remember that some of your readers make their lives in that neighborhood.

5. Respect the community standing of those you quote. Think twice before using a source in a way that advances your story, but severs his connection to the people he sees every day.

6. Cover your community's problems with all due vigor, but remember to cover what works as well.

UNDERSTANDING THE HUMAN DRAMA OF YOUR COMMUNITY

by STEVE WIEGENSTEIN, an Associate Professor at Culver-Stockton College in Canton, Mo., where he directs the journalism program and advises the student newspaper. He received his Ph.D. from the University of Missouri.

When I came out of journalism school I was offered a job at a weekly newspaper in rural Missouri, the Wayne County *Journal-Banner*. I took it with a slight pang of embarrassment, since like most students I assumed that the "big time" (i.e., large-market journalism) would have been a greater test of my abilities. I soon discovered that community journalism has its own challenges and rewards, and that one can be as creative and professional in the small markets as in the large ones.

Community journalism is not for everyone, nor should it be. The pay is less; the most recent AEJMC survey showed entry-level salaries on weekly newspapers at $327 per week, tied with radio for the bottom position on the scale, $96 per week behind the average entry-level salary in daily newspapers. I would point out, however, that this disparity is not as great as it seems. Compare the cost of living in Chicago with that of Pittsfield, Illinois, and the weekly journalist might actually have the advantage. Recognition is limited and slow in coming. And unfortunately, many so-called community weeklies and small dailies do little more than set wire copy and press releases into type, with minimal support for enterprise from their exploited staff.

But in the right situation, community journalism can be richly rewarding—and far from the dull experience of the stereotypes. In my years as a small-town journalist, I covered politics both local and large-scale, capital murder trials, airplane crashes, floods, fires, crime, accusations of governmental corruption, environmental issues, and antitrust actions. *And* I covered Fourth of July festivals, Little League games, deer season and mayoral proclamations, in addition to handling the darkroom work, copy editing, paste-up, feature writing, and the occasional trip to the front office to sell office supplies when the regular staff was busy. I learned something new every week.

For the student contemplating a foray into community journalism, I would make these observations:

Remember that word "community." Focusing on your community does not mean mindless boosterism. The last thing a community needs is another Babbitt thumping the praises of progress. Plenty of people will fill that job. Your job is to see your community steadily and whole, the good and the bad, the profound and the inconsequential. A community is an interrelated network of people. They have a history of their own, connections both official and unofficial, and unique sets of issues, hopes, and conflicts. As a reporter you can record, celebrate, and occasionally influence the life of that community.

Enjoy the competitive freedom. Community journalists rarely have to concern themselves with scooping the competition. When it comes to traditionally defined news events such as accidents and fires, you can take it for granted that the electronic media will get there first. With stories that reveal the deeper life of the community, no one else will bother. The artificial finish line of the "scoop" is, for the most part, gone. As a result, you can concentrate on creating the best report of your community rather than the first—though being first is, as always, nice.

Don't underestimate—or overestimate—your importance. I'll never forget coming into one of the town cafes one lunch time during a hot political season and seeing my newspaper, my words, being read at every table. At that moment I realized that journalism is not a game, that people's lives and fortunes were being influenced by words I wrote. This realization is perhaps more directly felt at the community level. The impersonalness of life in the larger cities enables reporters—if they choose—to separate their work from the human beings from which their work is drawn. In small cities and towns, those human beings are always with you. You pass them in the grocery aisle. Their children come to your door at Halloween. And if you treat them impersonally or arrogantly, they remember. Working in community journalism is both humbling and exhilarating, because you witness your effects, whether they be for good or ill.

Small-town life can indeed be boring, and there is a great deal of routine that the community journalist must come to terms with. But for the right person in the right place, community journalism offers as great an opportunity as any for the rewards that matter: exercising creative abilities, affecting people's lives, and developing a greater understanding of the human drama.

REPORTING CRIME

By DENNIS R. MARTIN, President of the National Association of Chiefs of Police, an organization of 11,000 police chiefs and sheriffs

Every officer of every police department who begins a tour of duty is, in his or her own area of patrol, "chief of police"; and, therefore, whatever action they take, from issuing a minor traffic citation to taking a human life, is of interest to the news media.

If I had my wishes for both new officers and new reporters, here would be my list:

1. That every news reporter ride with a police officer as part of his/her training in the community. That every police officer spend time in whatever setting to understand the needs of the media and how to address these needs.

2. That every law enforcement agency assign a senior officer (not the chief) as the source of public information. That the police public information officer meet weekly or monthly to discuss the state of local law enforcement.

3. Set up some ground rules for serious crimes in progress or on-going investigations so information is kept confidential until arrests can be made.

4. If accusations of public corruption are to be made, allow the accusations to be made by an independent agency. It is vital to

keep an honest department and at the same time not to assume that the media should act as a police agency.

5. It is just as important for police to understand that the media are the "court of last resort" and by having a good working relationship with them, we can serve the community better. Our standards must be the same—the truth.

6. Many reporters, like police, depend on informants who are paid in different forms. It is therefore vital that whatever leads or tips are provided be checked for accuracy and be documented. Some tips may endanger a police undercover operation and weeks or months of work. Some "tips" may, in fact, be the very tip of an iceberg of crime.

7. It is my belief that "no comment" is no answer at all—that if police need the cooperation of the news media, we are most likely to get it when we have learned to trust each other. That is something that is built and earned on both sides.

8. In emergencies such as hostage situations, where lives are at risk, the media should realize the role they play when every move is announced or televised. Our first objective is public safety, and we should be able to trust the media to limit their coverage for the safety of all concerned.

9. Keep in mind that there are 21,000 different police agencies of federal, state, county and local police—that 91% of all local police departments have fifty men or less and that on the average 2.3 officers cover the population per thousand. This is a small figure in any emergency. Police chiefs serve three years and two months on the average—and while the vast majority are well trained, we also are political animals.

10. New reporters can also look for valor and service among police officers that are quite common and unreported.

I have found most reporters to be effective, honest and always on deadline. In most cases I have been able to respond quickly with needed information. But not always. Some questions are very sensitive and need review. New or experienced reporters should be able to give the time needed for responses. Remember, our jobs depend a lot on how you report our responses.

REPORTING LEGAL ISSUES

By GEORGE E. BUSHNELL, JR., President of the American Bar Association, the world's largest voluntary association, representing more than 350,000 lawyers

When thinking about how the media cover events that occur

within the justice system—whether on television or in print—one is reminded of an old story about the actor John Barrymore. According to biographer Gene Fowler, Barrymore was assigned to deliver a small piece of paper obviously smaller than the message it should have contained. "Well," the other actor told the audience, "this isn't the right telegram, but I know what it would have said."

In this circumstance, as in the case of how the complexities of the justice system are addressed in the media today, it is tempting to "shoot the messenger." Such an approach is easy. It is simple to blame someone else for the manner in which the justice system has been perverted. But it would not be fair. For in this case, not only does the messenger have a responsibility; so do the actors.

The fact is that the justice system gets treated no better or worse than any other element of society. All issues are boiled down to sound bites and personalities. For example, rather than discuss the serious and compelling issue of the "right to die," we focus only on the activities of Dr. Jack Kevorkian. So it is in the justice system today. The media report on events within the system, focusing far too often on the fantastic, the strange and otherwise curious. O. J. Simpson, William Kennedy Smith, the Menendez brothers, and the Bobbitts are elevated to an exalted celebrity status simply as a result of their involvement with the system of justice. Talk shows fill with persons ready to condemn the system for the activity and results of such cases. But such cases do not reflect what is happening in the system.

Most Americans are familiar with the defense strategy in the Menendez case but have no idea of the existence of a five-year delay in the local civil courts. We hear about a large award for a woman burned by hot coffee at McDonalds but do not know about the need of the poor to have housing rights and child support orders enforced or to receive timely treatment by the Social Security Administration.

But we must realize that the justice system is not "just like any other element of society." The justice system belongs to each of us. It is our system to use to adjudicate our disputes and preserve our rights. The justice system provides the backbone for a society that has flourished economically and has helped us to reside together in relative peace. But that message is rarely heard.

But the fault lies not only with the media. It also rests with lawyers, judges and other players in the justice system. We have failed in our fundamental obligation to explain the justice system to our fellow citizens. We have not helped to explain how the system works or what its role is in our complex and fast-paced society.

The result is obvious. Across the nation people have lost faith in their system of justice. We see this result in the growing trend of business and corporate interests to use "private" judges to adjudicate their differences, rather than wait for a hearing in the public courtroom. A 1994 study by the American Bar Association showed that a growing number of poor and middle-income Americans fail to take any action when faced with a legal problem because they fear it will not "do any good."

Lawyers must take the lead for re-established confidence in the system of justice. The members of the media can help. They can start by re-examining some fundamentals. For example, more than 90% of the litigation in this country is civil, not criminal. This is where the law touches most of our lives. One does not get that impression, however, from flipping on the television or opening a newspaper with its focus on crime.

Decreased funding for the system has caused a plethora of problems for the system—adversely affecting any person who comes into contact with it. This problem can be addressed only through public awareness. The public's awareness will not change, however, if the articles that should be telling of the justice system's problems continue to shrink and cater to the lowest levels of human interest.

In "Fables For Our Time," James Thurber postulated satirically, "don't get it right, get it written," as a journalistic credo. That isn't good enough for the justice system. It is simply too important to all Americans—too basic to being American. If it should be read, make sure it gets written. If it must get written, get it right.

REPORTING BIOMEDICAL ISSUES

By STEPHEN G. POST, Associate Professor, Center for Biomedical Ethics, School of Medicine, Case Western Reserve University

Journalists sometimes do splendid work in reporting biomedical issues. There are some who have extensive background in biomedical ethics or policy and the life sciences. Their work is accurate, balanced, thorough, and clear.

However, because biomedical ethics is riding a wave of public commotion, such careful reporting is easily cast aside in the name of sensationalism. So-called "biomedical ethicists" are quoted not because they have nuanced views, but because the view of X clashes with Y on a matter of controversy. The net result is to convey the impression of sheer moral relativism to the readership, as though deeper analysis of clashing views cannot often lead to reasoned consensus.

For example, when X distorts the facts or obviously misinterprets them, a good reporter should point this out. In the negative sense of the word, "ideological" refers to the systematic elimination or distortion of empirical facts in order to support a particular perspective. Ideologue X is pitted against ideologue Y, giving the impression that there is no objectivity to ethics. The reader throws his or her hands into the air and utters, "Well, anything goes."

Visually, we see conflicting placards on opposite sides of the street or doorway. We hear one side shouting against the other. Acrimony rules, and reasoning fades. There is no sustained analysis.

Of course, on some issues, such as abortion or assisted suicide, conflicting opinions have been perennial and will remain so. But frequently, with the guidance of good reasoning and with careful communication, consensus can be forged. Reporters should look for the *unum* as well as for the *pluribus*, for the universal and the relative.

There is no substitute for careful study, both of the biomedical facts of an issue and of the social-ethical debates that surround it. Superficial reporting that uses unexplained and misunderstood terms is a continuing obstacle to moral progress.

My telephone rings regularly with calls from reporters on some issue about which I know rather little. I am in the habit of directing reporters to others more competent than I. Regrettably, some biomedical ethicists comment about anything and everything. This approach can benefit the source as his or her fame spreads. But such a temptation must be resisted, even though educational institutions love media exposure.

We need a return to the public world, to the spirit of enlightenment and reason that allows for serious conversation across traditions even when traditions disagree.

REPORTING ABOUT MEDICINE

By JAMES S. TODD, M. D., general surgeon and executive vice president of the American Medical Association

Journalism and medicine are alike in many ways. They involve highly motivated professionals, adept at examining a broad spectrum of data, who, by their observations, research, analytical skills and experience, are able to diagnose and illuminate some of the ills of society, with some hope of correcting them.

I work in a particular place where medicine and journalism come together. As executive vice president of the American Medical Association, this country's largest organization of medical doctors, I became the representative of American physicians and their principal spokesperson throughout an historic era of ferment and change.

As the badly needed reform of our health care delivery system became a top national priority, I testified on Capitol Hill and met often with President Clinton, the First Lady, key congressional leaders and many others involved in health care. I also met and talked to thousands of journalists, from all over the country and abroad.

Here are some guideposts that may help you to cover medical stories effectively:

• To be a science writer is to be a scholar. Seek the best information from the most authoritative source and learn and understand the complexity of health care. Don't expect the experts you interview to educate you on a whole subject. They will lack the time *and* the patience. As a courtesy, you should command some basic information on your subject's area of expertise. A two-day "mini-internship," seeing patients with physicians of different specialties, is available through many local medical societies and will be a real help in getting started.

• Understand that science is almost always uncertain, and medicine in particular is full of disagreement and controversy. No clinical trial is ever perfect. Understand statistics and polls. Try to achieve balance.

• Remember your audience and try to educate them. Remember, it's what you emphasize, as much as what you write, that will influence readers.

• Don't parrot conventional wisdom; instead, redefine wisdom. Don't write what you think readers want to read. Challenge their intellects.

• Bring no preconceived biases to your story; beware of those things about which you are absolutely certain! Try to educate objectively—opinions belong on the editorial page. Remember that working on deadlines may prevent full investigation of an issue and diminish the quality and completeness of your work.

• Don't seek controversy to assure publication. Remember that cynicism destroys objectivity and pejorative writing does a disservice to subject and reader. Don't be afraid to recognize and mention the good, as well as the bad.

• Recognize the ambivalence of being a physician today—that doctors have conflicting pressures unknown a generation ago.

They are torn between providing the best care for their patients and the confusion of red tape, regulations, and societal problems that now beset medicine.

• Finally, if you report on health care, try to specialize in it. The best journalists stay within a chosen field. Journalism—like medicine—requires constant study and continuing education. For the reader's sake, there should be no such thing as a general practitioner in journalism.

REPORTING RELIGION

By GEORGE M. MARSDEN, Francis A. McAnaney Professor of History at the University of Notre Dame

Suppose that a person who reported on music never played a musical instrument, had seldom paid attention to music, and knew next to nothing about the various types of music. That is the equivalent to how religion is often treated in the media. There are, of course, important exceptions. Some major newspapers and national magazines have outstanding religion reporters who are truly expert in their subject and judicious in reporting it. As a whole, however, religion stories are low on the list of media priorities. Beginning reporters are therefore liable to find themselves assigned to religion stories on which they have no accurate background knowledge.

Three major problems arise from this ignorance. The first is alienation of expert sources. Most experts are happy to talk to reporters, but they are not so happy to provide them with lengthy elementary instruction. Reporters who do not know the difference between evangelicals and fundamentalists, or even sometimes the issues that separate Protestants and Catholics, should not be imposing on expert sources to learn rudiments. It is as though a reporter called up Itzhak Perlman, but did not know the difference between brass and woodwinds.

The second problem, related to the first, is the stereotyped story shaped by endlessly repeated popular images. For instance, one is the Elmer Gantry story, the disgraced evangelist, now updated by Jim Bakker and Jimmy Swaggart. Stereotyping often controls what is seen to be religious news. The Pope may speak on a dozen important topics, but only what he says about sexuality may be reported. Or the vast majority of reporting on the African-American churches during the past thirty-five years has been variations of what might be called "the Martin Luther King story." African-American church leaders are recognized as newsworthy only to the degree that they participate in politics. Few people know anything about what else inner-city churches may be doing.

Stereotyping is closely related to a third problem, that of sensationalism. This problem, like stereotyping, is not at all unique to religion reporting. It is, however, exacerbated because of ignorance of substantial matters regarding American religion. The easiest way to deal with a complex subject that one does not understand well is to sensationalize it. Look for the extreme statements. Do not report the qualifications.

So what I would like beginning reporters to know is strikingly simple. Religion is too complex a subject to be reported on responsibly without prior preparation. Nobody should be reporting on religion who has not had at least one course in the history or the sociology of religion in America. The self-motivated could read the equivalent number of texts and supplementary readings on their own. Since the vast majority of American religion is Christian, they should have a solid grounding in the differences among major types of Christians. They should also be familiar with the other major religions prominent in our culture. Otherwise, they are likely simply to be contributing to misunderstanding about a dynamic and complex dimension of our culture.

Perspective...

WHAT THE WORLD'S PREEMINENT EVANGELIST WISHES JOURNALISTS KNEW ABOUT REPORTING RELIGION

By the REV. BILLY GRAHAM, who has preached the Gospel to more people in live audiences than anyone else in history—more than 180 million people in more than 180 countries. He is regularly listed in the Gallup poll's list of "Ten Most Admired Men in the World." The Gallup organization recently described him as the dominant figure in that poll over the last half century. The following comments are taken from an address that Dr. Graham gave to the American Society of Newspaper Editors in Washington, D. C., in 1994.

I've dealt with editors and journalists all over the world, and without hesitation I believe that the American newspapers have the highest standards of professionalism and integrity in the world.

I owe a great deal to the print media. Over more than 50 years of working together with you and your electronic colleagues, you have always been generous and fair in your reporting of me. My ministry would never have developed as it has without the coverage you have given it.

Some have suggested that the day of the newspaper is over because of television. But I believe the opposite is the case, for only newspapers can probe in-depth both the news and the background behind the news. In fact, I believe the role of newspapers in the electronic age is more important than ever. As Bill Moyers said about television, "Its god is brevity." Archbishop Keeler of Baltimore tells about being asked by one of the major morning television shows to discuss the Catholic church's position on abortion, birth control, and priestly celibacy—all in 30 seconds!

You have asked me to speak today on the topic of "Newspaper Coverage of Religion and How It Can Be Improved." I am not sure whether that means I'm supposed to talk about how newspaper coverage can be improved, or how religion can be improved!

I am convinced this is an important topic because religion continues to be an important part of American life. In fact, I sense that many people are alarmed about some of the trends in our society and are beginning to wonder if Professor Stephen Carter may not be right when he says we are paying the price of banishing religion from public life. George Gallup's latest poll indicates that 69 percent of Americans are members of a church or synagogue or another religious body. Furthermore, in any given week 42 percent of Americans attend at least one religious service. Someone has pointed out that this is more than attend all professional baseball games in an entire year.

I like the term Norman Lear used a few months ago at the National Press Club when he talked about "gropers"—people who are sincerely searching for religious values and beliefs.

And these people are your readers.

And yet I agree with Rabbi James Rudin of the American Jewish Committee who said, "Religion is one of the most under-reported activities in America." One religion reporter pointed out in *Editor and Publisher* some months ago that out of some 1,600 dailies in America, only about 50 had a full-time religion reporter.

As I travel from city to city, I find religious news is often relegated to a few ads and columns on Saturday and, in many instance, is on the same page as either the classified ads or the obituaries.

And yet I believe those of you in the media and those of us in religion have much in common.

Many people ask me what is an evangelist? An evangelist, in a sense, is a newspaper man because in the old Greek city-states they did not have television or newspapers, but they would have a town crier that would go up and down the streets announcing the latest news. He was called an evangelist. That's where the word evangelist comes from. He's an announcer, he's a writer, he's a crier of news. And the news is, of course, in the *New Testament* the Good News of the Gospel of Jesus Christ, that God loves you and that he is interested in you—whoever you are, whatever the color of your skin, whatever your ethnic background, He loves you.

Thus, you and I have in common that we both are in the business of communication. We also are both in the people business. In addition, truth is essential in your work just as it is in mine. But also we both want to make a difference in our world.

In its finest tradition, there has always been a reformist streak in the American press—revealing corruption, questioning misguided trends and policies, rooting out such social evils as racism and injustice. In this you share a common goal with America's religious heritage; and, I believe, this is one reason the founding fathers included both freedom of religion and freedom of the press in the same First Amendment.

In the long run the loss of one freedom will bring about the loss of the other. And I believe we need to learn to work together to reveal and reverse the problems that are threatening the very fabric of our society.

What is the problem? You are far more qualified than I to give an answer. But let me suggest several possibilities.

For one thing, much of what happens in religion is not news, by your definition, and I understand that. You are concerned with change; we are concerned with that which we believe to be changeless. You are interested in that which breaks the pattern of normal life—disasters, political upheavals, wars, the cruelties and foibles of human nature, conflicts between people and nations. We are interested in what goes on, often unseen, in the hearts of individuals: hopes reborn, purpose restored, guilt removed, love rekindled.

In addition, religion is such a vast subject that it must seem almost incomprehensible to those on the outside. Some of you may be afraid of offending some readers in our pluralistic society by dealing with religious topics, and you find it easier to avoid them altogether. Or the moral failures or extreme positions of a few religious leaders may have made you cynical of religion generally.

When we had some problems a few years ago with some religious leaders who were called evangelists—[although] several of them were evangelists, most of them [really] were pastors—I thought to myself, there are hundreds of airplanes that take off and land at our airports everyday, here in Washington, for example, and there's no news. But let one of them crash and it's news. There are thousands of clergy in America who are doing their job faithfully, and they need your support and your backing— but let one of them crash, and that's the big news. Many people get the idea that that's the church or that's religion, and they turn away.

And many of your reporters have little religious background and feel inadequate or uninterested when they come to religious news.

What can be done to improve the coverage of religious news?

Let me make four brief suggestions, which I hope will stimulate your thinking.

First: Make it a matter of policy to report more religious news for your readers, both from your local community and from the broader world.

I firmly believe the stories are to be found. In fact, some of those stories could add a whole new flavor to your newspapers. Our front pages are filled with stories of abuse, fraud, rape, mutilation, murder, war, starvation—the list is endless. And these are part of the news, for tragedy seems to be the rule rather than the exception of what happens in the world. But I believe the public is tired of a steady diet of unrelenting bad news—and I expect many of you are too.

Where is the good news? Much of it is to be found in the quiet work of people who are motivated by religious values.

The bad news is that our cities are crumbling under the weight of problems like poverty, gangs, drugs, unemployment, homelessness, poor education, and so forth. The good news is that there are countless new programs run by churches and individuals who are sheltering the homeless, feeding the hungry, developing special programs for job training and education, and rehabilitating those whose lives have been ruined by drugs and alcohol. For example, I have a grandson who is youth minister of a Presbyterian church in Coral Springs, Florida. He had 20 of his young people at Homestead, Florida, the day after Hurricane Andrew hit, and they went down day after day helping in every way they could.

There's an organization around the country today that is organizing to bring to Washington thousands of people, and also thousands and hundreds of thousands of pledge cards. It's called Love That Waits. It was started by an organization called Youth For Christ and carried on by the various denominations, both Catholic and Protestant. They are saying wait for sex until you get married. There are thousands of them. To me that's good news from any vantage point.

The bad news is that AIDS continues to ravage our society. The good news is there are thousands of small organizations throughout the country—Jewish, as well as Catholic and Protestant—that reach out to others in the name of Christ, sharing His love and compassion. There are thousands of groups that meet weekly for prayer in the most surprising and unsuspected places. There is hardly a professional athletic team that doesn't have within it a small group that regularly meets for prayer and Bible study. Each one could be an interesting story.

My *second* suggestion: Probe the religious, moral and ethical dimensions of some of the stories that make the headlines. Some of the major stories that cross your desks every day may have profound moral and ethical dimensions—dimensions that often are overlooked in the rush to report the bare facts. I think of many of the things that are happening today in medicine, for example, or science, or legal affairs, or even business. I don't think we can understand the conflicts in places like the Balkans or in the Middle East without understanding something of the religious dimensions and backgrounds to those stories.

There is often a religious dimension to the news that needs to be probed. And in the long run it may be the most significant story, because religion often sways whole societies and can even change the course of history.

My *third* suggestion: Reach out to the religious leaders, both clergy and lay people, in your own communities.

Many of the religious leaders in your community would welcome an invitation to lunch, or to visit in your offices once or twice a year. Be sure to include the lay people because many of the lay people are the religious leaders in some communities, and they would be honored and thrilled to get an invitation from you to come and have lunch with your editors. I've had lunch with editors in various cities throughout the country, including Mrs. [Katharine] Graham, who invited me to the Washington *Post* on two occasions to have lunch with their editors, and the Los Angeles *Times* and the Chicago *Tribune*; and they have been great enlightening periods for me.

It has been my privilege to sit with many editorial boards and have an exchange. I learned a lot when I was in Atlanta recently. Tom Johnson, president of CNN, invited all the editors and managers of the TV stations, news directors, etc., to a luncheon at CNN headquarters. And no one declined his invitation, and we had over an hour and a half of fruitful discussion. A couple of years ago Tom Murphy, president of Capital Cities, along with my longtime friend Leonard Goldensen, invited the top news men and women in television to a luncheon in New York. We had an excellent time of discussion and getting to know each other. Such people as Dan Rather, Peter Jennings, Diane Sawyer, and many others were there. These are just a few examples of what could be done on the local level if you took the leadership

Finally, I encourage you to seek qualified journalists for the "religion beat" who have an interest in or a knowledge of religion.

Those who have some knowledge of religion will be far better qualified to deal with religious news stories fully and fairly. And I believe such people are to be found. I would encourage seminaries to have courses on journalism to train journalists, who could go into the press with a knowledge of religion in their background. They should have the highest standards of objectivity, but they also should be expected to understand their field just as much as you expect a sports reporter to understand sports. If you sent a reporter out to cover a football game who knew nothing about football, he would come back with the most distorted version for the newspaper! The same is true in the field of religion.

Just as I have asked you to explore the religious dimension of human experience and to reflect it more thoroughly in your news coverage, I also appeal to you as an editor, as a person, as an individual here today to explore the religious dimension of your own life.

Our lamps must be lit, and we need a clear commitment to the things that really matter the most. Then we need to apply our faith to every aspect of our lives.

That is my challenge to you today—to let Christ, who is the light of the world, light your life and heart with the presence and purpose of God. That is what really matters.

REPORTING CHURCH ORGANIZATIONS

By PHYLLIS ZAGANO, Associate Professor and director of Boston University's Institute for Democratic Communication. Her books include *Religion & Public Affairs* (1987), *Woman to Woman: An Anthology of Women's Spiritualities* (1993), and *On Prayer* (1994).

There are over 1200 "primary" religious bodies or denominations within the United States, but the commonest are Roman Catholicism, Protestant denominations, Judaism, and various Muslim sects. Many of these religious bodies have official spokesmen; some have media-based ministries. All are part of the fabric of American society. Probably none receives adequate or appropriate coverage in the secular press.

The secular press may cover a religious or secular story. The problem many reporters have arises when the lines are blurred. For example, abortion can be either a religious or a secular story, or both. If the question at hand is how a particular denomination deals with that question internally, as a question of dogmatic teaching, the story is clearly a religious story. If the question is how the Supreme Court has ruled on a particular interpretation of the law, the question is clearly a secular story. Where things become confused is when a religious denomination makes specific intercessions relative to the law. Is that a secular story? A religious story? Or both? A number of studies have suggested that the secular press does not understand religious issues. Others have presented the view that religious denominations as a whole do not understand media.

Many, if not most, denominations have a collective distrust of the media. In this they are similar to other highly structured organizations—such as government or major corporations—whose very structures lend an inherent inability to react reflexively to media inquiries. The fact that bureaucracy, be it in government, business, or church, creates a lumbering reality that cannot quickly respond to media, intensifies the distrust the one has for the other. Media are willing to distrust official spokesmen, since they know that official spokesmen will always present the "party line." Bureaucracies, in turn, cannot fathom why their official statements are not believed. With religious denominations, the situation is exacerbated by the problem (and assertion) of truth, combined with an attempt to control information. One study succinctly presents the problem relative to the Catholic Church, and by extension to other denominations as well:

> Any attempt to consider the connection between church and press must contend with formidable obstacles concerning the Roman Catholic Church's historical distrust of the press and the popular media of television and film.

Clearly, if one party distrusts the other, no communication is possible. If each party distrusts the other, attempts at communication reduce to outright warfare. On many issues, church spokesmen and journalists are merely not communicating; on some issues they are quite frankly shooting at each other. In all cases, they need to recognize that the First Amendment works both ways.

It has become commonplace to say that religion is ill-served by the media. Some will even contend that media purposefully ignore religion and religious issues except when they involve scandal or when they are such major events that they cannot be ignored. The Catholic Church's stance on abortion is well known, but most press commentaries seem to center on an argument about the separation of church and state (conveniently forgetting that the First Amendment to the Constitution protects the free exercise of religion as well as speech).

Stories about religion are often poorly covered. There are many who contend that the reportage of essentially religious stories is biased. At least one recent study by the Media Research Center has found significant anti-religious bias in broadcast news coverage, while suggesting that print reportage is more balanced. The stories that often rely on scandal and unproved allegations too often overtake positive reporting of religion or religious belief in America.

Catholicism has the largest number of adherents of any organized religious body in the country—nearly 20% of the population—yet, it is often the target of both satire and scandal. For example, a recent editorial cartoon in *Newsday* by Doug Marlette depicted the Pope wearing a large "No Women Priests" button. A passage of scripture quoted nearby pointed like an arrow to his head: "Upon this rock I will build my church." One hundred letters protested, and *Newsday* felt obliged to issue an apology, to which Marlette replied in a Viewpoints piece: "It is always bad news when a newspaper apologizes for expressing an opinion—bad news for the First Amendment, bad news for journalism and bad news for readers.... The Catholic Church I know is big enough and secure enough to laugh at the cartoon."

Other matters are not so humorous—or so obvious. Several scandals relative to alleged priestly pederasty have rocked the media in recent years, from the eventually accepted 1989 allegations against Rev. Bruce Ritter, head of Covenant House in New York City, to the discredited allegations against Joseph Bernardin, the late, beloved cardinal of Chicago. An important fact of all the reporting on allegations is that when allegations are disproved, they are rarely, if ever, covered with the same intensity as the charges. In one other case in Chicago, the exonerated priest was brought to trial after one church and three state committees found no evidence for the allegations. When the case was adjudicated in his behalf, the Chicago *Sun-Times* ran a small piece that did not match his earlier excoriation.

Scandal aside, all denominational discussion moves into the political realm from time to time, and it is there that political writers often misconstrue denominational beliefs. The problem is complex to begin with. It is further complicated by the confusing patchwork of religions, religious spokesmen, religious organizations, and organizations that use denominational names. Because Catholicism is among the most highly structured of denominations, it serves well as an example. One is Catholic by dint of one's adherence to Catholic dogma, just as one is Lutheran by adherence to Lutheran dogma, Jewish by adherence to Jewish dogma, and the like. Certain beliefs are so central to Catholicism, as other beliefs are so central to Lutheranism or Judaism, as to put one outside the circle of membership. That is, some beliefs are such that, while holding them might not make one a Catholic, not holding them automatically excludes one from membership. Hence, the reporter must clearly distinguish among, for example, Catholics for a Free Choice or Catholic Coalition for Gay Civil Rights, both non-official organizations, and the National Conference of Catholic Bishops, the official organization of Roman Catholic Bishops in the United States. Other denominations have this confusing situation as well; for example, in North America the Unitarian Universalist Association of Congregations is far more an official spokesman than the Unitarian Universalist Peace Network, even though the latter may appear to have a political outlook identical to the former.

Where the reporter can be misled, therefore, is where religion and politics cross so completely that, although they are indistinguishable, neither part is properly covered or political motives are ascribed to a particular religious action. The murder of four missionaries in El Salvador in 1980 brought forth this comment in a letter to the editor of the New York *Times*:

> The media should resist the temptation to demean the death of those sister-heroes by ascribing ideological and political content to the cause of their deaths. The establishment of another kingdom was their sole motivation for being present among the rural poor of El Salvador.

But the comment itself presents the problem. "The establishment of another kingdom" is an easily misunderstood metaphor and can rapidly be translated into other languages in political terms.

A similar although quite distinct religio-political discussion arose with the publication of the United Methodist Church's statement on war and peace. While the United Methodist Church has official guidelines for dissemination of official information, a great deal of information and discussion about the Church's statement was not controlled by official channels—the media story of the statement took on somewhat a life of its own, and its text was first published by the Washington *Post*. While most newspapers accurately reported the real news story that the third largest denomination in the United States had rejected *any* use of nuclear weapons, even for deterrence—none really reported accurately on the reaction of members of the United Methodist Church at large. For example, it was at the end of a small piece that Marjorie Hyer of the Washington *Post* wrote that a survey conducted by the *United Methodist Reporter* found that, while two-thirds of

37,988 United Methodist congregations heard the letter read at worship services, "responses ranged from boredom to resentment at the intrusion of what was politics in worship sessions." Reporters often referred to the text for substantiation of its assertions, rather than to Methodist teachings, thereby missing the most interesting part of the story.

This is but one of many examples where religious discussion comes into the political realm. Many Americans recognize that political discussion in the United States has deep religious roots; so the reporter must be aware that the reader might actually *expect* to know what various religious bodies think of a political question. This attitude was underscored recently in a letter to the editor of the St. Louis *Post-Dispatch*:

> Religious folk have always been involved in American politics, whether it be Scotch-Irish Presbyterians supporting the independence movement, Congregationalists and Northern Methodists pressing abolition, liberal Christians pressing civil rights, nuclear disarmament and peace in Vietnam, or conservative Christians pressing traditional values.... There is nothing un-American about folks getting hip-deep in politics because they believe their opponents are wrong philosophically. We've been doing it for 200 years. What would be wrong would be to act as if religion were such a private affair we expect its proponents to keep their beliefs to themselves.

It would seem that the admixture of religion and politics in the United States is permanent.

Recommendations for Reporting

Where will religion—with or without politics—be in the pages of tomorrow's newspapers? How will this part of American life be portrayed? To what extent will other media report on these same issues?

Reporters and editors are increasingly aware of the critical role religion plays not only in American daily life, but in the lives of most of the billions of people in the world. Tomorrow's reporters and editors must be prepared to report professionally on religion. Ethnic and racial strife world-wide often have a religious component. We need only to look toward Salman Rushdie, and the stories of Waco, Texas, the World Trade Center, as well as those stories emanating from the Balkans, India, Northern Ireland, the Middle East, Iraq and Iran, to see how serious religious conflict can become. Churches and religious bodies world-wide are preparing to deal with the continuing media explosion, while complaining about the coverage they receive. And the American public in general is living a new spiritual awakening.

Various recent studies and major articles, including an eighty-six-page report entitled "Bridging the Gap: Religion and the News Media" from the Freedom Forum First Amendment Center at Vanderbilt University, have focused on the importance of religion reporting. At a recent meeting of the Religion Newswriters Association, Newhouse News Service Washington bureau chief Deborah Howell told the gathering:

> This is the best time for religion reporters. We're at a place where we can push editors for more time, more space and more resources. We can push these stories onto pages one and the metro front because they belong there....

Obviously, religion stories will get to the front pages when they are of such major impact that they would arrive there even without a religious component. No one would suggest that the World Trade Center bombing or the plight of the people in the Branch Davidian compound in Waco, Texas, would be any more or less covered without a religious component. What is unique in current analysis is the recognition of how important the religious component to these stories is, and therefore how important it is to have reporters and editors properly trained to cover the stories.

The argument that religion reporting is a more serious business than it has seemed to be in the recent past is supported by the fact that various newspapers—including the Dallas *Morning News*, the *News Tribune* (Tacoma, Wash.) and the Concord (N. H.) *Monitor*—have added prototype religion sections, while other media, such as ABC News, have added religion reporters. No longer can the religious component be left to chance, for the understanding of the entire story may depend upon it.

On the whole, the future reporter must be aware of the role religion and religious institutions play in American life and political thought. While more and more individuals will choose to become specialists, and more and more news organizations will develop the specialty, it is incumbent upon every reporter and editor to be aware of religion as a major component of the world news.

REPORTING MASS TRAGEDY

By RAY BROMLEY, Professor in the Department of Geography and Planning at the University of Albany, SUNY. Dr. Bromley is researching the impact of the 1990 Happy Land Social Club arson on victims' relatives and friends and on the seven survivors. The fire killed eighty-seven people, earning the grim record of being the biggest mass murder ever committed in the continental United States.

A mass tragedy can be defined as a single event causing at least 25 deaths and/or at least 100 serious injuries. Mass tragedies occur fairly frequently, but they are highly unpredictable in terms of location, type and scale. They include "natural" disasters (landslide, forest fire, flood, hurricane, earthquake, volcanic eruption, etc.), a wide range of "man-made disasters" (plane and train crashes, shipwrecks, dam bursts, building fires and collapses, industrial explosions, etc.), and "mass murder," including many genocidal massacres and war crimes. In reality, of course, "natural," "man-made" and "mass murder" are fuzzy terms with considerable overlaps. Thus, a flash flood may kill because settlement was permitted or even encouraged in flood-prone areas, and a forest fire may be started "for fun." An earthquake usually kills mainly through building, freeway and bridge collapses and through explosions in gas pipelines and chemical plants—all of which could be avoided if building and industrial safety standards were raised and strictly followed.

Sooner or later, almost every country and locality will be hit by a mass tragedy, but many people live their whole lives without direct exposure or involvement in such a tragedy.

However hard we try to "be prepared," tragedies may never come or may catch us by surprise. The timing of mass tragedies has no relation to journalistic work schedules or print deadlines. Without hundreds of teams of reporters deployed in a wide range of different locations and working shifts so as always to have someone ready to report a tragedy—an absurdly expensive option—there is no way that the media can rely on specialized mass tragedy reporters. Mass tragedies are not like sports, fashion, movie critiques, domestic politics or international affairs, with their specialized reporting teams. Instead, mass tragedy is lumped together with general news *and* local events—handled by generalists and often by the newest and least experienced reporters.

The coverage given to mass tragedies by the U. S. media varies enormously, and its volume is rarely related to the numbers of dead and seriously injured. Such common African, Asian and Latin American tragedies as ferry sinkings, bus crashes and landslides engulfing urban shanty-towns receive little or no mention. They mainly affect poor people and are considered of little importance by the media. Earthquakes, hurricanes, volcanic eruptions, plane crashes and other more "normal" tragedies in foreign countries receive more attention, with most detailed coverage when they occur in "sister" countries like Britain and Canada. Genocidal massacres and war crimes in foreign countries receive widely varying degrees of coverage, ranging from almost total avoidance of the topic to intense scrutiny when U. S. interests are considered to be endangered. U. S. mass tragedies usually get more coverage than foreign tragedies, but most fade from the news within a few days of the event. It is very rare that a mass tragedy, like the siege and burning of the Branch Davidian Compound in Waco, Texas, provides the opportunity for CNN-style ongoing reporting with abundant video coverage. Most mass tragedies take place without prior warning, filming or recording.

Journalists usually find it difficult to "personalize" mass tragedy, giving it a human dimension and a style suitable to the tabloid press. The conventional media wisdom is that the public wants more and more news about personable stars and people who could be "my next-door neighbor," but readers and viewers find it boring and depressing to be continually bombarded with reporting on mass tragedy. Thus, accusations against the rich and famous, suburban scandals and serial killers are reported *ad infinitum* (viz. Michael Jackson, O. J., Tonya and Nancy, Amy and Joey, the Bobbitts, Jeffrey Dahmer, etc.), while mass tragedies are rarely the subject of ongoing coverage or investigative reporting. Mass tragedies are usually "momentary infilling"—given a high profile when the flow of other news is sparse, but dropped quickly because it is presumed there is no ongoing public interest. They are *"what* news," not *"who* news" or *"why* news."

Despite the enormous diversity of mass tragedies, a few common features crop up again and again. First and foremost, the emergency workers and spokespersons who can be contacted in the immediate aftermath of a tragedy do not have a comprehensive knowledge of its causes or the range of victims. Most spokespersons have a legitimate concern to promote calm and order and to diffuse information, but some are engaged in "damage control," seeking to close off lines of inquiry and to avoid accusations of blame. Most mass tragedies have multiple causes and a considerable diversity of victims. Time and time again, reporters oversimplify both cause and effect, missing perspectives on mass tragedy stories that would merit investigative reporting. Most reporters fail to locate and consult "tragedy experts" and specialized information sources, and those who do often rely on inadequate materials and oversimplified indexes. As a result, the tragedy story dies quickly and no broader social lessons are learned.

Most mass tragedies have three key dimensions that together sometimes cause the tragedy and on other occasions simply increase its toll of deaths, injuries and damage: greed, negligence, and public apathy. Responsible journalism will seek out and expose greed and negligence and will seek to increase public awareness of risks and how they can be reduced. In major fire tragedies in night clubs and discotheques, for example, similar aggravating circumstances occur again and again: inadequate, locked or blocked fire exits; inflammable materials used in furnishings and decorations; malfunctioning alarms, sprinklers and emergency lights; angry, intoxicated patrons setting fire to the entrance or to garbage stacked outside; complex building and fire codes that insist on so many minutiae that every establishment is in violation and no priority attention is given to serious hazards; negligent and often corrupt police and inspectors who see major hazards but turn a blind eye; multi-tier bureaucracies that incapacitate diligent inspectors and bury their recommendations; and greedy club managers, landlords and building owners who disclaim all responsibility for the hazardous state of their premises.

One of the most distressing features of mass tragedies is that they tend to repeat themselves. The lessons of earlier tragedies are not learnt, and the public is often unaware of high risk situations. Journalists usually miss a vital advocacy opportunity—to represent the interests of the tragedy victims and their relatives and friends, most of whom are relatively poor, powerless and ordinary people. This interest is not just a search for "relief"—food, shelter, medical and funeral expenses, etc.—but also for a fitting memorial to the victims, and a sense of meaning and mission that emanates from the tragedy. Victims of Pan Am 103 provides a wonderful example of a successful grass-roots organization emerging from a mass tragedy, fighting corporate power, governmental red tape and international terrorism to ensure that loved ones didn't die in vain.

The media have tremendous outreach and command nearly universal attention. They can play a vital role in combating greed, negligence and public apathy toward mass tragedy, and in "enabling" and "empowering" grass-roots movements. In recent years, however, they have not played a major role in combating mass tragedy in the United States. Instead, the key role has been played in very self-interested fashion by the legal profession through investigation and tort suits on behalf of the victims. Tort suits usually last several years and are often settled out of court. Though a few court orders for punitive damages receive widespread publicity, tort suit settlements are usually confidential and are rarely reported by the media. Thus, mass tragedy, though often subjected to intense publicity for a day or two, tends to be resolved years later in the private domain. Attorneys, relatives and survivors may eventually get their compensation, and a few corporations may change their policies, but there is no social learning process to prevent tragedy from occurring again.

REPORTING PERSONAL TRAGEDY

By PATRICK SEAN MOFFETT, CFC, Ph.D., Christian Brother, former professor of psychology and pastoral counseling at Iona College, New Rochelle, N. Y. He has been President of Boys' and Girls' Towns of Italy since 1988.

The Boys' and Girls' Towns of Italy offer a unique perspective on yesterday's headlines. The "citizens" of these villages are the survivors of various forms of tragedy: natural calamities; domestic violence; war; terrorism; organized crime; physical, moral, and psychological abuse.

Democratic youth communities were a practical response to the tragic situation of homeless children in the wake of World War II. That they continue to exist today and that their system of self-government is viewed as a model for educational projects throughout the world is a tribute to the resourcefulness of the young people who, generation after generation, have shaped the development of these unique "towns."

Among the administrative functions of the young mayor of the Boys' Town of Rome are those ceremonial in which he officially welcomes visitors: heads of state and ministers of social affairs who arrive from all parts of the world to ask what the reality of this small village might suggest concerning the situations of the homeless youth of their own countries; educators, psychologists and social workers who are challenged to consider how they might be underestimating what young people can do for themselves; journalists who are fascinated by the untold sequel to stories that recently captured everyone's attention.

Visitors are impressed to find such energy, enthusiasm, and optimism in young people who have known so directly the problems of a troubled globe. Certainly the expression of such qualities is facilitated by the security and freedom of the new environment; however, these are gifts that the children bring with them. One cannot help but note their resilience, their capacity to deal with forced separations, to form new relationships, to pick up the pieces of their broken lives and move ahead with courage and hope.

In retrospect, the reports of the tragedies that rendered these children homeless seem incomplete. Some of the children have made scrapbooks of the newspaper clippings that tell of the war, or of the accident or the arrest of an abusing parent. Frequently there was a sensitive portrayal of the sorry details of human suffering and loss; however, there was no indication of what had to be present at that moment—the possibility of what has since been realized so beautifully. It is the rare journalist who identifies within the victims of tragic events the resources that will permit the person to go beyond survival to significant new life and new energy. And yet it is in such personal triumphs that we come to know the real story of our civilization.

In an era of information overload, that which is reported as "news" has a privileged role in shaping our understanding of the world we share. Because the happy endings of yesterday's stories are no longer "news," we are systematically deprived of information that could be a source of hope and encouragement. A new generation of journalists is challenged to find ways of discerning and communicating a fuller truth.

The discipline in which I received my professional training owes much of its wisdom to children who awakened us to the role of empathy in achieving insight into the dynamics of human motivation and therapeutic relationships. Empathy is the art of entering the life-space of another and seeing the world through her or his eyes. A capacity for empathy is present from early childhood and if practiced can develop throughout life. It relies in part on fantasy and imagination often associated with—but hopefully not restricted to—youth. We who are somewhat beyond the wonder-filled world of childhood do well to let a child reintroduce us to part of our story that may be hidden from those with a more rational and analytic mindset.

Were I ever to accept the great responsibility of a journalist for communicating to others what is happening in our world, I'd want to search out a child, on or off the scene, whose life will be dramatically altered by the story I am about to report. It couldn't be an interview—children rarely are at their best in such adult models of communication. No, I'd simply want to be present to the child and let the child animate the empathic vision that might let me see the good news that ought be told if the story is to be complete.

REPORTING SPORTS

By LESLIE FRAZIER, cornerback on the 1986 Super Bowl Chicago Bears and a football coach

If sports were reported simply as a chronology of facts, people would need to go elsewhere for entertainment. That is why it would be my wish that those who report sports embrace a different hierarchy of values. As a future sports journalist, consider what your attitude should be in reporting.

I would urge you to write with wisdom, informing your work with a purity of mind and consideration of spirit rarely seen in contemporary sports reporting. I would hope that sports reporters would show greater impartiality in their reporting and more sincerity. Don't blow something up just for the sake of blowing something up.

Be a wise teacher as a sports journalist. Remember that your number one job is to impart knowledge to people. So ponder and search out and organize material that will achieve that purpose. Be sure to find just the right words. Make certain that what you write is true, and avoid unnecessary embellishment.

Ask any athlete, and he will tell you that he wishes, the media reported sports with less bias. Many of us feel reporters all too often put their own slant on an event or a quote. Our hope is that reporters would be more scrupulous in reporting the facts of an event, whether they're covering a boxing match or a football game. As a former pro athlete and fan, I am not concerned with the opinion of a sportscaster or writer of an event. If I wanted an opinion, I would turn to the opinion page.

Those who write about sports and athletics should take their work seriously because the public does. I am among those who thinks sports has a profound influence on our society. The reason for this is that many Americans use sports as an outlet or getaway from their daily activities. They look to sports journalists to provide them information on this very important world.

One need only look at the salaries today's pro athletes are making to see the central place sports now plays in the lives of so many Americans. This is never more true than with the youth of America. Countless numbers of them look to pro athletes as role models; and since they cannot know the athletes personally, they turn to the media for glimpses of their favorite athletes. I would hope that sports journalists keep this in mind when they report athletics.

In the 1990s media coverage of sports has gradually taken on the tone of the tabloids. Outlets have busied themselves with reporting the personal lives of athletes, which has taken the story off the field. The media seem to take a personal delight in attacking the pro athlete who may make millions of dollars. It is in this kind of reporting that I see the greatest bias of the media.

Sports journalists need to look through the eyes of the sport they are reporting. They should be conscious of not taking an adversarial approach. The focus should be on athletic performance and not personality off the field. I often wonder whose values reporters use when they so quickly judge athletes. From my point of view that is the root of the problem in sports reporting. My own personal standard as a player, coach, and anything I am a part of is predicated on my belief in Jesus Christ. I am certain that the closer that we get to the values implicit in the Golden Rule, the better will be our sports reporting.

11

ORGANIZING THE NEWS STORY

The creation of a good news report depends on the quality and amount of the resources available. Those resources are facts—information obtained through the news gathering process. To write an effective news story, it's crucial that the reporter do a good job of organizing the facts. The task involves these requirements: (1) examining the initial facts imaginatively and thoroughly, (2) abstracting the essentials of the news event, (3) composing an accurate summary lead to introduce the story, (4) assessing the importance of information to be used in the story, (6) and anticipating questions that a reader would ask.

The quality and amount of information available for creating any news report are going to determine, obviously, the effectiveness with which knowledge and understanding of any new event or development can be communicated from writers to readers. Therefore, it becomes imperative that writers obtain as much relevant information as possible before committing to a

BY JOHN DE MOTT

Dr. De Mott is a former reporter and editor for the Kansas City *Star and Times.* He has taught journalism and mass communication at the University of Memphis, Temple University, Northern Illinois University, Northwestern University, University of Kansas, American University in Cairo, Egypt, and University of Missouri at Kansas City.

particular style of report.

To make certain that you know what you need to know before writing your report, review, extensively, the facts marshaled. Two good methods for doing that exist. Journalists have used both methods many years, more or less semi-consciously. Although no formal term has been assigned to either method, let's refer to them as (1) the three-dimensional exploration of news and (2) an anthropological approach to news.

THE THREE DIMENSIONS OF NEWS

Every news development, regardless of its basic character, has three dimensions: (1) time—chronological or historical context, (2) space—geographical context, and (3) social context. For superior reporting and interpretation, all three of those dimensions should be explored as extensively as practical. The point at which exploration of each dimension begins, of course, is the news event that attracted the journalist's attention originally. For purposes of discussion, let's take the discovery that a community's blood supply is polluted.

Exploring the time dimension backward, one examines the pollution's history. Do any previous occurrences shed light on the current situation's cause? Following the time dimension forward, one explores the pollution's possible consequences.

Exploring the space dimension outward, one looks at how the situation in one's own community fits into that of a broader geographical area—the entire country, perhaps. Exploring the space dimension inward, one looks for differences in blood from differing sources in the home community.

Exploring the social dimension, one looks for perspectives from people—individuals, groups, and organizations—on levels below and above those involved in the immediate news event. Which of them most logically will be affected, have expertise in the matter, or are positioned to have helpful insights into the situation? What persons or organizations are responsible for the situation? For solution of the problem? What do the people most affected have to say? Searching for such perspectives, one moves up and down the community's social hierarchy and also laterally across its organizational structure. The basic character of the event determines which dimensions can be explored most productively and eventually the nature of the report.

THE ANTHROPOLOGICAL APPROACH TO NEWS

For generations, anthropologists and other social scientists have been engaged in efforts to comprehend human behavior and analyze its essential features. One of the most interesting aspects of their study has been the attempt to identify and describe the enduring needs of all humans. From that attempt, anthropologists have developed several lists. One of the most popular is the following:

1. Food—its production and distribution
2. Shelter—community development
3. Sex—love, marriage, the family and child care
4. Physical security—public safety, law and order
5. Work—the exchange of labor for goods
6. Health—physical and mental
7. Education or training
8. Recreation
9. Faith—religion, morality, ethics, values
10. Beauty—"art for art's sake"

Using these needs—and the special interests derived from them—the journalist can obtain insights helpful in the creation of any story, whatever the nature of the news event or development being reported. Will the event or development have any kind of impact on the community's food supply and its use? On construction plans or projects in progress? Is there a sex "angle," or will family and children be affected? Have any laws or government regulations been ignored? Legal liabilities incurred? Is the marketplace being affected, are jobs gained or lost, or are new ways of doing work evolving? Does the new development raise questions concerning public health and its protection? Are new approaches to education suggested? Will the development lead to changes in patterns of play or provide more desirable entertainment opportunities? What philosophies of life, religions, faiths, or concepts of good and bad interface in difficult or painful ways with the development? Does the development satisfy anyone's search for the beautiful—or perhaps offend the sensibilities of others?

Walking around the news development in this way gives the journalist a grasp of its overall nature. The report, as a result of the news writer's anthropological "walk-around," will be much more comprehensive, rich, and insightful.

THE ESSENTIALS OF THE NEWS STORY

Wrapping oneself around the facts available for the report, before one begins to write, is the ultimate secret of good news writing. It is given short shrift too often, however, by news people eager to commit their initial impressions to paper or computer.

Before diving into the report, one needs to abstract the essentials of the news event or development. They are few, but they have stood the test of time as absolute necessities. Social scientists learn that in collecting evidence from observation, no hard and fast rules can be laid down. Observers must always be prepared to take their clues from unanticipated events. That is good advice for the news writer, also, and is precisely what a good editor would tell a journalistic "cub" being sent to cover a news story.

Journalists should follow the lead of social scientists when organizing news reportage. Our task is not unlike that of the anthropologist. Journalists need to be particularly aware of these five dimensions: participants, settings, purpose, social behavior, and frequency and duration.

The Participants

Here one wants to know: who are the participants, how are they related to one another, and how many are there? There are various ways of characterizing the participants, but usually one will want to know at least the following about any person who is being observed: age, sex, official function—e. g., teacher, doctor, spectator, customer, host, club president—in the situation being observed and in the occupational system of the broader community. One will also want to know how the participants are related to one another: Are they strangers, or do they know one another? Are they members of some collectivity and, if so, what kind—e. g., an informal friendship group, a fraternity or club, a factory, a church? What structures or groupings exist among the participants—e.g., can cliques, focal persons, or isolates be identified by their spatial groups or patterns of interaction?

That's the WHO of journalism's conventional news event.

The Setting

Let's look, now, at the second item of the cub anthropologist's checklist: *the setting*.

A social situation may occur in different settings—e. g., a drugstore, a busy street intersection, a factory lunchroom, a nursery school, a slum dwelling, a palatial mansion. About the setting one wants to know, in addition to its appearance, what kinds of behavior it encourages, permits, discourages, or prevents. The social characteristics of the setting may be described in terms of the kinds of behaviors that are likely to be perceived as expected or unexpected, approved or disapproved, conforming or deviant.

Again, the journalist is on familiar ground, for the preceding is the WHERE of a news event.

The Purpose

Let's go then to the third item in the checklist given the cub anthropologist. It's this: *the purpose*.

Is there some official purpose that has brought the participants together, or have they been brought together by chance? If there is an official purpose, what is it—e. g., to attend a funeral, to compete in a boat race, to participate in a religious ceremony, to meet as a committee, to have fun at a party? How do the participants react to the official purpose of the situation—e. g., with acceptance or with rejection? What goals other than the official purpose do the participants seem to be pursuing? Are the goals of the various participants compatible or antagonistic?

That's the WHY of a news "story."

Social Behavior

Now, let's look at the next item in the checklist. It's this: *social behavior*.

Here one wants to know what actually occurs. What do the participants do, how do they do it, and with what and whom do they do it? With respect to behavior, one usually wants to know the following: (a) What was the stimulus or event that initiated it? (b) What appears to be its objective? (c) Toward whom or what is the behavior directed? (d) What is the form of activity entailed in the behavior—e. g., talking, running, driving a car, gesturing? (e) What are the qualities of the behavior—its intensity, persistence, unusualness, duration, mannerisms? (f) What are its effects—e. g., what behavior does it evoke from others?

Although more complicated than a journalist's routine for creating a news "story," the preceding paragraph turns out to be about the same thing as the news writer's traditional WHAT and HOW.

Frequency and Duration

Let's look, now, at the fifth and last item on the checklist. It's this: *frequency and duration*.

Here one wants to know the answers to such questions as the following: When did the situation occur? How long did it last? Is it a recurring type of situation, or unique? If it recurs, how frequently does it recur? What are the occasions that give rise to it? How typical of such situations is the one being observed?

That's the WHEN of journalism, of course.

It's impossible, really, to over-emphasize the importance of these five points. They are essential to the reporting of any news event or development. Their identification and appropriate use involve, however, an exercise in abstract thought that many news people fail to perform competently.

THE INVERTED PYRAMID

As a result, the "inverted pyramid" form of news report has failed to be properly appreciated for its utility, efficiency, and speed of comprehension. The inverted pyramid form is an exceptionally able means of communication; and the form appears destined for greater and greater use as more and more news is disseminated through newsletters and similar media. Today's readers are suffering from acute data information overload and therefore are in need of news that can be grasped readily. That's the beauty of the inverted pyramid, with its focus on the essence of the news event or development near the top of the report.

Here the beginner is tempted to draw a conclusion that can prove fatal to his or her development as a skillful news writer. That fallacy, a tantalizing one, is this: that the inverted pyramid form is appropriate for reporting short, "straight," or "breaking" news only—not "feature stories" or long interpretative reports and certainly not in-depth articles like those found in magazine-type publications.

Wrong!

Except for narrative pieces, the articles found in magazines and the interpretatives found in newspapers generally are crafted in inverted pyramid form—an approach that leads into and through a summary paragraph or "nut" followed by an elaboration of that summary, which has given the reader an initial grasp of the subject's "Big Picture."

The approach and summary, conventionally called the article's *lead* (or, as it sometimes is called in journalistic jargon, the "lede"), may be several paragraphs. It may begin with an extensive description of one of the event's main characters. It may be a quotation explaining the "why" of someone's behavior. It may be an anecdote illustrating the situation or the "what" of the story. It may describe, in considerable detail, the locale of the event, the "where." The possibilities are endless, of course, for every situation is unique.

Generally, however, the approach to the story will lead into and through a summary paragraph composed of the essentials— the what, who, when, where, why, and how—of the news event or development being reported. In leading into the summary, the article's approach may make apparent one or more of the essentials. In such a case, that essential—what, who, when, where, why, or how—will be removed from the summary, to avoid pointless repetition.

In some cases, such as short hard-hitting reports of "straight" or "breaking" news, the summary will be the first paragraph. Such use of the summary as first paragraph is common, naturally, with wire services, in broadcast news scripts, and in newsletters.

Having reached this point, you may ask "what about feature stories?" All such stories are basically narratives or are crafted in a style resembling the inverted pyramid—except, frequently, for a short "kicker" at the end. One can conceptualize a scale in which "hard" news—news of major impact upon the lives of readers—is at one end and "feature" fare at the other end. Given such a scale, one would have to put any news report somewhere between the extremes. No news report is devoid of human interest, while no feature capable of stirring someone's emotions is totally lacking in impact. For that reason, every article in any news medium is a news-feature, to one degree or another.

In my experience as a city desk assignment editor for a metropolitan daily newspaper over several years, I found that reporters performed best when given free rein to create their reports outside journalism's hoary convention of dysfunctional news/feature dichotomy. Returning from an assignment, reporters trained in the news/feature tradition frequently asked whether the desk wanted a "straight news story" or a "feature story." If instructed to write a "straight" story, the reporter tended to eliminate all kinds of interesting information helpful in understanding the event. On the other hand, if instructed to write a "feature," the reporter tended to turn out an artsy-craftsy work with lots of fluff. I learned from that experience to instruct any news writer to simply explain, in the most practical structure he or she can devise, what has been learned on any assignment.

PUTTING THE PARTS TOGETHER

Creating a solid foundation for that structure, of course, involves exploring all three dimensions of any news event, doing an anthropological "walk-around," and rigorously abstracting the essentials of the news development being reported. Let's look again at how that works.

Vital to one's abstraction of the essentials is beginning with the WHAT. To WHAT does all the information that you've discovered add up? That's the journalistic take-off point for writing any news report. If you could use only a single word to communicate the essence of the "story," what would that one word be? Progress? Tragedy? Victory? Death? Success? Devotion? Ambition? Disruption? Failure? Guilt? Celebration? Corruption? Injury? Heroism? Achievement?

The WHAT of any news event corresponds, closely, to what is called the "theme" in literary works such as novels, novelettes, short stories, poems, and dramas.

For purposes of discussion, let's say you've decided that the single word that best tells the story is "victory."

Whose victory? You ask yourself.

Using a simple example from sports, you determine that the victory is that of the Metropolis Titans football team.

Now, having determined the news event's WHAT and WHO, you ask WHERE did the Titans victory occur?

In Bigtown.

WHY were the Titans victorious?

Because they scored more points, 28, than the 24 scored by their opponents, the Bigtown Bruisers.

HOW was this victory achieved?

By completing a 75-yard pass play as time ran out.

Now let's take those essentials and cast them into a single sentence—a sentence as short as possible—that gives the reader a firm grasp of the event's entirety.

Let's assume that we're given that single sentence to report the entire story. What should that sentence be?

Completing a 75-yard pass play as time ran out, the Metropolis Titans defeated the Bigtown Bruisers 28-24 last night at Bigtown.

Note that the story began with a participial phrase. Some news writers see that as a no-no. However, comprehension is the overriding consideration in news writing, rather than out-dated conventions such as admonitions not to begin a news report with a dependent clause, a quotation, a question, or whatever.

Let's move, now, to the elaboration that allows a news report's summary.

Beginning news writers tend to lapse into narrative style after their leads. From childhood, they have been told and have read stories in that form—"once upon a time," et cetera—and find it most comfortable. Using narrative, one avoids the challenge of news report organization. One begins at the beginning and ends at the end of a simple sequence. There is no job of organization, really.

For elaboration of the report, in real organization, there are available two processes. One is the creation of a *priority system* by which additional information is to be given the reader in the descending order of that information's relative importance. The other process involves *anticipation of logical questions* asked by a hypothetical reader after each piece of additional information is provided. In the hands of a skilled news writer, both processes are integrated in organizing the remainder of any news report.

The Priority System

After creating a report's lead, the writer lists, in descending order of importance, all the units of additional information he or she expects to provide the reader. Such units of information can be any of the following:

- Single paragraphs of factual detail
- Blocks of narrative relating the order in which certain things occurred
- Descriptions of persons, places, or things involved in the event
- Explanations of how involved things work, were done, or happened
- Comparisons to similar developments
- Comments made by a person involved, affected by, or possessing some special perspective on the development (reaction, assessment of effect, speculation about future developments, etc.)
- Acknowledgment of facts presumed to exist but unknown to the news writer at the time

Question Anticipation

Using this second process, the news writer imagines that an alert reader is sitting across the desk and asking a question at the end of each paragraph.

Immediately after composing the lead and then a list of priorities, the news writer asks, "Does the top unit in my priority system really answer the most logical question raised by a reading of the lead?"

It should, of course, but it sometimes doesn't. If that's the case, then the news writer must decide whether the answer to the question posed is perhaps more important than the information in the top unit in the priority list. If so, then the answer to the imaginary reader's question should be inserted ahead of the priority list's top unit.

That done, the news writer has this question: Is the question raised by the answer to the first question more important to answer at this point than the top unit in the priority list?

Perhaps so. In that case, the new question is answered then and there. If not, the question's answer is inserted in an appropriate place in the priority list and the news writer returns to the top of the list for the next paragraph of the report.

Paragraph by paragraph, unit by unit, the news writer works down the priority list, breaking into it as needed to answer questions asked by the imaginary reader and to organize the report in the way it can be comprehended best by a real reader.

Returning to one's priority list frequently, we find, is necessary. Knowing things about any news event or development that the average reader might ask about makes it imperative that the news writer retain firm control over the report's organization and not follow any logical string of questions off on some unproductive tangent. For that reason, the skillful news writer moves back and forth between the two processes, carefully weighing each unit of information in the priority list against the importance of information that answers questions suggested by the previous paragraph of the report.

THE CONCLUSION

In the organization of any news report, the report simply ends when the news writer exhausts his or her store of information that a reader needs to comprehend the event or development fully. That's the great advantage, of course, of the inverted pyramid form. Unlike a narrative or an essay, the inverted pyramid can be easily adapted to any given space, without rewriting or drastic editing that might destroy the report's integrity and leave the reader confused and frustrated.

The news writer needs to know when he or she has told the reader everything the reader probably wants to know about the news event or development.

Then one needs to stop.

Period.

Perspective...

WHAT A POLITICAL SCIENTIST WISHES BEGINNING JOURNALISTS KNEW ABOUT MAKING POLITICS MEANINGFUL TO READERS

By DORIS GRABER, editor-in-chief of the journal *Political Communication* and author of many books on political communication, including *Processing the News: How People Tame the Information Tide* and *Mass Media and American Politics.*

Average Americans are bombarded daily by hundreds, even thousands of messages. That makes it tough to attract their attention to political news, especially since most Americans are not deeply interested in the intricacies of government and politics. They are far more concerned with their busy work and home lives. To interest them in political news requires "hooking" them with a catchy newspaper headline or a tempting lead-in to a television or radio story.

What is a good hook? Unfortunately, there is no simple, straightforward answer. Audiences get hooked by things that fascinate them, by dramatic news that affects their daily lives, by stories that resonate with their experiences. Discovering what news subjects and what types of framing of news stories meet these criteria requires careful, *ongoing* audience research. In the past, such research has been all too rare. News story framing has been haphazard and intuitive.

Social science findings about information processing can provide journalists with guidelines for selecting and framing stories that appeal to average people. Most people want to understand all the forces, including politics, that they perceive as profoundly affecting their lives. They have developed basic ideas, attitudes, and feelings about their social and political environment through formal and informal education and through their experiences. Mass media stories must be framed so that they can be easily fitted into these conceptions—*schemata* is the scientific term.

If, for example, a story concerns a congressional mandate to lengthen the school year by one month, average news consumers are not particularly interested in the name of the Congressman who proposed the legislation, the legal tangles involved in teachers' contracts, or the implications for state and federal budgets. Political buffs would want to know these facts, which average people regard as confusing details that obscure the story's main thrust. Average Americans care far more about the "why" and "how" questions that explain the story. Why is an extra month of school needed, and how will it affect the lives of people in the community? If "expert" opinions conflict, how can the claims and counterclaims be evaluated? Currently, most print and broadcast news stories cover the traditional "who," "what," "where," and "when" questions of journalism well. But they slight the "why" and "how" questions.

For ease in processing, stories have to be framed in ways that match the experiences of average news consumers. That means that analogous examples have to be drawn from familiar events and that vocabularies should not strain the comprehension levels of people with less than a high-school education. It is particularly important to couch stories in a familiar vocabulary when they deal with subjects remote from the average person's life, such as events abroad or technological advances.

In audio-visual presentations, journalists need to consider the fact that it is difficult to process visual and verbal messages simultaneously unless the messages are mutually reinforcing. Camera movements, speech pacing, repetition patterns, and a multitude of other communication features should be designed toward making comprehension easy, rather than toward packing each story with as much information as possible. In a nutshell, if average Americans are your target audience, gear your story to their information processing propensities, rather than catering to your peers or policy wonks. Highlight the story's meaning for your audience, and avoid clutter. Finally, be realistic. Learning is incremental. Like grains of sand, a single story leaves few traces; but, over time, a solid knowledge structure does emerge.

12

WRITING THE LEAD

The responsible reporter takes writing the lead seriously, because a reader or listener certainly will. Good leads satisfy the "so-what" and "ah-ha" tests. The lead should immediately impress upon its audience the importance or the "so-what" of the story. A good lead leaves the audience with a desire to stay with the story. It makes contact with its audience. It causes readers and listeners to say "ah-ha, I see" and to want more.

The first thing a reporter says in a story is the most important thing in that story. It generally determines whether a reader will stay with your story or leave it. Since big salaries or even continued employment are not routinely offered reporters who are in the habit of losing readers, beginning reporters should spend more time on the first sentence of their story than any other sentence in the story.

In deciding what comes first, always remember your readers. You frustrate their legitimate expectation at your own peril. Most have read hundreds of news stories before they get to yours. They have in mind how a lead should look and what it should say. The reporter who fails to give them in the first sentence the most recent and relevant detail of the story will frustrate and lose them. Beginning reporters must work at putting themselves in the reader's place. That aspect of the story that has the greatest significance to the greatest number of readers is the lead.

BY BRUCE J. EVENSEN

SHARPENING THE LEAD

You should try to write every lead as if every word counts, because it does. But be particularly alert to certain hazards. Here are some common problems that beginning reporters have in writing leads and that you should avoid.

- *Treating a lead as if it is a bedtime story.* A bedtime story has a beginning, middle, and end and moves more or less chronologically from start to finish. But a news story isn't like that. Its beginning is often the ending of the bedtime story. It's not that Jack and Jill went up a hill to fetch a pail of water. Instead, the lead is that Jack fell down and broke his crown and Jill came tumbling after.

- *Putting two pounds of baloney in a one-pound bag.* Journalists sometimes put too much into the lead. They know that the who, what, when, where, why, and how should be in the first two or three sentences of a story, but they try to get all of them in a first sentence that seems to stretch from Toledo to Tucson and back again. Instead, reporters need to decide the kind of story they have on their hands. It is often a "what" story. Something happened. The something that happened is the lead. Many second-day stories are "why" stories. They are explanations of why something happened or what significance the happening has. Occasionally, "who" did something is the lead. In the current climate of personality news, that is increasingly the case. Rarely is "when" something happened, or "where" it happened, or even "how" it happened the most relevant detail of a story. So telling "when" or "where" or "how" something happened can often wait until later in the first sentence, or the second, or the third.

- *Setting the table.* Leads don't only set the table and serve as appetizers. They are the main course. The tendency to be so sweeping in your lead that you encompass everything in world history since the Peloponnesian War should be studiously avoided. The lead is not that the President gave a press conference in the East Room of the White House, but what he said or what others wished he had said. Offer not ubiquity in leads but specificity. Many journalists equivocate in leads because they are afraid to commit themselves to a concrete lead. But go ahead. Make a definite assertion in your lead. And be prepared to defend it when your editor wants to know why you made that choice and not some other.

- *Verbosity.* Keep your leads to twenty-five to thirty words as a maximum. That will give you words enough to describe the "what" and "who" and "when" or "where" of most stories. And what the reporter doesn't get into the first sentence is what the second and third sentences are for.

• *Inability to write declarative sentences.* Cognitive psychologists report that simple, declarative sentences—ones that begin with a noun, followed by a verb and direct object or predicate nominative—are the easiest sentences for readers or listeners to understand. Unfortunately, they are not always the easiest for journalists to write. So try to avoid beginning your lead with a prepositional phrase or gerund or dependent clause or past participle. Begin with a noun. Follow with a verb. Your reader will thank you for it.

• *Failing to let nouns and verbs carry a sentence's strength and fundamental meaning.* Avoid the Edgar Allan Poe effect that afflicts so many beginning reporters. They overload copy with big adjectives and adverbs. Modifiers that call attention to themselves should be quoted. If one candidate calls the other a "lousy" so and so, then let the candidate say so and not you.

• *Writing leads that contain two ideas, not one.* Each lead should contain the most recent and relevant aspect of a story. But sometimes reporters have a hard time separating out two ideas that seem equally attractive and linked. So they create compound, complex sentences where two different ideas sit uncomfortably side by side joined by an "and," "but," or "however." A better approach is to make two sentences out of the one longer sentence. It will make the lead easier to understand and underscore a simple unity—one idea per sentence. Each sentence in the lead paragraph should then relate to every other sentence in that paragraph. Together these sentences within the paragraph logically cohere.

• *Winding up for a pitch.* Often beginning reporters will write a lead that makes no sense until a reader reads further. But most readers will not read further. They will not be teased. They are busy, and the reporter is fighting for their time and limited attention. So every lead must be self-contained. It must be perfectly sensible in and of itself. A beginning reporter should never justify an enigmatic lead by saying, "If you read that second sentence, the first makes sense." Don't wind up for the pitch. Pitch.

• *Quoting too much.* Most quotations don't make sense unless a reporter contextualizes them. So it is a good idea for beginning reporters to stay away from long quotations in leads. It is better to lift a strong verb or adjective a source may have used and quote just that key word or phrase in a sentence that makes perfect sense in and of itself.

• *Using pronouns.* In many leads, where two or more subjects are involved, readers won't know who the "he" or "she" refers to. This is particularly annoying if a listener hears a story on radio or television and the proper noun is never repeated. It is maddening to hear "he" was shot and killed; when we don't know who he is. This leaves the audience wondering who the story is about. So reporters should simply repeat a person's last name after a first reference in which the full name is given.

• *Failing to update copy.* When journalists are filing multiple takes on the same story, leads must be updated to reflect latest developments in the story. The fact that a mother of three was killed in a car crash is the broadcast lead an hour after the accident. But several hours or a day later the coroner's confirming the woman was legally intoxicated at the time of the incident is the lead.

• *Assuming the audience has a running knowledge of the story.* Since a reporter's story gains and loses an audience all the time, each retelling of the story should be complete. Therefore, when rewriting the lead, never assume the reader knows the alderman has been indicted even though the mass media have been reporting little else for days. A week after the indictment, the fact of the indictment isn't the lead, but the fact of the indictment belongs somewhere in the story.

• *Failing the significance test.* Many leads don't make it because they don't pass a significance test. They leave the reader or the listener saying, "So what?" Ask yourself a simple question—why should the reader care about what I am writing? If the lead answers that question, you are well on your way to writing a good one.

• *Failing the "huh" test.* Many leads fail because they are obscure. The reader doesn't know what precisely the writer is claiming. Put yourself in the reader's place. How many times have you finished the first paragraph of a story and asked yourself, "What is this about?" If you paid reasonable attention and still missed the story's point, it is probable the lead didn't have one. A reader or listener can't puzzle over what a reporter just said and understand what that reporter is now saying. It is impossible. It leaves the reporter only one chance to make a story comprehensible, and that is from the very beginning.

• *Ignoring what's really relevant.* What's more important than the death of thirty-four-year-old Mary B. of 1414 Alpine Road is the fact that she is a mother of three. In a big, impersonal city, a reader may not know who Mary B. is but should have some sympathetic connection to the fact that the victim was a mother of three. Try to relate your story in any reasonable way you can to your reader. And don't wait to do it. Do it in the lead.

• *Overlooking relevance.* If the mayor's brother is one of three persons shot and killed in a bungled convenience store robbery, then include that in the lead. Death is the great equalizer, but not as far as news reporting is concerned. There is greater reader interest in certain deaths than others. That's why headlines on the obituary page are set in different sized type. So say, "The mayor's brother was one of three persons killed in a southside convenience store robbery." The reader who is not interested in a robbery story, even one with three fatalities, may well stay for a story in which the town's mayor loses a brother. And one of your primary concerns is that readers stay. So do every reasonable thing you can to make sure they do.

• *Failing to make it present tense.* Beginning journalists need to remember they are writing "news," not "olds." So when possible, use present, not past tense.

• *Writing clichés.* Many leads fall under the weight of clichés. Journalists are well served not to write the first thing that comes into their mind. The expression that occurs to you most naturally is often the exact phrase you should avoid using. It's probably in your mind because you've heard it before. More than once. And while you don't want to complicate the reader or listener's life unnecessarily, you don't want to bore them to death either.

• *Failing to attribute.* Leads are not conclusions you have drawn after looking at the facts of a story. You are not writing an op-ed piece or an editorial. The requirements of attribution are no less severe in lead writing than any other sentence in the story. The audience shouldn't know reading the lead what a reporter's position on an issue is. (That should be true also for every other sentence in the story.)

• *Delaying attribution.* When writing a lead for broadcast, attribution should always be at the head of the sentence, because listeners will have no way of measuring the veracity of the statement until they know who is making it. Print journalists, however, put attribution somewhere other than the beginning—unless the fact that someone said something is more important than what was said.

• *Reporting factual errors.* Nothing sinks the ship faster than a factual error. Once the reader or listener knows something you've said is false, your credibility is shot. Your audience won't be fully confident of anything else that you say. That's why when you lose the confidence of your audience you've lost everything. Reading or hearing a reporter's story is an act of faith that operates at the level of trust. If your partner has been unfaithful, it undermines the relationship. And when a story has even a single inaccuracy the reader's tendency is to turn the page or switch the channel, the journalistic equivalent of divorce. Because reporters don't always take their obligations to readers and listeners seriously enough, public confidence in journalists has sunk to the level of that of funeral directors. To extend the metaphor—when you get it wrong, you write your own obituary.

A REAL-LIFE EXAMPLE: A CAR WRECK

Here is a news story I covered early in my journalistic career. As you read the details of what happened, be thinking of how the most recent and relevant details of the story would be written as a lead and what choices you would make in arranging the information that immediately follows your lead sentence.

It's your third day on the job. It's late winter. A freezing rain has fallen overnight. You are driving to work in the early morning, westbound on U. S. Highway 51, a six-lane bypass south of the city. You are stopped in a traffic jam for twenty minutes on a stretch of highway approaching the Rock River bridge. What do you do? I got out of my car and walked a third of a mile in the direction of the bridge. There in the early morning light I saw a series of emergency vehicles with their red and yellow lights flashing. Who would you ask to speak to? If you are in a county jurisdiction, it will be a sheriff's deputy. Inside the city, it will be a police officer or police detective. In this case, I walked up to a sheriff's deputy. Before your first question, be sure to note to whom you're speaking, including a correct spelling of the name and the person's title. That will allow you to avoid one of life's most embarrassing moments, when the breathless cub reporter writes a wonderful account of the big story only to find he took no note of who he was talking to.

Winnebago County Sheriff's Deputy Randy Hines tells you that police received a call around 3:15 in the morning that a car had gone off the roadway, sped down an embankment, and plunged into the Rock River. He says a motorist ran down to the water's edge and attempted to offer aid but failed. He adds that the sheriff's department sent divers into the river. They attached grappling hooks, and a wrecker perched on the bridge above the water pulled the car out. You ask Hines what happened to the driver, and he doesn't answer. He simply points in the direction of the wrecker. As you walk over to it in the early morning light, you see the outlines of a late-model sports car, suspended in midair at the end of grappling hooks, with its headlights on and its front wheels a foot above the icy surface of the roadway. You circle the front of the car, and when you get to the driver's side you see a window partly rolled down and the head and shoulders of a woman in her early thirties dangling out. She is dead.

When you return to Deputy Hines, what would you ask him? The tendency, of course, is to ask the identity of the dead woman. But you will rarely get positive identification of a dead person at an accident or crime scene. Typically, next of kin must be notified and release of the victim's name will come from the nursing supervisor of a local hospital or the county coroner. That is the case in this story as well, but on the basis of what Hines told you you have a clue to follow up. He mentioned that sheriff's deputies had received a call regarding the incident. So you ask him if the person who reported the accident is still at the scene. He tells you yes.

Dave Sloan is standing shivering in the late winter chill; and before you ask him about the accident and after you get his name and its spelling, what might you ask him? If the car went into the river at 3:15 in the morning, your reader might want to know why he was out so late to report it to police. He tells you that he is a traveling salesman and that he was returning to his home in Pecatonica, a small town ten miles from the crash site, at the time of the wreck. He adds that he was driving westbound of U. S. Highway 51 in a freezing rain when he saw in his rearview mirror a car approaching his at a high rate of speed. "The car was swerving all over the road," he says. "I thought it was going to hit me. I slowed down and moved to the shoulder of the road. As I did, the car brushed by me, nearly sideswiping my car. Then the car spun. The driver seemed to lose control. The car raced over the shoulder, drove down an embankment, and plunged into the icy waters of the Rock River." You ask if he offered assistance. He tells you he stopped his car and ran to the river's edge. He could see the car's headlights in the murky waters below and knew the car had landed on its wheels. But "it was freezing," he says. "I couldn't do anything. So I called police."

It is now 6:30 in the morning. If you are a broadcast reporter, you are likely filing your story within the hour; but if you report for a newspaper, your deadline is probably hours off. How would you pursue the story during that interval? What crucial elements of the story are missing? Clearly you need to know the identity of the woman. That comes several hours later in a phone call to the coroner's office, where Winnebago County Coroner John DeMott tells you that thirty-four-year-old Mary B. lived at 1414 Alpine, and, according to information found on the body, you are told Mary B. was an employee of Sun Corporation, a major aeronautical parts supplier headquartered in your city. You have the woman's name but not her story. The further you move away from the time of her death, the more that other elements of the story take on relevance. For instance, you still don't know what killed her. If you assumed it was injuries sustained in the crash, you would be wrong. The coroner tells you Mary B. drowned when her legs were trapped beneath her car's crushed dashboard. This would explain why you saw the upper half of her torso dangling through the half open window. It explains why she was unable to escape the car.

On the basis of Sloan's description of how Mary B. was driving her car, what else might occur to you? A veteran reporter would know that, in any accident case, coroners will be routinely asked if alcohol or any illegal substance showed up in toxicology tests. And DeMott tells you that such a test was taken and that Mary B. was "legally intoxicated at the time of the crash." This prompts another even more fundamental question that your reader will likely ask and that you must anticipate. It moves to the "why" of the story. Why was this woman driving her car while drunk at three o'clock in the morning? You have her address, and you call the residence, which is listed under a William C. in the phone book, but there is no answer. You might drive to the address and ask questions of neighbors. But you are up against deadline, and there is something DeMott told you that might be even more efficient. Remember that he told you that Mary B. was an employee of the Sun Corporation. When you reach her extension, you get voice mail. So you try again and ask for "her best friends at the company." And in doing so you get a great deal more than you anticipated.

Shirley Carter should be established in the story by finding out how long she has known Mary B. She tells you that the two have been "close" friends for five years and that she only heard of her friend's death on the radio minutes before. "That no good husband of hers killed her," Carter tells you. She explains that William C. "has been running around" on his wife and "is threatening to take the kids." You ask the names and ages of the children and are told: Katharine, age seven; Jennifer, four; and Stephen, thirteen months. You also need to establish when was the last time Carter saw Mary B., and she tells you "last night, around eleven." You ask Mary's condition at that time and are told she "had been drinking. She was despondent. She said she was going to kill herself."

At this point you are right at deadline. You try reaching the husband, William C., one last time and find the couple's home phone has been disconnected. It's 2:30 in the afternoon, and you must file your story without hearing from the husband or anyone else. So, what's your lead?

Let's consider what you've got. You have a sheriff's deputy's account and a witness who was there. You have the coroner's report on the cause of death and a friend whose comments may reach to the "why" of the story. Most students in the introductory journalism class where I teach this story as an early assignment like to lead with the sheriff's deputy or the witness. This allows them a chronological summary of the day's events. So they'll start by saying, "Thirty-four year old Mary B. was killed this morning when her car...." Or they'll write, "Winnebago County Sheriff's Deputy Randy Hines says that a city woman was killed...." But why aren't either of these the best choices for a lead? Ask yourself, is the fact of the victim's death the most recent and relevant aspect of the story? In fact, her death has been reported for hours on the radio. Remember that Shirley Carter told you she heard about her friend's death on the radio. So the fact that we are several hours from the victim's death means we are not likely to lead with either the sheriff's deputy or the witness.

Your information from the coroner and the friend updates what you got at the scene, but can we treat the information from these two sources equally? The coroner tells us Mary B. drowned and that she was legally drunk at the time of the crash. The friend confirms that Mary B. had been drinking the evening before the crash and gives you a reason why she was disconsolate. Some students will take this information and lead with or without attribution the assertion that Mary B. committed suicide. They defend this choice by referring to the quotation in which she allegedly said she was going to kill herself. But did she attempt suicide? Certainly we can't say that without attribution because we don't know and Mary B. can't tell us. We do have evidence that Mary B. attempted to swim away from the crash. Remember that the driver's window was half down and her upper body was through it. The crushed dashboard appears to have prevented her escape. So the suicide angle is probably not lead material and if it's mentioned at all should appear much later in the story.

Most students will report verbatim Carter's claim that the victim's husband is responsible for her death because of marital infidelity. Sensing that this is a loaded allegation, they'll place the assertion late in the story or stick an "alleges" after Carter's statement. Neither, however, overcomes a potential libel suit in which the husband demonstrates you held him up to ridicule and scorn in the eyes of the community and that you showed reckless disregard for the truth. You cannot defend your decision to use the material by telling the court you were under deadline pressure and that you called William C. and couldn't get in touch with him, or by asserting that your use of the word "allegedly" gets you off the hook. You would be fired, as would your editor, and you would be making several lawyers as well as William C. very rich and the company for which you had worked very poor.

Does that mean a reporter couldn't use any of Carter's statement? Not necessarily. In fact, if you don't use it, you haven't spoken to the "why" of the accident, and that is a question many of your readers are sure to ask. The key in getting at Carter's statement is how you choose to frame it and phrase it. Some students will say that the couple was having "marital problems." But we don't know that that is the case, even if Carter claims it. A better choice would be to say that Carter said Mary B. had personal problems. Clearly, she did. One could argue that anyone out driving drunk and recklessly at three in the morning with three children at home is behaving irresponsibly regardless of the cause. In fact, later investigation demonstrated that Mary B. had a long and tragic personal history and that her problems went far beyond her marriage.

Some students will argue, well, why is it necessary to get into Mary B.'s personal life? Whose business is that anyway? Isn't it enough that a mother of three has died? Why does the press have to get into personal issues? There is much merit in this line of reasoning. Certainly the preoccupation of modern mass media with personality news and probing of deeply intimate issues in a person's life to feed an insatiable public appetite for gossip is one of the most regrettable tendencies in contemporary journalism. But the reporter must balance a public's right to know with an individual's right to privacy. Courts have ruled that there is a heavy burden an individual must meet to overcome the public's right of access to information. In this instance, it seems not unreasonable to satisfy a threshold reader interest in why this woman was out in the middle of the night driving drunk with three children at home. This is a particularly salient issue hours after the accident when it is learned the victim was legally intoxicated at the time of the crash.

One can argue persuasively that survivors of the deceased, including her children, are further harmed by revelations regarding Mary B.'s personal problems. But, again, a simple, brief statement indicating a friend's claim there were personal problems is an unobtrusive way to get at this delicate issue. It also satisfies a legitimate reader interest in what is, after all, not simply a private tragedy but a public event, in which a person has been killed and hundreds of commuters' lives affected when a major arterial highway is blocked as a result of the incident.

So what lead does one write? A good beginning is probably, "The coroner reports...." You don't need the coroner's name in the lead. Use the proper name in the lead only of someone who will draw readers or listeners to the story. Otherwise, simply use the office of the person. That is briefer and tells the story better. So what makes more sense: "The coroner reports 34-year-old Mary B..." or "The coroner reports a mother of three...."? I would argue that the generic is better than the specific in this case and that the victim's name can wait until the second sentence. The reason is that Mary B. is not well known in your community and reader interest is more likely to be captured with "mother of three." Realize that readers and listeners think in categories, or schema, cognitive psychologists tell us. That is how they process the news. They'll think, "This is an accident story," as you begin to tell the story. If you insert "mother of three," you are more likely to capture and hold their interest than if you use a proper name of someone they've never heard of. So look for the generic in writing leads. It helps in stimulating audience attention.

So, now you have, "The coroner reports a mother of three...," and your predicate should probably be "was legacy intoxicated," or some editors might prefer "drunk." This moves to the why of the accident and updates information your reader or listener might have gotten earlier in the day. So that brings you to, "The coroner reports a mother of three was legally intoxicated...." Then you add the cause of death "and drowned" and the where and the when of the story: "when her car crashed into the Rock River off U. S. Highway 51 early this morning." In twenty-seven words if you say "legacy intoxicated" and twenty-six words if you say "drunk," you have worked the who, the what, the when, the where, the why, and the how into the lead. You have followed a formula that sought the most recent, relevant information, and you have steered clear of allegations that embroil your paper or station in a nasty court case over libel. You have satisfied the public's right to know; and in a second sentence that might begin, "A friend of Mary B. of 1414 Alpine says the Sun Corporation employee's personal problems...," you have avoided creating a public spectacle by exploiting a private grief.

In a class of twenty to twenty-five students, generally only one or two will even note an aspect of the story that I would include within the first two or three sentences of the story. Can you guess which part of this story affected the greatest number of individuals and would therefore command a high place in the story? I am thinking of the traffic tie-up. Rush hour traffic is snarled on a major city highway because of the emergency vehicles that were brought to the scene. Hundreds of motorists were late to work as a result. They need to know the reason why.

It is interesting also to note how few students pick up on the freezing rain that may have contributed to the crash. It seems a more plausible cause for the accident than the attempted suicide that far more students seem interested in describing. So your second sentence might read, "A friend of Mary B. of 1414 Alpine says the Sun Corporation employee's personal problems may have contributed to the accident in a freezing rain that snarled rush hour traffic."

Then, depending on space, you can describe the fact the victim's legs were trapped beneath a crushed dashboard and even that her upper body was dangling from the open window when a wrecker removed the car from the river. You can paraphrase and shorten Sloan's summary of the accident itself and include from Deputy Hines only the detail of when emergency vehicles got to the scene and what they did there. Some will argue that identifying the husband and the three children by name and age is a further erosion of their privacy, and there is some truth in this. In other countries, neither the name of the victim nor the names of any family members would be given out. If you had positive identification beyond the single friend's recollection, it would not be inappropriate to use the children's names and ages, although some editors might argue that information serves no useful purpose.

When you are up against severe deadline pressure and are writing the first accident report you've ever done, or the first murder, or the first anything, it is an anxious time. But for those beginning journalists who persist, there is the gradual realization that the accident and murder stories that follow are easier to write because they've already written one. The facts of the story will differ, but the structure of the story remains the same, the choices you are faced with will seem similar over time, and breaking news will begin to fit into patterns of information you recognize and know what to do with. While writing a lead isn't as complicated as brain surgery, the act of writing does require you to organize the circuitry of your mind. You'll find that like weight lifting, the more repetitions you do, the easier the heavy lifting will become. You'll know what to look for and how to express it easily and professionally.

Beginning journalists would be well served to approach their work modestly and with a stiff upper lip. Making mistakes is the natural tendency in any line of work, particularly for the rookie or the cub. Mistakes are what the delete function in your word processor is for. The race is won by the one who perseveres. Learn from mistakes. Work to avoid repeating them. Be as accurate as you can. As fair. As balanced. Attribute. Don't let the reader know what you think but what others are thinking. Trust your readers or listeners to make up their own mind with the information you offer. Never assume. Check and check again. You will find pleasure giving way to a deeper satisfaction that you are providing readers and listeners with information they need to know. Perhaps that is why the Constitution takes the work of the press so seriously, protecting us from government intrusion in a way that other forms of commercial speech are not protected. Our work begins with writing the lead; and if we get that right, we are well on our way to meeting our obligations to sources, readers, and listeners.

13

INGREDIENTS OF GOOD NEWS WRITING

News writing can be—and should be—good. The keys to excellent writing are thorough reporting, unity of composition, and intensity of style.

If you asked journalists, most probably would say their news writing does its job. Many critics, however, would argue that it is dull.

The truth is, you probably can find examples of both kinds of news writing. Many reporters are excellent writers, but it also is true that much of the writing that newspapers publish is mechanical and bland. Why?

It is not that journalists don't have writing talent. Many enter the field of journalism because of a particular interest in writing. Unfortunately, that interest in good writing is sometimes whacked out of students and reporters—to be replaced by an insistence on a slavish adherence to mechanical rules. The rules—style rules, conciseness, objectivity, and so forth—may, in and of themselves, be good. The problem results when reporters, editors, and teachers assume that the rules account for good writing.

BY WM. DAVID SLOAN
Professor of Journalism at the University of Alabama, Dr. Sloan worked as a reporter and editor on four newspapers before becoming a teacher. He is the co-editor of six books on journalistic writing, including *The Best of Pulitzer Prize News Writing* and *Masterpieces of Reporting*, and of several other books on media history and education.

Rules themselves should not be the goal. They should merely provide the fundamentals to help assure that news writing fulfills its proper functions.

News writing can be excellent. It can make interesting, absorbing reading. To develop your own talents, you should be alert to the principles that account for good writing. You also should be alert to improving your writing. To do that, you must recognize that writing is the journalist's tool, just as the hammer is the carpenter's. As the carpenter must know how to use the hammer well, the journalist must know how to write well.

THE VALUE OF JOURNALISTIC RULES

Although simple adherence to rules will not assure good writing, the rules do have some important purposes.

The first purpose is *clarity*. The primary role of journalism is to provide information. Most rules, therefore, are aimed at assuring that news writing presents material clearly, that it is easily understandable to most readers. Such practices as using short sentences and simple words have one primary goal: to provide information clearly. Because so much attention has been devoted to clarity, it may be said of journalistic writing that, among all types of writing, it has one of the most easily understood styles. By emphasizing the basic rules of news writing, college journalism departments find it possible to turn out hundreds of graduates every semester who are able, more or less, to present information easily understood by the average reader. Of the requirements for good writing, journalism excels in this one. It is admirable for its ability to inform, to present information with exceptional clarity.

A second purpose is *consistency*. In journalism, an accepted principle is that all stories in a newspaper should follow essentially the same style. One story, for example, should not read "at 3 p.m. Tuesday" and another "tomorrow at 3:00 P.M." Readers expect stories to be understandable and free of confusion. Inconsistency can frustrate readers.

The most elementary purpose of some journalistic rules is to *save space*. That is the reason behind, for example, the rule that commas are to be omitted before the "and" preceding the last item in a series. One comma may not seem as if it would take up much space, but 100 commas eliminated from all stories in a newspaper would make a difference.

Another purpose of some rules is to *depersonalize writing*. Journalism is supposed to provide an accurate, unbiased account. Removing the reporter's personal perspective usually helps to accomplish that purpose. That is the reason behind journalism's emphasis on *objectivity*. It is also why for *attribution* reporters normally use the neutral word "said" rather than a word such as "screamed." Likewise, reporters normally are expected to omit evaluative words that might color meaning. That's why one finds few adjectives in news writing.

Some journalistic rules obviously have valid purposes behind them, and you not only should become familiar with them, but should master them. In learning the rules, however, don't let them become the end in themselves.

Instead, learn the principles of writing that account for quality, and learn to use them in your own writing.

WHAT IS "GOOD" NEWS WRITING?

Good news writing is, simply stated, *writing that achieves its purpose*, that does what it is supposed to do. News writing should do two things: (1) it should inform the reader, and (2) it should interest the reader.

Writing informs the reader when it provides all necessary and relevant details in a clear, understandable manner.

To be superior, however, writing also must interest the reader. Good journalistic writing does not only present information. An account of the most interesting event can lose the reader's attention if it is not presented in an interesting way. A reader may never get past the halfway mark of a story if the writing is dull. The writer must be concerned with story structure and presentation. The best journalistic writing appeals to the senses; it gives the reader the feeling of "being there," of experiencing what happened. It makes news events and information come alive.

But being interesting does not mean that writing should be ostentatious. Good writing does not draw attention to itself. It absorbs the reader in the content being presented. Writing fails if it makes the reader aware of the writing itself. Good writing focuses attention on what is being said, not on how it is said. Good writing is unobtrusive. It is not superficial or artificial or pretentious. It is natural and real. Effective writing carries the impact of the content by focusing the reader's attention on the story being told. While the reader should be oblivious to the writing style, however, it is the style that makes possible the wallop that the event inherently contains. Writing is good, then, when it delivers news material in its undiluted strength.

Writing that accomplishes those goals exhibits these characteristics:

1. It is based on thorough reporting.

2. It has a unity of composition.
3. It is marked by intensity of style.

These characteristics are demonstrated in the story about a lynching of two accused murderers that is reprinted at the end of this chapter. Written by Royce Brier for the San Francisco *Chronicle*, it won the 1934 Pulitzer Prize for reporting. You may wish to read the story now. It will provide illustrations of several of the points that this chapter emphasizes.

THOROUGH REPORTING

An adage in all types of writing—from novels, to histories, to news stories—is that *one must have good material before one can have good writing*. Some poems, for example, have lasting value not simply because of how they are written, but what they are written about. Today there are many exceptional craftsmen writing novels, but "classics" attain their stature because they deal with subjects of worth. The same principle applies to news writing. Every news story may not have universal meaning, but it should be based on substantial fact and detail.

Good news gathering is mandatory for reporting. That means that it takes time. Some reporters spend hundreds of hours gathering information. They talk to scores of sources. They spend days examining documents. They interview every expert they can. They retrace the footsteps of the people who are the major players in the story. They amass a huge stack of facts, dates, quotations, figures, and other details. By having a wealth of raw material, they are able to construct stories that come alive.

Gathering of information must be done thoroughly enough to allow the reporter to contextualize and to see larger stories from the factual circumstances. The reporter must be aware of all pertinent details, background, explanatory factors, related angles, contrasting points of view, and potential directions that events and issues might take. Such reporting requires an informed, alert, and energetic individual.

Because well developed stories are based on a *variety of sources*, you should be alert to one particular feature in stories that can signal that reporting has not been done thoroughly enough: Notice if you are relying too much on a single person or document. That can be indicated by continual attribution to the same source. If you find that your story has several quotations from the same person or document, that may indicate that you need to gather more material from more sources. The more variety in sources, the more substantial and interesting your story will be.

UNITY

Another characteristic of good news writing is unity. Unity gives structural meaning to a story that makes an impact on the reader more likely. It is achieved when all parts contribute to a central idea. All aspects are cohesive: they fit together; they all have their place in the story; extraneous and irrelevant details are omitted.

As an example of irrelevant details, notice how, in the following story about the impact of World Cup soccer being played in the United States, the reference to the sports of football and baseball (mentioned nowhere else in the story) is out of place:

> The world's game, the sport of kings, is coming to America. The World Cup tournament kicks into action Friday with 36 teams playing in 10 cities.
> Ironically, Americans' passion is not for soccer but for baseball and football.
> Orlando, Fla., is getting ready for the mass of people who will flood the city. Because of the enormous impact of the World Cup, finding parking will be almost impossible for fans....

Stories need to be planned. Although reporters are trained to write under pressure and turn out pages of copy—or computer screensful of characters—under hurried conditions, thought must be given to a story's overall structure and to its logical develop-ment. The reporter should know where a story is to end before the writing begins. When a reporter gets midway into a story and does not know where to go from there, the problem is that the story's development has not been planned. The solution is to determine the theme and then to decide the direction the story is to head, the structure it is to take, before the first word is typed into the computer.

Thematic Unity

The most obvious and important concept in the area of unity is *thematic unity*. It requires that the news story be structured around one central idea. A news story works best when it has a point. Without a unifying theme, a story falls apart. If it is no more than a collection of details or an odd, unintegrated assortment of pieces of information, it works poorly or does not work at all. To have an impact, a news story must do more than pull together a group of facts, quotes, dates, places, names, and other bits of "news." All of its parts must work together as a unified whole.

News writing, among the various genres, is especially prone

to thematic disintegration. Some short news stories may not offer the opportunity to develop a theme. At best, many news stories focus simply around a topic—usually an event, although sometimes around an issue—rather than around a theme.

As opposed to a topic, *a theme is a central "point" or "meaning."* The topic of Royce Brier's article at the end of this chapter, for example, is the lynching of two men. The theme is that the mob, seized with lynch fever, meted out a retribution to the murderers that was "terrible to behold." A topic is a subject; a theme is a statement. The best news stories always have themes. Too many newspaper stories are routine because they have only topics.

The theme that the reporter chooses to build the story around must be thoughtfully determined. It should not be artificial or unnatural. Neither should it be a mere summary of an episode, nor should it be cliché. At the other extreme, it should not be thought of as some great philosophical truth. Rather, it should be the essence of the episode or issue that the story is about.

To recognize the central theme of an episode, reporters must be scrupulously alert. They must develop the ability to determine what the salient features of an episode are. That ability requires continually working at sharpening one's faculties of observation and understanding of people.

Thematic unity also requires that a news story have only one theme. If a story has more, its focus will be diffused; its strength, diluted. Stories with more than one theme tend to confuse readers. When stories leap from one theme or point to another, they risk losing readers. A news story needs one central theme and needs to stick with it. Wandering from that central theme achieves nothing. Staying with it builds a story into a whole.

Reporters tend to wander for two reasons. The first is that they normally do not think in terms of thematic unity. They think in terms of details and pieces of information related to a situation involving a topic. A city council meeting, for example, is the situation, the topic. Things that occur at the meeting are the details. A convenience-store robbery is a situation; when the robbery occurred and how much money was taken are details. To provide a theme, reporters need to look for the point—or meaning—behind the event. They need to find the idea that unifies the details of the event. The theme in the robbery story could be that a clerk acted calmly in a threatening situation. The story then would be built— details selected and narrated—so that the characters in action are related to the governing idea.

The second reason causing reporters to wander is that they frequently assume that all information gathered from a situation is newsworthy. They tend to include all details without asking whether details are relevant to the point of the story. News stories tend to become hodgepodges of information. The reporter should ask whether details are relevant and necessary. What is the theme, the central idea? Does a particular detail relate directly to that idea? Does including it help build the theme? The rule for including or excluding a detail is this: if it contributes to the theme, include the detail; if it dilutes the theme, leave it out.

Paragraphs and Sentences

The same principle of unity should be used also in constructing paragraphs and sentences. Journalistic conventions call for *paragraphs* to be short, but reporters should not take that approach to mean that paragraphs should not be built around ideas. The journalistic approach is to design paragraphs as small blocks of type rather than as thematic units. The purpose is entirely visual. Each time a reporter begins a new paragraph, the reporter creates two areas of white space: one at the end of the previous paragraph and one at the beginning of the new one. Those white spaces break up what otherwise would be long columns of solid gray type.

In thinking of paragraphs as units of type, however, you should not think that they are to be constructed without regard for meaning. Bear in mind this simple principle: A paragraph should be about one idea and one idea only. After you have written a paragraph, a good practice is to read the first sentence and then check whether each additonal sentence focuses on the same topic. If any sentence does not, then remove it from the paragraph and place it in another or a new paragraph.

Apply the same principle to *sentences*. Be sure they focus on one point. The easiest way to do that is with simple declarative sentences (for example, "Help arrived too late to save the hostages"). Although you shouldn't write every sentence as a simple one—but should use variety in sentence construction—beware of the common problem of using "and" or "but" or other connectors to bring together two very different thoughts.

Logical Organization

Unity also requires that a news story have a logical organization. Parts should be arranged so that each has its appropriate place and seems to follow naturally the part that preceded it.

The organization most often used in news writing is the *inverted pyramid* arrangement, in which information is placed in descending order of importance. The most important material comes first in the story, and the least important last. The logic behind the inverted pyramid is that the reader may stop reading at any point and still have obtained the most important information, while editors may eliminate paragraphs from the bottom up if limited printing space requires that part of a story be cut. Neither reason for the inverted pyramid approach is based primarily on writing quality.

While the inverted pyramid may be adequate for brief stories and announcements, it tends to encourage haphazard arrangement of lengthier, fuller stories. It may work well for stories the reporter does not wish to develop beyond the routine, but it sometimes results in little more than a stringing together of actions, quotations, and facts. To make news writing good, parts of a story should be put together cohesively and coherently.

Leads

All news stories consist of at least two parts: (1) the lead and (2) the body. Those parts should be integrally related. They should fit together, and the fit should make sense to the reader. The lead should focus on the central point of the body, and the body should be an elaboration of the essential point presented in the lead.

Good *leads* have two characteristics. (1) They are *thematic*, and (2) they get the *reader's interest*. A thematic lead is one that contains the essence of the story. It reveals, in capsule form, what the story is going to be about. If you find that the body of a story you have written includes points that don't seem relevant to the lead, that means that either the lead or the body is constructed in the wrong way. The solution is to rewrite one to make it fit the other.

Leads to news stories normally get readers interested because of the subject of the story. If the reporter summarizes the main point of an event or issue in the lead, that often will keep the reader interested. Reporters, however, always should search for the most effective way to present the material in the lead. A well constructed lead can heighten reader interest in even those subjects that are inherently exciting.

The following leads illustrate these principles.

• Richard Harding Davis on the German army's machinelike invasion of Belgium at the start of World War I:

The entrance of the German army into Brussels has lost the human quality. It was lost as soon as the three soldiers who led the army bicycled into the Boulevard du Régent and asked the way to the Gare du Nord. When they passed, the human note passed with them.

• Herbert Bayard Swope on the murder of a police informant:

"Herman Rosenthal has squealed again."
Through the pallid underworld the sibilant whisper ran. It was heard in East Side dens; it rang in the opium houses in Chinatown; it crept up to the semipretentious crap games of the Fourteenth Street region, and it reached into the more select circles of uptown gambling where business is always good and graft is always high.

• William Bolitho on the death of actress Sarah Bernhardt:

The air was steady and bright, the day they buried Sarah Bernhardt. The crowd heard the wheel creakings as she passed and smelled the loads of costly roses like heavy incense in their faces. Even those at the back, who could see nothing, had this satisfaction: they grumbled less than is usual at so great a show.

Narrative Story Structure

Leads should fit neatly with the body that follows. The body then must have a logical organization. Along with the inverted pyramid structure, there are two other common story forms. One is the *narrative*, and the other is the *topical*. A narrative structure tells the story chronologically (from beginning to end of an episode), while a topical structure—which addresses the various parts of a subject point by point—is often more appropriate for descriptive and analytical stories. A narrative story typically would have these parts:

1. A *lead* that captures the thematic heart of the story.
2. A *body* that tells the story chronologically, during which time typically a situation would exist, intensify, and finally be resolved.
3. A *conclusion* that provides a denouement. (Remember, however, that a story in the inverted-pyramid structure normally has no conclusion.)

Royce Brier's lynching story at the end of this chapter illustrates the narrative structure.

Topical Story Structure

A topical story typically would have these parts:

1. A *lead* that captures the thematic heart of the story.
2. A *body* that incorporates material on major points.
3. A *conclusion* that provides a final thematic statement that ties up the entire story.

The topical structure can be seen in the following story:

Three city government committees looked at different angles Thursday—laws, lounges and leases—to defuse conflicts between students and University area residents.

[The body of the story discusses proposals for solving problems with student parking, consumption of alcohol, and noise.]

Officials, businessmen, residents and student organizations hope to resolve the problems to everyone's satisfaction. "We want to see if we can pass something without trampling on anyone's rights," Richards said. "These are complicated problems with no single solution."

Transition

With short news stories, reporters usually have little concern about how the material moves from point to point. In well developed stories, however, a reporter needs to be aware of *transition*. That is, *when moving from one part of a story to the next, the reporter needs to signal the reader that a change is being made*.

Various techniques may be used for transition. If the new part of the story is parallel or similar to the previous one, a word such as "similarly" or "likewise" might be used. If the subsequent part contrasts with the previous one, then a word such as "however" or "although" can be used. If one part stands out or is more important, its significance can be made clear with "primarily" or "mainly" or a similar transition. If parts are related by logic or time, words such as "therefore" or "then" can be tried. In the following passage, notice how the word "despite" and its reference to the idea in the previous paragraph provide a transition between two types of situations:

When Smith Community College moves from its present location, it will be leaving behind buildings with rusting plumbing and leaking roofs.

Despite the conditions of its facilities, Smith attracts about

7,000 students a year....

Transitional words should be used, however, with restraint. At times, the change in the thought from one part of the story to another will be evident without the reporter signaling the reader. In such instances, transitional words read awkwardly and slow down the reading. Transitions should not be used unnecessarily or repetitiously. They should be used only as necessary to make the structure of a story clear. Consider how in the following passage the word "however" is unnecessary:

The White House says getting a major crime bill is more important than passing a provision supported by the Congressional Black Caucus to let death penalty defendants show racial bias.
However, Caucus Chairman Muhammed Greene countered by threatening to block the crime bill....

INTENSITY

Good news writing has intensity that increases the story's impact. Intensity may be achieved through a number of devices. The most obvious is subject matter. Remember, however, that even a subject with great inherent intensity can bore a reader if the story is not written well. Too many stories that newspapers have published provide convincing evidence of that fact. Fires, floods, military battles, murders, gambling, and government corruption have made the dullest of stories. The best assurance of a good story is good material, but dead style can slay even the liveliest of events and personalities.

Many features of writing contribute to intensity. The most elementary is *mechanical correctness*. Grammar, punctuation, word usage, and other mechanics *must* be handled properly. If a news story contains errors in such matters, readers will begin to notice them rather than the account the story is trying to tell, and the story will lose its effect.

Clarity

News writing must be clear. News stories must be easily understandable to the average reader. All types of writing should be clear, but clarity in news writing is especially important because of the attitude that people bring to newspaper reading. Newspaper readers—unlike readers of novels, or scientific reports, or poems—will not stay with stories that aren't easily understood. News writing that is not clear—that is not easily understood on a first reading—loses power. News writing must avoid vague words and sentences, points, ideas, logic, and article structure. Reporters should use simple, strong words and sentences instead of complex or complicated or indecipherable ones. They should eliminate jargon, abstruseness, and fancy phrases. Effective news writing is direct. Its logic and meaning are plain.

Word Usage and Style

Various stylistic devices may intensify news writing. While some techniques of effective writing relate to overall story structure, word usage and style also intensify writing.

- Reporters should write with *precision*. Words should be chosen for their exact meaning. Writing should not ramble in the reporter's search to state, at last, the point. The right word should not be left to hope or chance. Obtuse writing is not forceful writing.
- Effective writing is *economical*. Journalists are prone to use the description "concise" for lean wording. While *conciseness* normally refers, in journalistic usage, to the use of one or a few words instead of many, economical writing suggests not only conciseness, but short words when they are best, short sentences when they are effective, simplicity of phrasing, and exact word choice. Reporters should not be slaves to rules requiring that sentences average only twenty words or so, but they should not use words needlessly. Declarative sentences taking a simple subject-verb-object structure are usually the most serviceable. If, however, an effective sentence can be stated in no less than fifty words, fifty words should be used; but two words should not be used when one makes the point just as well.
- *Nouns* and *verbs* should outnumber adjectives and adverbs. Adjectives and adverbs only qualify; nouns and verbs provide the substance and the action. Modifiers may be used occasionally to color and brighten, but the strength of writing bursts from things and people who are acting. Strength, decisiveness, power, and intensity come from verbs that act. Passive verbs should be used for victims. *Active verbs* suggest vigor, movement, action, life.
- Writing should use *variety*. Without it, writing becomes monotonous. Sentence structures should differ; word choice should vary. Sentence length and rhythm should change. Some sentences should have subordinate or coordinate clauses; others should not. Subjects and verbs should be placed at different points in sentences. Some sentences should begin with introductory phrases; others should not. Variety lends emphasis to words and ideas. Variety omitted, writing loses its spice.

Adequacy of Explanation

News stories must provide adequate explanation. Reporters must include all details necessary for a reader to understand events and issues. No questions should be left unanswered. The name of an individual, for example, should not be included in a story without an identification of the person. The newspaper practice is to identify even the most well-known people (for example, "*President* Bill Clinton"). You as a reporter may be thoroughly familiar with your subject, but remember that readers do not have the knowledge that you have. You must provide all information that the reader needs to comprehend every item in a story. One way to assure that you do so is by critically reading every sentence after you have written a story and asking if its meaning would be perfectly clear to an uninformed reader.

Natural Style

Style should be natural, not artificial. The reporter should write in a style that suits him naturally, rather than in one determined by mechanical rules. An effective style must be one's own style. Otherwise, articles will sound as if they were written mechanically. A reporter need not write like a robot, as if style rules are absolutes. A good, effective style begins inside a human, not in the circuitry of a computer.

Conversely, reporters should not write in an artificial, exaggerated style. Flowery attempts at "creative" writing are bound to fall on their face, and puffing of facts by careless use of adjectives and adverbs will not get past a seasoned editor or alert reader.

Likewise, a personal style does not mean a "subjective style." As much as possible, the reporter should rely on the concrete, observable details of the object under study. While complete objectivity may not be possible, the reporter should strive to reach it through hunting for evidence, using sources, and observing closely.

Concrete Detail

News stories should include concrete details. Without such details, stories seem vague and general. Concreteness makes them specific and particular. Physical descriptions of people help readers grasp characteristics better. Specific details of scenes help readers visualize where and how actions took place. Without concrete details, stories remain hazy, action and characters indistinct. Details bring them alive and make them real. They help readers to "see" what the reporter is writing about, to smell it, or to hear it.

Using concrete detail in writing requires, ideally, that the reporter be able to provide an *eyewitness* account. The reporters' presence at scenes of battle, tragedy, or heroism is one of the main reasons so many news stories from America's wars stand out as models of writing. The reporters were able to include story details that they observed themselves. Such reporting is more likely to be possible in war coverage because a reporter travels with the action. In many other types of coverage, whether a reporter is present at a news event depends on luck as much as anything else. A journalist is unlikely to know beforehand if, for example, an explosion will ignite a nightclub fire.

If the reporter does not witness an event, he or she must rely on others for accounts of the action and descriptions of the scene and people involved. Working under such restrictions, the reporter should attempt to gather as much concrete detail as possible. Even though secondhand, the detail will help make the account vivid and the event come alive for the reader. Descriptions gathered from witnesses must be more than general accounts, the reporter's story more than a collection of hazy descriptions introduced with the ubiquitous "he said." The job of gathering details must be so thorough that the reporter knows exactly what happened and is able to see, hear, feel, and smell specific actions, events, and characters—and is able to reconstruct them in such a minute degree that the reader can visualize them also.

Mood

Effective style evokes mood. Good news writing can create atmosphere, and one measure of writing is whether the reader indeed senses an atmosphere, or mood, surrounding the events and people in a story. Mood is not, however, a particular aspect of style. It is a result of all other features of writing. Mood is not created artificially but through theme, action, details, characterization, and other factors of a news story. Mood can be used as an indicator of whether news writing is effective. If the writing is good, it often will evoke mood.

Storytelling

Reporters should tell stories. Not all news accounts lend themselves to storytelling. Some require exposition. Many of the most effective news stories, however, have a narrative structure. Some lend themselves to plot development, characterization, conflict, pacing, and denouement. When an event offers the opportunity for narrative, the reporter should tell a story, introducing the situation and characters, building the action, and reaching the climax.

Even when a news account would not be served well by narrative storytelling, the reporter can make use of shorter stories—*anecdotes*—within the overall article. Anecdotes and examples may be used to illustrate points of exposition. They not only explain; they add a human dimension and make reading livelier and more interesting. Because of the secondary place they play in a large story, anecdotes and examples must be brief and should focus on a single point. The insightful reporter may, within a pithy example, reveal character, capture the essence of an event or situation, or create a sense of place or action.

Reveal Character

Effective writing includes people and reveals character. News is important primarily because of one reason: *people.* It involves people, and it affects people. An inanimate topic takes on importance when and usually only if it has an effect on people. Even atomic energy, a major news topic today, has little news value in and of itself. It's critically important because of its potential impact on people. People are the reason for news. Every reporter should explore the human angle in news writing. The more a reporter writes about people, the more interesting and important a news story becomes to the reader.

News stories can offer two types of treatment of people. One involves the event, action, or issue that has the potential for affecting large numbers of people. The other involves only one person or a small number of people who are interesting in and of themselves or who serve as representatives of larger numbers or of humanity in general. By examining the individual, the news story captures in one person's life significance that extends to others. That approach helps the reader comprehend the totality of an issue or event.

To write effectively about people, the reporter must think in terms of *characterization* and should make use of a number of principles. A character in a news story, whether the subject of just one paragraph or of an entire article, must seem real to the reader. A character is made real through physical characteristics (features such as eyes, facial details, and skin texture), typical gestures and movements, details of the person's surroundings (decoration of the office or tidiness of the home, for example), and dress (which may reveal pride, economic class, taste, or another characteristic).

In deciding which details to include, the reporter should ask which ones are pertinent to the particular characteristic of a person the story is showing. Obviously, a story cannot include every detail—weight, height, color of hair, cleanliness of fingernails, shape of ears, and on and on. Even if it could, details unrelated to character would sidetrack readers. The reporter must first recognize the essential characteristic and then select those details that are best for revealing it. The following excerpt demonstrates this principle. It is from a Pulitzer Prize-winning news story, written by Margo Huston of the Milwaukee *Journal*, about a cranky and artful old woman confined to a wheelchair.

...At 91, her blue eyes still twinkle, her smile beckons, and she manages, ever so slowly, to raise her saggy arms and motion, come here, with her fingertips.

Her stringy hair matted, she cocks her head coyly and, smiling like a contented but shriveling babe, softly pleads to this stranger, "Come here, lady, and give Bertha a little kiss."

What a person says and how she says it, if noted accurately by the reporter, will make the characterization come alive. Quoting someone's speech should be used for more than information in news stories. It should reveal character. The reporter should be especially alert to words, quotations, conversation, and dialogue that will help the reader understand the speaker as a real person.

Most important in revealing character, however, is *action*. How does a person act or react in a real situation or at a crucial moment? How does he behave when facing a major decision? Character revelation can be strengthened when the reporter has done enough research and alert observation to be able to analyze the motives behind actions. Readers understand character better when not only the actions taken by a person are shown but also the reasons behind the actions.

Despite its importance to effective news writing, characterization is not often done. The reason: it is not easy to do. It takes a reporter who is observant of exact features and alert to the minutest details. If done well, it can add a fuller dimension to news writing.

USING QUOTATIONS AND ATTRIBUTIONS

Good news writing is not merely stringing together facts. Reporters are particularly prone to string together material without evident plan, however, when they work with quotations. The result is that large blocks of stories are made up of direct quotation after quotation introduced and divided from one another only by the perfunctory "(the source) said." Such an approach is not only boring, but it fails to separate the important from the unimportant.

A number of principles will help you use quotations effectively.

• When a quotation is used to provide information—as opposed to developing a character—it should be *introduced with an explanation*. A quotation itself should elaborate on a point explained by the reporter. Don't begin a quotation with no preparation for it. Introduce it, indicating what its relevance or significance is. Be certain, though, that the introduction doesn't simply repeat the content of the quotation. Notice how violation of that principle causes awkwardness in this Associated Press story:

President Smith issued a statement saying his son had not told him he was engaged and he just recently learned of the relationship.

"He did not inform me that he was considering getting engaged. In fact, I only recently became aware of a relationship between him and a student friend," the president's statement said.

• *Strings of direct quotations should be interrupted occasionally for the reporter to provide perspective.* When a story is composed of extensive quotation, the reporter serves as little more than a stenographer. The reporter must serve as guide for the reader, pointing out the contours of an issue or explaining the high points of an event.

• *Use the word "said" when it is the most correct form for attribution, but use other words of attribution when they more accurately capture the sense of how a speaker made a statement.* "Said" can be used properly when the reporter is trying simply to indicate that a quotation conveyed information, but the neutral "said" is not precise when the tone of a quotation needs to be indicated. Effective attributions can do more than indicate the source of a quotation. They can add to characterization or reveal the tone of how someone said something. The word "said," while impersonal and "objective," should be omitted in favor of more revealing words such as "argued" or "vowed" or "snapped" when the reporter's intent is to show character through tone of speech. If, for example, two city council members carried on a heated shouting match, it would be misleading for a story to report it in the following manner:

"You don't have the faintest idea what you're talking about," Smith said.

"At least I don't go around showing off my ignorance and making a fool of myself," Jones said.

• *Attributions should be placed in a spot within a quotation where they are least conspicuous.* Remember that attributions normally are mechanical devices and should not be overused or made too obvious. Unless you have a reason to emphasize the attribution, you should place it where the reader will least notice it.

That principle suggests, then, that an attribution should not begin a sentence, since the first part of a sentence is normally the most noticeable part. Begin a sentence with the attribution only if you want to draw attention to the fact that a particular individual is the source of a quotation or if the quotation is from a different source than a preceding quotation. In the latter case, beginning with the attribution alerts the reader to the fact that the quotation is not a continuation of one from the previous speaker.

The best place to insert an attribution usually is the point where there is a natural pause in the flow of a statement, as in these examples from two Pulitzer-Prize winning news stories:

A man, distraught, came sprinting after the police car. "That's my kid in there," he yelled. "Help me get my kid out."

"After all," her mother put in, "Linda's whole life was art. She had a burning desire to do something in the art world."

• How much attribution should you use? The basic principle is to *use enough to let the reader know who is speaking, but no more than is necessary.* In a continuing direct quotation, one attribution is enough. In indirect quotation, you need to insert attributions frequently enough to remind the reader that the statement is from a speaker and not from you. The following passage illustrates the problem of using unnecessary attributions. Consider how you would rewrite it using only one.

Donald Stewart, an attorney representing Walters, *said* he is pleased matters are resolved for his client in relation to the criminal proceedings.

"What we were trying to do was preserve what rights we could for our client on the civil side and protect his interests on the criminal side," Stewart *said*. "I feel like we've done that with this settlement," Stewart *said*.

- Unless you have a particular reason to use extensive direct quotation, *mix direct and indirect quotation*. Lengthy direct quotation can become monotonous. Intermingling indirect quotation will create variety. If you are using quotations simply to provide information, consider whether you as a reporter are able to write more economically and pointedly than the speaker was able to talk. Consider using direct quotations only if they reveal the character of the speaker or if the speaker's wording is distinctive.

- Similarly, recognize the value of sometimes *quoting a key word or phrase* rather than a whole sentence. Avoid quoting more than words or phrases unless there is a compelling reason to do so.

- *Never make an error in quoting a speaker.* Accuracy in news is critical. One of the most frequent complaints of sources against newspapers is that they were misquoted.

- Most of us use awkward expressions and sentence structure when we are talking. Unless you have a specific reason to include such awkwardness in a story, *correct a speaker's grammar in printed quotations*.

- *Use punctuation correctly* with quotations. Particularly note these two rules:

1. Commas and periods *always* are placed inside quotation marks.

2. An attribution within a quotation normally is set off with commas, and the remaining punctuation marks remain the same as they would have been if there were no attribution.

Examples:

"If you plan to join us in taking a stand," she said, "then you must be prepared to make a sacrifice."

"I did not intend to get involved," he explained; "I was just planning to watch."

Perspective...

WHAT SOME OF AMERICA'S GREATEST JOURNALISTS WOULD TELL BEGINNERS ABOUT GOOD WRITING

An old woman of upstate New York was asked in the 1880s if she were afraid living alone in the countryside. No, she replied, for every evening the carrier threw her copy of the New York *Evening Post* onto her porch, and it "just lay there and growled all night."

The *Evening Post's* editor, E.L. GODKIN, like other outstanding journalists, knew one of the secrets of really good journalistic writing: really good writing. They knew that how something was said is almost as important as what is said.

If the greatest writers of American journalism were standing before your reporting class today, what would they say?

GODKIN enjoined a youthful writer: "Never write without conveying information."

WILLIAM CULLEN BRYANT, editor of the New York *Evening Post*, 1829-1878, observed: "The necessity of attending to many subjects prevents the journalist from thoroughly investigating any." As a result, journalism "begets desultory habits of thought, disposing the mind to be satisfied with mere glances at difficult questions and to dwell only upon commonplaces." A journalist's writing style tends to "become, in consequence of much and hasty writing, loose, diffuse, and stuffed with local barbarisms and the cant phrases of the day." The problem can be avoided, however, if journalists will always write their best. The key is to "be simple, unaffected; be honest in your speaking and writing. Elegance of language may not be in the power of us all, but simplicity and straightforwardness are."

WALT WHITMAN, editor of a dozen newspapers in the mid-1800s, noted: The journalist "should have a fluent style: elaborate finish we do not think requisite in daily writing. His articles had far better be earnest and terse than polished.... Have something to write about.... Write short; to the point; stop when you have done.... Read it over, abridge, and correct it until you get it into the shortest space possible."

LAFCADIO HEARN, writer for the New Orleans *Item* and *Times-Democrat*, suggested in the 1880s that the journalist help readers "see the colour of words, the tints of words, the secret ghostly motions of words; hear the whispering of words, the rustling of the procession of letters, the dream-flutes and dream-drums which are thinly and weirdly played by words, the weeping, the raging and racketing and rioting of words; sense the phosphorescing of words, the fragrance of words, the noisesomeness of words, the tenderness or hardness, the dryness or juiciness of words."

CHARLES DANA, editor of the New York *Sun* from 1868 until 1896, declared: "The invariable law of the newspaper is to be interesting. Suppose you tell all the truths of science in a way that bores the reader. What is the good? The truths don't stay in the mind and nobody thinks any better of you because you have told them the truth tediously." Some critics "measure our journalistic production by an English standard which lays it down as its first and most imperative rule that [newspaper] writing shall be free from the characteristics of the writer. This is ruinous to good writing and damaging to the sincerity of writers.... Men with actual capacity of certain sorts for acceptable writing have been frightened off from doing natural and vigorous work by certain newspaper...doctrinaires who are in distress if...the temper and blood of the writer actually show in his work."

JOSEPH PULITZER, editor-owner of the New York *World* who established the Pulitzer Prizes, demanded: "Accuracy, accuracy, accuracy. Also terseness, intelligent, not stupid, condensation."

ERNEST HEMINGWAY, war correspondent and general reporter for newspapers in the 1920s and 1930s, claimed: "I'm trying in all my stories to get the feeling of actual life across—not to just depict life—or criticize it—but to actually make it alive. So that when you have read something by me you actually experience the thing."

To a young writer on how to capture the details that make a good story, Hemingway said: "When people talk, listen completely. Don't be thinking what you're going to say. Most people never listen. Nor do they observe. You should be able to go into a room and when you come out know everything that you saw there and not only that. If that room gave you any feeling, you should know exactly what it was that gave you that feeling. Try that for practice. When you're in town, stand outside the theatre and see how the people differ in the way they get out of taxis or motor cars. There are a thousand ways to practice. And always think of other people.

"Watch what happens today. If we get into a fish, see exactly what it is that everyone does. If you get a kick out of it while he is jumping, remember back until you see exactly what the action was that gave you the emotion. Whether it was the rising of the line from the water and the way it tightened like a fiddle string until drops started from it, or the way he smashed and threw water when he jumped. Remember what the noises were and what was said. Find what gave you the excitement. Then write it down making it clear so the reader will see it too and have the same feeling that you had."

• • •

MODEL STORY:
A LYNCH MOB'S "SWIFT AND TERRIBLE" RETRIBUTION

Notice how a variety of principles for good news writing are used in the following story by Royce Brier—the winner of the 1934 Pulitzer

Prize—of the lynching of two jail inmates. He wrote it after eleven hours of strenuous reporting and dangerous work. Gripping fiction can hardly compare with his straight report of human beings obsessed with lynch fever and victims terrified by a mob. By selecting vigorous verbs and revealing detail, Brier conveyed the realism and emotion of the event.

As you read the story, answer these questions:

1. What is the theme of the story?
2. What structure (inverted pyramid, narrative, or topical) does it use?
3. How does the lead reveal the theme?
4. Where does the lead end?
5. How, in outline form, are the main points of the body (beginning, intensification, and climax of the episode) organized?
6. Where does the conclusion begin?
7. For what purposes are direct quotations used?
8. How are details used to create a sense of the sights and sounds of the episode?

Murderers Meet Violent Death at Hands of a Mob
by Royce Brier
San Francisco *Chronicle*
November 27, 1933

SAN JOSE, Calif.—Lynch law wrote the last grim chapter in the Brooke Hart kidnapping here tonight. Twelve hours after the mutilated body of the son of Alex J. Hart, wealthy San Jose merchant, was recovered from San Francisco Bay a mob of ten thousand infuriated men and women stormed the Santa Clara County Jail, dragged John M. Holmes and Thomas H. Thurmond from their cells, and hanged them in historic St. James Park.

Swift, and terrible to behold, was the retribution meted out to the confessed kidnappers and slayers. As the pair were drawn up, threshing in the throes of death, a mob of thousands of men and women and children screamed anathemas at them.

The siege of the County Jail, a three-hour whirling, howling drama of lynch law, was accomplished without serious injury either to the seizers or the thirty-five officers who vainly sought to defend the citadel.

Help from San Francisco and Oakland officers arrived too late to save the Hart slayers.

"Don't string me up, boys. God, don't string me up," was the last cry of Holmes as the noose was put about his neck in the light of flash lamps.

Thurmond was virtually unconscious with terror as the mob hustled him from the jail, down the alley, and across the street to his doom.

Great cheers from the crowd of onlookers accompanied the hoisting of the two slayers. Some women fainted, some were shielded from the sight by their escorts, but the gamut of human nature was here in the park. Old women with graying hair and benign faces expressed satisfaction at the quick end of the murderers, and young women with hardened faces broke down and wept.

King Mob was in the saddle and he was an inexorable ruler.

And here was a sovereign whose rise in invincible power stunned San Jose and will stun the nation and the world.

Brooke Hart's torn body was found in the water this morning. Barricades went up before the County Jail, and the crowd gathered and stayed all the day. It was a good-natured crowd. It knew the deputies and the police and the state highway patrolmen who stood guard. It bandied words with them.

There had been talk of an organized mob, and as the crowd grew in the evening there was no organization. There was shouting, and good nature still ruled.

"This crowd won't do anything," was the constant reiteration of Sheriff Emig's deputies.

Yet as their words of confidence were being spoken there flashed, like a prairie fire, the word through San Jose—eleven o'clock! Eleven o' clock!

The constant bombardment of that hour on the ear was monotonous and ominous.

Indeed, when that hour came the mob was well on its way to its prey, and they were dangling from limbs before midnight.

It was shortly before nine o'clock that the front line at the barricade made its first move of violence. Ten or fifteen patrolmen and deputies were against the barricade, which was not more than thirty feet from the jail door.

There was some pushing from behind, and the good-natured jeering, which had prevailed for almost an hour, took on a deeper tone of muttering. Strangely enough, there was little shouting of "lynch them" at this critical stage. It was a growl which was not unlike the throaty shouting in an African film.

Newspapermen stood behind the barriers; a few deputies stood about. Cameramen snapped flashlights.

Suddenly that front line lunged.

The police locked arms to hold them back. There were fifteen police and a hundred men exerting pressure against them. They swayed for a moment, locked in one another's embrace.

The police shouted orders, but they were mere shrill nothings as the mob behind began a deep rumble, dreadful in its menace.

Out of this twinkling of struggle, while the men behind the barriers held their breath, came a blast like that of a gun. The mob was temporarily quelled and uncertain, staggering back. "Shooting! Shooting!" went up the cry.

But it was a tear-gas bomb which had exploded.

The police suddenly gave way, taking one officer who had been burned back into the jail. The mob, after a moment of uncertainty, surged forward but was still a little cautious.

Out of the jail poured five or six deputies armed with tear-gas sticks. Again the leaders of the mob, those who bore the brunt, staggered back.

But even as they staggered they jeered, and the first shouts of "lynch 'em" stabbed through the tumult.

"We'll get 'em now boys....Bring

'em out....Bring 'em out...." And another dreadful cry went up, a kind of chant which lasted but a minute: "Brooke Hart—Brooke Hart—Brooke Hart—Brooke Hart."

This chant, all of these shouts and screams were choked off in an instant as the first tear-gas bombs were fired.

"Boom—boom—boom," went the bombs. Again smoke, blue and lazy, drifted in the night air of the besieged jail, as lazy in the arc light as cigar smoke before a hearth.

The crowd broke and ran, women and children went screaming out beside the courthouse, handkerchiefs went to eyes everywhere, and the jail for a moment stood deserted, a grim old fortress which seemed in that moment impregnable.

"That's the end of it," everyone said, deputies, newspapermen, everyone.

And everyone, unable to plumb the depth of fury which has swayed San Jose for seventeen days, was wrong.

This was about nine o'clock.

The women and children had run, but there were hardy spirits who stayed. They were the leaders, they were the men who ultimately hanged Holmes and Thurmond.

They couldn't get in close to the jail. The lazy smoke burned their eyes. But they could stand off and throw rocks, and throw rocks they did.

The first rock came soon after the gas started to dissipate. A new post office building is being built near by.

There was tile aplenty about and bricks. There was also a vantage point from which to throw.

Sixty seconds after the first stone came, a steady shower was beating a tattoo on the stone wall of the jail, clanking against the steel door, making musical tinkles as it struck the bars.

Every rat-a-tat on stone or steel brought cheers from the crowd, and when a window in the jail fell, the cheers were redoubled. The sound of a smashing window seemed by some alchemy to get them all, and they roared at the tops of their two hundred voices.

The alleyway before the jail door was now wholly untenable for human beings.

The scene in so far as concerned the pavement was not unlike the front steps of a church during the World War. Debris was everywhere. It was no man's land—no mistaking that.

Now not all of the officers on guard were besieged in the County Jail. Across the alley in Sheriff Emig's office were ten or twelve San Jose police officers, also armed with tear gas.

The situation was complicated by the splitting of forces in this manner, but once accomplished, nothing could be done about it.

The officers fired out the side windows and even sent a bomb out the front window of the courthouse, but the crowd seemed to survive this gas, and went about choking.

The leaders in the front-line trenches, so to speak, most of them boys between eighteen and twenty-three, were not dispersed by any of these bombs.

They stuck. There was some grim and terrible determination in them to get Holmes and Thurmond. There were scarcely more than fifty of them.

After about an hour of this rain of missiles at the jail, the leaders seemed to realize that they were getting nowhere. You can't knock a jail down with bricks.

It was then, about ten o'clock or shortly afterward, that the first settled attack was made on the steel door.

From the post-office construction job came a nine-inch iron pipe, weighing several hundred pounds, but there were willing hands to lift it.

Into the lazy smoke went fifteen or twenty men, charging from the crowd across the no-man's land straight for the ancient steel doors of this jail, which had stood unbreeched since 1866.

"Boom," went the great pipe against the doors.

"Yeeoweeeeeeh," went a strange animal cry from the throats of the onlookers.

"Bang—bang—bang," went the tear-gas bombs from the second story of the jail.

"Ping," went a rock through the arc light at the corner of the jail, and the greatest cheer of all rent the air.

An eerie gloom swam in the courthouse alleys. It was like a stage set for the deepest of blue lights, and here was transpiring a drama the like of which has seldom been seen in America—a drama of a life brutally ended and two more to end.

There was no mistaking this mob now. It was out for Thurmond and Holmes, and nothing short of an army would stop it.

Who held that first iron pipe doesn't matter. They are known in San Jose, but ask someone who was there.

Here was the darkness and here was the mob out in the street. A policeman at the corner tooted his whistle. He was directing traffic. If the courthouse had blown up, if the sky had fallen, that policeman would still toot his whistle, directing traffic at the corner of St. James and First Streets.

He kept on sending 'em down First Street by the courthouse. Traffic was in a terrible snarl. All about the courthouse, about St. James Park to the east, wandered thousands, youngsters and their girls, women with children in their arms, men and their wives, nice old ladies with their daughters.

They milled about, went up as close to the howling front-line boys as possible, wandered away, wondering if they would get them or if they wouldn't get them.

It was a carnival, nothing less, and, after all, you couldn't drum up a straw of sympathy for Jack Holmes and Thomas Thurmond in this valley city.

But what was going on in the front lines? Darkness like a blanket wrapped the alleyway and the box-like old prison.

Out of the darkness leaped another sound, the ominous sound the iron pipe battering ram made on the steel door. Cheers, cheers, cheers, and more blasting of tear gas bombs, more staggering back by the men who held the ram.

Somebody said help is coming. San Francisco's and Oakland's inexhaustible supply of peace officers were speeding this way in automobiles and on motorcycles.

Armed with gas, more gas, and more gas, armed with riot guns.

It must have got about by telepathy, traveled to the front lines as surely as though an army had phones hooked up to the bombproofs.

"Get 'em! Get 'em! The cops are coming!" galvanized the mob and the leaders to more strenuous efforts. Still the bricks beat like an interminable tropic rain on the jail walls and bars and the steel door. Still the scene was plunged in darkness, blue darkness in which the slowly drifting smoke of the tear gas seemed to take the reflection from the very sky.

The third ram went into action. The

leaders leaned as they strained at the great pipe, and in the darkness lunged at the door again. This time the double door gave way. It gave way with a tremendous crash, which stirred an entire block to frenzy.

Into the front corridor went the leaders with their ram. Screaming madly for vengeance, they had come to close quarters with the defenders, men they had known all their lives.

Across the corridor is a heavy barred grating, with a door. This door was open. The ram went through the grating, tearing it from its moorings. On went the ram to the brick wall behind, where it stopped.

In the darkness below, in the no man's land of a few minutes before, surged the mob, sending up yells in waves like the ocean surf. It was a steady drum of sound, in which words were indistinguishable.

In the second-story window at this moment appeared two of the leaders. "We're getting 'em....We're bringing 'em down."

If it was possible the sound from below rose to a greater volume. Those below could not get into the jail. There wasn't room for them in the narrow corridors and cells.

And while the crowd screamed, here was the scene inside a jail occupied by men who had stood by valiantly, whatever may be said, against overwhelming odds.

They all knew one another—remember that—the mob and the officers. This was not a masked job.

Howard Buffington, veteran jailer, wept. He knew he was helpless before those men. They ran up the stairways, through the jail. No one could shoot them down. What is the law? No one had been hurt yet. Joe Walsh and Felix Cordray, all of them veterans, were helpless.

The mob knew where their prisoners were, and there was little chance of mistake. The mob leaders knew Thurmond and Holmes personally.

They went to Thurmond's cell on the third floor, the old northeast cell of David Lamson. Buffington went along with the leaders. They took the keys from Buffington. Thurmond, in mortal terror, was clinging to the grating in the toilet of his cell.

Then there occurred a scene probably never enacted before in a lynching in the history of America.

The leaders prayed for Thurmond's soul.

They knelt in that jail cell, five or six of them, in the midst of the turmoil and the shouting, and they prayed to God Almighty for the man who was soon to meet that God.

They arose with the whimpering prisoner, arms grasping him on either side, and he stumbled down the stairs. He stumbled along tongue-tied with his last great terror.

The scene in the Holmes cell on the second floor of the prison was a different one. No one prayed for Holmes, the so-called leader of the Brooke Hart slaying.

Holmes was also concealed in the washroom off his cell, and when the crowd went in he denied he was Holmes.

With a last bravado he shouted: "I'm not Holmes."

But his destroyers laughed in his face. Too many of them knew him well. One man struck him in the face.

"By God you are!" shouted the men jammed in his cell. He fell to the floor. Grasping him by the feet, they dragged him down the steps and out into the open, where Thurmond had just arrived.

For a moment there was bedlam about the jail. A few on the outskirts of the crowd shouted that one was the wrong man. There was some doubt at first that two men had been taken. But those next to the men knew whom they had.

There had been some howling in the jail for Tony Serpa, a youth recently convicted of manslaughter, when he had been charged with murder. It was a short-lived cry. The mob leaders were not to be diverted from their purpose.

The snarling mob with the half-conscious prisoners did not tarry before the jail. They moved with a kind of mindless precision down the alley beside the courthouse to First Street, and across that street to St. James Park.

That movement across First Street seemed instantaneous. One moment the men were in the jail alley; there was yet a ray of hope for them, even though policemen were wandering away in a bewildered manner. The next moment the mob had the prisoners in the park, and their end had come.

A great murmuring went up from the thousands who had thus far taken little part in the actual seizure of Holmes and Thurmond. These spectators, men, women, and children, streamed like a mighty surf toward the park.

They climbed the statue of William McKinley, and they milled about, gorging the entire west side of the big park.

There was not the remotest doubt where the sympathy of these people lay.

"String 'em up!" came from a thousand throats, from grammar-school boys, from businessmen with spectacles, and from workingmen in rough garb.

There was some delay in getting a rope, some impatience from the crowd. Several men started climbing trees, and every man was given a cheer. The light was dim in the park, but there were a couple of arc lights and hundreds of flashlights.

After a delay of almost fifteen minutes, ropes were produced, and Thurmond, who was at the south end of the park, was the first man to be hanged. He was benumbed with fear, and his crazed mutterings were without meaning.

Thurmond was hanged to a low limb. As his body was hoisted, the crowd broke into frantic cheering. Someone in that crowd must have had the technique of hangman's knots. Thurmond thrashed as he hung there, swaying to and fro, seeming to bend his body at the hips in a last spasm of life.

For perhaps three minutes he swayed there, his face blackening slowly, his tongue extended, although he was obviously unconscious.

"Brookie Hart—Brookie Hart," cried his executioners to the man who could no longer hear them.

The taunts went on as the man's body dangled at the end of the rope, slowly turning, now this way and now that, as though some mocking power were giving all a full view of him.

The crowd ran hither and thither, children scampering through the crowd to get the best view. Some children in arms were held twenty-five feet from the dangling man as the mob of onlookers milled about and gave vent to cries of triumph.

Holmes' execution followed that of Thurmond by a few minutes. In a despairing voice, which was nevertheless clear, he kept denying that he was Holmes, but the crowd knew better, and those immediately about him did not bother to fling his words back at him.

Holmes, his bloody face turned on his captors, took death with more stamina than did Thurmond. As the rope was let down from a limb, he begged:

"Don't string me up, boys.... Don't string me up."

"Yes, I'm Holmes," he gasped, and held his head up, and in the next instant the noose dropped over it, and with a cheer his body was flung into the air.

Holmes did not struggle as long as did Thurmond. It seemed that that last relinquishment of hope had taken the life from him. The rope about his neck, too, seemed to have left him nothing but reflexes to cause motion.

There was a report that both nooses were the hangman's knots which crush into the skull behind the ear, and destroy consciousness.

While Thurmond still dangled, his feet even with the faces of the crowd, Holmes was thrown far into the air. The crowd gasped for a moment as it observed that his body was stark-naked.

Now, as the men swung there, both playthings of the winds and the twisted ropes, many who had cried for their execution turned away. Several women fainted in the crowd, but there were thousands who did not faint; there were hundreds who looked on with smiles.

And the burden of all the talk was:

"Well, there won't be any kidnapping in this county for a long time."

The dead men swung there. Some of the more violent spirits were for cutting them down and burning them with gasoline. Thurmond's trousers were stripped from him, and some of the mob set fire to his rubber coat, which burned for a few minutes.

The bodies hung in the park for almost an hour. Shortly before midnight came squads of San Francisco police officers. The crowd ran. These were the police for whom Sheriff Emig called when he ran out of tear gas about half an hour before his prisoners were seized. They were too late to save anything but the dead clay of the murderers.

14

WRITING WITH
AN EDITOR'S EYE

Editing and revision are essential parts of the writing process. For every well-written news story, a good reporter and a good editor are at work. Reporters often grow frustrated with the changes editors make in their copy. It seems almost unfair that someone who did not do the actual reporting for the story can be allowed to have the final say on what should go in the story. However, this is the very reason why editors have the final say. In the natural course of learning everything he or she can about a given subject, the reporter tries to become an expert. Unlike the reporter, the editor is more likely to bring to the story a fresh eye, which the reader is more likely to have. The secret to writing with an editor's eye is to temporarily step out of the role of expert and try to see things through the eyes of the reader.

The traditional relationship between news reporters and editors tends to be characterized in popular culture as an ongoing love-hate affair. At best, the editor is described in terms similar to a teacher, parent, coach, or confidant—a calm voice of reason

BY JOSEPH A. MIRANDO

Dr. Mirando, Associate Professor of Journalism at Southeastern Louisiana University, worked as a reporter and copy editor for five daily newspapers and a weekly. He served as the Executive Secretary of the Southeastern Journalism Conference from 1988 to 1996.

ready to help a reporter put the facts into proper perspective. At worst, and probably more often, the editor is seen as a mean, picky, ruthless, uncaring individual who could never quite make it as a reporter and now thinks nothing of cutting the heart out of many a good story. Like most myths, there are probably some bits of truth to this image, but most of it is overstated or based on a few but memorable reporter-editor confrontations.

A survey conducted by the Associated Press Managing Editors provides a more accurate picture of the typical reporter-editor relationship. In putting together its "Agenda for Journalism Education," the APME polled managing editors and beginning reporters. Both groups of journalists were asked to rank the skills that schools of journalism and mass communication should emphasize in their classes. In the movies and in novels editors and reporters are never able to agree on anything, but in the APME study the nation's youngest reporters and the most veteran editors showed surprising agreement over what were the five most important traits all journalists must have:

- Thinking analytically
- Presenting information well
- Understanding numbers in the news
- Listening to readers
- Writing concisely

Just as interesting were skills to which both editors and reporters gave the lowest rankings: "personal affairs reporting," managing and marketing newspapers, why newspaper penetration has dropped, desktop publishing, and multi-culturalism.

A strong sense of respect for what constitutes good writing and reporting is what the best editors and reporters share. They have their disagreements, as in all healthy, vibrant relationships. But agree or disagree, reporters and editors are bound by a common goal—to help readers gain a clear understanding of the world around them.

It is a mistake for reporters to view working in a newsroom as a type of cat-and-mouse game, the object being to see how they can sneak as much of their original copy as possible into the newspaper. Antics include such devices as trying to avoid tough copy editors and turning in a story near deadline in the hope that an editor will give it only a quick read. No doubt such antics go on in college journalism classrooms and student newspaper offices, and in many cases they may even have their roots there.

However, the best reporters resist the temptation to engage in such tactics even when they are confronted with the stereotypical ogre editor of popular fiction. Hiding parts of stories, playing favorites, or lying merely promotes a haphazard form of journalism that only occasionally allows reporters to do truly excellent work.

Rather than playing games, the best reporters try to write with an editor's eye. That is, they understand the importance of revision. They realize that checking over copy, cutting, and making changes are essential parts of the writing process. No one turns in copy so perfect that it never contains anything resembling an error of grammar or logic. And the reasons for editing changes are not necessarily because the reporter got it wrong. Segments of news stories may need to be reworked for practical reasons—a tight news hole, a similar story already in the newspaper or possibly new developments in your story after you've filed it.

Writing with an editor's eye involves a dedication to editing one's own copy as thoroughly and as critically as possible.

ACCURACY

Most journalism textbooks discuss the qualities students need to become journalists, and they tend to describe these qualities in vague or arbitrary terms. A doctoral dissertation found that 130 different qualities appeared in 250 news reporting and writing textbooks printed between 1867 and 1987. Typical textbooks maintained that journalists needed such attributes as alertness, intelligence, knowledge, and perception.

The results of the APME survey are a bit more useful to journalism students because of their clarity. And it's no mistake that the top choice among the editors participating in the survey was the ability to think analytically. Simply put, analytic thinking means the practice of breaking down information into its most important parts in a critical manner to understand the importance and relevance of the information. In reporting the news, the analytic reporter places less emphasis on formulaic aspects of the story and devotes far more attention to providing proper perspective. This forms the basis of all editors' No. 1 concern—accuracy.

A commitment to accuracy involves a lot more than just a constant reminder to follow Joseph Pulitzer's famous motto, "Accuracy, Accuracy, Accuracy." Making sure the facts are right must dominate all phases of the reporter's work. Reporters often find themselves in a position to assume truth. They witnessed what they're reporting on, or they talked to the people involved or saw the documents; so they may naturally trust that they have the whole story. But copy editors are trained differently. They weren't there, and they're not close to the sources; so they do not develop this natural trust. Reporters who are serious about ensuring the accuracy of their stories can adopt the copy editor's point of view by maintaining a healthy sense of skepticism about everything they see and everyone they talk to. Here are some hints on how to do it:

• *Be careful about word choice in providing description*, especially when dealing with extremes. The easiest way to cause a newsroom to be deluged with complaints is to describe anything as the "first," the "most," or the "oldest." An extra amount of documentation is needed whenever those adjectives are used, and it's quite likely that the extra effort still won't be enough because the documentation needed may not exist. An article may appear to be watered down in describing something as "one of the first" or "one of the earliest known," but it will be more likely to be true. Be careful about assumptions when you may not have all the evidence. Besides, in many cases the distinction of being first or earliest can be an insignificant distinction.

• *Pay strict attention to context.* Breaking down information in smaller, more visual terms can be an effective device in analytic reporting. In trying to make readers understand how vast a library's book collection was, an enterprising reporter reported the number of books in the library and multiplied the number by the average size of the books to come up with this description: "...If all the books contained in the university library were laid down edge-to-edge along Highway 10, the collection would stretch from the campus to the state line." However, in describing how a town lost money in sponsoring a festival, another reporter wrote, "...The final bill amounted to a figure that would have been enough to pay for a spare uniform and a bullet-proof vest for every policeman in the town." The subtle political criticism contained in this passage implied the inaccurate view that the town council refused to maintain its police force. In this case the reporter would have been better off just reporting the simple facts—that ticket sales at the festival fell $20,000 short of the expenses paid to put on the event.

• *Choose sources cautiously.* It's possible the sources themselves have been misinformed; so the information they pass on may be inaccurate. Some sources want to be helpful and try to tell reporters what they think the reporters want to hear. Other sources try to manipulate reporters to create the best possible image for themselves in the paper. All of these problems may occur unintentionally or for what sources consider legitimate reasons. The best policy for a reporter is to take the time to identify what or who would be the most authoritative source, the source most likely to have the most reliable information. Even if reporters don't particularly like to deal with a particular source, in the interest of accuracy they must.

• *Make sure all the important questions are answered.* Even if everything in a story is true, it may still be inaccurate if certain facts are left out. To report that the local state representative was absent for almost half of all votes during a special legislative session would be truthful if state records backed up the statement. But the records won't say that the representative was involved in an auto crash and was unable to attend.

• *Be selective about the minor details* to be included in a story. Providing background or secondary facts doesn't always enhance a story and may even harm it. Just because somebody said something doesn't make it so, no matter how interesting it is. To help understand why a mayor opposed a new zoning ordinance, a councilman who was the sponsor of the proposed ordinance once told a reporter, "It's because the mayor is a Communist." It was the ugliest thing the councilman could think of at the moment, and the reporter thought it would be okay to put that comment in the story. "I know he really doesn't think the mayor is a Commie, and the story is mainly about how the ordinance failed; so that's why I thought it belonged deep in the body of the story rather than the lead," the reporter explained. When the editor deleted the comment altogether, the reporter protested, pleading with the editor, "But he said it." Without proof that the mayor was a member of the Communist party, the councilman was slandering the mayor, and the newspaper would have libeled him if it had printed the information. Even without the legal risk, the comment had no place in the story because the reporter had done nothing to show any connection between Communism and zoning laws, and the reporter even admitted that the councilman didn't believe it himself.

• *Check facts.* Some reporters think that verifying information is a tedious chore that takes away time from putting the story together and moving on to the next assignment. Having to bother a source at home with yet another phone call is hardly something reporters look forward to. They seem to feel time is wasted when they call a source and hear the same information repeated. However, making sure a story is correct is always time well-spent. Sources often appreciate the effort and come to respect a reporter more for commitment to the truth. Reporters who take pains to confirm the facts strike a blow for journalistic credibility.

An elaborate fact-checking policy that has gained prominence over the past decade exists at the *Columbia Missourian*, the University of Missouri School of Journalism's daily newspaper. Stories generated by the *Missourian* staff are checked through a phone call to sources, who are read segments of stories or even whole stories. The sources are asked to correct misspellings and errors of fact, and the integrity of the reporter is protected because the sources are not allowed to edit the stories or change their quotes.

PROMOTING UNDERSTANDING

In journalistic writing, unlike personal essay writing, the writer does not write primarily out of a desire to form an impression. Readers are trusted to form their own impressions. The best journalists try to help readers understand the important issues of the day. The APME survey findings on the need to present information well, make sense of numbers, listen to readers, and write concisely all attest to the value both editors and reporters place on promoting this sense of understanding.

Information presented well to a copy editor means that the reporter's story is kept simple and to the point, technical information is explained, the impact on readers is examined, and quotations and attributions are all clear.

The advice to *keep copy simple* often earns journalistic writing a bad rap from scholars and teachers because it implies elementary words and choppy sentences. But simple writing actually has two meanings that, when it's done well, do not deserve such criticism. In a general sense, simple means to emphasize topics and terms that are the most familiar to readers. Words like "prognosticate," "rubric," or "fuliginous" may impress a teacher in an essay written for an English composition class, but they don't do much to increase understanding in a news story read by thousands of subscribers representing a wide range of education levels. Instead, "predict," "directions," and "smoky" are going to be the words that help a reader concentrate on the substance of a news story rather than the way it's written. In a grammatical sense, simple means to confine sentences to one main clause— one subject-verb relationship. Readability research going back to the 1940s has consistently shown that complex and compound sentences, structures that employ two or more subject-verb relationships, are not as readily understandable. Notice how the three clauses strung together in a single compound-complex sentence below are easily improved by simply putting periods after the clauses.

Compound-Complex Sentence:

The state public health office reported that the number of teenage pregnancies had risen last year within the tri-county area, and to counter the problem community organizations are busy organizing a massive advertising campaign targeting the public high schools while social service agencies are hoping to add federal assistance.

Simple Sentence:

The state public health office reported that the number of teenage pregnancies had risen last year within the tri-county area. To counter the problem, community organizations are busy organizing a massive advertising campaign targeting the public high schools. Social service agencies are hoping to add federal assistance.

The use of *technical information* probably represents the most pressing need for a reporter to write with an editor's eye. In becoming familiar with a particular news beat, reporters learn the specialized language that goes with the territory, and they learn that they must frequently speak that language in dealing with their sources. When they become close to their sources and knowledgeable of the language the sources speak, it is almost inevitable that specialized terms creep into their copy if they don't watch out. That's why when a story on the nearby community college points out that "The number of FTEs made only 75 percent of formula funding necessary," the education reporter will feel that it makes complete sense, but the copy editor will say that it sounds like a foreign language. It's most likely going to sound like a foreign language to anybody not involved in higher education administration, too. The reporter needs to explain somewhere in the story that FTEs are numbers of students taking the equivalent of a full-time course load and that formula funding is a method of allocating money to the college based on the enrollment.

The easiest way to promote understanding is to give readers a clear reason why they should want to read a news story. They have to contend with an information explosion taking place today, and the only way they can keep up with it all is by being choosy about what they read. They're most likely to choose to read news stories that are especially meaningful to them. In recognition of these conditions, strong copy editors constantly ask "Who cares?" and "So what?" as they edit stories. Reporters can easily do the same as they revise their stories.

USING QUOTATIONS

For years journalists viewed *quotations* mainly as effective devices for sustaining interest in a news story, but recent legal decisions have caused concern among editors.

Direct quotes, those statements that are within quotation marks, appear to be safe only when they are a source's exact words. Direct quotes that contain even minor changes for grammar may be troublesome. This is a big reason why the typical news story should have just one or two direct quotes. Few people speak in complete sentences without er, ah, or um mixed in. Besides, direct quotes, like any literary device, tend to lose their impact when there are too many of them.

Partial quotes, one or two-word statements within quotation marks, can be equally troublesome because they often imply the opposite of what is said (i.e., The president said he had a "good" time).

Indirect quotes, those statements that are still attributed but are not within quotation marks, consist of paraphrased and condensed versions of what was said. Editors tend to prefer these because they remove concern over the specific words actually spoken and allow the writing to place emphasis more on context and clarity.

USING NUMBERS

The ability to *understand numbers* in the news was rated highly in the APME survey because newsmakers often use a wide range of statistical information to justify their actions. A number by itself is an easy concept to grasp, but when a bunch of numbers are thrown together in comparisons, formulas, and equations, more effort is required to sort out what they all mean. Readers find sentences and paragraphs that stuff numbers together tedious, like this one: "When oil dropped $1 a barrel, gas stations cut their prices by 5 cents per gallon, but an estimated $25 million was lost in tax revenue, forcing an across-the-board cut of 4.4 percent for state agencies."

Editors may make the problem worse. In their attempts to improve readability, they may try to remove at least some of those numbers, but their choice of which numbers to include and which ones to take out may not be as strong as the reporter's choice. Reporters therefore cannot shy away from numbers. They are so important.

The solution is for the reporter to consider which numbers are the most vital to the story, to avoid bunching numbers close together, and to provide explanations and examples to give the numbers meaning. Describing how much families save at the gas pump or what state agencies have to do to contend with the budget cuts will be a lot more interesting to readers than general numbers will.

PAY ATTENTION TO READERS

The call to *listen to readers* may someday top a future APME survey. The Detroit *Free Press*, the Charlotte *Observer*, and the Wichita *Eagle* all received accolades for employing a reader-centered approach throughout the 1992 presidential campaign. While papers like the New York *Times* and the Washington *Post* continued to stress horse race-style polls and candidates' charges and counter charges, the *Free Press*, *Observer*, and *Eagle* focused on citizen-identified issues, replaced the usual newsmakers' views with comments from average citizens, and even organized community forums to encourage more local residents' responses. More newspapers and broadcast stations used similar devices during the 1994 elections and expanded on them to include stories on how communities were dealing with race relations, crime, education, and health care.

The trend is now being identified as a movement called *Public Journalism*, and many editors are working to advance it by encouraging reporters to use innovative methods involving citizens in their news stories. "Public journalism is a form of reporting, writing and presentation that treats readers not merely as residents, but as citizens with a stake in the processes that shape their communities," Marty Claus, vice president/ news for Knight-Ridder, explained in a recent issue of *Knight-Ridder News*. "It provides readers with the critical information they need to participate in public life. It creates opportunities for them to participate and opportunities for journalists to listen to the people we serve, not just the usual sources. It emphasizes reporting of solutions and success stories—not just problems. It is not journalism that advocates a particular point of view, but it does advocate every citizen's participation in a healthy dialogue."

BE CONCISE

The reporters who write in the most *concise* manner are typically the ones most prized by editors. There's no getting away from the reality that newspapers have a limited amount of space and readers have a limited amount of time to devote to reading. It is difficult to boil down an article as the deadline approaches, and the reporters who adopt the attitude that they need not be concerned about how long their story runs can be a liability. The irony is that the length of the story by itself is not the key issue. To make an article concise does not necessarily mean to make it short. Conciseness should never be used as an excuse for not reporting the whole story. To write concisely means removing as much unnecessary information as possible so that the whole story is still there but has been told in as few words as possible.

Perspective...

WHAT A VETERAN EDITOR WISHES BEGINNING JOURNALISTS KNEW ABOUT WRITING AND REPORTING

By FREDERICK R. BLEVENS, an editor and reporter on six newspapers, including the Houston *Chronicle*, Fort Worth *Star-Telegram*, San Antonio *Light*, and Philadelphia *Bulletin*, and now an assistant professor of journalism at Texas A&M University

I. F. Stone, the quintessential practitioner of personal journalism, once explained the dangers facing novices in the fictional case of a cub reporter sent to a fire. Consumed by allegiance to a higher being who obviously provided this disaster as a means to demonstrate journalistic skill, the reporter actually forgets its tragic consequences.

Stone, blacklisted in the mid-century Communist purges, founded, wrote and edited one of the most influential weeklies in American history. He was motivated by a healthy sense of outrage; his hard-earned autonomy allowed him to question authority, expose injustice and explain consequences without outside manipulation from sources, advertisers and editors. Stone predicated his personal autonomy on the ability to think and act responsibly, to see stories as ends as well as means, to report and write with integrity and ethics beyond reproach.

Every new generation of journalists has its own personality and values, all of which seem to differ from—yet correspond to—those of the past. For Ben Hecht and Ernest Hemingway, journalism was a craft whose rudiments and conventions were best learned by up-from-the-bootstraps routine. The value and worth of apprenticeship were positively correlated with the difficulty and pain of training.

Like many of the myths of journalism history, that period has been characterized inaccurately as one of "anything goes" and "every man for himself," with autonomous reporters chasing, creating and embellishing "scoops." Those, in fact, were the *collectively* established norms.

Since mid-century, journalists have been operating under the theory of social responsibility with collectively established ethics and "truth behind the truth" as their new conventions. Again, the individual journalist has been pushed into a double bind that seldom recognizes personal autonomy and intellectual diversity. The guerrilla sensationalism of pack-like urban journalism has been replaced by "we feel good" four colors and the sweeps mentality of network infotainment.

Every network is airing news sensationalized by fast-paced footage and hidden cameras. Newspapers, looking to "reconnect" to their readers, promote journalism of community consensus. They give away homes, cars and "repackaged" local news in hopes of maintaining double-digit profits. Colleges and universities profess rudiments and conventions established by megamedia conglomerates that endow the schools, then hire and sometimes exploit the graduates.

With two halves of a century on such parallel tracks, why are editors surprised when today's beginning journalists value quick over quality, deceit over decency, docudrama over straight, if qualified, truth? More than ever before, novices must develop a sense of self, a personal philosophy and ethic associated with telling and, more important, *feeling* a story.

Editors do care about writing and reporting; and, to their credit, most will admit that they, too, were not grammarians and stylists at the start. But to them, a cub reporter who can see the internal conflict—the outrage—in the news is much more valuable than a cookie-cutter factoid journalist who can craft a lead and four bullets to fit a five-inch hole on the page. Beginning journalists must ferret inequalities and injustices with fundamental inspiration from fully grounded personal autonomy and ethics.

Without those, the cub reporter is likely to forget the fire is actually burning.

15

ANALYTICAL STORIES AND EXPLANATORY WRITING

The explanatory journalist probes, analyzes, and explains, using all the tools at his or her disposal. Explanatory writing requires much of the reporter but is playing an increasingly important part in analyzing our world on the eve of the 21st century.

In this Future Shock world of accelerating complexities, journalism serves no higher purpose than to explain. While reporting the news is fundamental to all news media, analyzing the news—detailing the why—traditionally has been the purview of print media, especially newspapers.

David Halberstam, author of *The Powers That Be* and several other books analyzing American society, once declared, "Print defines what television magnifies." Dramatic pictures do not necessarily give meaning to events; but printed words, based on comprehensive research, do.

Newspapers today have an impressive array of tools to help readers understand the world's complexities. For collecting in-

BY RON TAYLOR AND LEONARD RAY TEEL
Mr. Taylor has been a reporter, editor, and writing coach at the Atlanta *Constitution* for the past twenty-five years. He also teaches reporting at Georgia State University.

Dr. Teel, Associate Professor in the Department of Communication at Georgia State University, has more than twenty years' experience as a newspaper reporter, editor, and columnist.

formation, there are computerized databases and data analysis systems. For presenting information, there are computerized graphics to design everything from fever charts to maps of natural disasters around the world. The Society of Professional Journalists even gives an annual award for "informational graphics."

At bottom, though, analytical newspaper stories require that the writer make from something very complex something relatively simple and understandable.

TWO TYPES OF ANALYTICAL WRITING

The most common types of analysis appearing in newspapers are *opinion* and *sourced*.

What often is labeled as *analysis* is the authoritative opinion of some expert or veteran reporter regarding an issue. Such articles usually run as companions to news stories or as columns and are written in a relatively short time.

A report on the decline of the stock market, for instance, may be accompanied by an analysis by an economist. Or a reporter who covers city hall may write an opinion article for the perspective section on how a bribery scandal in the city council is affecting city politics.

Sourced analysis takes the form of traditional news stories, including plenty of attributions, supporting evidence, and multiple viewpoints. In the profession, stories of this type are aptly called "explainer pieces."

Since newspapers generally turn to outsiders or old-timers for opinion-type analysis, we will focus on sourced analysis, or what we shall call, as the Pulitzer Prize committee does, *explanatory journalism*.

To some extent, all thorough articles explain, giving the reader some understanding of the *why* behind an event or issue. What sets apart pure explanatory journalism is comprehensiveness and the commitment of time to improve accuracy.

Explanatory journalism is typified by the following characteristics:

- It defines an event or issue of considerable complexity in simple and understandable terms and relates it to everyday concerns.
- It connects disparate segments of an event or issue to form a comprehensible whole.
- It represents the latest knowledge about a complex event or issue.

- It gives context to a multitude of opinions and experiences.

For newspaper management, explanatory stories can represent sizable investments in hours and resources; so projects are undertaken only after careful planning. The reporter must first convince the editors that a story or series is worth doing.

IDENTIFYING THE NEED FOR ANALYSIS

Trends come and go; so not every one is worth developing into a major work of explanatory journalism. And some trends are quickly analyzed into triteness. Thus, imagination and insight can make a vast difference in story quality. When veteran science writer Mike Toner of the Atlanta *Journal-Constitution* began looking into the resurgence of tuberculosis, one problem was finding something truly new to say on the subject. The resurgence had been recorded in scores of news stories, and practically every other health and science writer in America was looking for a new angle on the subject. What Toner discovered in his research, however, eventually won him a Pulitzer Prize: The TB bacteria was not the only bug fighting back, but hundreds of others were defying scientists' efforts to keep them out of our food and bloodstreams. Toner's series, "When Bugs Fight Back," won the 1992 award for Explanatory Journalism.

Stories that explore a trend or a convergence of trends are the most common type of explanatory journalism. But explanatory stories also are built from historical patterns, demographics, and sheer fascinating detail. Let us discuss briefly each of these four foundation factors.

Trends

Trends are pretty easy to spot. If it seems new and everybody suddenly is talking about it, it's a trend. Television comedians will be telling jokes about it, popular magazines will be highlighting it, and newspaper lifestyle sections will be telling you where to find it and what to wear with it.

Explanatory stories, however, usually reach beyond merely assessing a particular trend. Instead they explore how one trend is converging with others to alter culture and the environment.

While looking into the resurgence of TB, Mike Toner found not only a multitude of other bacteria and viruses that had become resistant to the latest antibiotics designed to stop them, but also an alarming number of crop-destroying insects that had become resistant to most pesticides. Moreover, he found, weed killers weren't working well either. The thread that wove bugs and weeds together was mounting evidence that pests have as much will to survive as humans have to kill them. From the convergence of trends—microbes increasingly resistant to antibiotics, insects increasingly resistant to pesticides, weeds increasingly resistant to herbicides—emerged Toner's creepy, hairy tale of the ugly side of nature coming to get us. The original concern about the resurgence of TB became a side issue, discussed in a sidebar.

Historical Patterns

If it's happening now, it probably happened—with some variation—before. History may not exactly repeat itself, but it does provide patterns and guideposts for understanding and explaining current events and giving them context.

As scary as Mike Toner's series on bugs was, he provided some comfort to readers by assuring them that the problem had happened, to varying degrees, before, and we had survived. At times, he reached back to biblical times for precedent, and throughout he reminded readers of the evolutionary history of survival of the fittest.

The American history of gobbling up frontier and threatening distinct cultures came into play in Leonard Teel's prize- winning articles on Persimmon Valley, an isolated north Georgia mountain community still cherishing its traditions but encroached upon by values of a New South. By spending weeks with the families of Persimmon Valley, Teel immersed himself in the culture. In the end, he portrayed what was at risk in the push for progress, as well as a personalized history of a vanishing society.

Demographics

The story of Persimmon Valley also was, in many ways, a demographics story, a description of the movement and changing habits of people. While the story took a largely narrative approach, the trend in demographics stories today is toward statistical analysis. One reason is that there are so many statistics available to us. While there is danger in overburdening readers with numbers, explanatory journalism based on demographics and polling information offers a more precise view than anecdotal material does.

Many newspapers are just beginning to use this technique well. One of the pioneering reporters is Hyde Post, leader of the "innovation team" at the Atlanta *Journal-Constitution*. As projects editor in 1988, he directed reporter Bill Dedman in digging through demographic surveys, census data, and federal bank lending documents to prove finally what many had suspected for years, that blacks were significantly less likely to get mortgage loans than whites. By matching demographic data on various metro Atlanta neighborhoods with the bank lending information, Dedman was able to show—in maps and words—that people living in predominantly white neighborhoods were nearly twice as likely to get loans as people living in predominantly black neighborhoods. The *coupe de grace* came in an interview with an African American who had been denied a loan—the chairman of the county commission. The series—"The Color of Money"—won Dedman a Pulitzer Prize.

Fascinating Details

Sometimes events are so filled with fascinating detail that recounting them is an elaborate explanation unto itself.

Reporter David Hanners and photographer William Snyder of the Dallas *Morning News* won the 1989 Pulitzer Prize in Explanatory Journalism for their detailed report on the investigation of an airplane crash from beginning to final report. They had arranged in advance with the National Transportation Safety Board to follow an investigator as he helped piece together the fragments from a typical crash to attempt to determine the cause. NTSB officials kept their commitment to cooperate when a business jet crashed in a thunderstorm near Texarkana, leaving seven people dead. Sharing the Pulitzer was Karen Blessen, the graphic designer who helped illustrate the report.

Susan Faludi won a 1991 Pulitzer at the *Wall Street Journal* by detailing the leveraged buyout of Safeway Stores Inc. not through financial documents but through the sad stories of ordinary employees who suffered because of the buyout.

RESEARCH

To explain a subject, a reporter must understand the subject; and to understand the subject, the reporter must do thorough and comprehensive research.

In explanatory journalism a review of the literature is essential just to find out if a subject is worthy of detailed exploration. That is how you identify the convergence of trends and determine whether someone else already has written the definitive article or series of articles on the subject.

That is not to say that a subject that has been written about has been adequately explained to the broad audience of general circulation newspapers. Often details of developments important to large numbers of people lie buried in academic journals or alternative publications, discussed only among scholars or social scientists until an explanatory journalist discovers them. These articles then become pieces of an elaborate puzzle to be assembled by the journalist through research.

Publications

At major newspapers, reporters—particularly specialists in fields such as medicine and demographics—routinely receive academic and government publications from which early information about important developments can be garnered. AIDS first came to the public media's attention, for instance, through the "Weekly Mortality and Morbidity Report" mailed to newspapers by the Centers for Disease Control. From a relatively small item in that newsletter in 1982 about a mysterious new disease that destroyed the immune system grew the thousands of articles and broadcasts that since have described and explained the disease.

Many academic and professional publications can be obtained from government agencies and university libraries. Also helpful are newsletters and booklets published on behalf of trade associations and special interest groups, representing everything from the soft drink industry to gun collectors. Most libraries carry reference books listing the names and addresses of agencies and associations, as well as indexes of books and periodicals.

Data Bases

Increasingly, reporters do the brunt of their research by computer. Most publications, in fact, are indexed in data bases, and many articles—and even books—are now available through computer data services. For quickly finding a business telephone number in another city, for instance, there is an electronic yellow pages.

Experienced reporters rarely embark on a serious project without first checking Nexus, a data base pioneer that provides articles from many major newspapers. That way they quickly learn what their competitors have done on the subject and get background information on which to build their own articles. A growing number of newspapers are offering their articles through local data base services. Such services usually provide both fresh articles written for the newspaper and archived articles stored in the newspaper's library files.

Huge amounts of government information also are now accessible by computer, including census data. In some metropolitan areas, court records that once could be obtained only by regular visits to the courthouse are available through court data bases, allowing reporters to review lawsuits and bankruptcy petitions without leaving their office.

And don't forget E-mail. This computerized message writing phenomenon has become a valuable research tool. Through E-mail reporters can contact hard-to-reach interview subjects or get someone to send the latest economic information from Prague. More generally, E-mail provides a way to find out what the generation plugged in to electronic mail is talking about.

Data Analysis

Merely having information from data bases sometimes is not enough. Especially if you are dealing with statistics, the information may require additional computations and cross-referencing—"crunching," as it is sometimes called. A few newspapers have begun to create data analysis teams for this task, setting up personal computers programmed for shuffling data. In that way, a massive file on toxic waste pumped into the air statewide, for instance, can be broken down—if the information is sufficiently detailed—to show what industries are contributing to air pollution in specific communities. With the proper software, names of the industries can be sorted according to zip codes, or resorted according to the amounts of waste they put into the air, to provide a Ten Worst Polluters list.

If the place you wind up working does not have someone with this expertise, you probably can find someone in business or government willing to crunch information for you. Better still, learn to do it yourself. Data analysis is a growth segment of journalism.

Interviews

Fundamental to all journalistic research, of course, are interviews. In explanatory journalism, the people you usually need most to talk with are the experts and pioneers in the field you have chosen to write about. For every trend, there is somebody who started it. For every issue, there is somebody who has studied it. And usually there are experts on both sides of any given issue. For every expert certain that there is a greenhouse effect about to overheat the planet, there is an expert certain that it does not exist. Offering a spectrum of opinion is what separates explanatory journalism from alarmist journalism.

The names of experts and pioneers normally can be found in the publications and data bases you should research before planning any interviews. Government agencies, businesses, and trade associations also can provide the names of experts and pioneers. Additionally, comprehensive research has a chain-reaction quality: one interviewed expert inevitably leads to another. You probably will have less trouble finding enough experts to interview than deciding which ones you can afford not to contact.

All interesting stories, of course, have victims, villains, and heroes; so no work of explanatory journalism is complete without "real people" to illustrate the effects of the issue or event. Mike Toner began his series with an anecdote about a fifty-eight-year-old man who died after four months of treatment with antibiotics failed to stop a bacterial infection in his chest. Throughout the series, Toner described the heroic efforts of scientists fighting to keep resistant bugs in check and the unwitting villains who helped create superbugs by prescribing too many antibiotics and spraying too many chemicals.

NOTE KEEPING

In doing the comprehensive research necessary for explanatory journalism, keeping track of your notes is as important as taking them. We won't attempt to tell you where best to put everything, but here are a few things to consider:

- Analytical pieces require as much documentation as you can find. Develop a system for filing documents you will need when it comes time to write.
- Set up computer files for storing the computer data you collect. This may be difficult at some newspapers where guardians of overloaded main frames urge you to purge files as often as possible. Access to disk-loaded personal computers helps.
- Treat illustrative materials such as maps and charts as valuable documents to be carefully filed and stored. When it comes time to assemble your massive work of explanatory journalism, the first question likely will be: Where's the art?

THE VISUAL CONCEPT

Explanatory stories are concept stories, and increasingly that concept is as much visual as narrative. Along with an outline of what the story or series will say, you should prepare a plan for how the story is going to look. The design ultimately is controlled by layout editors, but you must provide many of the elements the layout editors will use. Let us discuss briefly some of the key graphic elements.

• *Charts and graphs.* Most developments, whether they be in crime or the price of lemons, can be measured in increases and decreases; and they usually can best be presented in the form of a chart or graph to show that. Art department designers will take care of making the chart pretty, but you will be expected to come up with the facts to put in it.

To help illustrate his point about the increased toughness of bugs, Mike Toner provided this chart:

> In the past 10 years more strains of salmonella have become resistant to drugs.
> 1980 . . . . 16%
> 1985 . . . . 24%
> 1990 . . . . 32%

A quick glance tells the reader the salmonella demons were twice as strong in 1990 as they were in 1980.

• *"Infographics."* This is a term of fairly recent newspaper coinage used to describe elaborate illustrations. For example, not long ago *USA Today* carried one depicting the effects of the economy on one town as a kind of Monopoly board of factory shutdowns and store closings. The 1994 winner of the Society of Professional Journalists Informational Graphics Award was a half-page effort showing how Air National Guard helicopters were used to airlift sandbags during floods in Des Moines. For his series, Toner provided information for an infographic on how parasites from a mosquito bite enter the bloodstream and multiply, causing blood cells to rupture.

• *Maps.* Few newspapers today carry major stories that don't include some kind of "locator map" showing the reader the segment of town or state where the event occurred. Improved color reproduction and graphics software that made possible the multi-hued weather map are routinely used to show demographic shifts and environmental threats.

• *Boxes.* Newspapers use boxes in a variety of ways to display complementary information with stories. Sometimes boxes include lists of things or tips on how to do or find things. Other times they simply include wacky details. Toner's series included a box with these facts on fleas:

- More than 2,400 species exist worldwide.
- A female flea consumes 15 times its body weight in blood daily.
- Fleas accelerate about 50 times faster than a space shuttle does after liftoff.
- Fleas can jump up to 150 times the length of their bodies—sideways or up—equivalent to a man jumping nearly 900 feet.

- *Photographs.* Pretty pages are not made from charts and boxes alone. Your editors will expect you to help photographers come up with a few eye-catching pictures to break up the type and help establish the tone of the project.

- *Visuals: The next generation.* As major newspapers move from page design controlled by makeup editors and printers in a separate "composing room" to "pagination" on computers in the newsroom, reporters and editors will assume more responsibility for how stories are displayed. At a few newspapers, reporters already are learning to use graphics software to put icons and other symbols onto their charts and to build their own bar graphs. Reporters soon may be expected to translate their explanatory vision—words, pictures, charts, and all—directly to the printed page.

WRITING THE EXPLANATORY STORY

In writing an explanatory story, as in writing all newspaper stories, the lead is the most important part. And with this type of story, you usually are inviting readers to take a very long journey. You have to give them a darn good reason for getting on board. Here is how Mike Toner started his first installment:

The death certificate attributed the 58-year-old heart patient's demise to "complications" following bypass surgery. The real reason made even his doctors cringe. Antibiotics didn't work anymore.

Key words and phrases make it clear this is going to be a scary ride: "death," "demise," "made even his doctors cringe," and, finally, "antibiotics didn't work anymore."

Once on board, the riders on the great explanatory express are likely to want to know pretty quickly where they are going. In other words, the writer has to make clear early on, in the "nut graph," what the whole enterprise is about. After six short, snappy paragraphs, Toner provided this summary:

> On city streets, in remote jungle clinics, on the farm and in back yards, the world's simplest creatures—bacteria, viruses, insects and weeds—are unraveling the chemical security blanket that has nurtured a half-century of progress in both public health and agriculture.

Also fairly high up in the story, the writer should relate the tale to ordinary people and situations. Readers inevitably want to know what their stake in all this is. Toner did it with this example:

> Have a child with an ear infection that won't go away? Deep in the recesses of your toddler's ear, there is probably a resistant bug to blame.

That particular detail is what sold Managing Editor John Walter on the story. He had treated his own two children for stubborn ear aches.

Toner also used images from popular culture with which readers could identify:

> Like the villains in a late-night horror show, resistant strains of mankind's oldest enemies are finding ways to sabotage our most sophisticated technology. And even the malevolent microbes of "The Andromeda Strain" or the angry hordes of "Killer Bees" aren't as scary as the real-life "superbugs" that are now emerging throughout the world.

The passages also illustrate some fundamental rules of explanatory writing:

- *Use simple, understandable words*. The whole point of explanatory journalism is making complicated events and issues comprehensible to a wide audience.
- *Limit jargon*. When you draw material from specialized material and expert opinions, a major risk is putting too much of the specialized and expert language in to your articles. Some jargon may be necessary to convey the way in which experts discuss the subject, but it should be used sparingly and with plain- spoken definitions.
- *Avoid obfuscating quotations*. Better to use almost no quota-

tions than to use quotations that don't make sense. Larding stories with meaningless quotations is a disservice to readers—and a sure sign the reporter doesn't understand the subject he or she is endeavoring to explain.

Like all good writers, Toner confined his use of quotations to those that had impact. The first quotation in his series was this one:

> "If he hadn't had such a resistant strain, he would have made it," says Dennis Schaberg, professor of medicine at the University of Michigan medical school in Ann Arbor. "I hate to sound like Chicken Little, but with certain microorganisms, we are back to a point in time where we have no options left. It's tough to explain something like that to a family of the patient. Very tough."

Toner did not use another quotation for more than twenty paragraphs, but it was another impact quote:

> "The problem is not chemicals; it's the irresponsible way they are used," says University of Illinois entomologist Robert Metcalf. "Our shortsighted and irresponsible use of antibiotics and pesticides is producing strains of monster bugs resistant to nearly everything in our arsenal. The outlook is dismal. And it is getting worse."

The spare use of quotations is another way explanatory stories differ from basic news stories. While quotations certainly are used to authenticate and give support to the information, the reporter does most of the telling in his or her own words. That is, after all, how we usually explain something when we are talking.

Pursuit of clarity in explanatory journalism has led to the use of a controversial device called *voice of God*. Because qualifiers must be limited, the explanatory journalist often will state facts as givens—as if God said so. Toner stated emphatically early in his series: "The bugs are fighting back. And they are getting very good at it." No "according to experts," no "some scientists say"— just a stated fact, which he proceeded to back up with considerable evidence.

Even the voice of God requires some verification in journalism; and explanatory journalism, like all good journalism, is loaded with *evidence and compelling facts*. Bill Kovach, curator of the Nieman Fellowships and a former editor of the Atlanta *Journal-Constitution*, told his reporters that newspaper stories should have "fact upon fact and detail upon detail." This is especially true in explanatory journalism.

Here are but a few facts from Toner's series:

• Because drug resistant germs are twice as likely as other germs to be fatal, they contribute to 50,000 hospital deaths a year. And because they take twice as long to cure, they add as much as $30 billion a year to hospital care.

• The clouds of pesticide-resistant sweet-potato whiteflies that devastated last winter's vegetable crops in California, Texas and Florida triggered supermarket sticker shock that gave us $3.50 cantaloupes and $2-a-pound tomatoes.

• Bacteria have been on the Earth for at least 3 billion years; insects, for at least 850 million years. Like all living things, they are constantly mutating, testing new traits that may give them an edge in a hostile environment.

• Today, resistance has been documented in 504 species of insects and mites, 273 weeds, 150 fungi and other plant pathogens, and five kinds of rats—and there are at least 17 insects that are resistant to all major classes of pesticides.

• Americans use 700 million pounds of pesticides and herbicides and 30 million pounds of antibiotics each year to treat everything from acne and gum disease to farmed catfish and feedlot cattle.

To believe that explanatory stories are told mostly by numbers is a misconception, however. *Explanatory stories describe and demonstrate, and to do that they must be laced with vivid descriptions, images, and examples.* Here are a few examples from Toner's series:

Sequestered behind the double-locked, airtight doors of the Centers for Disease Control's $23 million virology laboratory, researchers handle the most dangerous bugs known to man— the causes of exotic, incurable diseases like Marburg, Ebola and Congo-Crimean hemorrhagic fever. They work secure in the knowledge that, for the bugs, escape is virtually impossible. But even at Biosafety Level 4 there is one bug that makes researchers nervous—one microbe on which no one wants to experiment.

On Long Island, where the Colorado potato beetle is now resistant to every major class of pesticides, potato farmers use tractor-towed blowtorches to kill the insects.

Unlike the humans they hitch a ride with, the bugs need no passports. Health officials are worried, in fact, that healthy Americans returning from the Olympics in Spain this summer, where resistant pneumonia bacteria are common, will carry resistant strains home with them.

If farmers are running out of magic bullets, one reason is that they have been shooting themselves in the foot for so many years. Much of this $7.6 billion-a-year chemical blitz misses its target.

Doctors, eager for an oral antibiotic that would work against almost anything, voted with their prescription pads.

There is no great mystery about what is happening. The bugs, whether single-celled microorganisms or the six-legged variety, are doing what comes naturally. They're surviving.

While organizing and writing the articles for an explanatory journalism project are the main parts of the work, there are a few other things to consider in this age of graphics:

- Reconcile the story with illustrations. Having the story describing something one way and the illustration showing it differently is a definite no-no.
- Limit repetition between stories and graphics. If something is shown in a graphic, it usually doesn't need to be described in the story.
- Box facts that interrupt the flow of the story. Information boxes not only are a good layout device but a good way to get in the tidbits and oddball facts that just don't fit in the story.

Endings

In long, intricate stories, endings can be almost as important as leads. Jim Naughton, associate managing editor of the Philadelphia *Inquirer,* sees a good conclusion as a way to reward readers for having taken the long journey. Toner ended his series with this quote:

"When you try to eradicate an insect, you are going up against a billion years of evolution," says University of Illinois entomologist Robert Metcalf. "Pests have survived long because they are very good at adapting. We will probably never completely eradicate any pest. We shouldn't be trying. We should be looking for a way to live with them better."

HOW ONE PROJECT EVOLVED
By LEONARD TEEL

Bringing together all the elements for a work of explanatory journalism can take weeks, even months. Here is how I compiled my articles on Persimmon Valley:

I started by attending a funeral in Young Harris, Georgia. Whose funeral it was didn't matter. The managing editor wanted me to go into Georgia's Appalachians, find a relatively isolated valley, and document how values had changed there in the past three generations. The key to explaining this would lie in the stories of old-timers. I found some at the funeral. One of them, pointing to the east, told me the valley I was looking for was just over that series of ridges.

Several miles west of the city of Clayton in Rabun County, a narrow county road sneaks off to the right, cuts through a gap, and climbs a rise. From the top of the rise, the view widens to the whole of Persimmon Valley.

In the next six weeks I immersed myself in this tiny pocket of civilization. I tried to appreciate its institutions, traditions, and, most of all, its people. I went wherever the people went, to church, to the store.

The small general store was where I first heard the names of two of the valley's old-timers, the Addis brothers. More names and history were waiting in the graveyard opposite the Baptist church. I drove up the rocky dirt roads to Lester Addis' clapboard home where he lived alone with his mule and cow. In his humble front room he offered me white cornbread. I visited his brother, Ralph, who had sold land and now lived in a modern brick home along the main highway.

Patterns emerged and became clarified. The old-timers told stories of their years as farmers. That was before the great growth of Atlanta, two hours to the south. By the 1960s, real estate scouts entered the valley. City folks soon followed, seeking sanctuaries from busyness and traffic. Land values increased. The prices tempted the old-timers and the next generation. The prettiest spread in the valley now belonged to the Nash family, refugees from crowded Atlanta.

The youngest generation in the valley became landless, working for wages at jobs in the nearby town. This was not by choice in every case. Some longed for land. But theirs was a dream difficult to realize.

There were many subplots. One farmer in the middle generation had been drawn away from the fields by higher profits from selling moonshine liquor. He had been caught and imprisoned. He felt he had no choice but to sell his farm. His remorse was genuine. He walked through the graveyard where his mother lay and said he felt he had betrayed her and the way of the valley.

The stories from the valley people took four weeks to gather and more time to understand so that they could be explained. In the end, the narrative took on the nature of fiction. There unfolded the continuous, interwoven stories of the old men, the sorry moonshiner, the land agents, the Atlantans, and the new generation, wage-earners with a dream.

This chapter has analyzed the qualities of good explanatory writing. While the "why" is an important part of most stories, journalists in the 21st century are likely to be required, as never before, to report the context that gives the fact meaning. That is why the need to explain very simply something very complex has never been more urgent.

16

WRITING A NEWSPAPER FEATURE STORY

Feature writing is a highly disciplined method that journalists use to enable readers to gain insight about people, their character, and behavior. Feature writing requires an immense amount of reporting, and feature writers, in order to capture the essence of their subjects, become "flies on the wall." Feature writers have also adopted literary techniques to shape their stories and make them attractive to readers.

A feature story is distinguished from other stories by the way it is written and the focus it takes. A feature story focuses on *people* in events, not on the events, and should help readers gain insight about why and how people behave. Such a feature story captures the flavor and character of the people in it. As in all other journalism, facts inform feature writing.

Feature writing has come a long way from the penny press days of the 1830s when stories were hyped, overwritten, and, even worse, made up, and from more recent days when a reporter would

BY R. THOMAS BERNER

Mr. Berner, Professor of Journalism and American Studies at Pennsylvania State University, is the author of *Writing Literary Features, The Process of Writing News, The Process of Editing, Editing,* and *Language Skills for Journalists.* He teaches news writing, feature writing, and the literature of journalism. He invites you to contact him by e-mail at BX2@PSU.EDU.

interview someone and then write a story roughly structured as lead, direct quote, indirect quote, direct quote, mundane ending. Thanks in part to the work of such newspaper notables as Gay Talese, Jimmy Breslin, and Tom Wolfe, feature writers have begun to apply the techniques of fiction to non-fiction. Wolfe called it New Journalism; a more current label would be Literary Journalism.

Literary journalism, like all good journalism, relies on thorough reporting. It differs because it aims to put readers in the story through the techniques of story-telling. Rather than functioning like a scribe in the he-said, she-said mode, the literary journalist becomes the teller of a story based on detailed reporting.

FLY ON THE WALL

Beginning feature writers sometimes behave as though feature writing is easy. All one does is imagine the story and then fill the computer screen with purple prose. Nothing could be farther from reality. In some ways, a feature story represents a more challenging reporting task than a hard news story. The good feature writer is first a good reporter. He or she functions as a fly on the wall, discreet, unnoticed, able to observe everything going on, not interfering in what is unfolding before him. The good feature writer learns to look and learns to listen. Here is the opening of a story about people who were discharged from mental asylums. It was written by Donald C. Drake of the Philadelphia *Inquirer*.[1] What did Drake see and hear?

Dawn was just beginning to brighten the eastern sky. It was a sunrise that went unnoticed by the man asleep on the steam grate opposite Rittenhouse Square, folded up between a concrete trash receptacle and a newspaper vending machine.

An electric digital display in a nearby bank window gave the time: 5:54.

The sleeping man was wearing baggy corduroy pants, a wool hat, a shirt and a dirty blanket worn over his shoulders like a shawl.

His eyes still closed, the man reached into his open shirt to scratch at the lice, as he had been doing all night. A bread truck roared by on Walnut Street, followed a few minutes later by a milk truck. Then it was quiet again.

---

[1]"The Forsaken: How America Has Abandoned Thousands in the Name of Social Progress." July 19, 1982, p. 1. Reprinted by permission of the Philadelphia *Inquirer*.

The sidewalk, which in two hours would be crowded with people hurrying to their jobs, was deserted now. The only signs of life were the man and a lone car that waited obediently at an empty intersection for the light to change.

The man started to stir and, still without opening his eyes, pushed himself up to a sitting position, leaning back against the concrete trash receptacle. Joggers began to appear across the street, resolutely circling the park, too intent on their exercise to notice the solitary man.

It took a long time, maybe 15 or 20 minutes, for the man to wake up fully, but by 6:15 his eyes were open wide, staring down the elegant street that had been his home for three years. At first he did nothing but sit, stare and scratch.

Another day was beginning for Jim Logue Crawford, 69, former mental hospital patient.

This excerpt is part of a seven-part series that Drake reported on for eighteen months. He tracked mental patients who had been released from hospitals in Philadelphia. He wanted to know how they lived, and he found out not by asking social workers or even the patients themselves, for that would have given their interpretation of how they live, but by unobtrusively observing the patients themselves. He became a fly on the wall. Be more than a facts-and-figure reporter, Drake urges. Look and listen.

TYPES OF FEATURE STORIES

When editors and educators talk about feature writing, they have a short but useful vocabulary. As you read, look for words and phrases such as voice, character, foreshadowing and flashback, dialogue, transition, overwriting, rewriting, quote lead, authority of fact, show don't tell, logical development, enduring ending, people focus, perspective, drama, tension, plotting, relevant detail, scene setting, focus. These words represent a list of qualities found in good feature writing.

One type of feature story is the *brite*, which means light-hearted. Such stories are short and tightly written. Despite that, they are as well written and well structured as the longer feature—that is, have a beginning, middle, and end—and, because of their compactness, are more challenging to write. Unlike the short news story, which puts the least-important information at the end, the "brite" has a logical ending or a kicker. It rewards the reader for reading through to the end. Here is an example from the Philadelphia *Inquirer*:

Two is the ultimate lucky number for 75-year-old twins Doris and Dorothy Shell, who were chosen to appear in two TV commercials advertising twin packs of corn chips. The Shells, of Winnfield, La., even were second choice for the ads. They finished second in August in the look-alike competition at the International Twins Day Festival in Twinsburg, Ohio.

They were there with their brothers, Dennis and Denton, 71, also identical twins—a one in 57,600 chance occurrence—and 2,700 other sets of natural-born pairs.

Representatives for Doritos corn chips, made by Dallas-based Frito-Lay, came to the event seeking male twins in their 70s for the ad campaign. Dennis and Denton Shell were picked.

"They weren't looking for women at first," said Dorothy Shell. "They wanted our brothers." But health problems interfered, and the brothers recommended their sisters. From then on, it was off to Hollywood. They shot two commercials at a beach.

The sisters had to be careful about eating too many chips, though. "Cholesterol problems, you know," Dorothy Shell said.[2]

Longer feature stories can range from single-interview accounts about someone to elaborate and detailed stories written from multiple points of view and exhibiting all the tension and drama of a short story. Longer feature stories include profiles about someone in which the writer attempts to show an individual's character through a Herculean reporting task. No matter the length of the story, to succeed it must focus on a narrow event and then bring out the emotion, behavior, and character of the people in that event.

Feature writing presents an opportunity for the writer to show individuality in style. Usually, a reader can hear the voice of the writer in a feature. That does not mean, as some beginners believe, that a feature gives a writer license to spew out opinion or emotional drivel wrapped in purple prose. It does not mean that a feature is an advertisement for the writer. Just the opposite. A good feature writer distances him/herself from the people in the story and writes a story that calls attention to the people in the story, not to the way the story is written.

THE OPENING
Just as in any other successful writing, the opening of a feature

---

[2]Philadelphia *Inquirer*, January 13, 1992. Reprinted with permission.

story must either tell what the story is about or "hook" the reader so the reader continues reading to find out what the story is about. Consider the following lead from a short feature story written as a classroom exercise:

The romance between Xu Huainan and Qian Lijun began by accident.

In eleven words, the writer, Li Xiaohong, has managed to set the tone of the story by incorporating an event, the accident, and the result, romance. Her second paragraph explains what happened:

One winter afternoon, a car hit a bicycle, leaving the rider, Xu Huainan, with three broken ribs. Last Saturday, three months after the accident, the driver and the rider got married.

The remainder of the nine-paragraph story explains, using information from the people involved, how the accident victim and the driver of the car evolved into wife and husband. The story was based on a police report and interviews with two people. The writer had enough information to write 1,200 words, but the editor limited her to 400. Any story can be overwritten, and while a predetermined length may at first seem unfair, it really disciplines the writer and enables him or her to produce a tighter and better story. Overwriting can ruin any feature. The writer needs to recognize when to summarize and explain rather than go on at length.

Sometimes a good lead is hidden within the lead the writer has already written. Ma Zhan of the China School of Journalism produced this lead on a feature story written after a classroom speech by an American:

During Dick Carter's seven-month stay in China, he toured many places, such as Hangzhou, Suzhou, Ningbo and several other cities in south China. He says one of the most impressive experiences is that a lot of Chinese asked him many interesting questions during his trip.

"They asked me where I am from, how old I am, how much I earn," Carter says, "and the main question they asked me on the train or elsewhere is 'Do you have a gun?'" Carter says he was greatly surprised that so many asked him the same question about the gun.

Carter is an American lecturer teaching in the Institute of

Tourism in Beijing. He says Chinese people gain their impression of American people from television programs, in which Americans often carry guns and shoot people.

Ma was not happy with the lead and re-examined it to see what might work better. His writing coach asked him what stood out in Ma's mind, and Ma said the question about the gun. Ma decided that some of the direct quotations could be more effectively paraphrased. He produced this rewrite:

"Do you have a gun?" That's the question Dick Carter has been asked frequently during his seven-month stay in China.

Chinese also ask Carter where he's from (America), how old he is (68), and how much he earns ($2550 a month). He's toured Hangzhou, Suzhou, Ningbo and several other cities in south China and he keeps getting the gun question.

Carter says he was greatly surprised that so many ask him the same question about the gun. Carter is an American lecturer teaching in the Institute of Tourism in Beijing. He says Chinese people gain their impression of American people from television programs, in which Americans often carry guns and shoot people.

Ma realized that if the gun question surprised Carter, it would surprise others. By leading with the gun question, Ma improved his lead and maintained his theme, which was the questions Carter was asked when traveling.

Ma also demonstrated that the best writing is rewriting. A writer can always improve on the first words put on paper or on the computer screen; and good writers edit themselves critically, rewrite frequently, and welcome suggestions from their editors.

At one time editors and journalism teachers were almost unanimous in their injunction against using "quote leads" (direct quotations). They argued that direct quotations lacked context and would not help the reader enter the story. Now editors and teachers appreciate the value of quote leads in feature stories when the direct quotation is especially strong and can capture the reader's attention, as demonstrated by the "Do you have a gun?" type of lead. A good quote lead needs to be clear on its own; being catchy is not enough. Will the reader understand it immediately, without having to go back and reread or without reading five more paragraphs? The quote lead has to be something the reader can identify with.

USING LITERARY TECHNIQUES

Literary journalism is based solely on fact, not flights of fancy, using the techniques of fiction and writing in a compelling way to present information, not imagination, to the public. Mike Sager, a practitioner of literary journalism, believes that video is a threat to print and that journalists must "give the readers vivid stories, stories that supply their own soundtrack and internal visuals."

Literary journalists use scene-setting, relevant detail, description, storytelling, logical development, plotting, and perspective. They use these and other techniques to give shape to the facts they have gathered. Because they have done a great deal of reporting, because they have accumulated detail and knowledge, their stories ring loudly with "the authority of fact." And so the reporting that goes into a literary feature is as much of the essence of the story as is writing style. Documentation is essential. Gather as much information as possible; trust, but verify; mine and re-mine sources.

A narrative is an account of something. It is a story. A subset of narrative is the anecdote, which newspaper feature writers have relied on for a long time. The anecdote illuminates a point in a narration, and a good narration may contain several anecdotes.

THE JOURNALIST AS STORYTELLER

By using narrative, by becoming a storyteller, the journalist is able to show how something happens. As the late John Hersey, the author of *Hiroshima*, once put it: "Journalism allows its readers to witness history; fiction gives the readers an opportunity to live it."

This is where *authority of fact* comes in, for the journalist cannot be a storyteller without first being a reporter, without first gathering as much information—and from as many points of view—as possible. Facts underlie the work of literary journalists.

Paul Shinoff, the author of a feature story on two men who dig graves by hand, discusses how he pressed the gravediggers for details:

I spent a good part of one day at the cemetery, was there for both the digging and the filling of the grave. I stood next to them, asking questions about the most minute aspects of their work. In such situations, I generally ask a worker to describe what he is doing as he does it. Often, I am asking someone to articulate something that has never been put in words before. And in such situations, the hands move faster than the mouth. "I'm digging," Fitzpatrick would say, feeling a bit silly about the whole thing. I would continue with specific questions. "Why are you holding your hands like that?" "Why that shovel?" We talked a lot about tools.

Literary journalism is not possible without relevant detail acquired through good reporting. Literary journalists attempt to put the reader in the scene in a variety of ways. Literary journalists also work exceptionally hard to convey the character of the people in their stories. Most of them say they achieve this through detail. Here is an example of detail:

> Kintzel fumbles with a pair of thick black glasses that fence in his pale, serious features. Then he starts the pickup, carefully backing it out to the dirt road that will now carry us to the brothers' mine. The ride is particularly bumpy; the road, slashed uneven and stained black from 80-odd years of coal being hauled over it.

Is Kintzel just wearing glasses? No. They are thick and black, and they fence in his face. Kintzel backs up his truck "carefully," which, while not very precise, still gives the reader a feeling for his driving. Anyone who drives or who has been in a car can understand backing up carefully. Note that the road is bumpy, dirt, and stained black. Detail that helps the reader see and feel the story is relevant detail.

In the typical news story, the journalist functions almost like a scribe. But in narration, the journalist becomes the storyteller by assembling the facts into a story. The journalist, backed by facts, presents the facts in a readable form. Some of the facts, by the way, come to the journalist through observation. He has the "authority of fact" because he has seen what is happening. The opening of Drake's story on mental patients is but one of many examples.

Literary feature stories *move forward scene by scene*. Editors tell reporters to *show, don't tell*. That means using scenes. In standard news writing, reporters tend to tell rather than show, to use summary instead of scene. Here is an example of summary:

> John Fitzpatrick and Maurice Hickey begin their jobs as gravediggers at Holy Cross Cemetery at the crack of dawn. They know which gravesite to begin work at because their assignments are written on a piece of yellow paper Fitzpatrick has in his pocket.

Here's is how Paul Shinoff of the San Francisco *Examiner* wrote it, as a scene:

The early morning sun had barely cleared the top of San Bruno mountains as John Fitzpatrick and Maurice Hickey trudged across the wet, well-manicured lawn of Holy Cross Cemetery carrying shovels and spades.

Fitzpatrick paused, took a folded yellow slip of paper from the pocket of his faded blue overalls and glanced at the name on the marble headstone.

Measured against Sager's advice to provide vivid stories, this lead stimulates the reader's visual side. The reader is present. It is like watching a movie. The writer is a storyteller.

Scenes enable the literary journalist to show how something happened and to show drama and tension. As each scene passes, the reader is seeing a story unfold, seeing the story happen. Even when the reader knows how the story turns out, the reader can still feel the tension.

Going from one scene to another—*transition*—means more than just writing "And then ..." Some journalists, when changing scenes, will use what can be called scene markers (* * *). Other writers prefer to create a seamless story. One such writer is Doris Wolf, who has worked for several newspapers in upstate New York. She uses transitional techniques that are so economical they are almost unnoticed.

In a story she did about the funeral of an undercover policeman shot in the line of duty, for transition Wolf relied on the action of the police officers who had come to pay their respects. For example, she described the scene outside the funeral home, including the ranks of police officers. Suddenly, their commander ordered them to attention and then to march into the funeral home. Using that action, Wolf in one very brief sentence got the reader inside the funeral home.

Good transition is economical. Instead of trying to wax poetic and at great length, the literary journalist attempts to advance the story as efficiently as possible. A word or two. A sentence. A paragraph, if it's necessary for a major shift. Transition indicates the writer's hand in the story and should be as unobtrusive as possible. Let the reader see the story, not the writer writing the story.

Literary newswriting does not rely as much on *direct quotations* as some feature writing does. While some journalists pride themselves on using many direct quotations in their stories, such quotes, unless they are direct and clear, do not help the reader understand the story. The writer helps the reader. A writer does that by paraphrasing what people say rather than quoting spontaneous remarks. People are at their most inelegant when speaking off the top of their head. Of course, direct quotations are invaluable when they make a point about a character in a story. But direct quotations can impede the narrative flow, especially when they are used to provide biographical or other factual information that the writer could more easily summarize.

Direct quotations can, however, play an important role beyond just making a point about a character. The best direct quotations are those that are part of *dialogue*, of people talking to each other. Dialogue represents a dimension of realism because it enables the reader to "hear" people talking. Dialogue gives readers the voice of the characters in the story. Dialogue helps move a story forward.

The best dialogue, like the best direct quotations, reveals a telling point about a character. Don't use dialogue for the sake of dialogue. Use dialogue when it provides a deeper understanding of someone in the story or enables the reader to feel the tension that might exist or sense the direction the story is going.

Examine how Drake uses dialogue in the story about his daughter. (The story, entitled "Valerie's Been Injured," is printed at the end of this chapter. You may wish to read it now.) Even more importantly, look at the times he could have used dialogue and did not. Imagine if Drake, instead of writing about his conversation with Dr. Langfitt—"Quickly, I relayed the facts."—had instead gone through the conversation line by line, pause by pause, false start by false start. And that is just one time out of many that Drake chose a paraphrased summary over a verbatim conversation. Drake is economical in his use of direct quotations, and he uses dialogue when it reveals something about a person, explains a major point, or advances the story. Look at the section in which Drake first has a dispute with Valerie's doctor and then with the hospital administrator. It is just enough to give a flavor of the moment. The dialogue shows the tension and says a lot about the father, the mother, the doctor, and the hospital administrator.

Other valuable techniques are foreshadowing and flashback. *Foreshadowing* enables the reader to see ahead and have a reason to continue reading. *Flashback* enables the writer to fill in the "holes" of a story with background as it is needed to explain the present. Flashback allows the writer to begin the story in the present and then reach back and insert historical information as needed. If writers did not use flashback, every story would start almost with the birth of the characters.

Another story by Drake provides an example of foreshadowing. Drake was given the assignment of assembling the reporting work of thirteen people into a narrative that looked at the days leading up to the attempted assassination of President Ronald Reagan.

In his opening, Drake used foreshadowing in referring to the gunman John C. Hinckley:

> He carried with him a suitcase, a $47 handgun and a letter describing how he intended to assassinate the President of the United States.

The reader wants to keep reading this story because while the reader knows that Hinckley tried and failed, the reader wants to know "how" Hinckley intended to do it. Again, this is a strength of using the literary approach because it enables the writer to show "how" something happened.

Drake also uses flashbacks to great effect in this story. They provide background on Hinckley and help the reader understand the larger story. Drake, while putting together a story on what Hinckley did just days before he attempted to assassinate Reagan, uses flashbacks to tell what Hinckley was like in college, later his childhood, his affiliation with the American Nazi party, and his circuitous route to Washington, D. C. Flashbacks function as pieces of the puzzle that the writer is putting together for the reader. In that way, flashbacks, just like foreshadowing, add drama and tension to the story.

Drake approaches writing a literary feature the way a playwright or filmmaker might. He *plots his stories and thinks in terms of scenes*. He breaks the story into segments of related information and writes a segment at a time.

Examine the organization of Drake's story on his daughter. It opens with the telephone call. Immediately, the reader is focused. Drake very quickly brings in the tension and pain he is feeling and then in paragraph six sets up the rest of the story. Notice how Drake does not tell the reader something until the reader needs to know it. The mid-story reference to pneumothorax, which could complicate the transfer, is not revealed for the red herring it is until Drake learns about it first hand. The writer must decide when the reader needs to know a fact in order to understand the larger story. Not all facts are equal, nor can all facts be dumped on the reader at the beginning of a story. Just as life and the understanding of it unfold and evolve, so too must a story.

Drake also writes about the conversation with Dr. Langfitt;

then he explains the problem a depressed skull fracture can mean and why a small hospital is not equipped to handle such a case. The tension keeps building as Drake keeps adding detail after detail—the authority of fact. He foreshadows when he writes about transferring his daughter and then asks: "But what if her doctor on Long Island should refuse?"

In order to return to the action, Drake employs the ringing of the telephone. He does it simply: "The phone rang." The doctor gives Drake what he thinks is good news, but Drake, who has already warned the reader about how small-town hospitals are staffed, adds more tension when Dr. Langfitt reveals why he had a difficult time reaching the surgeon. Again, Drake does it simply: "I felt the muscles in my jaw tense."

Drake's *simple writing style* is a model for beginning writers to imitate. He writes so simply that his style does not call attention to itself. He does not use rhetorical tricks. He relies on shorter sentences and paragraphs when the action is nearing a climax and uses longer sentences and paragraphs when the action slows.

In his story on Hinckley, Drake ends the story this way:

He fired.

Drake avoided overwriting. He did the same in his story on his daughter, where because of his personal attachment he could have easily gone overboard. Here is the ending of that story:

Soon all we could see was the blinking red light of the helicopter in the dark sky and then not even that. It was quiet now and we could hear our feet squishing in the sodden grass as we left. No one said anything. We were each lost in our own thoughts.

Drake follows this with an epilogue. (The *epilogue* is something added as an overview of the larger story.) But the story Drake wanted to tell is not how his daughter recovered, but the dramatic one of getting her into the hands of skillful doctors. In fact, her recovery is almost routine when measured against the touch-and-go nature of her rescue from the jaws of death.

It is also important to note that Drake did not identify the doctor, hospital, specific town in which the hospital is located, or the hospital's administrator. To do so would have invited a lawsuit, since the story suggests misfeasance and malfeasance, claims that, if the named people had chosen to sue, the newspaper would have had to prove. In another time and context, with full documentation, names might have been published. But this is a story about getting Valerie into a Philadelphia hospital. That is the story's focus, and by not naming the culprits, Drake actually helps keep the focus where it belongs.

THE ENDING

A good feature story has an ending that flows logically from the facts presented and endures after the reader puts down the paper. If feature writers make any mistakes in ending stories, they are these:

1. Raising a new point in the last paragraph
2. Writing too much

A writer can determine if he or she has committed Sin #2 by applying the "hand test," as the writing critics Don Fry and Roy Peter Clark call it, in which the writer covers the last paragraph of the story with his hand and decides if the next-to-last graph doesn't make a better ending. Then the writer covers that paragraph and sees if the third-to-end paragraph doesn't make an even better ending. Then the writer covers that paragraph. The nugget of wisdom in this advice is that some people tend to overwrite, cram their stories, and don't know when to quit. Keep the story's focus narrow and you won't have such a problem. In avoiding Sin #1, ensure that anything stated in the ending was mentioned or foreshadowed earlier so the reader is not surprised.

In Li Xiaohong's wedding story, she ends with a paragraph that not only captures the story to date but points to the future:

They said they believe fate brought them together and will protect them forever.

Such a story lends itself to an overwritten ending, but Li resisted that approach and stayed with a paraphrased quote. Another representative ending that came out of the assignment:

And the bicycle? Although it is beyond repair, the couple said they keep it in their apartment as a symbol of their love.

Similarly, the ending on the earlier story about the Shell twins and potato chips is designed to bring a smile:

The sisters had to be careful abut eating too many chips, though. "Cholesterol problems, you know," Dorothy Shell said.

The ending that endures is the one that the reader can add to vicariously. In "brites," an enduring ending brings a smile to someone's face. In a feature on a serious topic, the enduring ending leaves readers feeling that they have gained insight, some lesson or understanding about life. The ending that does not endure is the one that drives the point home through overstatement or overkill. That's why the "hand test" is so important. A now retired journalist once told a story about his first day on the job. He did not have a degree in journalism and so had not learned some of the basic news writing techniques taught in journalism schools. In fact, he had a degree in English literature and thus was more knowledgeable about the literary approach to writing, the one with a beginning, middle and end. He was sitting at his typewriter with a nearly completed story when his editor walked by and noticed that he was staring at his typewriter.

"What's the matter?" the editor asked. "I'm trying to come up with an ending for my story," the then-budding journalist replied.

"Newspaper stories don't have endings; they just stop," the editor snapped back.

Well, that's not true for literary journalism. How well a story ends is an indication of how well the journalist gathered relevant material and how well the writer controlled the material and understood the literary process. The best endings stay with the reader long after the reader has turned the page. The best endings endure.

Perspective...

What an Award-Winning Reporter Wishes Beginning Journalists Knew About Narrative Writing

By DONALD C. DRAKE, assistant metro editor for narrative writing and medical writer at the Philadelphia *Inquirer* and winner of numerous national awards for writing

The two most important things a reporter must keep in mind when doing a narrative story are that (1) it requires detailed reporting, beautiful writing and hard work and (2) it's worth the effort.

It's especially important to keep point Number Two in mind because it's so easy to lose faith in yourself when attempting something so difficult. Everyone fails at their first attempts, and their stories are gruffly rejected by editors, who don't know how to fix them. Most newspaper editors do not understand narrative techniques. Some even resist them because they go against everything they've been trained to do as journalists.

Good narrative writers do not cram all of the information in the top of the story, but hold back facts until the reader has been prepared by the story to appreciate the information intellectually and emotionally.

They build rather than kill anticipation, as journalists have been trained to do by answering every question in the next paragraph. Nothing drives a story more than the reader's anticipation of what's about to happen.

They use quotes sparingly because quotes, as given in interviews, jerk the reader out of the narrative, unless they're dialogue that is part of the scene.

They try to avoid attribution, which also disrupts the integrity of scenes, even though this forces the reporter to do a lot of extra reporting to verify facts. Narratives don't let you hide behind attribution.

Narratives, by their nature, take a long time to report and write and require a lot of space to tell. Narratives are not editor friendly. You must have faith in the technique and yourself, because far too often no one else does.

But all of this is worth it because a well written narrative is the best read story in the newspaper. Of this I am convinced. I have no readership surveys or focus-group assessments to support the assertion. I base it on personal experience and the experience of many colleagues over the years.

When you write a good narrative, colleagues and readers shower you with compliments. Even the skeptical editor will give you a begrudging "well done," unless you've gotten into a shouting match with the poor soul and his/her ego must be defended.

When people tell you how much they like your story, you know they're not just complimenting you to be friendly because they'll talk about intricate details of the story found way back on the jump page. Years after the story appears, people will still remember it and talk to you about it at parties and other gatherings.

It is not surprising that this happens because narrative journalists use the same techniques that novelists and playwrights have been using for years to entice their audiences. The narrative writer thinks more like a film maker than a journalist. He sees stories in terms of a collection of vivid scenes with building action.

At the Philadelphia *Inquirer*, we even use playwriting terms in planning and writing stories. We talk about the opening scenes and dramatic arches and curtain lines and primary and secondary characters. We're more interested in the subtext of what is happening and bringing it out clearly than the surface facts.

And we don't just think out the lead and nut graph and then start writing, letting everything else take care of itself. We plot the story, scene by scene by scene—a process that can take hours and in the case of series days—before the first word of the story is written.

Because narratives often deal with subtle events that don't meet conventional, dramatic, breaking-news criteria—many killed, millions stolen, laws violated—they're much more dependent on the reporting and writing skills of the reporter than other types of news stories.

And this is the most scary part of narrative writing. If you're not good, you've got nothing. But if you are good, they'll love the story and you'll love doing it.

• • •

MODEL STORY:
A FATHER'S EFFORT TO SAVE HIS DAUGHTER'S LIFE

The following story by Donald Drake illustrates the various techniques that make for effective feature stories. Pay particular attention to how the writer plotted the story, builds tension, and uses dialogue, foreshadowing, and characterization.

"Valerie's Been Injured"
by Donald Drake
Today (Philadelphia *Inquirer* magazine)
December 28, 1975

It was late at night when the phone call from my estranged wife came. She spoke quickly, with obvious urgency. Valerie, our 14-year-old daughter, had been hurt in an automobile accident. She had a depressed skull fracture and was unconscious in the intensive care unit of a small hospital on eastern Long Island. The doctor said it was too early to say how bad it was. My wife answered a few questions and hung up, promising to call

back as soon as she knew more.

I sat stunned, looking at the silent phone.

"Do they have any idea how serious it is?" It was Patricia, my companion, who had overheard the telephone conversation. She was already crying. After five years she and Valerie had become good friends. I shook my head and reached for Dorland's Medical Directory to get the home phone number of Dr. Thomas W. Langfitt, a neurosurgeon. Only four weeks earlier I had written about him and a special intensive care unit he organized to treat patients with brain injuries.

A thousand disconnected thoughts and images filled my mind. Skull fracture. A mangled car on a rainy, deserted country road. My daughter on an emergency room litter. Unconscious. Policemen and doctors crowded around her. How bad was it? Would she live? Would she be normal?

Other thoughts of better times. My daughter running to meet me at the railroad station. A big smile. Her red hair askew. Sailing together on the Chesapeake Bay. Fighting about silly and sometimes important things. Why did we fight so much?

And so, with wrenching suddenness began the longest time of my life, 27 hours of exhausting tension and intense conflicting emotions. Before it was over I would be filled with a screaming outrage against inadequacies of our medical system and the self-interest of some of its practitioners. But at the same time I would also be overwhelmed by the generosity and love of dozens of other people who would spend this day helping a girl they didn't even know.

As I dialed Dr. Langfitt's number, I couldn't believe that this was really happening to me. The coincidence of having just written about the head trauma unit at the University of Pennsylvania Hospital was just too great. It was a story of the many medical advances being made there. But it was also about how people were dying needlessly of head injuries in small hospitals where they couldn't get such good care. I wrote about doctors who attempted surgery they weren't equipped to handle and of others who held back in referring patients to medical centers until it was too late.

So many of the victims were teenagers. So often the pattern was the same—an automobile accident, a head injury, inadequate care at a small hospital, irreversible brain damage or death.

Mrs. Langfitt picked up the phone on the third ring and put me right through to her husband. "Hello," I said, relieved that I was able to reach him so quickly. "This is Donald Drake. My daughter's just been hurt in an automobile accident." Quickly I relayed the facts. I told him that I was anxious to get her transferred to a hospital with a neurosurgical service. He said there was a good unit at New York University and agreed to contact the doctor on the case to see how Valerie was doing. He would call me back immediately.

It was 10:20. Only five minutes had passed since the phone call from Long Island ended the cozy calm of the evening, but it seemed like hours. Everything before the phone call had been wiped from my mind—the television program, the science meeting I had covered that morning in Ann Arbor, Mich., the flight back home and being stacked in a holding pattern over International Airport. For the moment there was nothing to do. I paced the floor, pausing now and then to stare out of the window into the darkness and heavy rain that had made the roads here and in Long Island so slippery.

Talking out loud more to myself than Pat, I tried to find something positive to hang onto. But all I did was think of things that made me worry more as I waited for the phone to ring.

The depressed skull fracture that Valerie had was far worse than a simple break because in such injuries the bone is pushed into the brain. The seriousness depended on the location and extent of the depression. Also Valerie was still unconscious an hour or more after the accident. And she was in a small community hospital on the eastern end of Long Island, more than 100 miles from New York City and its sophisticated medical facilities. That would be particularly bad if Valerie needed surgery. At least 10 percent of such patients do require surgery, a fact I knew from the head injury story I had just written.

I knew there was little chance that the small hospital had a neurosurgeon, and brain surgery is beyond the capabilities of general surgeons. I worried that there might not even be a qualified physician in the emergency room. So often at night the only physician small hospitals can get are foreign medical graduates who can't qualify for larger hospitals and speak little English. Knowing only that Valerie had a depressed skull fracture was enough to convince me that she should be transferred. But what if her doctor on Long Island should refuse?

The phone rang. I picked it up in the middle of the first ring. It was Dr. Langfitt. He spoke calmly and with gentle firmness. His tone made me realize that I now had an ally in this terrible business, and it felt good.

"I have just spoken to Valerie's doctor, and he feels things are progressing satisfactorily at this point," Dr. Langfitt said. "Her neurological signs are good." He went on to explain that he would be much happier if Valerie were conscious, but added that it wasn't uncommon for someone with such an injury to be unconscious for hours or even days without permanent ill effects.

I told him again that I wanted Valerie transferred. He said he had discussed this with the doctor and they both felt it would be better to wait until daytime because it would be difficult to make transportation arrangements so late at night and her condition seemed satisfactory. The Long Island doctor agreed to call Dr. Langfitt at 8 the next morning to discuss the transfer.

"What kind of doctor is he?" I asked. "He's a general surgeon, but," Dr. Langfitt said, anticipating my concern, "he said he's handled many cases like this before and he is familiar with the head trauma unit at NYU." That seemed encouraging. Just before hanging up Dr. Langfitt apologized for taking so long in getting back to me. The physician in the emergency room—the physician most directly associated with Valerie's care—was apparently a foreign house staff physician, and it took a while for Dr. Langfitt to reach the surgeon at home. I felt the muscles in my jaw tense.

It was 11:30 now. We would, of course, go to Long Island. The only question was when. Nothing could be done before the 8 o'clock phone call between the two doctors; so we didn't have to leave immediately. At night and with the heavy rain the trip would probably take five or six hours, which meant that we wouldn't have to leave until 1:30 or 2. But we were too tense to take what would amount to a nap; so we decided to leave immediately and rest when we got there.

The second call from Valerie's mother came just as we were making arrangements to borrow a car. "I think we have some good news to report," she said. "Valerie is conscious. She recognized me and is complaining about everything hurting so much."

That was good news. But the peak

period of brain swelling wouldn't come for another 24 hours. I didn't go into detail about this with Anne, Valerie's mother, saying only that I was coming out immediately and I thought we should think about transferring Val to another hospital just to be safe.

The rain was coming down hard by the time we got on the road. Lights glared off the macadam, making it difficult to distinguish oncoming traffic. And the windshield wipers could barely keep up with the rain as they thumped back and forth across my vision.

Half way to New York we stopped for a 1 A.M. snack, and Pat took over driving until we reached Nassau County. The going was awfully slow, partly because of the weather and partly because we were so tired. I was beginning to wonder now if I wasn't being hysterical about this whole thing. "Why not wait and see how Valerie does tomorrow?" I said to myself, thinking for the moment that his late night race was foolish. Then I'd answer myself with the same statistics. Ten percent of such head patients will need surgery. To wait until the need is obvious is to have waited too long. I would learn later that with the type of fracture Valerie had, the odds for complications requiring surgery or other sophisticated therapy was 30 percent. By the time we reached the Nassau-Suffolk line, both Pat and I were too tired to go any further. It was 3 A.M. and we had to take a nap; so we pulled the car off the road and fell into a restless sleep with Pat in the back and me in the front.

We slept only an hour before a policeman in a yellow raincoat was standing at the door, knocking on the window. He asked for my license and asked why we were sleeping there in the car. I told him. He nodded without saying anything, handed back my license and drove off.

It would probably take us more than two hours to reach eastern Long Island; so we started off again. It had stopped raining, and we picked up speed as a grey dawn began lighting the horizon in front of us.

Soon it was daylight and we could see the flat land and scrub pine of eastern Long Island racing by us. We were now beyond the commuting range of New York City, and the split-level suburban sprawl of western Suffolk was behind us. Out here it was potato fields and duck farms. Even though it was a grey morning, the daylight felt good and the fears that filled me during the night seemed less threatening. We turned off the highway and onto the small country roads.

Even under the grim circumstances, the small village Valerie lived in looked beautiful in the early morning, still damp from the heavy rain of the night. We followed the "hospital" signs that led us through the still sleeping village and arrived at the side door of the hospital at 7:30. Few people were about at that hour. A nurse walking through the parking lot directed us to the door that would take us to the intensive care unit.

The surgeon was examining Valerie when we arrived. Seeing us, he came to the doorway and edged us outside, saying we could see Valerie as soon as the nurses had moved her bed.

The surgeon was in this late 40s and wore a turtle neck sweater and sports jacket. "Your daughter's doing fine. I was just going to call your boy in Philadelphia," he said, referring to Dr. Langfitt. I asked him a few questions, but I could tell from his curt replies and manner that he wasn't given to long explanations.

"Will there be any problems transferring her?" I asked.

"Nope," he said, pushing through the swinging doors of the hallway leading to the operating rooms. "Go right ahead if it makes you happy." The doors swung shut behind him. His casual, almost carefree maner, was disconcerting, but I didn't think about it for long because the nurse came out of the intensive care unit to say that Valerie was ready.

"Hello, daddy. Hello, Pat," Valerie said, recognizing us immediately. "Oh, I hurt all over. I can't move my arm." Her face was swollen, but her skin wasn't cut and her color was good. She wore a hospital gown and had an intravenous line running from her hand. She struggled to sit up, but I got her to lie down again, and soon she was asleep. I was very surprised and happy to find her so alert. It bothered me a little bit to see her drop off to sleep so quickly, but I brushed this worry aside.

"Let's call Philadelphia," I said to Pat, who was still holding Valerie's hand and caressing her arm. Dr. Langfitt answered the phone himself because it was still too early for his secretary to be in. He said he had just spoken to the Long Island surgeon and everything looked good so far, but he agreed that it would still be wise to transfer Valerie.

I would handle the ambulance arrangements from my end. In Scotland and other European countries, transfers for head injuries like this are arranged routinely, with smaller hospitals automatically referring to regional specialized centers. But in most U.S. areas, it's up to the concerned individuals to work things out as best they can.

We were just preparing to leave when Valerie's mother came down the hall, having just finished breakfast. We exchanged information, and then she went home to rest while we had breakfast and the arrangements for the ambulance were worked out. Everything was moving along nicely, but our luck was running out.

"Gonna have to renege on my promise to let you take your daughter out," the surgeon said the moment we got back to the hospital. "X-rays show what looks like a little spot up here on the top of her lungs, and she may have a couple of broken ribs. Her pelvis is also separated slightly."

It was now 12 hours after the accident, and it amazed me that they were just getting around to looking at the chest x-rays. "You mean she's got a pneumothorax," I said, more concerned about the "spot" than the other findings. For the first time, and only for a moment, his breezy style disappearted. "Yes," he said studying me. "It's not definite, but it looks like that. In any case we're going to have to keep her here another day." And with that he was off again.

I wasn't at all happy with this development, especially after I saw Valerie again. Her condition had obviously deteriorated since we last saw her only an hour or so earlier. It was difficult to rouse her now. She'd ask a question and fall unconscious again before I could answer her.

"That's normal for someone to be sleepy after a bump on the head," the nurse said.

I was not so easily reassured. I knew such "sleepiness" is a very disturbing sign when it's associated with a head injury. It could mean any number of very serious things. A life-threatening blood clot might be forming. Her brain might be bleeding. It certainly was swelling. In any case, it was imperative that the pressure inside of Valerie's skull was monitored and that plans be made for intensive drug therapy and possible surgery to control the swelling.

But then it's terribly dangerous to move someone with a pneumothorax. This is a condition in which air escapes from a ruptured or collapsed lung, filling the pleural cavity between the lung and the chest wall. This is serious but the air can be vented through a tube, which can be easily inserted in the hospital, but is difficult to install during a long ambulance trip.

Back we went to the telephone, which fortunately was in the lobby of one of the little used wings of the hospital. It would become our headquarters for the afternoon as I tried to get Valerie to the head trauma unit.

The doctors in Philadelphia agreed that it would be dangerous to move Valerie without a physician if she had a pneumothorax. But they also thought that Valerie's somnolence was a disturbing sign and said that a neurosurgeon should be brought in as a consultant right away.

The general surgeon said he could contact a neurosurgeon in western Suffolk if I wanted, but I mistrusted him now and wouldn't feel comfortable with anyone he recommended.

I was disturbed that it took him 12 hours to read the x-rays that revealed the chest problem, when in most hospitals such studies are done as soon as an accident victim comes into the hospital. I couldn't understand why he wouldn't immediately transfer a patient with a depressed skull fracture on his own initiative or at least insist on a neurosurgical consultation. And finally I just didn't like his breezy, almost indifferent manner. I wanted to at least try to come up with someone I could feel confident with.

I had two options. I could get a qualified neurosurgeon and hope that he would make the trip out to examine Valerie. Or I could push on with my plans to transfer her and get a physician willing to ride in the ambulance as a safeguard should the pneumothorax cause problems.

I preferred the transfer option, because I knew the best neurosurgeon could do little if he didn't have adequate support personnel and facilities. Neurosurgery has become so complex that it requires a team of anesthesiologists, nurses and radiologists trained in this specialty, as well as such modern and costly equipment as three-dimensional x-rays, brain pressure monitoring devices, neurological intensive care units for post-operative care, etc. Even the best community hospital can't afford to provide all this for the few head cases it might get each year.

Before medicine became so complex, and also more effective, it was good enough to get accident victims to the nearest hospital because then there weren't many things that could be done. But the newest concept is to take the injured to the proper specialized center even if it is many miles further away. They have found that with such problems as burns, head injuries and newborns with birth problems—it is safer to transport the patients than let them linger in a hospital not equipped to provide the most modern care.

My first call went to my friend and city editor at *The Inquirer*, Maxwell King. Quickly I told him my problem, explaining that I vaguely remembered that the Air National Guard or some military outfit provided air ambulance service in such emergencies. Max said he would get to work on it immediately and call me back right away at the pay telephone.

Then I called up David Zinman, another friend and my medical writing counterpart on *Newsday*, a daily newspaper that serves Long Island. Dave gave me the names of two people in major hospitals on the western end of Long Island. I would call them while he checked out other names that he had.

My first few phone calls revealed that the nearest neurosurgeon was 40 miles away and the nearest fully-equipped hospital was even more distant. I got the names of a couple of neurosurgeons, but was unable to find anyone willing to ride with Valerie.

Max called back quickly. He had no word on the military planes, but The Inquirer photo department, which frequently hires planes for aerial photos, had gotten hold of a helicopter ambulance service, which was now standing by for word from me. The problem was that they wouldn't take a patient in Valerie's condition without a physician on board.

Anne came back from the intensive care unit and said that Val seemed to be getting worse. She couldn't rouse her. The thought of staying here another day was becoming terrifying.

It was 12:30 now. The rain had started up again, and with it my frustrations were mounting. So many things were ready to happen, but important segments were missing from the puzzle. There was a helicopter ambulance waiting for word from me, ready to fly immediately to a medical center, but a doctor wasn't available to make the trip. In New York and Philadelphia were two of the best head trauma units in the country, but one doctor in Long Island refused to release my daughter so she could get this care.

The stately grandfather clock in the lobby sounded the half hour. I really didn't expect anyone to get a doctor to make the trip, and I was resigning myself to calling in a neurosurgeon and hoping that he would get Valerie out if necessary. But before I did that, I thought I would try one other thing. Maybe a helicopter could get Valerie to a head trauma unit fast enough to make it unnecessary for a physician to accompany her. Whatever was decided I wanted to have clearly established options to present to this surgeon, who offered me none.

For the fourth time I called Dr. Langfitt. His secretary, who obviously had been alerted to the growing drama, put me right through. Before I could say anything, Dr. Langfitt spoke. "Don, I've discussed Valerie's case with Dr. John Laurent, and he's agreed to go out there and see your daughter." Laurent was one of the neurosurgical residents I knew from the head trauma story.

I choked. For the first time since this terrible thing began, tears started to well up in my eyes. I covered the phone, and then, trying to keep the quaver out of my voice, told him about the helicopter. "Would Dr. Laurent have any objections to riding in a helicopter?" Dr. Langfitt said he wouldn't. I told him I would get right back to him.

I hung up and dialed Max. "You won't believe what just happened," I said to Pat and Anne, sniffing back tears. "They're sending a neurosurgeon up from Penn."

I explained the latest development to Max. "Would it be possible," I asked, "to get the helicopter down to Philadelphia first, pick up Dr. Laurent and then come here?" Max said he didn't know, but he'd work something out. Max took the names and phone numbers of the various doctors. He said he would call me back as soon as he had something definite. I hung up and collapsed on the couch in the deserted lobby. The rain was really getting bad now; and I was beginning to wonder if helicopters could fly in such weather. It was 12:45.

With nothing to do for the moment, I was becoming aware of a headache that was coming on. With the exception of the short nap in the car, I had been awake for almost 30 hours now. I didn't feel it, though, because of the tension. Leaving Anne and Pat by the phone, I went down the hall to Valerie. She was still unconscious. Anne was gone by the time I got back. No phone calls.

A delivery man with flowers came into the lobby, shaking the rain from his hair. "Boy that weather out there ain't fit for ducks," he said, unaware of my grimace. The grandfather clock sounded 1 P.M. The phone rang. It was Max.

"OK, it's all set up," he said. "This is what we're going to do. A small helicopter will pick up Dr. Laurent at Penn and fly him out to the hospital. Meanwhile the ambulance helicopter will leave from New York and fly directly out there. They should both arrive at the same time. The best we can figure it is that they should reach you at about 2:30."

I was ecstatic. "But there's one important thing," Max continued. "We've got a problem with daylight. Once they get there they've only got an hour to examine Valerie, get her into the plane, fly back here and land in Philadelphia. You've got to have everything ready at your end to move as soon as they get here. The helicopter can't land in the dark."

"When do they leave?" I asked.

"They should be in the air now," Max said. I looked at the grandfather clock. It was a little past 1. I had only 90 minutes to wait. Valerie would go to Philadelphia instead of New York City. With a helicopter the extra distance wouldn't mean much, and it meant that Dr. Laurent could stay with the case from beginning to end.

No sooner did I get off the phone than Anne returned followed by the surgeon, who was raging mad. "I've had your daughter's case up to here." he said, indicating the top of his head as he charged into the lobby. "What's all this nonsense about taking that girl out of this hospital?" I tried to explain, but he wasn't listening. "She's not leaving this hospital. I'm not going to let you pull this crazy stunt of yours. She's my patient . . ."

"What?" I screamed back at him, the anger suddenly overwhelming me. "She's my daughter and I don't want her under your godd---n care anymore." People standing in nearby halls were looking at us.

"We'll see about that. I'm going to the hospital administrator to see just how much control you have over a minor," he said, marching down the hall. Minutes later he returned. The administrator wanted to see Valerie's mother. I followed both of them down the hall.

"He doesn't want to see you," the surgeon said. "He only wants to see the girl's mother."

I pushed past him. "Well I'm Valerie's father and he's going to see me too."

The administrator ignored me, addressing his questions to Anne.

"Do you want your daughter taken out of this hospital?" he asked. Anne was bewildered by this sudden hostile turn of events.

"I don't know," she cried. "I only want what's best for my daughter."

I turned on the administrator, who was obviously intimidated by the doctor.

"Are you trying to tell me that I can't have a consultant of my own choosing brought into this case?" I demanded.

"You've got to remember that this doctor is legally responsible for your daughter's care. We're holding him responsible. He's the one that's legally liable." I could feel it coming, and it was going to make me want to punch someone. "If something happened to your daughter, then he's the one who would be sued for malpractice."

"Screw your malpractice," I yelled. "I'm talking about my daughter's life. I want a consultant on this case. Are you trying to tell me you're not going to allow this? I'm not talking about some quack. I'm talking about a neurosurgeon from the University of Pennsylvania. At this very moment he's in a helicopter flying here and you're not going to let him see my daughter when he arrives? Is that what you're saying?"

I couldn't believe that they would resist this. Not only is it proper for a patient or guardian to ask for consultations, it's unethical for a physician to resist. Most self-assured doctors welcome consultations because the expert advice is helpful and it spreads the responsibility.

The administrator looked at the surgeon.

"That's not what you said in the hallway," the surgeon said.

Finally they agreed to my request and I returned to the lobby. It was 1:30. I walked to the front door and looked outside. The rain was getting worse. Oh, what irony if after all this

the weather prevented the helicopters from getting in. I looked down the road across an empty field, a distance of 500 yards at least. The visibility must not be too bad if I see that far, I thought. But this is horizontal visibility. What about vertical? I looked up and saw only grey.

I had to do something to calm myself down. My mind and body had been racing so fast all day that I still didn't feel tired, even though it was now 31 hours since I woke up a lifetime ago in Ann Arbor. I ran outside and walked around the hospital in the pouring rain. Above the grey clouds and rain I thought I could make out the sound of a fixed-wing plane. That was good, I thought. If one plane can make it in this weather, then the helicopters should be able to get through. I was so wet by the time I got back to the lobby I needed a towel to dry my face off. But I felt a little better.

Now that school was over for the day, the hospital was beginning to fill with Valerie's friends, who had heard about the accident over the radio. They were in the hall outside of the intensive care unit, in the front lobby and wandering around us in the little used side lobby that we had taken over.

Rumors spread among them that the hospital had asked the radio station to stop broadcasting the story about Valerie because the crowd of teenagers was disturbing hospital routine. I chuckled at that. The other rumor wasn't so funny. Supposedly the local newspaper had already written Valerie's obituary on the chance that she died just before press time.

The time was dragging now. Visiting hours were beginning, and people with dripping umbrellas and wet coats started arriving to visit their relatives and friends. I looked at them walk by and felt very much a foreigner, very much separate from them.

This was their hospital. Many of them were probably even born here and themselves gave birth here. They had faith in the hospital and undoubtedly the doctors. Yet here I was, a stranger from a big city 200 miles away, doing everything I could to take my daughter out of their hospital because I didn't share this faith, at least not in a case of this type.

Then I started getting angry. It looked like I would be able to get my daughter transferred because I was special. I had specialized knowledge of medicine, as well as connections with a medical center and a newspaper accustomed to dealing quickly and efficiently with crises. Because I was a medical writer, I knew enough to question the care my daughter was getting, but more important I knew what the best possible care consisted of and where to get it.

Most people aren't so lucky, and they're stuck with the level of care that happens to be provided by the hospital nearest them. Terrified by the emergency that brought them to the hospital, people are intimidated by the authoritative doctors who may or may not have their best interest at heart.

Finally it was almost 2:30, and I was up and out before the grandfather clock could chime. I knew it was unreasonable to expect the helicopters to arrive right on schedule, but I wanted to be ready. I asked an old woman entering the hospital where helicopters for the hospital landed. She pointed to a field on the other side of a nearby nursing home. The rain was just awful and accompanied now by a strong wind. I got the car out of the parking lot and double parked in front of the side entrance. Leaving the motor running, I stood next to the open door and peered up into the rain.

Exactly at 2:30 I heard what I thought was the motor of a helicopter. It's funny how the mind will play tricks on you, I thought, when you want something desperately. Then I saw it—the biggest, most beautiful, most wonderful helicopter I had ever seen. It was a great big plane with sliding doors and a big red streak painted across the body. It came right out of the overcast, no more than 300 feet above me, so close I could almost read the writing on the side.

"It's here," I yelled to Pat standing in the doorway of the hospital. "It's here." I jumped into the car and gunned the motor, sounding the horn all the way to the field behind the nursing home. The helicopter was just putting down on the soggy grass as I screeched to a stop a few yards away. I looked for Dr. Laurent, but recognized neither of the two faces peering at me from the open, side door of the plane. Then I realized that this was the ambulance helicopter. Dr. Laurent was on the other one. Disappointment swamped me. Without him all of this would be useless. I looked up into the sky and tried to hear the motors of another plane over the whine of the ambulance helicopter's motors, but there was nothing. I spoke to the helicopter pilot, told him that we had to wait for a second plane and went back to the hospital to tell Pat and Anne the sad news.

Anne had already left for home to bring all the things for the trip. We waited a half hour and still no second plane and no call from Max. We had only two hours of daylight left. That didn't leave much time.

I didn't know it at the time, but the helicopter Dr. Laurent was in wasn't equipped to fly in such bad weather and had been forced down in Ambler. Ordinarily that would have been that, but the spirit driving these people to get Valerie to the medical center was extraordinary. The helicopter pilot had radioed ahead; and by the time they landed, a twin engine, fixed-wing plane with bad-weather navigational equipment was waiting to take Dr. Laurent the remainder of the way.

I was to learn later that this was typical of the camaraderie that had built up during a daylong series of telephone calls among the dozens of people involved in this project. As far as they were concerned, the object was to save the life of a 14-year-old girl none of them had ever seen, but all could identify with as parents of children themselves. No one was about to give up easily.

Max had no time for his normal work this day, and another editor filled in for him while he coordinated the transfer. Gary Haynes, the head of the photo department, and his assistant, D. Gorton, spent much of the day talking to pilots. A neurosurgical team of surgeons, anesthesiologists and special nurses at the University of Pennsylvania had been alerted to stand by for possible surgery. And Anne Budrew, Gary Haynes' secretary, had typed up a prayer for Valerie's recovery, which she distributed to a dozen other secretaries in the building.

The fixed-wing plane solved the immediate problem of getting Dr. Laurent to Long Island, but it created a new problem. The airport was 25 miles from the hospital. A way had to be arranged to get the doctor from the airport to the hospital.

As the plane headed eastward through an opaque sky, Larry Eichel, an *Inquirer* reporter who used to work for *Newsday*, called a friend there. The friend got in touch with the Suffolk County's sheriff office which had a patrol car and Deputy Sheriff Alan Croce waiting at the airport when the plane arrived.

Finally at 3:15 Max called to bring us up to date on the latest events, and I went out and told the helicopter pilot. All this time the helicopter's motor had been kept running because there was no auxiliary power on the ground to restart the engine. The pilot was getting low on gas. They would have to refuel en route to Philadelphia, but they'd continue to stand by.

The hospital administrator was waiting for me when I got back to the hospital. With a huge, whining helicopter sitting on a field a few hundred yards from his hospital, he realized that I had every intention of moving Valerie out if the surgeon from Pennsylvania decided it was necessary. He was not happy about my determination, and told me in no uncertain terms that no doctor was to see Valerie without seeing him first. At this point I wasn't about to argue and agreed.

Excusing myself, I returned to the lobby. I told Pat to pick up Anne at her house and load all the stuff for the trip to Philadelphia in the car so we could get it out to the helicopter right away. Then I passed the word to all of Valerie's friends who were still hanging around the hospital. I told them that a sheriff's car would be arriving soon with the doctor from Pennsylvania, but I didn't know what entrance they would come to. I told them that it was very important that I know as soon as the doctor arrived.

Immediately teenagers started dispersing to different entrances of the hospital, while I waited at the main entrance, looking down the road for the flashing red or blue lights of a patrol car. I waited no more than five minutes before a young boy came running up to me.

"A sheriff's car just came into the emergency room driveway," he said, out of breath.

"Where?" I said. Running ahead of me, the boy led me through a labyrinth of halls, reaching the emergency room just as Dr. Laurent arrived, a red tool box in one hand and a black medical bag in the other. The black bag contained the conventional instruments doctors use. The red box had enough drugs and equipment to sustain life for four hours. He was still wearing his green surgical gown covered by a long white coat.

We recognized each other immediately. He was smiling. I could have kissed him. Briefing him on the problems we were having with the hospital administrator, I led him down the hall to the administrator, followed by Deputy Sheriff Croce and a contigency of teenagers.

The administrator wasn't there when we arrived, but a harried secretary ran out and fetched him. He came in, sat down behind the desk in his small office and, without inviting Dr. Laurent or me to sit down, explained just what could and could not be done.

"You may examine the patient," the administrator said, "and convey your findings to the doctor of record, but you cannot administer drugs or write anything in the chart, and nurses are not to fill any orders you have." Dr. Laurent asked if he would be able to examine Valerie's medical chart. The administrator was so nonplussed by this request that he sidestepped it by telling Dr. Laurent to discuss this with the doctor.

Dr. Laurent and the small group of people now following him marched down the hall, passed two more groups of Valerie's friends and went into the ICU. Valerie was still unconscious. A nurse stepped in between her and Dr. Laurent. "You can't see her until we get permission," the nurse said, pulling the curtains shut around Valerie's bed. Dr. Laurent and I waited while she called the administrator, dismissing our explanation that we had just seen the administrator.

The administrator wasn't at his phone; so we waited while they went looking for him. The local surgeon wasn't on hand either, even though he had been alerted to the urgency of moving fast because of the flying problem.

While we were all waiting, Valerie rolled over in bed and moaned. That was too much. Dr. Laurent strode over to the bed, pulled back the curtains with a sweep of his arm and bent over Valerie's head.

"Valerie! Valerie!" He yelled into her ear. "Valerie, can you hear me?" She didn't respond. Giving up on the phone, the nurse came over and sent me out of the ICU, but left Dr. Laurent alone.

We waited outside for a half hour that seemed 10 times that long while Dr. Laurent conducted his examination alone and consulted by phone with the local surgeon. It would be impossible for the helicopter to reach Philadelphia before darkness now. Did that mean that after all this we had lost the race? I was afraid to call Max for fear the transfer would be called off, but if I had I would have been reassured.

Max realized the moment Dr. Laurent was diverted to an airport 25 miles from the hospital that the transfer couldn't be completed by nightfall. So he prepared a contingency plan in cooperation with the University of Pennsylvania and the Philadelphia police and fire departments.

The helicopter would be directed to land at an athletic field next to the Schuylkill River, a couple of blocks from the hospital. A dozen or more fire trucks and police cars would ring the field, lighting it with spot-lights and pin-pointing the field with their flashing emergency lights. Shortly after the helicopter landed, traffic on roads crossing the route from the field to the hospital would be stopped and the fire department's crack ambulance, Rescue 7, would be given a clear, non-stop run to the hospital.

Finally Dr. Laurent emerged from the ICU and we huddled in an empty room down the hall from the ICU. Valerie's condition was potentially extremely serious, Dr. Laurent said, even worse than I had thought. The fracture occurred on the meningeal groove, a point in the skull that lies over the major artery feeding the brain.

It was quite possible, he said, that the blow caused a bruise or blood clot that would close this artery off with lethal consequences. The odds were about 30 percent that Valerie would need surgery or some other form of intensive therapy. Looking at it from the opposite perspective, this meant that there was a 70 percent chance that Valerie would be transferred immediately.

Anne would go back in the helicopter along with Valerie and Dr. Laurent. Pat and I would follow in the car. Pat insisted that I go in the helicopter also, but she was exhausted and I didn't want her making the long trip by herself for fear she would get into an accident.

As we hurried back to the ICU, I asked Dr. Laurent about the pneumothorax that had forced us to fly him to Long Island to accompany Valerie back.

"She doesn't have a pneumothorax," he said.

"What?" I said shocked.

"There's no pneumothorax," he said. "The x-ray film was over-developed."

Deputy Sheriff Croce, Anne and I rushed out to the helicopter. Anne would wait in the helicopter while Croce and I returned to the hospital with the litter to get Valerie. It was raining hard.

Dr. Laurent was ready to move the moment we got back. Keeping Valerie attached to the intravenous bottle, which was held above her, we slid her onto the helicopter's litter. We wrapped her up tightly with a towel because of the rain and then strapped her in.

A very official looking woman, probably the director of nursing, suddenly appeared. "What are you doing?" she demanded. "You can't take that girl out in the rain like this?"

"What's the alternative?" Dr. Laurent asked.

"You have to get an ambulance," she said.

"How long will that take?" he asked.

"I don't know," she said. "A half hour or so."

"Let's get going," Dr. Laurent said, refusing to even consider a delay of that length at this point. We pushed the litter down the hall, leaving the unknown woman standing in the middle of the hall.

Out the front door we went, down the driveway and onto the sidewalk. Dr. Laurent tried to keep the rain out of Valerie's eyes by holding the towel over her head.

The four of us—Dr. Laurent, Pat, Deputy Sheriff Croce and I—half pushed, half carried the litter across the soggy lawn of the nursing home. We were all out of breath by the time we reached the helicopter.

Quickly we got the litter into the helicopter. Dr. Laurent fastened the fluid bottle over Valerie's head, the helicopter pilot tied the litter down and Anne tried to comfort our still unconscious daughter.

Too many things were happening around Valerie for me to kiss her good-bye, so I squeezed her foot and got out of the helicopter. Dr. Laurent and Anne came to the door. I shook their hands. The helicopter crew member waited for us to finish and then slammed the door shut. Pat and I moved back, instinctively ducking under the helicopter propeller that was slowly beginning to rotate.

The three of us who remained stood in the rain and a darkening dusk, waiting for the helicopter to take off. Slowly the giant propellers picked up speed. Red glowed from an engine exhaust in the dark.

The propeller went faster and faster until it became a vague blur, but the plane just stayed there, almost as though the earth refused to release it. Then, awkwardly, the giant helicopter lifted off the ground. It took off at an angle, reached a couple of hundred feet altitude and then headed east to the ocean and beach it would follow to Nassau County and then to Philadelphia.

Soon all we could see was the blinking red light of the helicopter in the dark sky and then not even that. It was quiet now, and we could hear our feet squishing in the sodden grass as we left. No one said anything. We were each lost in our own thoughts.

EPILOGUE

Valerie reached the hospital safely. A variety of tests revealed that her brain was severely swollen, but no surgery was necessary. A bolt to monitor the pressure within her brain was inserted through her skull, and the swelling was controlled with drugs. After five days in the neurosurgical intensive care unit and three days in the general hospital, Valerie was released. She is now recuperating back home on eastern Long Island.

Reprinted by permission of Donald Drake and the Philadelphia Inquirer

17

WRITING BROADCAST NEWS

Write as if your life depended on it. Your livelihood will. Broadcast journalists should write clearly, concisely, and understandably and be fair and accurate as well.

Writing is one of the skills you must have to be a broadcast journalist. The other skills are reporting, editing, using the technical equipment, and performing.

Of all the skills required to be a successful broadcast journalist, the one that is most under your control is writing ability. You may not get a chance to be on-the-air because a news organization's management may not think you have the diction, the voice, or the "look" it is seeking to present to the public. The labor situation, i.e., union rules, where you intern or work may preclude you from becoming or being a technical wizard, or you may simply think that type of work is too "blue collar" for you.

Satellite feeds have made "talent" available with "the" look and sound to the smallest of markets. The miniaturization of equipment means that fewer people will be needed to do the technical jobs required by older and bulkier equipment. Ultimately,

BY JAMES PHILLIP JETER

Dr. Jeter is Professor of Journalism and Director of Graduate Studies in the School of Journalism, Media and Graphic Arts at Florida A&M University. He earned his Ph.D. in communication arts (radio/television/film) from the University of Wisconsin—Madison.

writing ability will be your key to longevity in the business because the need for good writers will remain.

If there is a patron saint of broadcast journalism it is Edward R. Murrow, who is credited with pioneering a style of journalism that took advantage of the capabilities of the medium he would use to become a household name. Although Murrow was not trained in journalism, his skill in public speaking and debate and being well-read were qualities on which he relied to achieve renown. Murrow could also write. His journalistic breakthrough came as technology created possibilities for doing the news differently than it had been done by newspapers. He was there, for example, when the Allies liberated the Buchenwald concentration camp during World War II and described the scene for CBS radio:

...There surged around me an evil-smelling horde. Men and boys reached out to touch me. They were in rags and the remnants of uniforms. Death had already marked many of them, but they were smiling with their eyes....

Although these words were written in April 1945, anyone who reads newspapers can see how this style of writing is different from print. The excerpted passage has no words over three syllables; the sentences are short and direct; and the word choice is exact and descriptive. Murrow's words were written with the knowledge that people would not read them but *hear* them, that the audience was not at Buchenwald but Murrow was and Murrow's task was to tell the audience what he had seen, heard, and smelled.

There is a technological revolution underway in the telecommunications environment. It is now true that never have so many been able to say so much to so many with (often) so little time to think about what is being communicated. In the future, there may be more information to communicate, but the need will remain to communicate it clearly.

This writer does not subscribe to the idea that news has been, or can be, objective—because a reporter is a not a blank slate without any prior experiences in life when that reporter goes to events.

Rather than seeking imagined "objectivity," the broadcast journalist should write clearly, concisely, and understandably and be fair and accurate as well.

The changing telecommunication environment will mean cooking channels, gardening channels, and home improvement channels, to name a few, added to the myriad of current and announced channels that already exist. "News," i.e., presentational information programming, will likely be a part of the programming of these new outlets.

In this chapter, the writer's bias for precise, simple, clear, and direct writing will be apparent. Two memories from my early days as a news writer provide reasons for this. When I worked for United Press International, I could always gauge how I was doing by the number of calls I did *not* get from editors calling for clarification of stories I had written. No calls meant that scores of experienced professionals reading a story I wrote understood it and had no problems with it. It was a good feeling.

Another memory is more ominous. Shortly after I started work at UPI, we ran a series of stories on an area football stadium construction project, and allegations surfaced that organized crime was involved in bidding for the concessions contract. One day when I arrived for my shift I was told of a telephone call a staffer had received the night before. He said the telephone rang and on the other end was a voice that sounded like a character from *The Untouchables* who said "we are reading what you are writing about the [XYZ] company" and hung up. From that moment on, I decided to take great care to make sure my copy was clear, the sources attributed, and my stories contained facts. If there is one point I could make in this chapter that will remain with the reader, it would be the following: Write as if your life depended on it. Your livelihood will.

Journalists do not always get to choose their subjects. While enterprise is usually welcome in organizations, beginning writers get assigned stories or topics, and their task is to produce usable copy. You usually will not receive "voice in the night" calls that carry with them a sense of apprehension because of something you have written. You will likely get calls from a politician's aide saying your story might ruin a campaign. Maybe it will be an athletic director saying "We've done nothing wrong in our recruiting" or someone who implores you not to "air dirty linen."

The fact is that frequently the subjects of and participants in news events may not like it that you have chosen to write about them. They do have a right to expect that you will be accurate and will give them a chance to respond to the facts.

BROADCAST STYLE

The best way to develop your broadcast writing ability is to practice it and critically assess what is currently being aired. Tape newscasts; transcribe them. If you have access to *CNN Newsource*, look at the scripts that are available. Find a newspaper version of a story you have on tape and compare what was written. If you had to use the print story as source copy, what would you include in a radio or television story?

What makes something newsworthy centers around whether the event or person has prominence, geographic proximity, timeliness, human interest, uniqueness, or impact on a large number of people. It also helps if the elements of controversy, conflict, and, increasingly, sex and violence, are present. Visual images and sounds of the event or person help move the story closer to getting on the air. You will find yourself in an environment where it will become clear (fairly soon) where each of these factors fits into your organization's hierarchy. No matter what you may think of programs like *A Current Affair, Entertainment Tonight, Hard Copy*, and *Inside Edition*, the news writers for those programs perform the same tasks as writers on the local news, ABC's *World News Tonight, The CBS Evening News, The NBC Nightly News*, or any of the CNN programs.

The process of preparing each broadcast story is essentially the same. A news director, producer, or assignment editor decides a story is important enough to devote air time to it and assigns it to a staff member. A reporter/writer determines which facts are important and assembles them in some order. There is often audio or video to accompany the story. The writer then matches the written script with the available audio tape or videotape. If the visuals are not compelling, then the attempt might be made to tell the entire story with words (a form known as a "reader"). The assignment editor, producer, or news director reviews the match and says "air it."

The basic difference between broadcast writing and print writing is style. The subject may be the same, but the way the reporter tells the audience about it and sequences facts is different. Because all the words in a thirty-minute commercial television network newscast will fit on less than one page of a full size newspaper, the reporter is giving the audience a summary of an event. Because reporters have less time to convey a sense of the story, they need to decide what new aspect of an event they can bring to the audience. Another major difference between broadcast and print is that broadcast news is fleeting. While the printed page is a tangible item, a broadcast is literally gone with the wind. While some of your listeners may videotape a newscast, the majority of them will not.

The Lead

The classic newspaper lead attempts to cram as much information as possible into the first paragraph. Known as the inverted pyramid, the traditional story structure dates back to the days when news reports were often transmitted to newspapers by tele-graph. Since communications lines could be cut or lost at any time, the writer made sure the lead contained the who, what, when, where, why, and how of the story up front. Although transmission methods are now more reliable, this style endures, as this recent lead from page one of the New York *Times* indicates:

> Millions of voters across the 12-nation European Union chose a new European parliament today in elections that reflected re-cent trends toward the right and that voters saw as a chance to deliver a message on the popularity of their national govern-ments. The vote also produced a surprise boost for Chancellor Helmut Kohl in Germany.

Such a lead would not make it to the air. At over fifty words, it's too long and has too much information. A broadcast lead might have been:

> Elections returns indicate voters want the European parlia-ment to be more conservative.

What's missing from the broadcast lead are names, numbers, and many of the specific facts in the newspaper lead. If you had to deliver the opening part of the above story, which of the two leads would you be most comfortable with giving people one shot at un-derstanding what the story was going to be about?

Because you should not include in the lead all the Ws and the H of the story, you will have to use your judgment of which of the 5 Ws or the H is important. "Who" and "what" are important in the following lead:

> Former President Richard Nixon is dead.

In natural disasters or catastrophes, the "where" becomes im-portant:

> Hurricane Andrew is about 100 miles from Miami at this hour.

Choose one or two "Ws" or an "H" for the lead. Try to get the attention of the audience with a good setup and add the important details to the setup. Do not tease your audience in the story. Any promise in your lead should be quickly explained:

The jazz world loses a giant. Miles Davis has died. Authorities say the beebop pioneer died in Santa Monica. He was 65-years-old.

Question leads should be avoided unless the subject matter is a feature or light material. Consider the following lead:

Could interest rates be headed higher?

This lead could be written anytime. If you have an expert who is predicting this, say so in your lead:

One Nobel Prize winner says interest rates will have to rise.

Humor
Humor is fragile and has the potential to offend as much as evoke a chuckle. Because of today's sensitivities, be careful with jokes about ethnic and racial groups, women, and the disabled. Material about sexual activity and crime can be the start of a slippery slope as well. Light or feature material is the best candidate for a laugh. Usually, the facts told clearly will provoke a smile. Humor might be appropriate in a story about a winning lottery ticket retrieved from an unusual place (i.e., the cleaners or a trash can) or a story about a duck that acts like a dog.

Sentences
Sentences in broadcast news copy should be written to imitate the way you would tell the story in a conversation. Keep the sentences short and linear with the subject first, the verb second, and the object last. Try to avoid introductory phrases, complex sentences, appositives, or dependent clauses. Watch out for sentence length, and read your copy aloud after you have written it. If you have to take a breath to get through a sentence, it's too long. Split the thought or make two sentences.

No: After being indicted for the embezzlement, Roberts pleaded no contest.
Yes: Roberts pleaded no contest to embezzlement charges.

No: Laura Tyson, chair of President Clinton's council of economic advisers, says the administration is very concerned about the fall of the dollar.
Yes: Laura Tyson says the Clinton administration is very con-

cerned about the fall of the dollar. Tyson is chair of the President's Council of Economic Advisers.

Unlike formal prose, you can occasionally get away with sentence fragments in broadcast writing. Since we sometimes talk in fragments, the audience is used to hearing phrases like these:

Big accident at the Thomasville Road overpass.

No word yet on new transit contract.

Used occasionally, this technique is perfectly acceptable. Don't try to tell an entire story with such cryptic phrases. The style becomes old to an audience if used too much in one story or back to back.

BASIC RULES

There are some basic rules that you need to start using as soon as possible. The more you use them, the more they become second nature. You will then have more time to spend with your stories rather than a stylebook.

• 1. No handwritten copy. Neatness counts. Since typewriters are no longer the writing instrument of choice, you will have to learn how to use a personal computer. Using is not programming. Many word processing packages are available. While personal computers have been a boom to writing, the ease of making corrections makes it always possible to tweak your copy until you literally have to let it go.

• 2. Copy should be double-spaced. This makes it easier to read and to make minor corrections.

• 3. Slug/Identify every story. Copy with slugs can be quickly identified. On the top left of each page, put the story name, your name, the date, and the time of the newscast:

EUROPARLIAMENT
P. Jeter
6/21/97
5 p.m.

• 4. Line spacing and timing. Use a 65-character line for radio copy, and estimate no more than four seconds a line. Television uses a split page format with video cues/information on the left side of the page and the audio information and script on the other. Estimate approximately two seconds a line for a video script.

• 5. Use only one story per page. If the story runs more than one page, type "(MORE)" at the bottom and add the slug with a page number for each subsequent page. Some editors prefer indicating how many total pages of the script there are: 1 of (total), 2 of (total), 3 of (total), etc.

• 6. Do not write in all caps. Use upper and lower case when preparing scripts.

• 7. Don't hyphenate or split words or jump sentences from page to page. This minimizes the chance of reading the wrong word or injecting a pause while the deliverer's brain catches up with the eyes and hands.

• 8. Radio copy does not use paragraphs, but television news scripts normally divide the copy into units of two or three lines.

• 9. The end of a story should be indicated by placing 30, -0- or #### centered below the last line of the copy.

• 10. Editing—Copy corrections should be kept to a minimum or the item should be reprinted/retyped. Words, not letters, can be deleted, substituted, or added if the corrections are likely to be understood. If not, or there is any chance of being misread, retype the material. Appearance does count.

Punctuation

The most commonly used punctuation marks in broadcast journalism are the period, the comma, apostrophe, the hyphen, the double dash, quotation marks, ellipses, and parentheses.

Periods indicate the end of a sentence or thought:

There are no more American troops in Somalia.

Commas indicate a pause or separates items, words, or phrases:

The governor said he would not ask the legislature to raise property taxes, sales taxes or inheritance taxes, but revenue would have to come from some source.

The use of a comma for a pause usually works for radio, but for Teleprompters the ellipses is best to avoid the probability of a comma being misinterpreted as a period.

Use the *apostrophe* for contractions. *Contractions* are acceptable because people use contractions in their normal speech. Because you are striving for conversational style, "don't," or "won't," and "can't" are acceptable:

The governor says he won't sign any bill that raises sales taxes.

The *hyphen* is used to connect words or letters: Y-M-C-A, F-B-I, 12-hundred dollars, three-billion dollar deficit.
Dashes indicate an abrupt change or clarification:

The governor—who is not running for reelection—said he will raise sales taxes.

Ellipses are three consecutive dots that indicate a pause that should be longer than that for a comma. Perhaps the best known practitioner of the use of the ellipses is radio news commentator Paul Harvey. Here is an example of his style:

TASS...the official Russian News Agency...said it would be wrong to make a political scandal out of the spying charges against a former C-I-A official.

Quotation marks appear in the copy but are not read. They are used to indicate the exact words of a newsmaker or the titles of books, movies, plays, songs, and television shows.
Underline words or type them in *full caps* for emphasis:

The Rockets came back to win the series AFTER losing the first three games.

If you will not be reading the copy, you can take additional steps to indicate emphasis by placing *slash marks* where you would like the anchor or reporter to pause:

The wildfires have burned 12-thousand acres // three times as much as last summer's blazes.

Parentheses indicate material that should not be read over the air but provides information for the reporter or anchor. Information on soundbites or word pronunciations is enclosed in parentheses. Stories with sexual content frequently contain "(Note sexual content)" before the beginning to let an editor decide if the story will be used on the air at all.

Pronunciation

If there is any chance a word could be mispronounced or cause an unwanted pause, use a pronunciation guide to standardize the word. Munich would be written (MEW-nick) with the stressed syllable in capital letters. The standard pronunciation guide is to use the following phonetic styles for word sounds:

Consonants
K for hard "C" as in cat
S for soft "C" or soft "S" as in ceiling, seal
CH for hard "CH" as in cheese
SH for soft "CH" as in machine
G for hard "G" as in graduate, go
J for soft "G" as in geranium
KW for "QU" as in quart
Z for hard "S" as in music

Vowels
A
AY for long "A" as in day
A for short "A" as in cat
AI for nasal "A" as in dare
AH for soft "A" as in arm
AW for broad "AW" as in walk

E
EE for long "E" as in meet
EH for short "E" as in met
AY for French long "E" with the acute accent (as in passe)
EW for "ew" diphthong as in dew

I
IGH for long "I" as in slime
EE for long "E" as in machine
IH for short "I" as in city

O
OH for long "O" as in notable or though
AH for short "O" as in shot
AW for broad "O" as in broad
OO for long double "OO" as in pool
UH for short double "OO" as in boot
OW for "OW" diphthong as in how or plow

U
EW for long "U" as in due
OO for long "U" as in rule
U for middle "U" as in put
UH for short "U" as in mud

Sometimes, particularly for names, you have to resort to rhyming technique, e.g., Tiar (rhymes with TIRE) or Blough (rhymes with go) or (like blow).

Attribution

This is one area where more work could be done to improve broadcast journalism. Avoid writing a story like this:

> The tobacco industry has been using high nicotine tobacco in its cigarettes.

Who says so? A newspaper lead might look like this:

> The tobacco industry has been using high nicotine tobacco in its cigarettes, according to Dr. David Kessler, chairman of the Food and Drug Administration.

In print we see that the source is the head of the FDA but only when you can look at it. The lead could be written for broadcast this way:

> The tobacco industry has been using high nicotine tobacco in its cigarettes. That from the head of the Food and Drug Administration.

It would be better, though, to write the following:

> The head of the Food and Drug Administration says the tobacco industry has been using high nicotine tobacco in its cigarettes.

We now know who said what and not what was said by whom. The last lead minimizes the biggest source of the greatest confusion to your audience: making it clear who said what. *Your goal as a writer is to minimize confusion.* Tell your listeners who is saying what before you tell them what was said. The audience cannot see quotation marks or commas. Anytime you have a story that contains allegations that are not fact, tell your audience who is saying them. Put the source before the charge, prediction, or statement.

A fact is information about which there is no doubt. Consequently, such information as the following need not be attributed:

- George Washington was the first president of the United States of America.
- The University of Nebraska won the 1995 Orange Bowl.
- Thurgood Marshall was a Supreme Court Justice.

Facts are also historical (in the context of the story). The first report of the death of a prominent person should be preceded by attribution from a hospital or family spokesperson. Later stories on the person's funeral, however, require no attribution for a reference of death.

Quotations

Listeners can't see quotation marks in your copy. The best way to handle quotations is to avoid them. This is where actualities (excerpts from interviews with newsmakers) come in. If you want to use a quotation, decide if it adds to the story. If not, omit it. If the information needs to remain, try paraphrasing the quotation, being careful to maintain the integrity of the context in which the statement was made.

If you decide that you must use a portion of the quotation verbatim, you need to signal to your audience that what follows are the exact words of someone:

Governor Jones says the legislature must not approve what he called..."a travesty in the tax code."

or

The President said—and he put it this way—"Mistakes were unintentional and regrettable."

If a story has a long quotation, break it up and identify the source as often as needed for the audience to connect the quote with the speaker:

The President said—and he put it this way—"Mistakes were unintentional and regrettable." The President said—still quoting—"nobody will lose their job unless they are indicted."

Although you sometimes hear an anchor or reporter say "quote" and "unquote," the consensus is this is a hackneyed method of handling a quotation.

Actualities

Actualities are excerpts of taped interviews. As such, the tape allows the use of the capabilities of the broadcast medium to bring the words, inflection, and tone of newsmakers or eyewitnesses to the telling of an event. Because the voice on the tape will be different from the anchor or reporter on radio, you need to prepare the audience for the change in voice. In radio, there are numerous conventions that can be used:

Police captain Bob Smith described the arrest....
(Smith interview)
Teamster spokesman Bill Brown details the union's demands.
(Brown interview)

On television the newsmaker will be identified by name and agency affiliation; so no name may be required, but the need to set up the actuality remains:

Video	Audio
(Jeter on/camera)	Jeter: The police describe what happened...
Officer Smith on camera w/super	Smith on tape (:20 sec) incue: "The red car swerved..."
Ofc. Bill Smith Miami Police	outcue: "....and slid into the underpass."

Abbreviations

The rules for using abbreviations are these:

- Generally, avoid abbreviations. They can cause errors.
- Write out avenue, boulevard, parkway, lane, and street.
- Write out the name of states and countries. An exception is the U-S for United States.
- Write out days of the week and months of the year.
- Write out titles with the exception of the courtesy titles of Mr.,

Mrs., and Dr.
• Some abbreviations are familiar enough to be used. Using YMCA in your copy is okay, but it should be written as Y-M-C-A (indicating that each letter is read separately). Well-known acronyms such as NOW, NASA, and NATO can be used when they are written in full caps and should be pronounced as words.

Titles
Titles should precede names and be shortened. "John Jones, assistant secretary of state for Middle Eastern affairs" should be "Assistant Secretary of State John Jones...."

Numbers
Do you really need to use them? If so, round them up or down. Remember that numbers will be heard, not seen. A sum like $9,235.13 becomes "more than nine-thousand dollars" or "over nine thousand dollars" in a broadcast script. Spell out numbers one through eleven and use numerals for higher numbers through 999. Above that use a combination of numbers and words, three-billion for 3,000,000,000 (you can see why), 45-million or eight-thousand. The exceptions are dates, times, and scores: 8 P-M, June 2nd, 3-1. For ordinal numbers add ND, RD, ST, or TH as in 2ND, 23RD, 41ST, or 65TH.

Use precise numbers only when important:

Mortgage rates are up three-tenths of one per cent this week.

Symbols
Use words for the symbols $, %, and #.

Tense
The preferred tense in the lead of a broadcast story is the present tense. Any other tense fails to take advantage of the immediacy possible from broadcasting. You want to tell your audience what's the latest. Suppose there was a fire at the largest furniture plant in town last night. If you write for an afternoon newscast the following day, "The largest furniture plant in the county burned to the ground last night," the reaction of your audience will likely be "Hey, tell me something I don't know." A better lead would be:

Fire officials say they don't know what caused last night's fire at the Big Furniture Company.

or

> Fire officials say it will be weeks before they have a cause for last night's fire at the Big Furniture Company.

If you can't use present tense in your lead, try to use present perfect (has or have plus the past participle):

> Business has been booming for Chrysler, Ford and General Motors so far this year.

is better than:

> The three major American automakers reported record earnings for the first quarter of 1994.

A final option might be to look at some future development:

> Chrysler, Ford and G-M say they will raise new car prices next year even though each automaker is earning record profits.

In the following pair of leads, the first one is better than the second because of the emphasis on the future rather than the past:

> The F-C-C will decide next month if a portion of the information highway will be auctioned off.

> The F-C-C announced today that a decision on personal communications services spectrum auctions has been postponed.

The past tense is acceptable for sentences later in the story, but avoid it in the lead.

Predictions

It is preferable not to make predictions. When they are made, attribute them, preferably to someone with expertise on the subject matter in question. A Nobel Laureate may be a whiz at molecular biology, but his opinion on a labor dispute is beyond his realm of competence.

Voice

Avoid the passive voice. Try to write in the active voice using the subject-verb-object approach.

"The satellite was launched by NASA" would be better written as "NASA launched the satellite."

Time Element

If the time element of a story is important, use it and be as specific as possible. Today could be this morning, this afternoon, this evening. However, don't make your audience count the days between today and the 29th. Make it tomorrow, next week, next month, in four days.

Word Choice

Keep it simple. Mark Twain asked, "Why should I write 'metropolis' when they pay me the same for the word 'city'?" Your audience will not have a dictionary handy when listening or watching the news. Any word in your copy that makes the audience go "huh" was the wrong one. Some of the more common examples of wordiness or inappropriate word choice would be using "laceration" for "cut," "surgical procedure" for "operation," and "transmit" for "send."

Similarly, the words "say," "says," and "said" carry less connotation with them than "claimed," "contended," "charged," etc. Again, the facts should be colored as little as possible by the writer.

Pronouns

Avoid pronouns unless the antecedent is clear:

> The dean said the professor has academic freedom, but she decided to resign anyway.

or

> The governor and the senate president disagree on how to fund the bill. He said higher taxes are needed.

To whom does the "she" or "he" refer? Remember your audience cannot read your sentence or place a mental pin in the antecedent. Don't make your listener or viewer spend time trying to figure out a version of the old comedy routine of "Who's on first?" The best technique here is repetition of the antecedent:

> The dean said the professor has academic freedom, but the dean decided to resign anyway.

or

The governor and the senate president disagree on how to fund the bill. The senate president wants higher taxes.

You should avoid pronouns in the lead if there is more than one possible antecedent.

Adjectives

Avoid using adjectives unless they are descriptive. Writing "The witness told police the robber was driving a red car" is one thing; but words like "belligerent," "brutal," and "grisly" may be an opinion of yours that is not universally shared. If an event is tragic, the facts will convey this.

PUTTING IT ALL TOGETHER

Your first task is to understand the story and think it is important. If you do not take this attitude, your writing will convey it. You need to be aware of current events and well-read. Reading daily newspapers and weekly magazines and watching C-SPAN and newscasts will help. You should have some idea of what the topics are that are likely to be around awhile. Particularly as you read, you should clip statistics, factoids as they are sometimes called, on issues like health care, the inflation rate, interest rates, and the local municipal budget.

If you do not maintain such a file, you need to know where you can obtain this information, preferably in written form. One advantage of having facts and statistics in front of you is that if you need to talk with sources—e.g., college professors who have done research on a topic, elected representatives, or lobbyists—you will be in a position to challenge or press them on their responses when their data differ from yours. Skills in using databases such as NEXIS and LEXIS will be invaluable.

Your first assignments will be the staple stories (fires, accidents, conferences, speeches, meetings, crime, trials, sports, and weather).

Let's look at the following facts for such a story and suggest one way to write it:

Facts: Action at the Red Bank City commission meeting last night.... Commission 5-0 approved a one per cent raise for city employees.... Mary Brown made a motion to fire Paul Smith, city manager.... Smith has been city manager for last 19 years and 7 months.... Smith has a national reputation as a competent city manager.... Brown is the newest commissioner and was elected last month during the regular election.... Brown's motion never put to a vote.... Two (Roger Wilcox and Susan Strict) of four other commissioners complained of manager's lack of communication, poor budget management and allowing staffers to call commissioners by their first names.... The commission ordered a study to be done on enlarging a neighborhood playground.... The city denied a request to sponsor a free Labor Day concert in a city park.... Ernest Green and Rachael Foote, the other two commissioners, supported Smith....

Obviously, there are numerous activities to report. However, the dissatisfaction of the majority of the city commissioners over the long serving city manager is probably of interest to most people and has the widest impact because it could affect the delivery of city services if the city manager is replaced or resigns. The worst lead would be a nothing lead like this:

The Red Bank City commission met last night.

The audience's reaction would be "And????"
My 30-second story would be the following:

CITY COMMISSION
P. Jeter
6/1/97
8 a.m.
Three city commissioners say they are not happy with the performance of city manger Paul Smith. Commissioner Mary Brown moved to fire Smith. Two other commissioners—Roger Wilcox and Susan Strict—complained about the city manager's lack of communication. Wilcox and Strict say they were also unhappy about the city manager's poor budget management and his allowing city employees to call commissioners by their first names. No vote was taken on Commissioner Brown's motion at last night's meeting. Commissioner Brown has been on the commission for less than one month, and she gave no reasons for her motion. Smith has been city manager for nearly 20 years.

# # # #

The commission's other actions are less significant or can be added if you have more time to summarize the meeting.

UPDATES

If you find yourself covering a breaking story, the challenge is to give your audiences something new. For the 1994 Los Angeles earthquake the first story might have looked something like this:

An earthquake has hit Los Angeles. Sources say the ground shook for about 40 seconds about half an hour ago. No word yet on injuries or damages.

As more information becomes available, you change the lead and move the new information up front. Any word on injuries or deaths? What was the exact location, the magnitude of the quake on the Richter scale? How bad was this quake compared to previous ones? No matter where your station might be located, many members of your audience may have friends or relatives in the Los Angeles area. Consequently, any information on deaths or injuries should lead when you get it:

Los Angeles authorities confirm at least three deaths because of this morning's pre-dawn earthquake. One was a motorcycle policeman on his way to work.

The general rule is that people are more important than property in the order of sequencing facts.

By midmorning your story might have looked like this:

Seismologists say this morning's pre-dawn earthquake in Los Angeles was the strongest in the area in seven years. The quake hit about two hours before dawn and measured six-point-six on the Richter scale. The earthquake's epicenter was actually in Northridge...about 25 miles northwest of L-A. So far, authorities confirm 16 deaths, including one California highway patrol officer who was killed when his motorcycle fell off a section of a collapsed freeway. Three other major freeways have been shut down. This is L-A's worst quake since 1987.

By the next day your lead might have been:

Aftershocks are still being felt in L-A more than 24 hours after yesterday's early morning quake.

or

Damaged freeways are being torn down as Los Angeles starts

digging itself out of its worst earthquake in seven years.

COVERAGE TIPS
Fires
Television is driven by visuals, and cameras are drawn to fire like moths to flames. Besides videotape of the fires, you will want to get information on location, injuries, and the amount of time it took to get the fire under control. The people to talk to would be the ranking firefighter at the scene to determine any information on suspected cause, suspicious nature, special equipment used, injuries, and so forth. There may be paramedics or ambulance drivers willing to talk about the nature of the injuries received. Finally, any victims or witnesses who were near when the fire started would provide eyewitness accounts. Again, be concerned about people (personal injuries or deaths) over property (damage dollar figures).

Road Accidents
Road accidents are a staple of local news. Like fires, you are concerned with the location of the accident, injuries, and a description of what happened. The best source of what happened is the police officer at the scene. Here, being well read may result in another story. An enterprising reporter might check to see how many accidents have occurred at this location in the last year or two. Is the location poorly lit or marked, or is the volume of traffic too much for the intersection at that time of day?

Speeches and News Conferences
Can you get an advance copy of the speech or statement that will be read? If so, you can look through it to determine which remarks might have the most newsworthy qualities. However, videotape and audio tape are cheap. You could record only the selected portion of the speech you have deemed newsworthy, but what if the speaker deviates from his or her prepared remarks? Will you miss the "bite of the story" because you were being lazy? Sometimes speeches and news conferences are notable for the topics the speaker does not discuss. Being well-read or up on current events will help because questions are frequently taken.

Crime
Too many news organizations limit their definition of "crime" to murder, robbery, rape, burglary, and grand theft auto. Usually, the crime itself is covered, and there may be a follow-up on the

second day. Unless the crime was grisly, gruesome, or heinous, you won't hear much about it after the second day. If the crime was grisly and there is no plea bargain, there may be public interest in the trial. Although the emotional aspects of the trial often receive the most attention, the legal points of the trial are the most important. While it is compelling video to show a sobbing witness or report that fact, it is better to tell your audience whether a witness tied a defendant to the scene of the crime or said the defendant was somewhere else. A coroner may have said a victim had been stabbed twenty-seven times, but did the coroner cast doubt that one person could have done it or the weapon held in evidence could have produced the kind of stab wounds found on the victim?

By choosing to report a crime story, you must understand the legal process as well as the criminal justice system. There are nuances from state to state, but overall there are some broad similarities. The job of the police is to investigate a crime, arrest someone if they think that person is guilty, and turn him or her over to the judicial system. Once in the judicial system, a person must be arraigned (where formal charges are lodged or the case is dismissed). A preliminary hearing may be held to determine if a trial is warranted. The judicial system conducts a trial, if warranted, on the guilt or innocence of the person charged on the alleged violations of specific criminal laws.

During the course of an investigation, police might question witnesses at the scene or ask one of them to come in to make a statement. That person may or may not be under suspicion. The presumption in American jurisprudence is that persons accused of crimes must be proven guilty beyond a reasonable doubt. Police arrest people and then frequently release them, dropping the charges. Giving a statement does not mean one is under suspicion. An arrest does not always result in charges, and charges do not always result in conviction.

The events surrounding the O. J. Simpson case should serve as a reminder of the need for reporters to exercise caution when writing about a story they are not covering first-hand, to refrain from speculation that might hamper the right of the accused to get a fair trial, and to refrain from reporting information that indicates their feelings on the guilt or innocence of the person charged. Too frequently news organizations report that someone was arrested but fail to let their audience know if and when charges against that same person were dropped or the case dismissed.

THE BROADCAST WRITING ART

Some say broadcast writing is an art; others argue it is a craft. The easiest aspects of it to master are the craft components, the stylistic considerations and conventions (handling numbers, quotations, and abbreviations). The art comes when you write a story that in the competition of all the din of activities makes someone go "Shhh" to others in the room or makes others pause to hear what you said about a person or an event.

18

WRITING FOR PUBLIC RELATIONS

Despite bells and whistles on the information superhighway, the ability to write well still determines one's success in public relations.

One of the questions frequently posed to students in a media ethics class asks: "Would you go to work in public relations for a tobacco company?" Although legislation someday may make that question meaningless, similar hypothetical examples are sure to surface.

Public relations certainly has a credibility problem. It is too often viewed as an occupation that distorts facts, withholds information, and presents subjective statements as simple truth.

Such charges came crashing down upon Hill & Knowlton, at the time the largest PR firm in the United States, shortly after the Persian Gulf War. It was discovered that Citizens for a Free Kuwait had hired Hill & Knowlton to help move the United States toward military intervention by spreading false stories about Iraqi atrocities.

Public relations professionals condemned the controversial public relations firm, a division of WPP Group of London, which

---

BY RANDALL W. HINES
Dr. Hines teaches in the Department of Communication at East Tennessee State University. His Ph.D. is in public relations from Texas A&M University.

had caused havoc earlier this decade with such clients as pro-life Roman Catholic bishops and the Florida-based Church of Scientology. Hill & Knowlton shot back with a classic and solid defense—it was only helping a client articulate its side of the story. No stranger to controversy, Hill & Knowlton was hired by the tobacco industry forty years ago to refute scientific claims about smoking's harmful effects.

Asking if a person with morals can work in public relations is an ambiguous question, since people with varying degrees of ethics are involved in every career. A demanding profession, public relations is aware of skeletons in its closet. The Public Relations Society of America, the nation's largest body of professionals in the field, continues to demand ethical decision making of its members.

Constantly evolving, the PRSA ethics code was born in 1950 and revised in 1954, 1959, 1963, 1977, 1983, and 1988. Members, in following such a code, pledge to conduct themselves professionally with truth, accuracy, fairness, and responsibility to the public. If a member violates the code, the organization can reprimand, censure, suspend, or expel the guilty party. The downside of such standards is that they apply only to members of PRSA. Critics quickly point out the ineffectiveness of an ethics code when a majority of the field's practitioners are not bound by it. However, the entire industry has become more cognizant of professional standards.

A related organization second only to PRSA in size, the International Association of Business Communicators, acknowledges that its sanctions apply only to members. But its code states that such principles of conduct are for IABC members as well as all other communication professionals. Only as individuals rightly respond to ethical decisions will the profession itself be lifted to a higher plane of morality. This view is reflected in a recent book, *Public Relations Writing*, in which authors Kerry Tucker, Doris Derelian, and Donna Rouner argue that "public relations practitioners should make it their business to maintain the organizational conscience and ensure that ethical issues are aired at the planning table."

If an individual is faced with a job assignment that goes counter to his or her moral conviction, the obvious options include completing the task anyway, quitting the job, or trying to alter the assignment so that it does not conflict. Such choices, of course, are not unique to public relations.

As part of their job description, PR professionals usually encounter three major tasks (ranked from easiest to most difficult):

1. Maintain favorable opinions of their clients or organizations
2. Solidify potential support for their clients or organizations
3. Change/neutralize antagonistic attitudes toward their clients or organizations

Ivy Lee, considered the father of public relations, faced such tasks after muckraking journalists exposed the "evils" of an expanding industrialized society early in the twentieth century. His revolutionary approach to the media was to provide them with as much information as they wanted, quite unlike most publicists up to that time. (This approach remains a struggle for some professionals today, especially those not on the management team.) Ten years after forming the first modern public relations firm in 1904, Lee took on as his client John D. Rockefeller Jr. Lee convinced the unpopular multi-millionaire to visit striking employees at his family's Colorado mine. He arranged for photographers to be on site when Rockefeller mingled socially with the workers and their families. Lee is also credited with the idea of the equally disliked Rockefeller Sr. giving dimes to children he met on the street. Through Lee's efforts of publicizing Rockefeller's many donations to charity, the multi-millionaire was considered a great philanthropist at his death.

Such efforts still make public relations an exciting but challenging career option. Too often students opt for a major in public relations for all the wrong reasons. "I like people," they say. Or worse, "I like parties."

The *one* quality that is essential for success in the public relations field is being neither a hand-shaking extrovert nor a congenial social butterfly. It is merely *being a good writer*. Public relations professors cringe every fall when at least one aspiring major invariably utters, "I don't like to write; so I decided to major in PR."

For those who may be thinking that writing is not important for a career in public relations, reflect on the daily newspaper's sources for information. Much of the material found in its sports, entertainment, business, features, and sometimes even news sections originates with public relations departments or agencies—although few newspeople might be willing to admit this.

Consider a college sports information department, for example, as just one minor contributor to a newspaper's barrage of news releases. Its SID (sports information director) and staff will mail or fax stories about schedules, updated statistics, player profiles, game promotions, coaches' comments, post-season honors, high school recruits, and other topics. An energetic SID is always looking for ways to promote the school and its athletes by providing the media timely news and features. Is a former player who made it to the professional level returning for a visit? Will a professional team be using school facilities for practice or an exhibition game? If the college participates in an athletic conference, of course, the league office also will send the newspaper numerous releases.

Multiply that small example by the myriad corporations, nonprofit organizations, civic groups, educational institutions, health organizations, government agencies, churches, manufacturers, book publishers, movie studios, sports promoters, entertainment centers, small business owners, public relations firms, advertising agencies, other media outlets, etc. They all send releases regularly to the media. This fact should not be taken to imply that the only valid measurement of PR success is the number of releases that the print and broadcast industry use! Not all releases will be printed. In fact, according to several surveys, the small percentage of such mailings making it into a paper is surprising even to public relations professionals. Anywhere from just one to ten out of 100 releases are published.

Then why—with such a low success rate—are public relations practitioners still churning out releases by the pound every day? Maybe it is the numbers game. If a company's success rate averages 5%, then sending out 200 releases should guarantee ten placements in the media. Unfortunately, that faulty logic must have caught on. Releases continue to pile up in newsrooms across the country, wasting postage, paper, and personnel. A more logical response is to improve the writing—not the volume—of news releases, which has been the main stumbling block for their use since popularized by Lee back in 1906.

MAJOR FLAWS IN WRITING RELEASES

One of the principal reasons for the subtle animosity existing between journalists and public relations people is the quality of the news release. As Tucker, Derelian, and Rouner point out in *Public Relations Writing*, "Editors love to boast of the hundreds of news releases that end up in the daily 'round file.' Many enjoy maintaining files of the 'worst-of-the-worst,' bringing them out with glee when asked or surveyed."

Questionnaires asking editors what rankles them about news releases produce interesting results. Experienced communicators who have both written and received hundreds of news releases over the years say their principal weaknesses are easily detected.

Writing in *Public Relations Review*, Bill L. Baxter summarized the major complaints from managing editors of dailies across the country. In rank order of gripe, categories were

1. localization
2. newsworthiness
3. advertising puffery
4. length
5. timeliness
6. writing style

This Isn't for Our Readers

Failure to localize stories ranks as the most common complaint from newspeople. Too often releases are sent in a blanket mailing nationwide with hopes that enough papers might decide to use them, especially if they come from a national company. Yet the same release might be sent to every media, without regard to their regional differences, retail outlet locations, market share strengths, and so forth.

One of the major determinants of news has always been its proximity to media audiences. A company's major expansion plan means little if it is across the country, but quite a bit if it is in a neighboring county. A superior outdoor swimming pool liner might be an important news release for all southern newspapers. But it would be out of place for the Cadillac (Mich.) *Evening News*, unless a local individual or company designed or produces it.

With computers allowing insertions of names of individual businesses or outlets in releases, there's little excuse for not localizing stories to the media. Localizing takes extra time and effort, of course, but it could probably triple the chances of a release seeing print.

The John Deere tractor company a few years ago mailed such a release touting its system to successfully recycle Freon from industrial and agricultural equipment. Reducing chlorofluorocarbon (CFC) is a major breakthrough, but the informative, one-page release was never *localized* with an area dealer's name, address, and quote about the new clean-and-recycle system helping the earth's fragile ozone layer. (John Deere perhaps assumed that an editor would think to do this.)

This Isn't Even News

Usually near the top of the list of complaints from newsrooms about public relations writing is that releases contain little if any real news. The appointment of a company vice president to an executive VP post is hardly earth-shattering news to anyone outside the organization or the appointee's family. Yet that is one of the typical examples of what journalists term "trivia" sent to newsrooms constantly by many in public relations. Here's a typical example:

Jerry Hilliard, president and CEO of the Kilowatt Edison Company, announced today the appointment of Jane Morgan as executive vice president of its marketing department.

Most journalists would look at this short, opening paragraph and toss the release in the recycle bin. A business editor, if space allows, probably would save it for a one-paragraph-only news brief on the business page.

A quick glance at the above lead reveals that the writer fell into the common trap of writing to please the bosses. Hilliard is certainly not the news, yet he is featured as the main aspect of this key sentence. He may be the one who approves all company releases and rewards those writers who pay him homage. Releases should not employ this technique of unnecessarily mentioning the president, especially early in the story.

Instead of using the original term of "public relations release," many practitioners thought if they called it a "press" release or "news" release it would be considered news. Such is not the case. A student driving a Plymouth Neon can call it a Rolls Royce, but it is still a Chrysler Corporation compact car.

This Is in the Wrong Department

Some practitioners have wrongly confused public relations with advertising. They send promotion pieces encouraging people to buy a particular product, use a service, or visit a certain establishment. But such releases are nothing less than advertisements, containing no news of any consequence. The frequency of such occurrences is too high among public relations departments, ranging from large international corporations to small local businesses. (We will not show examples—in order to protect the *guilty*.) Editors can usually spot this category immediately because the name of the product or business is blatantly used four or five times in the first couple of paragraphs.

Realizing that releases are not the place to try to get free advertising, some professionals are warning their public relations colleagues about the practice. After all, if newspapers react negatively to the practice by one business, then all legitimate releases by that company and others may also get recycled without even a quick reading. Charles W. Hucker, division vice president for public affairs and communication at Hallmark Cards, realizes the fine line between puffery and publicity. "We avoid too much self-promotion," he has explained. "We get the Hallmark name into news releases, but we don't load the release so heavily that it stinks when it lands on the desk of a newspaper."

This Is Too Long To Read

Rejecting the common newspaper style of short words, short sentences, and short paragraphs does not impress journalists. Rather than wasting time—often under deadline pressure—reading a four-page release, many news directors or reporters will pick a release that makes a clear and concise statement of the news. One medical school sent a news release about a student paying his way through graduate studies by conducting science-theme birthday parties for children. The first page was fine for print or electronic use. But then the release bogged down with three more pages, describing in great detail the varieties of parties available.

Overwriting relates to another problem. Readability studies indicate that the ideal average sentence length is now seventeen words. Yet many writers exceed forty words often enough that their sentences average thirty, almost double the goal. Both sentence length and overall release length need to be regulated for maximum results.

This Is Too Old To Use

Even a well-written release will fail to inform readers of an important event if it arrives late at the newspaper office. Editors at both daily and non-daily newspapers cannot use information that is outdated. It is always best for releases to be mailed, faxed, or delivered (determine the medium's preference) long before an incident is to occur. That gives the reporter a chance to clarify information, obtain additional facts, or revise the writing style so that the release still makes it into the paper to announce the upcoming event. It might even get printed twice, once a week or so before the event and then as a smaller brief a day or so before.

Thinking ahead is a prerequisite for organizations if they want to promote through the press. They simply have to understand—and meet—the various deadlines used by the newspapers. For church sections, for example, which appear on Saturday, the deadline for all material is more than likely Thursday noon. Waiting until Friday afternoon to deliver an important news item because the paper is not printed until Friday night is an inadequate excuse that will make more enemies than friends. Some sections are actually printed a day or two early on several major dailies.

Non-dailies, of course, also have deadlines—usually two days before the day of publication. Some inside (non-news) pages are finished long before deadline. So even if a quality release arrives by the deadline, a newspaper simply may not have room for the story, especially if it would involve pulling another story already set in type or pulling (heaven forbid) an ad that pays the bills. As is the case with the bird and the worm, the earlier release may get the space.

This Is a Waste of Time

Harried editors are easily depressed by the quality of writing that comes across their desks. From sloppily handwritten notes to computer-generated news releases, mistakes are so numerous they easily could fill a book. One Ohio school district decided to honor coaches with winning records from the previous year. So it presented them with *plagues*. What, we wonder, did the losing coaches receive?

News stories should be produced in an objective, third-person style. Yet releases still are written in the first or second person, using flowery adjectives and adverbs, with an overuse of personal pronouns (*our, we*).

Inaccuracy is another major problem editors face with releases. The lead paragraph may say five persons are being honored but list only four. Or the release may say an event will be Tuesday, Dec. 11, when a check of the calendar by an alert section editor tells her there's no such date remaining this century. With so many media battling for their share of the audience, the paper does not want to handicap itself with mistakes. If a newspaper loses credibility with its audience, it loses everything.

Misspelling continues to be a common complaint of editors. Whether a word (*occurred, it's*) or an individual's name is misspelled (a problem that has libel potential), releases with such blunders quickly make credibility suspect. An editor understandably presumes that if news release writers are indiscreet with spelling, they may be careless with other details as well. Although spell checks on computers should be used, they are not foolproof.

A spell Czech can dew a grate job most of the thyme. Butt eye can knot rely on it four all my miss steaks, oar I May bee inn big trouble.

Well-written news releases that avoid these and other flaws are used daily by the media. A public relations practitioner is saving the print and broadcast industries both time and money by bringing credible news stories in a ready-to-use fashion to their attention. Both the preparation and writing of those stories help determine if they will be passed along to readers, viewers, and listeners.

PREPARING RELEASES THE RIGHT WAY

With time such a precious commodity in deadline-conscious newsrooms, few editors will waste it by trying to decipher a handwritten news release. Although such releases are extremely rare now, in the pre-computer era releases might have been handwritten, typed on a manual typewriter with a ribbon that had 100,000 words on it, smudged on a carbon-produced onionskin copy, or produced on a spirit master duplicator.

Despite technology advances, releases, unfortunately, often are not prepared in an orderly fashion that encourages their reading. Because of both budget and environmental concerns, many businesses and organizations have been conserving paper by printing on both sides of their releases. Some, too, considering the sheer volume of their media communication, have been squeezing more on the page by using one-and-one-half spacing rather than the typical double spacing.

Others are putting four or five short releases on both sides of three sheets of paper. This has caused problems with news outlets that prefer one story per release, especially if individual articles are distributed to different journalists on the news staff.

Some other standard copy preparation guidelines for journalists should be followed to make the news release resemble as much as possible an actual news story. Customs include

- Having at least a one-inch margin all around the page
- Placing the day's date and a release date at the top of the page
- Not hyphenating words at the end of lines
- Not splitting paragraphs from one page to the next
- Using the word "More" at the bottom of page one and the word "End" or "30" or the symbol "#" at the bottom of the final page
- Using a two- or three-word description of the release (called a slug) with a page number at the top of all subsequent pages

Although not necessary, companies frequently print special

stationery for all news releases. In any case, the first page of the release must contain full identification of the sender. It also should list a contact person (who can answer additional questions concerning a story) with both office and home phone numbers. A release may even list two names since it is vital for the media to reach someone who thoroughly understands all aspects of the article. If a journalist has doubts about release details and cannot confirm such facts, the decision to hold the story could just as easily kill it (by making it too old).

Consensus is impossible on one final point—whether to place a headline atop the release. Those who object to the practice say that it is insulting to journalists, as if one were telling them how to do their job. After all, a release essentially is a story idea and has nothing to do with final page layout or design. Headline responsibility rests with the copy editor.

But what's the purpose of a headline? Is it not to attract attention and to summarize the main aspect of the story for its intended audience? For a public relations writer, the immediate audience is the media gatekeeper (a city/section editor or a broadcast news director). If the object is to attract that person's attention and let the individual quickly know what the release is about, why not use a fourteen-point, boldface headline as well? Public relations writers know that the journalist has the right to change all copy on the page, including a headline; so why would there be any misunderstanding regarding the latter?

Thus, a good news headline can be used as a favor to the busy journalist. Essentially, it says, "I value your time; so in six words or less here's what this release is all about":

Morgan Heads Kilowatt Edison Marketing Division

Traditional newspaper headlines employ these devices:

- Short, simple words
- Few (if any) adverbs, adjectives, or articles
- Active voice verbs rather than passive voice
- Present or future tense verbs rather than past tense

Of course, the six-word limit is merely hypothetical. But a good headline should be able to tell the story in just a few words.

WRITING RELEASES THE NEWS WAY

Making the release, whether geared for print or broadcast, conform to proper journalism style will enhance its chances of being used. So the earlier chapters of this text certainly apply to the writing of the public relations news release. Press releases use the straight, inverted pyramid news story structure. The lead tells the most important information; the body expands on the lead, presenting information in an order of decreasing importance. The structure allows editors to cut stories from the bottom up.

Public relations writers must think, act, and *write* like journalists if they want their releases to show up in the media regularly. That will involve developing a lead that sounds like a legitimate news story—which at times could mean placing the name of the sending organization in the second or third paragraph.

That action could provoke internal office questions such as, "Why in the world did you bury us in our own release?" However, effective placement results—which are achieved by writing news releases as a journalist does—could qualm such future outbursts.

Writing the news way undoubtedly means a decrease in the use of loaded adjectives and adverbs. Use instead *colorful* quotations from authoritative sources to get subjective viewpoints into the media. Note the emphasis on colorful. Direct quotations should not be used for mundane or generic information. Quote, instead, something said that is unusual or something that is unusually said. Even a single word can be extracted as a quote from a boring statement to make a sentence sing.

ASSOCIATED PRESS STYLEBOOK

A huge part of that conformity to newspaper format results from the *Associated Press Stylebook*, used by an overwhelming majority of newspapers. Arranged like a dictionary, the $10 to $12 paperback *Stylebook* provides the definitive word on abbreviations, capitalization's, grammar, numerals, punctuation, etc. In the introduction to the stylebook, Louis D. Boccardi explains that journalists "approach these style questions with varying degrees of passion. Some don't really think it's important. Some agree that basically there should be uniformity for reading ease if nothing else. Still others are prepared to duel over a wayward lowercase."

Even if the public relations writer is not in complete agreement with every AP rule—which requires Tenn., for example, instead of the common postal abbreviation of TN—it is wise to follow religiously what has been called "the journalist's Bible."

Most versions of the *AP Stylebook* also contain an important libel manual that is must reading for every public relations writer.

Because the stylebook is constantly being updated and revised, it would be smart to pick up one of the latest volumes. The first edition was published in August 1977; the twentieth-ninth edition, in March 1994. Furthermore, some major metropolitan newspapers and many magazines have their own style manuals. Always determine what manual is being used by local media to avoid sending them improperly written news releases.

When writing for broadcast outlets, keep in mind that their style varies tremendously from print. For example, the number 111 is spelled out, according to many broadcast stylebooks, so that it is not confused on air with the Roman numeral III. The *AP Broadcast News Handbook* and *A Broadcast News Manual of Style* are two frequently consulted sources. (See Chapter 11 for more details about electronic writing tips.)

DON'T FORGET NON-DAILIES

By targeting only daily newspapers for its news release efforts, a company is shortchanging its reach and effectiveness. Outnumbering dailies by almost a 5-1 ratio, non-dailies have a strong tradition of being read more thoroughly by their customers. Circulation of U. S. dailies is slightly over 60 million (64 million Sundays), but newspaper readership almost doubles when the non-daily circulation is added in. Moreover, from suburb to small town, these newspapers print more local news on a percentage basis than their daily counterparts.

What that means for a public relations writer is that the smaller staffs on non-dailies rely on releases regularly for a larger proportion of their news hole. Chances of a press release appearing in its original form are much stronger in the local-oriented, non-daily press.

In a discussion about the lack of any AP or national news in the award-winning Homer (Alaska) *News*, editor and publisher Mark Turner said, "Our readers simply want local news." That does not mean his Thursday tabloid will print fluff about visits by Aunt Roberta from West Virginia. It does mean, he said, that the staff looks for thorough articles about a variety of local issues. Homer *News* stories include such items as an analysis of local political candidates, a proposal to turn a coastal area frequented by birds into an RV park, and a biologist's opinion about eagles preying on seagull chicks. Local residents could not read such stories anywhere if the Homer *News* not print them.

Erroneously called weeklies—since many are published two or three times per week—non-dailies are eager for solid, local news. Sometimes editors are so zealous that they will invite a public relations staff writer from a major local corporation to produce a regular column on a topic of general interest.

North American Precis Syndicate (NAPS), a firm specializing in the preparation and distribution of news releases, promotes its service frequently in full-page ads in *Public Relations Journal*. NAPS claims to increase a company's effectiveness by writing and mailing a company's news releases to all papers, not just major dailies. "Give your management the pleasure of 1,000+ placements" is a frequent headline in such NAPS advertisements.

Other outlets for news releases include monthly business publications, magazines, trade journals, government agencies, and associations.

VIDEO NEWS RELEASES

A growing method of distributing news releases expensively but effectively to television stations is through a short video tape. A video news release (VNR) is potent when it appears to be a news feature produced by a network affiliate or the local station itself. In other words, it cannot blatantly use the name of the sponsor or product too soon or too often. (Does that sound familiar?) In *Effective Public Relations*, authors Scott M. Cutlip, Allen H. Center, and Glen M. Broom estimate that "the number of VNRs distributed each year range up to 5000, with about 80 percent of television news directors reporting that they use VNR material that they judge to have news value."

Probably a majority of viewers are not even aware when a segment on their local news has been produced by an outside source. Whether done by a state poultry association or a national lottery promoter, VNRs are being criticized for—of all things—being too realistic. Writer David Lieberman blasted VNRs in a *TV Guide* article aptly titled "Fake News" for deceiving viewers into thinking that the pieces are produced by an objective news source. He places VNRs in the same classification as the longer infomercials—paid subjective programs that only appear to be news—and suggests that VNRs identify the source for viewers when they are aired.

VNR how-to workshops are popular among corporations and businesses eager to display visually the operation of a new product or service. Numerous companies advertise that they are willing to write, produce, and distribute by satellite video releases to specific markets.

FEATURE STORIES

Rarely do public relations practitioners send feature stories to newspapers or broadcast stations. Because features are written in such an individualized subjective manner—usually requiring a byline or an on-screen broadcast personality—and would not be repeated by competing media in the same market area, PR practitioners simply offer suggestions for features to journalists.

Often two or three such news feature possibilities with tips and background information are sent to media organizations. Since the feature is lighter than a straight news story, it is often easier to propose several ideas that could be adopted by local staff writers. Such features are often found in the larger Sunday editions of the daily paper and in the expanded early evening television news slots.

A bank president, for example, who volunteers a weekend every other month building houses for Habitat for Humanity would be an ideal candidate for a reporter-written human interest story. Or consider company employees who could be feature candidates because of unusual hobbies: a collector of 500 different businesses' magnets, a successful weekend mystery writer, a Star Trek national fan club officer, a ten-gallon Red Cross blood donor.

OTHER COMMON WRITING TASKS

Although the news release is the most common weapon in the public relations worker's arsenal, other writing assignments consume much effort as well. Some are geared to an internal audience, some to an external, and others are mixed. Even if the writing style is unlike a straight news story, adherence to grammar and punctuation rules and to all elements of quality communication is required.

Newsletters

College students fulfilling public relations internships often find themselves working on a newsletter. It provides practical training in using a common tool of public relations. Newsletters are one of the most effective ways to communicate with internal and specialized audiences. Each year in the United States about 50,000 corporate newsletters are published.

Because most readers of a newsletter are familiar with its topic or the sponsoring body, its writing style is often less formal. For example, familiar terms will not need explaining (but go easy on jargon or highly technical terms). Writing in a journalism feature style is often recommended for such publications.

Newsletter writers must be brief. Limited space on the typical four-page, $8\frac{1}{2}$ x 11 format calls for practical, lively, and to-the-point articles. With a relatively long shelf life, influential newsletters should reflect a company's quality image to all readers, both inside and outside the organization.

Fact Sheets

Commonly found in media kits, fact sheets are usually simple outlined lists of items about a group. They could be historical (merely citing significant dates) or oriented to special events (who does what, where, and when).

Objective fact sheets are useful for busy editors who need a quick profile as a background resource for an issue or a company. A typical one-page fact sheet could include a description of an organization, its history, its location, key personnel, and additional facts relevant to the occasion.

Backgrounders

Also inserted in many media kits, the backgrounder goes into much more detail than the abbreviated fact sheet. Written objectively, a three- to six-page background piece provides a thorough overview on an issue or organization. After extensive research, a public relations writer produces a backgrounder with a statement of the issue, an historical overview, and lots of factual information devoid of opinion. Using subheads, bullets, and/or graphics provides a helpful format for readers.

Backgrounders help news gatherers supplement their stories with additional information. They can also help authors within the association as they prepare speeches, news releases, advertisements, or annual reports.

Position Papers

Unlike objective fact sheets and backgrounders, the position paper must be written persuasively on an issue. After a brief introduction, a position paper loads up on evidence supporting the organization's stand. Using the research found in the fact sheets and backgrounders, the position paper tells why the company's management has selected the stand it has.

Similar to an editorial, a position paper may point out opposing arguments, but it then convincingly shows why one method is considered the best overall solution.

Annual Reports

Because of a 1987 Security and Exchange Commission ruling, summary annual reports can be written now more for a reading public than veteran CPAs. Since that change, many annual reports have been shortened and, more importantly, have become a public relations showcase of good writing and graphics in communicating a message. With the typical production cost at a hefty $3.52 each, annual reports by U. S. public companies average forty-four pages. In *Effective Public Relations*, authors Cutlip, Center, and Broom explain that some companies use the annual report for most of their external communications, sending it to a "wide range of publics, from employees to analysts, educators, and business media. This tool has evolved to a high degree of technical and graphic excellence, due in large part to its public relations objectives for so many different publics."

A Churchill Downs annual report, for example, uses a full-color cover and color spreads on several inside pages. A helpful table of contents is found on the inside cover along with a one-third page financial summary titled "Story in Brief." Material is presented in short copy blocks with lots of space between the lines.

Still, in working with SEC guidelines, chief financial officers, outside auditors, and legal counsel, the annual report is not an easy task for any communicator.

Advertising

Unlike news releases, an advertisement gives the public relations practitioner total control over its contents, its placement, and its timing. A new corporate emphasis on integrated marketing communications (using a variety of marketing communication tools along with packaging, special events, sales, etc.) means that advertising people also may be writing news releases and PR people may be handling some ads.

To produce effective advertising copy, *AIDA* is a common acronym helping ad copywriters focus their efforts on the consumer target market:

- Attention (the ad or commercial grabs the consumer's attention)
- Interest (the consumer now takes interest in the product or service)
- Desire (the consumer now wants to see or sample the product or service)
- Action (the consumer decides to go to the store or order the

item or service).

Although the AIDA formula has been around since the 1920s, the progression from the first A to the last A is not an easy one.

Etcetera

Because the jobs of public relations practitioners are so varied, PR employees could be called upon to produce a plethora of other written documents. Such activity includes (in alphabetical order):

- Advertorials—advertising that promotes a company's viewpoint on an issue
- Biographies—informative, factual summaries of key individuals' lives
- Collateral pieces—brochures, catalogs, counter displays
- Crisis communication plans—guidelines on who does what during those unexpected emergencies
- Handbooks—publications providing details about organizational guidelines (for students or employees, for example)
- Letters—correspondences primarily directed to external audiences
- Memos—usually more informal correspondences primarily directed to internal audiences
- Proposals—persuasive reports attempting to convince an audience
- Public service announcements (PSAs)—broadcasts made by stations at no charge in the public interest
- Questionnaires—survey instruments used to collect information and opinions
- Reports—common methods to keep track of ongoing activities of an organization
- Scripts—audio portions of slide shows or videos
- Speeches—verbal information and opinion conveyed to an audience

In *Handbook for Public Relations Writing*, Thomas Bivins contends that any public relations writer "worthy of the name" must be "familiar with all forms of writing—from business letters to press releases. After all, good writing is good writing, no matter what the form." A good writer, "like the good artist...is able to work in any medium."

CAREER PREPARATION

Writing has to top the list of preparatory skills for a student interested in a public relations career. One should love all aspects of the written word (even grammar and spelling). But what other traits will help?

Because of the complex nature of the job, *organizational skills* are a must. Consider the following tasks encountered during *one* typical day: proofreading a corporate newsletter, writing and mailing original version news releases to three area newspapers, checking on the progress of a brochure, scheduling a photographer and a florist for a special event, consulting with clients, and keeping up with general correspondence. (Perhaps being a juggler relates to this task.)

Research is becoming more important for the entire public relations industry. Realizing that two-way communication is vital for the success of any organization, practitioners must conduct original research and obtain already accessible data in a usable form. Questionnaires, surveys, and communication audits are examples of research a person could be conducting in the field.

A related skill for students to acquire is *computer* knowledge. Fortunately, most college requirements include at least one computer literacy course. Taking at least one other class in publication design or production on the computer will give insight into some of the popular software packages available.

Decision-making ability cannot be found in a college catalog. Yet, creatively solving problem situations in classes or at part-time jobs can serve as good preparation for a public relations career. Being able to rationally appraise a predicament and select the best course of action is a skill that does not come easy for everyone. Fortunately, learning from mistakes is allowed.

An *inquisitive mind* is essential for anyone working in the communication field. Students need to read widely, keep up with current events (both locally and globally), and have a desire to know more than superficial information about issues.

Completing an *internship* during college—even if not required—will give students a big advantage over otherwise equal applicants. An intern experiences many of the tasks that one will encounter on the job. So students often return to the classroom with a better understanding of "book knowledge" after seeing it put into practice during an internship. Some employers flatly refuse to hire graduates who have not worked in their major field during school. Even working on the school newspaper provides essential writing experience for a public relations student.

19

ADVERTISING COPYWRITING

A career in advertising copywriting offers opportunities for developing truthful and persuasive communications in a global marketplace of increasingly diverse products, consumers, and media.

The answer to the question "What is advertising?" may be examined from a number of perspectives, which form the basis for most discussion about advertising's role in society and as a form of communication.

Consumers attend to advertising for information about a product or service, as a source of entertainment, and as an aid in the decision-search process. Producers and advertisers depend upon its function in a free-marketplace and its role as a mirror of the enlightened economic self-interest on which our capitalistic system functions. The mass media increasingly rely on the economic role of advertising as the vehicle for the delivery and transmission of news, information, entertainment, and the cul-

BY SHIRLEY STAPLES CARTER
Dr. Carter is Professor and Chair of the Department of Mass Communication and Journalism at Norfolk State University in Virginia. Her professional background includes positions as weekly newspaper managing editor, public broadcast producer, and institutional public relations and marketing practitioner. A specialist in values analysis in advertising and marketing, audience analysis, and consumer behavior, she is co-editor of the book *Mass Communication in the Information Age.*

tural values prevalent in our society.

Because of its pervasiveness—indeed, advertising messages are ubiquitous—advertising has the potential to affect its audiences with unintended consequences. Critics of advertising claim that one of its most harmful social effects is its predilection to cause over-consumption and dissatisfaction in the quality of life among lower income and poorly educated people. Another criticism is that it transmits middle-class values, a distorted picture of reality that extols the virtues of the so-called good life, and inadequately or stereotypically portrays women, the elderly, and members of ethnic or racial groups.

Such criticism has been refuted by proponents of advertising who counter that advertising does not create societal trends such as a culture of consumption, narcissism, ethnocentricity, discrimination, and pursuit of a higher quality of life—it merely reflects what already exists.

The focus of this chapter is to present advertising copywriting as a viable career choice within the context of advertising's social responsibility. The chapter includes an examination of the role of the copywriter, the creative process, advertising strategy, product strategy, audience analysis, and the media environment. These issues will be examined in terms of the creative process (how to create persuasive communication), social responsibility (ethical considerations), emerging technologies that affect media choice, and the impact of a global marketplace on the development of commercial messages.

ROLE OF THE COPYWRITER

Advertisers must know and understand the nature and characteristics of the product, the medium best suited to the sales pitch, and something about the audience or consumer to whom the pitch or message is directed. Understanding the product, medium, and audience becomes increasingly crucial given the emerging new technologies and global marketplace. Advertisers who enter the Eastern European, Pacific rim or Caribbean markets must have a sense of what product attributes the prospective consumer is interested in, convey persuasive communications in a cultural context that elicits the desired response and conveys the intended meaning of the message, and select the medium most effective to reach targeted markets. Advertisers must know how to take a product theme and develop it in the style of each medium and the appropriate language of the targeted consumer, and must understand that although the message may be the same—"Buy Brand X"—the presentation must be tailored to the form of the particular medium in which the product is advertised.

The advertising copywriter has to remember two principles: (1) the goal of advertising is to sell goods, and (2) selling occurs as a result of well-written, well-presented persuasive communication, targeted to a receptive audience.

The advertising copywriter's task is similar to that of any communicator. The copywriter, in the creation of an ad or campaign, serves as author of a message, whereas the consumer or audience serves as the interpreter. The copywriter as communicator should understand his or her collaborative role with the consumer, that is, being able to convey meaning in an advertisement that will be interpreted by the consumer as the copywriter intended. Sometimes consumers may read into an advertisement additional meanings beyond those that were intended or miss the point altogether.

THE CREATIVE PROCESS

Jaye S. Niefeld, in the book *The Making of an Advertising Campaign*, identifies the following steps in the creative process:

1. Define the target group.
2. Determine the most effective appeal or creative strategy for the target group.
3. Execute the creative strategy.
4. Select the most cost efficient and effective media for the target group.

In an ad campaign, according to Russell Colley, the creative process should include the following objectives:

1. Make people aware of a product's existence.
2. Create a favorable emotional disposition toward a brand.
3. Plant information about benefits and features.
4. Combat or offset competitive claims.
5. Correct false impressions or misinformation.
6. Build recognition of a package or trademark.
7. Build a corporate image and favorable attitudes.
8. Build a "reputation platform" for new brands or product lines.
9. Plant a unique selling proposition in the minds of consumers.
10. Develop leads for sales personnel.

These objectives are designed to answer three basic questions:

What do you want to accomplish? Who are your target consumers? And, what do they want?

ELEMENTS OF ADVERTISING COPYWRITING

Most advertisements contain the following elements:

- *Headline*. The headline should catch the attention. Whether the ad is designed for mass appeal or for an individual, the aim is to attract the attention of the targeted consumer.
- *Subheads*. The subheads emphasize the main selling points to guide the reader through the ad.
- *Text*. The text follows up on the headline and illustration and presents the ad's main message.
- *Slogan*. Slogans essentially use repetition to create an image or brand awareness.
- *Logotype*. Logotypes are corporate symbols.
- *Illustration*. Illustrations add a strong visual appeal.

The basic message elements of an advertisement are designed to emphasize the consumer's needs or desires, to introduce a product as singularly capable of fulfilling those needs or desires, and to call for action—either subtly or directly— on the part of the consumer.

ADVERTISING STRATEGIES

Advertising strategies were introduced in the 1940s and 1950s as creations of advertising agencies with the primary objective of differentiating products or laying stake to a product claim. Some of the more prevalent strategies and the agencies responsible for their development are cited below.

Unique Selling Proposition (USP)

The USP was developed by Rosser Reeves of the Ted Bates agency. USP makes a claim that a particular product is unique or that in effect suggests its superiority to other products in its class. In reality, the claims may only be preemptive—if indeed all toothpaste is the same.

Brand Image

Brand-image advertising was first promulgated by David Ogilvy of Ogilvy, Benson, and Mather. The intent of brand imaging, which usually emphasizes status, is to lift a parity product above all others. The clever introduction of a new line of luxury cars, such as Toyota's Lexus or Nissan's Infiniti, using mere symbols and teasers is a contemporary example of brand imaging.

Motivational Research

Norman B. Norman of Norman, Craig, and Kummel, and Ernest Dichter, president of the Institute for Motivational Research, introduced motivational research as a means of supporting Norman's belief that consumers were motivated to buy as a result of deep-seated Freudian impulses. This collaboration between Norman and Dichter heralded the popular use of sex as an advertising appeal or theme.

Subliminal Advertising

This much debated strategy evolved from an experiment conducted by James Vicary in the 1950s. Subliminal advertising—supposedly operating below the conscious threshold of perception—has been the subject of much controversy. Vicary claimed that by inserting such messages as "Hungry? Eat popcorn" and "Drink Coca Cola" during the showing of movies in a theater, advertisers induced moviegoers to buy more of these products. Whether subliminal messages can effectively sell an idea, product, service or political candidate is still debatable.

Positioning

This strategy was developed in the 1960s by Al Ries and Jack Trout. The objective of "positioning" is to attract a dependable market share. Marketers use market segmentation or targeting to achieve the same result. An illustration of how this technique works is the advertising of a product such as coffee. As coffee experienced a consumption decline in the past decade, advertisers positioned coffee as a lifestyle drink, promoting its use among younger people and introducing coffee beverages such as Cappuccino and International Foods flavored coffee drinks. Another example, of course, is the advertising of the tobacco industry, which used the slogan "You've Come a Long Way Baby" to position Virginia Slims as the female cigarette in the same manner as the Marlboro Man targeted the male smoker. Arm & Hammer baking soda represents one of advertising's success stories in product positioning. As the use of baking soda declined as a baking ingredient, it was effectively re-positioned as a multiple-use product for everything from all-purpose household deodorizer to toothpaste and laundry detergent ingredient.

Audience Participation

This innovation of the 1990s may have first been popularized by Benson and Hedges "For people who like to smoke" and the Taster's Choice coffee "lifestyle ads" that featured soap operas. In audience participation, the prospective consumer is invited to actively participate in the print advertisement or commercial by supplying meaning to a seemingly vacuous illustration and copy, as in the Benson and Hedges ad. The ad featured a man clad in pajama bottoms, standing in a room adjacent to a group of fully clothed people seated at a table. One of them appeared to be toasting the out-of-place character. The audience was left to supply meaning to an advertisement that attracted attention by being intentionally vague. In the Taster's Choice commercial, coffee is supposedly being sold against the backdrop of a drama that for years has successfully sold soap. Again, the audience was being invited to supply meaning.

MACRO ADVERTISING STRATEGIES

When one considers that consumers are exposed to more than $100 billion worth of advertising each year, the primary challenge to advertisers is to break through the clutter and effectively communicate their messages to target audiences. Researchers have identified the following four macro advertising strategies:

• 1. *Name Identification.* The objective of commercial or political campaigns is to build awareness of the brand or candidate. Political candidates are heavy users of television advertising to boost name identification and image awareness among voters. The 1996 political campaigns showed a tendency of candidates to blitz the television market and use a combination of media exposure: town meetings, focused entertainment shows such as Larry King Live and MTV, and 30-minute blocks of commercial air time. The common strategy employed by advertisers such as Rosser Reeves to gain name identification was to take simple points and repeat them. This repetition of messages over time is also used to maintain awareness of established brands.

• 2. *Advertising Themes, Affect, and Testimonials.* Generally, advertisers use themes or appeals to promote an image of the brand or candidate. Themes may be cognitive, thereby emphasizing a specific product attribute, candidate quality or position, or social action goal; or affective, as in commercials that involve the way consumers feel about a brand.

Political campaigns tend to rely on themes (which say the same thing in a different way) and slogans (which always say the same thing in exactly the same way) to influence voter behavior. During the 1992 presidential campaign, President George Bush's strategists focused on character issues whereas the Clinton strategists focused on change, thus forming the basis of themes and slogans embodied in both camps' advertisements. In 1996, change didn't work for Bob Dole, but staying-the-course was a winner for Bill Clinton.

Commercial themes are usually conveyed in terms of the existential codes—having (materialism), doing (functional and practical), and being (self-focused and self improvement)—that relate to specific product attributes. The Nike brand of shoes has promoted awareness by the use of the simplistic slogan "Just Do It." The Swedish auto maker Volvo has successfully built image awareness around the simple theme of safety.

Advertisers' use of affect is based on the belief by some practitioners that feelings are influential in consumer decisions. One of the ways in which advertisers use affect in political campaigns is through resonance, or linking an image of a candidate with the kind of person the consumer is or wants to be. This was effectively demonstrated in the 1988 presidential campaign by the Bush camp as compared to the Dukakis campaign, when one considers at least two of the most indelible images: Bush against the backdrop of the American flag evoked images of patriotism while Dukakis riding in a combat tank did not.

Commercials and print ads use affect to promote brand image by evoking appeals to warmth, esteem or sex appeal. Most advertising critics decry the use of such appeals to promote brand image of harmful products such as tobacco and alcoholic beverages. Increasingly, advertisers are beginning to use positive appeals as embodied in AT&T and Sprint commercials promoting "family" as the link to long distance calls and in McDonald's family pride commercials.

The function of testimonial advertisements in commercial, political, and social action campaigns is to capture consumers' attention. Research has supported the use of testimonials as an effective visibility tool. Advertisers believe that the key to using celebrity endorsements is to match the celebrity to the product; hence we get a parade of celebrity athletes endorsing a variety of products from Nike shoes to Hyundai automobiles. Some long-gone celebrities were resurrected in 1994, most notably Kentucky Fried Chicken's late Col. Sanders.

• 3. *Attack Advertising*. The "attack" advertising strategy focuses on a negative aspect of the competing brand or political candidate, using either a negative or comparative tactic. One of the most often cited examples of the effectiveness of attack advertising is the 1988 George Bush campaign's "Revolving Door" commercial that portrayed his opponent Michael Dukakis as soft on crime, supposedly based on his state's prison furlough policy.

Pepsi skillfully used the comparative approach to challenge Coca Cola's dominance in the soft drink market. Although advertisers have been criticized for their use of attack ads, research supports their effectiveness because consumers tend to process negative information more deeply than positive information.

Ethical considerations that guide this strategy when used in a political or advertising campaign are derived from the following question: Are the charges that form the basis of the attack against the opponent or product true? Critics of attack advertising point to the 1988 Bush campaign's "Revolving Door" ad that featured Willie Horton, a black inmate, as being racially offensive and divisive.

• 4. *Response to Attack*. Once a product or candidate has been struck by attack advertisements, the target has the option to ignore the attack, which can be fatal, as demonstrated by the 1988 Dukakis campaign; or refute the attack, which has its disadvantages when the attacked product happens to be the market leader or the attacked candidate is the front runner in a campaign. Conventional wisdom is against admitting competition. The best strategy is to refute the attack by preemption. Advocacy advertising, or advertorials, a technique pioneered by Mobil oil company, also has inoculation effects.

The underlying techniques of the four macro advertising strategies discussed in this section may be summarized as follows:

1. Bolstering messages that are designed to convey information about the candidate's character, qualifications, or positions on the issues

2. Attack messages that are designed to identify weaknesses in the opponent

3. Response or rebuttal messages that are designed to respond to an attack by an opponent

4. Inoculation messages that are designed to preempt the lines of potential attacks by opponents

PRODUCT STRATEGY

Advertisers frequently use Rosser Reeves' unique selling proposition to gain marketing advantage for their products. This usually evolves into a product's distinctive brand image such as Campbell Soup's "MMmm Good," or BMW's "Ultimate Driving Machine." The effective copywriter must be guided by a fundamental knowledge of the product he is selling, as the advertising campaign to some extent is "product driven." Products may represent two types of goods: *Search goods*, in which advertisements offer a great deal of factual information (ads for department store clothing sales), and *experience goods*, in which advertisements use lifestyle or sensory appeals (ads for tuna that tastes good or long-lasting deodorant protection).

Products may be classified as (a) thinking or feeling and (b) high involvement or low involvement.

Thinking	Feeling	Ad Characteristics
High Involvement		
Car, House, Furniture	Jewelry, Cosmetics, Apparel, Motorcycles	Information; Long Copy
Low Involvement		
Food, Household Items	Cigarettes, Liquor, Candy	Satisfaction of Personal Tastes

Advertising is also influenced by a product's life cycle: new products generate advertising that stimulates demand; established products emphasize brand loyalty; and mature products emphasize retention and product differentiation.

AUDIENCE ANALYSIS (MARKET STRATEGIES)

The opportunities for those studying advertising and interested in pursuing copywriting careers lie in the understanding that communication campaigns directed to a mass audience are less effective than those targeting specific consumer groups. People of various ages, income levels, and occupations do not all want the same things or to live by the same set of values.

Advertisers use three traditional approaches to target audiences:

• *Geographic*—Refers to place of residence, as in regional target markets. The makers of "BC" headache powders, for instance, only target Southerners.

• *Demographic*—Refers to socioeconomic characteristics, including gender, age (such as baby boomers, those born between 1946 and 1965), ethnicity, family life cycle, education, income, and social class.

• *Psychographic*—Refers to values, emotions, and lifestyles. These form the basis of most advertising appeals and are considered by most marketers to be a reliable predictor of consumer behavior.

In the 1970s, the Stanford Research Institute developed one of the most widely used typologies of values and lifestyles analysis, VALS. The categories are the following:

• *Integrated:* Represents 2% of the population; individually are powerful and sensitive.

• *Inner Directed:* Represents 19% of the population. Includes the "I am me," "Experiential," and "Societally Conscious." Buy to please themselves.

• *Outer Directed:* Represents 68% of the population. They are "Belongers," "Emulators," and "Achievers." Buy to impress others.

• *Survivors:* Represent 11% of Americans. They are need driven; seek life's basics.

Recently, VALS II, a variation of VALS typology, has emerged, combining consumer psychological orientation and their psychological and material resources. VALS II typology has eight basic components:

1. *Strugglers*: People who lack basic financial resources.

2. *Experiencers*: Young people who seek variety and excitement in their lives.

3. *Makers*: People who are bound by traditional values and possess the practical skills to use in pursuit of self-sufficiency.

4. *Strivers*: People less sure of themselves who look to others for social approval.

5. *Achievers*: Successful, career-oriented people who feel in control of their own lives.

6. *Believers*: Conservative and deeply moral people who follow established routines.

7. *Fulfilleds*: People who are more mature, satisfied, and comfortable; who value order, knowledge, and responsibility.

8. *Actualizer*: Take-charge people with high self-esteem and

abundant resources.

The reality is that in a fluctuating economy and across cultures, income, and other demographic and psychographic characteristics may cause a consumer to move from one stage of VALS or VALS II to another.

In its 1993 annual survey of 4,000 U. S. adult heads of household, the DDB Needham Worldwide advertising agency found a growing pattern of skepticism and frustration among American consumers. Consumers were polled on their views of the following institutions:

• *Politics:* An upward trend toward doubting first-year presidents, as opposed to giving them the benefit of the doubt. Of the men surveyed, 55% felt an honest man could not be elected to high office, compared to 46% of the women surveyed.

• *Big Business:* About 75% of the respondents are skeptical of big business motives.

• *Financial Optimism:* The number of people who felt their family income was high enough to satisfy all their important desires dropped to 64% of men and 65% of women from 75% of men and women in 1976, the year the survey was introduced.

• *Religion:* Trend watchers, advertisers, and media companies believe religion is on the comeback: the 1993 results were 66% of men and 81% of women felt religion was important to them, compared to 60% of men and 76% of women in 1985.

• *Jobs:* Approximately 85% of respondents in 1993 felt good jobs were hard to find, compared to 65% of respondents in 1988.

• *TV:* According to respondents, there is too much violence on prime-time TV: 82% of men and 90% of women, compared to 75% of men and 88% of women in 1985. Respondents also felt there is too much sex on TV, 76% of men and 88% of women and too much emphasis on sex in advertising, 80% of men and 89% of women.

• *Personal Malaise:* If the 1980s were a decade of greed, trend forecasters think the 1990s may be shaping up to be the decade of doubt. While 71% of men and 73% of women said they were very satisfied with their lives, 37% of men and 33% of women said they would choose something entirely different from their present lives.

Advertisers see these trends as an opportunity to establish empathetic themes of trust, friendliness, credibility, and guarantee.

TARGETING MARKET DIVERSITY

The contemporary advertising student preparing for a career in copywriting has an opportunity to contribute to the balancing of power as depicted in secondary messages of advertising, particularly to those groups of consumers who are distinguished by gender, ethnicity, and cultural and geographic characteristics.

Advertising has been criticized for the images and content in commercial messages targeted to children, women, and members of ethnic or racial minority groups. Much of the criticism has centered around stereotypical portrayals of women, African Americans, Latinos, and Asian Americans. The stereotypes include the following:

• African Americans have been portrayed as simplistic, monolithic, athletic, and entertaining; Native Americans are usually portrayed as savage; Asian Americans, the model minority. Latinos have endured stereotypical portrayals as Speedy Gonzales and Chiquita Banana.

• Women have been portrayed in ads as "Super Mom," sex symbols, or as subordinate to men.

• The elderly have been stereotypically portrayed as unattractive and incompetent.

• The disabled consumer has been stereotypically portrayed as helpless and, to some extent, invisible.

Those who create media images have an obligation to understand the sensitivities of all consumers. Marketers have recognized the tremendous economic impact of more accurately and adequately portraying ethnic and racial minorities, especially considering their combined spending power of more than $400 billion and distinct consumer behavior. The Latino market, for instance, is considered by many as a sleeping giant, given its propensity toward product brand loyalty and willingness to pay extra for name brands. The African American consumer is a heavy purchaser of "aging" products that have reached the maturity stage in the product life cycle. African American consumers, according to most research studies, should not be treated as monolithic.

Advertising representations are an important social legitimation for most ethnic and racially diverse consumers who seek visibility and validity in advertisements. The copywriter should possess a knowledge of cultural traditions, histories, and experiences along with other strategies for developing effective messages to reach these markets.

The globalization of goods and services poses opportunities for the advertiser and raises the issues of universal human wants and aspirations, and whether universal symbols and representations can be used in advertising around the globe or to develop local selling messages to promote global products. Generally, advertisers should think globally and act locally.

Coca Cola has developed an advertising strategy that reflects its sensitivity to its role in global markets. The company is guided by a complex structure for producing messages that contain universal themes but are sensitive to local cultural differences. To get around the language barrier, for example, international Coca Cola commercials almost never include any speaking person on camera.

Examples of successful global campaigns:

- L'Oreal's "It's expensive and I'm worth it" brand position.
- Proctor & Gamble's Pert Plus/Wash & Go shampoo and conditioner successfully employs convenience and ease-of-use-oriented brand positioning and advertising in widely different countries.
- Snuggle fabric softener's brand concept and teddy bear brand property work remarkably well across borders without a limiting brand name (it's called Kuschelweich in Germany, Coccolino in Italy, and Mimosin in France).

THE NEW MEDIA ENVIRONMENT

Emerging new technologies, media fragmentation, and the increasing desire among consumers to seek information about products and candidates tailored to their own specific needs are some of the recent trends and developments that pose challenges and opportunities to advertisers. As far as new media environments go, the future is now.

Infomercials, interactive cable home shopping networks, the convergence of the telephone, computer, and television set, and computer on-line advertising are some of the innovative media that advertisers should add to the traditional media of newspapers, magazines, radio, television, billboards, and direct marketing. The ability to construct appropriate messages for these non-traditional channels will become even more critical to the successful launching of advertising campaigns. Other trends suggest a blurring of editorial content and entertainment programming in increasingly popular half-hour infomercials.

In their efforts to reach market segments such as the Latino and African American markets, advertisers may begin to advertise more heavily in ethnic publications and media.

ADVERTISING AND SOCIAL RESPONSIBILITY

As with all media practitioners, the advertising copywriter should be guided by a sense of social responsibility and professional integrity. This principle of honesty and social responsibility is reflected in the Advertising Code of American Business: "Advertising shall tell the truth and reveal significant facts, the concealment of which would mislead the public." The Federal Trade Commission issues guidelines for truthful and ethical advertising and has the authority to require remedial or corrective advertising.

Common practices advertisers should avoid are deception, false advertising, and puffery. According to ethics professor Lewis A. Day, misleading or deceptive advertising practices constitute a breach of faith with the consumer, because it is usually more difficult for the consumer to discover the truth about commercial speech than about political speech.

Day further asserts that although advertising and public relations practitioners, as purveyors of persuasive communications, have no ethical mandate to provide balance in their public proclamations, the moral imperative to disclose fully is more acute if the health or safety of the public is at risk. That is the dilemma of the advertising copywriter who develops the slogan for a Newport cigarette ad such as, "Alive with Pleasure." That particular ad appeared in a magazine targeted to African American women at a time when smoking-related diseases are the number one cause of death among African Americans, according to the National Center for Disease Control.

The free marketplace of ideas is based on the belief that rational individuals will make informed decisions if they have sufficient information to do so. The consumer's responsibility, according to Day, is to seek alternative sources of information on which to base buying decisions.

One of the major criticisms of advertising is the messages targeted to children, particularly on television commercials. This criticism is based in part on children's perceived inability to reason and seek alternative sources, yet they are often exposed to the same messages as adult consumers.

Creating truthful and ethical advertising is the high call to copywriters. Those who create media images and messages have an obligation to the audience for whom these messages are intended.

20

EDUCATION AND THE JOB MARKET

This chapter discusses what and who the competition is in mass media, where the graduates are coming from, what they are being taught, what they are not being taught, what employers would like to have them taught, and where traditional and nontraditional jobs are, or will or will not be.

Shortly after arriving almost penniless in New York City in 1925, reporter Ben Hecht received a telegram from a friend in Hollywood: "Will you accept $300 per week to work for Paramount Pictures? All expenses paid. The three hundred is peanuts. Millions to be grabbed out here and your only competition is idiots. Don't let this get around."

Although the offer was made to the talented print journalist nearly seventy-five years ago, there is still a great deal of truth to it for journalism and communication school graduates in the 1990s. Despite a steady decline of traditional full-time print and broadcast jobs due to deregulation, mergers, elimination of jobs, reductions in force (RIFS), firings, and other economic factors,

---

BY ALF PRATTE

Dr. Pratte, a former newspaper reporter, is Professor of Journalism at Brigham Young University. He received his Ph.D. in American Studies from the University of Hawaii. He has served on the board of directors of the American Journalism Historians Association and as the association's president, newsletter editor and advertising director.

opportunities are still available to those who have mastered the basic journalistic skills of reporting, analysis, and writing and can apply them to other related fields of work.

Hecht followed in the tradition of some of America's best-known movie script writers, poets, short story writers, novelists, and others who began their careers in journalism before moving on to related fields, or who continued in the business while working and writing in other genres: Benjamin Franklin, William Cullen Bryant, Margaret Fuller, Edgar Allan Poe, Mark Twain, Ernest Hemingway, Sinclair Lewis, and many others.

Of course, not all journalists or journalism school graduates will go as far as Hecht and the others. Hecht parlayed his newspapering skills to the movies and became one of the most successful screenwriters in the history of motion pictures. In a career that spanned forty years, he was credited with writing the screen stories or screen plays for more than fifty films and worked without credit on many others. Despite the slim pickings for journalism school graduates as well as the hostile economy facing thousands of other white-collar oriented college graduates, limited opportunities remain for those able to adjust.

With the elimination of many traditional newspaper, radio, and television jobs over the past two decades, opportunities are no longer available on big city dailies and broadcast holdings as they were in the past. One study shows only about 25% of today's journalism graduates find jobs on newspapers or wire services after graduation, and about 60% of communication graduates do not enter traditional communications related occupations. There is growing industry-wide commitment to hiring minorities in a traditionally, mainly white and male industry. Thus, the opportunities for minorities have increased. And even as some doors have closed for other graduates, other doors have opened in smaller communities, in business, entertainment, government, and in other nontraditional areas not always considered in journalism folklore and history.

HIGHER ENROLLMENT—FEWER JOBS

Despite the job outlook, things look bright at the college level, both in enrollment and quality. As noted in annual studies conducted by Ohio State University, the total (about 36,000) number of students enrolled in nearly 415 U. S. journalism and mass communications departments increased in interesting ways from the latter 1980s to the first part of the 1990s. While undergraduate enrollment increased 2%, graduate enrollment increased 9%, led by a dramatic increase of 39% in doctoral students. Women today constitute more than 60% of the bachelor's and master's degree recipients in journalism and mass communications, although doctoral programs remain predominately male in enrollment. Inasmuch as many of the graduates with masters and Ph.D. degrees will seek jobs in teaching, students will face the interesting situation of being taught not only by those with limited practical experience, but also will confront a professional world that is rapidly changing.

In contrast to the 1950s and 1960s, public relations and advertising now account for a larger percentage of the enrolled students (31%) than do news editorial—broadcast news and journalism combined—the Ohio State survey shows. However, inclusion of magazine specialization, community journalism, agricultural journalism, and photojournalism in the "journalism" group boosts the journalism numbers to 33%, just slightly more than the estimated number of students in public relations and advertising. These two almost equally sized groups of students account for a bit under two-thirds of all mass communications students enrolled nationally.

CURRICULUM AND THE CRITICS

Notwithstanding a close relationship between journalism educators and professionals since the 1920s, as well as joint academic/professional accrediting committees and many other means of coordination, professionals continue to complain about journalism education. In a 1990 American Society of Newspaper Editors' survey, editors said they hired predominately journalism program graduates, although by and large they did not have strong feelings about what degree a job applicant held. Editors of small newspapers expressed a preference for journalism graduates, but a majority of those at medium-sized and large newspapers said they had no preference or they preferred graduates from other disciplines. One survey conducted by the Associated Press Managing Editors (APME) listed ten journalistic skills that professionals thought were important for students to learn in order to prepare for the job market: thinking analytically, presenting information well, understanding numbers in the news, listening to readers, writing concisely, storytelling, our multicultural society, desktop publishing, why newspaper penetration has dropped, managing and marketing newspapers, and personal affairs reporting.

Similarly, a nation-wide poll of 381 editors emphasized the following points as essential for job applicants:

- Basic skills, such as writing, spelling, and grammar, are essential qualities in candidates.
- Internships, knowledge of journalism ethics and a broad background in liberal arts and sciences also rank high.
- Nearly three-quarters of the editors say they wish their new hires had taken more coursework in the liberal arts and sciences.
- Half of the editors said they had no preference whether new staffers have a journalism degree or are liberal arts majors.
- The least important quality, according to the editors who responded, is familiarity with communications theory.
- The most significant improvements in journalism schools, the editors say, would be to add more media professionals and to put more emphasis on nuts and bolts journalism.

This last point is the traditional sore point between professionals and educators and the continuation of a debate that has gone on since journalism schools came into existence in the post-Civil War period. Should institutions of higher learning with their liberal arts tradition and trained faculty permit professionals to foster a trade school mentality and curriculum? Although both groups agree on a predominately liberals arts approach, the image of a trade school department persists in some areas. Some journalism schools still take their cues from the industry where they seek to place their students and in so doing harm their status on the college campus.

Work for a campus newspaper remains a significant part of the curriculum in most, but not all, programs. Work for a college newspaper is part of the curriculum at nearly 60% of schools. Work for a college radio station is part of the curriculum at 45% of the programs, and work for a college TV station at one-third of the programs. Nearly all programs give college credit for communication internships.

CAREERS IN THE NEWSPAPER INDUSTRY

Notwithstanding the quality of their academic preparation, many students find themselves in a state of shock after they graduate and begin to look for traditional jobs that are no longer available. One of the reasons is because of the dramatic restructuring of American business that has contributed to major changes in the job market both in journalism and other parts of the economy. As noted by one newsmagazine, "Work is more specialized, information is harder to come by, employers are smaller and exceedingly cautious about hiring. In searching for a job, what you don't know can hurt you badly."

One of the most brutal facts in the decline of jobs is the decline in the number of major dailies, as well as the failure of newspapers to attract readers. With about 475,000 workers, the newspaper business is an industry whose employment needs are on the decline. Of this total, about 70,000 are employed on the editorial side, and the rest in promotion, advertising, and administration. About 45% of the work force in 1990 was female.

A 1991 survey showed for the second straight year a pessimistic job market for those seeking entry-level journalism jobs. The survey conducted by Lee B. Becker and Gerald M. Kosicki showed that by six to eight months after graduation, 16.1% of the bachelor's degree recipients still had not found work. The percentage of those holding bachelor's degrees with full-time work was 62.2%, 3.1% lower than the previous year. The picture was equally bleak for those holding master's degrees. Six to eight months after graduating, 23% of the M. A. recipients were unemployed. The percentage with full-time work was 61.5%, or 15% lower than the previous year.

A similar study for ASNE showed the number of newsroom professionals hired for their first full-time jobs fell 30% from 1990 to 1991 due to an economic recession and the closing of a number of newspapers. There appears to be little chance that jobs lost in recent newspaper closures will ever be resurrected.

John Blodgett, vice-president of human resources at the American Newspaper Publishers Association, attributes the decline in opportunities to a "structural change" in the industry: newspapers have learned to do more with less. And newspapers are certainly not going to be beefing up at the same staffing levels, even if things turn around, he says. Newspapers are going to be more cautious about hiring.

A number of other job opportunities have appeared in the last two decades, however, because of new print technology. Three of them are suburban newspapers, city and regional magazines, and "shoppers" distributed free to every address in a market area. Some of these publications consist entirely of a one-person staff who primarily rewrites press releases and other handouts. Others, like the *Utah County Journal* in Orem, Utah, have hired as many as eight full-time writers to gather and interpret the news. As for suburban papers, they vary in size from small dailies and weeklies such as the *Kettering-Oakwood Times* where Erma Bombeck started her humor column to *Newsday* of Long Island, New York, which now rivals some metropolitan papers in size, coverage, and profitability.

Newspaper experience also puts graduates in line for other interesting and sometimes lucrative work. The opportunities include corporate public relations, lobbying, writing newsletters, teaching, government, photography, government public relations, and broadcasting. Other newspaper-related opportunities include arts reviewing for weekly newspapers, book reviews, local columns, copyediting, copywriting, dance criticism, drama criticism, editing/manuscript evaluation, fact checking, feature writing, writing obituary copy, picture editing, proofreading, science writing, and stringing for larger newspapers.

MAGAZINE INDUSTRY

Although there are many opportunities available with smaller magazines and publications, it is equally as hard to find full-time jobs with major magazines as with major newspapers. One of the most difficult print journalism jobs to acquire is in the magazine industry, where only about 113,000 people are employed. Many major magazines are located near New York City. Most jobs, however, are found at small publications or at business or trade magazines. The most common entry level job is that of an editorial assistant.

In addition to the traditional jobs in the magazine industry, the following opportunities are available for those in the magazine and trade journal industry: abstracting, article manuscript critiques, book reviews, consultation, editing, fact checking, feature articles, ghostwriting, indexing, columns, picture editing, production editing, research, rewriting, science writing, and translation.

BROADCAST INDUSTRY

More jobs are available in the television industry. According to recent figures provided by the Federal Communications Commission, about 110,000 are employed in commercial TV; 100,000 in CATV; 10,000 in non-commercial TV; and about 16,000 at TV networks. These 236,000 employees compare with General Motors' 775,000 and IBM's 383,000. There are, however, at least two people looking for each available position. In the so-called glamour jobs of television—reporter, network page, on-camera host for interview shows—competition is more intense.

Vernon Stone, journalism professor at the University of Missouri and research director for the Radio-Television News Directors Association, says that the workforce in television journalism has held steady in recent years. He was surprised to learn that the well-publicized layoffs by the networks were largely offset by new jobs added at other stations. "There are more jobs out there than people think," Stone says. "There are always openings for good entry-level people. They don't cost as much."

Among the places Stone advises graduates to look for jobs are commercial TV stations, commercial radio stations, public television stations, public radio stations, broadcast networks, cable television outlets, wire services, newsfeed services, syndication services, corporate television, and public relations. Examples of those working on a TV staff in a middle market include a news director, executive producer/assistant news director, assignment editor, weathercaster, producers, photographers, reporters, news anchors, anchor/reporters, sportscasters, and multi-duty staff.

As is the case with those seeking jobs in newspaper work, advertising, and public relations, internships are important, perhaps essential for those who wish to be taken seriously. Many internships don't pay a salary, but they add credibility in getting applicants hired. Other steps recommended by Vernon Stone are to use your school's placement service and to write a businesslike letter of application accompanied by a relevant, direct, concise, and forthright resumé and a professional resumé tape.

ADVERTISING JOBS

Closely related and strongly supportive of the news gathering industries is that of advertising, which faces financial problems similar to those already cited. Jobs in this area are also competitive in creative positions, client liaison, media buying, and market research. Many agencies also employ technicians and producers who turn ideas to camera proofs, colorplates, videotape, film, and audio cartridges, although a lot of production work is contracted to specialty companies. Besides full-service agencies, there are creative boutiques, which specialize in preparing messages; media buying houses, which recommend strategy on placing ads; and other narrowly focused agencies. Students are now being urged to expand their career goals beyond the traditional agency-client arrangement and seek careers in direct-response advertising and sales promotion.

PUBLIC RELATIONS

In contrast to the bleak job picture for those trained in gathering, writing, and editing objective news, prospects are brighter for those in public relations. During the image conscious 1980s, independent public relations companies expanded rapidly, and, at the same time, corporations welcomed their in-house people into management ranks. Other opportunities are available in lobbying, political communication, image consulting, financial public relations, fund-raising, contingency planning, polling, and events coordination.

Whereas the field was once recruited from the ranks of burned-out or underpaid journalists, increasingly students with writing and communication skills go straight to public relations. Nationwide in the fall of 1992 there were about 16,750 students majoring in print reporting and editing compared with 18,220 majoring in PR, according to an Ohio State University survey.

According to figures published in *Jack O'Dwyer's Newsletter*, an industry tip sheet, the top ten public relations firms cut their payrolls by an average 7.5% in 1993, a downsizing that will affect PR students. The growth areas are the health care and high-tech fields, not exactly what students have in mind after four years in the communications fields.

ALTERNATIVE OPPORTUNITIES

In addition to the traditional places for public relations, advertising, broadcast, and journalism jobs, in the 1990s there are numerous alternative opportunities for those trained in writing. Some of the best kept secrets are hidden within the business community. Business people always need writers for one thing or another, and they like to hire freelancers rather than full-time staffers so they can save on benefits. Among the opportunities are those of resumé writers, translators, writers of scripts, and protocols for videotapes and computers. Other jobs are available writing annual reports, sales letters, direct mail packages, corporate histories and anniversaries, capability brochures, and collateral materials.

COMPUTER LITERACY

Although market needs vary greatly, there is general consensus on one issue during the 1990s: computer literacy is paramount to getting freelance assignments. Writers who work out of their homes are expected to be equipped at the very least with a computer and a telephone answering service. Many are finding it worthwhile to invest in peripheral equipment such as fax machines, modems, copy machines, and laser printers.

THE FUTURE

Although the journalism job market isn't overly inviting, it isn't much different from many other professions during the last decade of this century. The cover article of a major national newsweekly in 1993 plaintively asked: "Where did my career go? The white collar lament of the '90s." The old refrain to students at commencement that "It's rough out there, brother" is that things are rougher. And it isn't over yet. A hostile economy where big corporations continue to make big profits partially by trimming news staff has helped cut short careers for many of America's best and brightest.

Mary Kay Blake, director of recruiting and placement for the newspaper division of Gannett, a corporation that while doing much to foster minorities in the workplace has also helped to reduce the journalism workforce, advises that since the jobs are hard to come by, graduates will need to be more flexible, willing to work for smaller publications and relocate—and accept small starting salaries. One study finds that the median salary of a 1990 bachelor's degree recipient who found full-time employment with a daily newspaper was $348 per week; for those at TV stations it was $289; and at radio stations $254. For graduates who found full-time work in public relations agencies, the median salary was $378 per week.

Graduates can do $5,000 to $10,000 a year better at entry-level trade associations, in public relations, or even in government jobs, according to Phil Robbins, director of journalism at George Washington University. "A lot of people," he explains, "are coming into the news editorial sequence without any intention of ever working in journalism."

Another long-range implication of the less-than-bright job market is that journalism may lose the appeal generated through its public-service oriented history. There is also a danger that journalism, which benefited from the Watergate generation of youth who flooded journalism schools, may become a backwater for students who lack the ability to succeed elsewhere. That may be one of the most sinister legacies of the news industry's emphasis on economics in the 1980s and 1990s.

University administrators are already eyeing the once burgeoning journalism schools as prime areas for cutting, merging, and even elimination as can be seen at the universities of Oregon, Arizona, and others. The responsibility for maintaining the schools as homes for some of the best and brightest students and practitioners, ranging from Ben Franklin to Ben Hecht and Ben Bradlee, not only rests with the faculties at journalism schools but with an industry that at least during the past two decades has been more consumed with profits than the contributions good students could make to America's newspapers and magazines.

Perspective...

WHAT TO DO NOW IF YOU WANT
TO BE A FOREIGN CORRESPONDENT

By WESLEY G. PIPPERT, Associate Professor of Journalism and Director
of the University of Missouri's Washington Reporting Program

When my managing editor approached me at a farewell party for a
colleague and asked if I wanted to take an overseas assignment, I was
delighted and quickly said yes. The posting would be in Israel, a land
I had learned to love from afar primarily through uncounted Bible
stories from Sunday School and my mother's bedtime reading. The
taste that I had acquired as a child had been cultivated in later
years by a master's degree I had earned in biblical literature.

Within a few weeks, I was dropped into the middle of the complex Israeli society. There were perpetual struggles galore—the political standoff between the centrist Labor Party and the right-wing
Likud Party; the cultural clashes between the Ashkenazi Jews, the
ruling class that hailed mostly from Europe, and the Sephardic Jews,
largely poor Jews from Arab countries; the religious tug between the
Ultra-Orthodox Jews and the secular Jews.

Somehow I got through those early months; and, eventually, I
came to feel I had as good a grasp on Israel as I did of Washington,
D.C., where I have been a journalist for nearly a quarter of a century.
But when I returned to the United States, I sought a fellowship at
Harvard, where, *ex post facto*, I studied the modern history of the
Middle East and other subjects. Then I saw how really unprepared I
had been in going to Israel.

Later, I took a poll of my American colleagues in the Middle East
to see what they thought a new foreign correspondent ought to know.
I was not surprised to learn that we came to the same conclusion. Here
is what a foreign correspondent ought to have studied:

- Modern history of the region where the correspondent has been
  assigned
- U. S. diplomacy
- International economics and trade
- And perhaps most important, cross-cultural sensitivity.

There are solid reasons for the above choices. The geopolitics of nation states as we have known it seems past. The global battles of the future are likely to be economic and trade in nature; yet we see the multiplicity and complexity of ethnic and cultural clashes on every hand.

Curiously, none of us listed a course in the language. There is a reason for this: To be confident of one's translations of newspapers, broadcasts and interviews, one must become very proficient, particularly in a language like Hebrew or Russian. I decided that by the time I was that proficient, my three-year posting would be over. So I relied on translators and the abundant number of fluent English speakers in Israel.

But I also made use of that master's degree in biblical literature. Time and again, I would pinpoint a dateline in terms of its occurrence or significance in the Bible. A recent example of this was the 1994 massacre of more than a score of Moslems while they were praying at the site of the burial of the patriarchs Abraham, Isaac and Jacob; the location was a key part of the story. Other stories were less significant, yet were greatly improved by this biblical reference. One such story was the reopening of a newly blacktopped road between Jerusalem and Jericho. My lead read:

JERICHO, Occupied West Bank —Israel reopened a stretch of road between Jerusalem and Jericho today that had been blacktopped and improved for the first time since Jesus walked it nearly 2,000 years ago.

That story was picked up and printed.

APPENDIX

STYLE GUIDELINES

For the sake of uniformity—and to save writers, copy-editors and keyboard operators from mild insanity—most publications prescribe a specific way to present many commonly used words, phrases and symbols. Some of these prescribed ways merely reflect a generally accepted rule, while others arbitrarily represent a choice of one way over one or more other equally correct ways. Many newspapers (mostly smaller ones) do not emphasize a particular style; larger and better organized papers, however, generally stress strict conformity to their preferred style. It is therefore important, since a reporter's style usage is considered indicative of his or her overall journalistic capabilities, that the staff member of any publication be thoroughly familiar with style rules. Most styles are based generally upon the *AP Stylebook*, the most widely used by newspapers and other mass media. This stylebook is far-reaching in usage. It prescribes and includes a large set of specific usages, rules for virtually every instance of the use of language a reporter may ever employ. In the beginning, you may find it difficult to memorize them all. To help you get started, following are some style usages accepted and employed by almost all publications. You may come across them on many of the stories you write. As a starting point in mastering style rules, learn them as quickly as you can and begin applying them to your own writing. While writing as a journalist, be especially observant of these guidelines.

GENERAL

Write in the third person. Avoid use of *we, us* and *our*.

Generally avoid use of direct address (*you*).

The source of all information should be stated or definitely implied.

Verify spelling of names. Verify addresses. Verify times and places. Be skeptical of sources; they may be wrong.

Reporters must take full responsibility for their stories. Do not depend on someone else to catch your errors.

An essential of any news article is completeness. Write for readers. Do not say when the circus will start and omit where. Be a good news hound; keep after the elusive facts until you get them— all of them.

Do not identify victims of sex crimes or children under 16 accused of crime.

News stories of coming events should not contain material that is more promotional than factual.

Avoid credits such as 'The office said...." Human beings make statements.

Put the speaker's words in standard English prose unless there is some reason for indicating illiteracy, clowning or talking down. Changes in quoted words should be minor and corrective. Do not substitute words the speaker would never use.

In listing addresses or places, begin with the smallest unit and progress to the largest: 2029 N. Jones St., Pittsburgh, Pa.

TIME

In writing news stories, use the day of the week, as *Monday* or *Thursday*, instead of *yesterday*, *today* or *tomorrow*. Write the day of the week (such as *Monday*) if the date is within six days. Write the date (such as *Aug. 12*) if the date is more than six days away.

Consider *night* to be from 6 p.m. to 6 a.m., *morning* from 6 a.m. to noon, and *afternoon* from noon to 6 p.m. Many papers avoid use of *evening*. It is preferable to use *a.m.* and *p.m.* instead of *morning* or *night*.

The proper sequence in which to list time is (1) hour, (2) day, (3) month, (4) year. (Begin with the smallest unit and progress to the largest.) The main thing to remember here is that hour comes before day: 6 p.m. Tuesday.

When noting both place and time, time is written before place: Thursday in Dallas; *or* at 8 p.m. in the auditorium.

Normally, numbers of only one digit should be spelled; in stating time, however, this rule does not apply: not *six p.m.* but *6 p.m.*

Make it 2 p.m.—not 2:00 p.m.

Convert times to those in your own time zone.

Normally, do not use the words "o'clock," "morning," "afternoon" or "night": *Not* 6 o'clock at night *but* 6 p.m.

The name of a month is spelled when it is used without a day, but it is abbreviated (if possible) when used with a day:

not in Oct.	*but* in October
not October 20	*but* Oct. 20

PLACE

Spell and capitalize the word "street" if a street name is given without a house number (Elm Street), but abbreviate and capitalize the word "street" if a house number is given (2020 Elm St.); spell and lower case the word "street" if it is not used as part of a proper name (the street).

Abbreviate the name of a state (if possible) when it is used with a town name (Miami, Fla.), but spell the name of the state if no town is given (in Florida). Notice that state names use the traditional abbreviation, not the two-letter postal designation (Wis., *not* WI).

When writing for a publication in your own state, omit the state name with the name of a town in the state unless the state name is needed for clarity: Athens, Ga.

WORDS

Never use useless, ambiguous, unnecessary or repetitious words (such as the following):

not	*but*
German language	German
12 midnight	midnight
located in Sacramento	in Sacramento
a period of two hours	two hours
well-known group	group
prominent speaker	speaker

Do not use the word "active" in the following kind of context:

"...an *active* member of the club..."

Never use "etc." in a news story.

Should an individual die, state that s/he died, not that s/he "passed away," "went to meet his maker," "kicked the bucket," "went to his just reward," "is deceased," "is pushing up daisies," "bit the dust," etc.

When a woman's husband has died, she is a *widow*. (Some papers make exceptions to this rule, and others even emphasize that the word "widow" should never be used. Follow the style established by your publication.)

Identification by race, religion or national origin is justified only when this information is essential to understanding a story. Current usage and good taste should be followed in referring to racial groups.

Adult males and females are men and women, not gentlemen and ladies.

Unintentional overtones may be suggested by careless words such as "claimed," "admitted," "refused to deny," "withheld support," "dodged reporters," etc.

Do not use contractions (won't, don't, isn't, etc.) except for special reasons or circumstances or in quoted matter.

Do not fail to use enough conjunctions in compound series. Write: "Guests were Mrs. John Doe *and* Misses Ann Cox and Mary Dodd." Also: "She studied in Paris *and* Berlin *and* lectured at Swarthmore."

Make sure the verb agrees in number with the subject.

PUNCTUATION

Do not place a comma before the "and" or "or" that precedes the final object in a series: "the flowers, trees and clouds."

Omit the comma in a name before *Jr., Sr., III*.

Always place the comma and period within quotation marks: "Keep pencils sharp."

Do not separate a verb from its direct object by interjecting a colon—*not* officers are: Joe Smith, John Brown....; *but* officers are Joe Smith....

Use a comma in giving a name and city: "John Jones, Topeka." However, omit the comma if "of" is used: "John Jones of Topeka."

Put a comma in figures indicating thousands, millions, billions: 15,275.

Use the semicolon in lists of officers: John Jones, president; Joe Smith, vice-president; and Bob Brown, treasurer.

Do not underscore names of publications, movies, etc.

NUMERALS

Use figures for 10 and above. However, for large sums it is all right to round numbers to "thousands," "millions," "billions."

Spell out numbers below 10 in general use, but figures are used in technical and statistical matter, election returns, times, speeds, temperatures, distances, dimensions, scores, heights, ages, ratios, proportions, numbers of military units, dates and betting odds.

Do not let two figures stand together, causing confusion; rewrite the sentence.

TITLES

Identify the person by full name in first reference and by last name only in later references.

Capitalize titles preceding and attached to a name. In general, lower case most titles standing alone or used after a name. Do not capitalize occupational titles preceding names, such as "defense attorney Smith" or "shortstop Jones."

Do not precede a name with a long title; place the title after the name.

Do not use as titles the names of organizational offices: *not* President Tom Jones of the YMCA *but* Tom Jones, president of the YMCA.

Do not use the designation "Mr." except in the phrase "Mr. and Mrs." and sometimes in reference to past and present U.S. Presidents and Supreme Court justices. Do use "Mr." in the proper reference to a member of the clergy.

In first references to clergy, write: "the Rev. John Smith." In later references call the person "Dr. Smith," "Bishop Smith," "Mr. Smith," etc. Be sure to use the correct title for various religious offices.

INDEX